Parents of children in placement.

# Parents of Children in Placement:
*Perspectives and Programs*

# Parents of Children in Placement:

*Perspectives and Programs*

Edited by
PAULA A. SINANOGLU AND ANTHONY N. MALUCCIO



Published in collaboration
with
The University of Connecticut
School of Social Work
by the
Child Welfare League of America, Inc.

Publication of this book was supported through a grant from the University of Connecticut.

Child Welfare League of America, Inc.
67 Irving Place, New York, NY 10003



Current printing (last digit)
10 9 8 7 6 5 4 3 2

Manufactured in the United States of America

**Library of Congress Cataloging in Publication Data**
Main entry under title:

Parents of children in placement.

Includes bibliographies.
1. Foster home care — United States — Addresses, essays, lectures. 2. Parent and child — United States — Addresses, essays, lectures. I. Sinanoglu, Paula A. II. Maluccio, Anthony N. III. Child Welfare League of America.
HV875.P344 362.7′33′0973 81-4937
ISBN 0-87868-205-8 AACR2
ISBN 0-87868-181-7 (pbk.)

# Contents

## Part IV Sociocultural Perspectives



## Part V Legal Issues



## Part VI Importance of Parents for the Placed Child



## Part VII Impact of Placement on Parents

## Part VIII Perspectives on Programs and Methods



## Part IX Special Aspects

# Preface

The field of child welfare is witnessing a burgeoning interest in practice with, and in behalf of, biological parents of children in placement. Parents in many cases receive limited service, but there is growing emphasis on working with the family as a unit, viewing the family or the parent(s) as the primary client, and providing effective services that promote reunion of children with their parents or some other form of stable, permanent placement. Consequently, child welfare personnel—administrators, policy makers, practitioners, educators, and students—are seeking to enhance their knowledge of the issues and their skills.

Responding to this need, the editors brought together from a variety of sources a collection of articles reflecting different perspectives on, and approaches to, parents involved with the foster care system. The book may be read for itself or used in conjunction with formal educational programs as well as inservice training.

Most of the articles were originally published in social work journals during the 1970s. Several additional papers were written especially for this volume. In choosing from a range of available materials, the editors were guided by a number of criteria, including timeliness of content, diversity of views, and significance for practice.

In addition, the selections were tested in special courses and workshops on "Working with Biological Parents" offered for personnel of public child welfare agencies in two states. The criticisms and suggestions of participating workers and supervisors were most useful to the editors, especially in identifying practice-relevant materials.

This book is addressed primarily to direct service personnel and others interested in direct practice with parents. Consequently, it does not include articles specifically considering policy, organizational, and funding aspects that could appropriately be the focus of another volume. Most of the contributors, however, explicitly or implicitly touch on these issues and consider their impact on direct service.

Following introductory chapters examining the emerging focus on parents and presenting an overview on practice, the book is divided into the following sections: early professional perspectives; ecological perspective; sociocultural perspectives; legal issues, importance of parents for the placed child; impact of placement on parents; perspectives on programs and methods; and special aspects. Each section is prefaced by a brief discussion of the particular readings and their relevance, including suggestions for further study.

Selected writings, earlier and more recent, present the complexity of the issues involved—psychological, legal, cultural, institutional. Other writings describe tested programs and methods of working with parents. Together they offer an overview that we anticipate will stimulate questions while also offering answers in the form of pertinent practice guidelines and principles. The reader, it is hoped, will generate creative ideas and programs leading to positive outcomes between parents and children, in keeping with this book's key goal: to provide those in child welfare a background with which to seek more effective solutions in working with parents of children in foster care.

# Acknowledgments

During 1978–80 the University of Connecticut School of Social Work carried out a special child welfare training project, "Toward More Effective Work with Biological Parents," in collaboration with the Connecticut Department of Children and Youth Services and the Rhode Island Department of Social and Rehabilitative Services. The project was funded through Grant No. 90–C–1441 from the U.S. Department of Health, Education and Welfare, Administration for Children, Youth and Families, Children's Bureau. Its overall purpose was to develop and test courses, workshops, and curriculum materials designed to help child welfare personnel to work effectively with parents of children in placement.

This volume is one in a series of publications resulting from the project. We gratefully acknowledge the support of the Children's Bureau and the many persons who have contributed to the book: the social workers and supervisors who participated in related courses and workshops; the instructors and guest lecturers; and our faculty colleagues. We especially appreciate the encouragement of Dean Robert Green and the suggestions offered by Charles Horejsi, Alice Y. Moe, Scott Mueller, Kathleen Olmstead, John Smey, and Florence Walker.

We would also like to thank the contributors, publishers, and copyright holders for permission to reprint their materials. Specific acknowledgments are given at the beginning of each chapter. Finally, as always, a special vote of thanks to our outstanding secretarial staff, particularly Margaret Partridge, Lois Pye, and Barbara Salwocki.

PAULA A. SINANOGLU
ANTHONY N. MALUCCIO

# Part I
# Overview

# Part I

## Overview

Child welfare literature increasingly reflects interest in practice with parents of children in foster care. Part I provides an overview of this interest and related themes and trends.

In Chapter I, Maluccio reviews the emerging focus on parents. Following a brief discussion of the practice concerns and research findings that have helped stimulate such a focus, he outlines the range of practice innovations in the field and the practice guidelines that are being developed or strengthened through increased activity in behalf of parents in many agency settings.

Chapter 2, also by Maluccio, focuses on casework with parents of children in foster care. The author highlights the multifaceted role of the worker in practice with parents and considers such aspects as the meaning of placement for family and child, the worker's attitudes toward the placement and the parents, and some of the generic principles useful in services to this client population. Although written nearly two decades ago, this paper prefigures a number of themes now prominent in child welfare practice, such as recognition of the needs of parents as human beings, emphasis on comprehensive services to families of placed children, concern about children drifting in foster care, and clarification of long-term planning.

### SUGGESTIONS FOR FURTHER READING

Beck, Bertram M., *The Lower East Side Family Union: A Social Invention*. New York: Foundation for Child Development, 1979.

Fanshel, David and Shinn, Eugene B., *Children in Foster Care—A Longitudinal Investigation*. New York: Columbia University Press, 1978.

Kadushin, Alfred, *Child Welfare Services*—Third Edition. New York: Macmillan Publishing Co., 1980.

Maluccio, Anthony N., "Foster Family Care Revisited: Problems and Prospects," *Public Welfare*, 31: 2 (Spring 1973): 12–17.

Sinanoglu, Paula A., "Working with Parents: Issues and Trends as Reflected in the Literature," in Maluccio, Anthony N. and Sinanoglu, Paula A., Editors, *The Challenge of Partnership: Working with Parents of Children in Foster Care*. New York: Child Welfare League of America, 1981.

# 1

# The Emerging Focus on Parents of Children in Placement

ANTHONY N. MALUCCIO

The field of child welfare has long recognized the significance of parents of children in foster care and the importance of involving them actively in the placement plan and the helping process; but, in practice, emphasis has not been on direct work with parents. In general, most attention has been devoted to the children themselves and/or their surrogate parents or caretakers [Fanshel and Shinn, 1978; Gruber, 1978].

The situation is now changing, as interest is burgeoning in practice with—and in behalf of—parents. This chapter examines this emerging focus and highlights pertinent practice innovations, implications, and guidelines.

## BACKGROUND

Although it is a widely accepted belief in the field of child welfare that every child has a right to a "secure and loving home," this goal has been

---

An original article prepared for this volume. This work was supported by Grant No. 90–C–1794 from the Children's Bureau, Administration for Children, Youth and Families, U.S. Department of Health and Human Services.

Portions of this chapter have been adapted from Maluccio (1977 and 1981a).

difficult to achieve. From the first statement of a bill of rights for children at the 1930 White House Conference on Children to the recent publication of an extensive, longitudinal study of children in foster care [Fanshel and Shinn, 1978], the quest for permanency in planning for children has persisted.

Yet today nearly half a million children are in foster care. "These children characteristically experience the impermanence of moving to one home after another, frequently resulting in lasting emotional damage" [Zigler and Hunsinger, 1978: 12]. As the number of children in placement has steadily increased, concern has mounted over the issue of permanent planning. But the problems inherent in the child welfare field have remained unresolved.

Many studies have shown that the foster care system has not fulfilled its ultimate mission of reuniting children with their parents following a temporary placement, or providing alternate permanent plans. Over two decades ago, Maas and Engler [1959] reached startling conclusions on the basis of a nationwide survey: Many children in foster care had at least one parent living, but the parents rarely visited them and generally had no plans to assume responsibility for their care; and nearly two-thirds of the children were unlikely to return to their own homes; for most of the children in foster care, future plans were indefinite and there was little sense of permanence.

These early findings have been supported by subsequent investigations demonstrating that many foster children are likely to grow up in foster care [Fanshel and Shinn, 1978; Gruber, 1978; and Wiltse and Gambrill, 1974]. Thus, following a comprehensive review of a large public foster care program, Wiltse and Gambrill [1974: 14] asserted:

> The fact remains that public foster care programs tend more to be long-term child-caring programs than short-term or crisis-oriented treatment programs . . .

Other researchers have pointed to the damage resulting from the tenuous status in which many foster children find themselves—a status that makes it very difficult for the child to develop his or her identity, to achieve a sense of belonging, to establish meaningful relationships with people, and to deal successfully with developmental tasks [Bryce and Ehlert, 1971]. The phrase "children adrift in foster care" has been used to describe the instability, uncertainty, and prolongation of the child's experience within a program that is supposed to be temporary and remedial. Consequently, questions have increasingly been raised about the adequacy of child placement services and programs. In effect, the foster care system has been undergoing a critical period of intensive reexamination and reassessment. For instance, Fanshel and Shinn, [1978: 479] have concluded: "We emerge from our research with the view that all children should be afforded permanency in their living arrangements if at all possible." Others have similarly emphasized the critical importance of permanence and the child's need for continuity of parental relationships [Goldstein, Freud, and Solnit, 1973].

The goal of permanency for each child has consequently begun to shape the overall philosophy of many foster care programs and is reflected in the commitment of the federal government. Federal legislation now promotes programs such as periodic case reviews and permanency planning, encourages services to parents in public welfare agencies, and stresses prevention and reunification services (P.L. 96–272—the Adoption Assistance and Child Welfare Act).

To maximize permanency planning, various measures have been carried out in different agencies, including time-limited service contracts combined with availability and enhancement of legal expertise; periodic internal and/or external case reviews; and a range of services involving parents. Especially noteworthy are practice innovations that have been successfully tested in work with parents in residential group settings, as well as foster family care.

## PRACTICE INNOVATIONS

A number of such innovations are presented in Maluccio and Sinanoglu [1981] and also in a later section of this volume (Part VIII—"Perspectives on Programs and Methods"). They reflect such emphases as:

1. Use of the residential treatment center as a resource for parents, along with active participation of parents in the program of the center. The staff recognizes the importance of parents to the child as well as the parents' own needs, and mobilizes agency and community resources in behalf of parents and the family as a whole.
2. Systematic case management based on principles of decision making, contracting, goal setting, and/or behavior modification. These approaches help clients not only to enhance their parenting skills but also to reach decisions as early as possible regarding the best long-term plan for the child. The ultimate purpose is to prevent drift and promote permanency or continuity in the child's care.
3. Formation of self-help groups and parent organizations that lead to new and more effective helping roles for parents of children in substitute care. Self-help approaches are gaining

attention in child welfare, albeit slowly, as practitioners recognize the untapped resources and latent potentialities in clients themselves.

4. Provision of intensive services and varied social supports to families during placement and in the aftercare period. These comprehensive programs reduce the duration of placement and reunite children with their own families by strengthening the parents' coping and adaptive capacities and providing them with necessary resources.

5. Redefinition of the relationships between parents and foster parents or other substitute caretakers such as child care staff. Particularly significant is the involvement of foster parents as resources for parents through such means as role modeling and serving as parent aides. Various programs show the value of having parents, foster parents, and child welfare personnel regard themselves as partners in a shared undertaking, with common goals and mutually supportive and complementary roles. This perspective leads to new helping systems that are ultimately more effective and rewarding for everyone concerned.

6. Use of parent aides such as home management aides, homemakers, and older persons who model effective parental behavior and coping skills. These aides help meet the basic needs of parents, strengthen the family's environment, and prevent placement or re-placement.

Renewed emphasis on understanding and working with parents is seen especially in group settings such as children's institutions, many of which are moving toward family-centered services. A recent book, for example, presents the concept of group child care as a *family service* and stresses the development of the "family-centered children's home" [Keith-Lucas and Sanford, 1977].

The literature offers many examples of practice innovations, along with long-established approaches. For instance, a child care agency has demonstrated the effective use of "family residential centers," that is, group homes where parents of placed children are given almost unlimited visiting privileges and encouraged to participate fully in their children's placement [Simmons, Gumpert, and Rothman, 1973]. This program has been found to be beneficial not only for the children but also the parents: with agency support of continual interaction between parents and children in placement, it is possible "for parents with severe problems to increase, sustain, and improve upon their parenting role" (p. 232).

Other agencies have experimented with "parent-child foster placements," in which single mothers and their abused or neglected children are placed for time-limited periods in specialized foster homes. Along with immediate protection of the child, the placement facilitates assessment of the mother's functioning and provision of intensive services so as to strengthen her parenting roles and skills [Nayman and Witkin, 1978]. Furthermore, some authors have suggested that the concept of parent-child foster placement could be extended to others, such as two-parent families and their children [Nayman and Witkin, 1978: 257], and young mothers and their infants [Benas, 1975].

Spotlighting the value of parental visiting is another promising development. Researchers' findings have underlined the profound effect of visiting not only on the child's ability to return home but also on his or her well-being while in placement. According to Fanshel and Shinn [1978], "the finding that discharge rates are quite closely linked to the frequency of parental visiting underscores the need to assign high priority to monitoring this phenomenon" (pp. 110–111). The same authors also stress "that agencies should be held accountable for efforts made to involve the parents in more responsible visitation" (p. 111). Moreover, other studies have shown that frequency of caseworker contact with parents is a major factor in parental visiting and continued involvement with the child [Jenkins and Norman, 1975; Jones, Neuman, and Shyne, 1976]. And White (Chapter 30 in this volume) formulates guidelines for using parent-child visitation as a means of promoting competence in parents and achieving permanency planning.

The practice focus on parents has also been reinforced by studies dealing with the feelings and reactions of parents of children in foster care—a long-neglected area. A case in point is the examination of the impact of foster care placement on mothers and fathers, particularly their separation experiences when their children enter foster care. Jenkins and Norman [1972] have formulated the concept of "filial deprivation" to explain the feelings of loss and consequent reactions of parents following placement of their children. In a later followup study, Jenkins and Norman [1975] explored the mothers' views of foster care and recommended policy and practice changes on the basis of the mothers' perceptions of placement. Above all, these authors underscored the importance of a family focus rather than a child focus in foster care, urging full involvement of parents in the helping process as a whole and greater emphasis on their "strengths and capacities rather than pathology and deficits" (p. 142).

## IMPACT ON SERVICE DELIVERY

The emerging focus on parents and the resulting practice innovations are encouraging. Many practitioners are increasingly sensitive to the needs and feelings of parents and some agencies have translated this sensitivity into efforts to involve parents actively in the service. As reflected in subsequent sections of this volume, a variety of issues such as parents' rights, services to minority groups, impact of placement on parents, are receiving attention.

At the same time, how much the service delivery system in general has changed in relation to parents is questionable [Maluccio, et al., 1980]. Practice continues essentially to be child-oriented rather than family-oriented. Although innovations mentioned in the preceding section move an increasing number of children into permanent plans, studies show that a significant proportion of "permanent placements," such as return to the child's home, do not work out satisfactorily [Claburn, Magura, and Chizeck, 1977; Fanshel and Shinn, 1978; Fein, Davis, and Knight, 1979].

In many agencies, parents receive little in the way of preventive or concurrent help or aftercare services, even though it has been demonstrated that maximal involvement of parents and availability of aftercare services and supports are essential to the success of child placement [Taylor and Alpert, 1973]. The service delivery system apparently reflects a continuing anti-family bias. Following a comprehensive, nationwide examination of policies and programs for children in out-of-home care, the Children's Defense Fund concluded that the service delivery system is so fragmented and inadequate that it appears that families and children "don't count": "Pro-family rhetoric notwithstanding, a pervasive, implicit anti-family bias often shapes decisions about children at risk of removal or in out-of-home care" [Children's Defense Fund, 1978: 5].

In agencies in which the commitment to families is fully translated into practice, intensive services to parents, in conjunction with other supports and resources, are effective in achieving higher rates of permanency planning (Jones, Neuman, and Shyne, 1976). In a three-year demonstration project undertaken in Oregon by the Regional Research Institute for Human Services, intensive casework services resulted in successful outcomes for many foster children for whom return home had not been considered possible [Lahti et al., 1978]. The Oregon Project has developed methods for overcoming barriers to permanency planning and demonstrated the effectiveness of working intensively with children and their families [Emlen et al., 1977].

## PRACTICE GUIDELINES

Although much remains to be done, the renewed focus and changing perspectives on parents have served to enhance our knowledge and our practice approaches in work with parents of children in foster care. At the same time, new knowledge and theoretical developments have sharpened practice principles and guidelines.

A promising theoretical framework for practice specifically with parents is provided by the ecological perspective and the life model of social work practice derived from it [Germain and Gitterman, 1980]. This framework relies on a broad array of knowledge from such disciplines as general systems theory, ecology, evolutionary biology, cultural anthropology, social psychology, and ego psychology. Its main thrust lies in addressing social work intervention to the *interface* between people and their environments. Practitioners seek to change the transactions between people and their impinging environment to enhance adaptive capacities as well as to improve the quality of the environment [Germain and Gitterman, 1980].

The ecological perspective encourages practitioners to shift from a narrow focus on the parents' pathology to a multifaceted interventive approach to children and their families in the context of their real-life situation and environment. It enables workers to understand more clearly the relationships between families and their social situation and to identify the crucial sources of stress and conflict [Laird, 1979]. It underscores the urgency of identifying, supporting, and mobilizing the natural adaptive processes of parents and families.

The value of the ecological perspective is reflected in various practice guidelines and action principles that have been developed or highlighted through the demonstration programs, practice innovations, and research findings noted in this chapter. As discussed elsewhere [Maluccio, 1981a and 1981b], these include the following:

1. viewing the family as the unit of treatment and, in particular, making aggressive and systematic efforts to help children and parents preserve their connectedness and maintain family identity and continuity [Laird, 1979];

2. involving parents actively in the child's placement and the overall service;

3. linking traditional services and formal helping methods with informal approaches and natural helping networks in the parents' own ecological context;

4. restructuring and enriching the environment of parents and children to make it more supportive of their coping and adaptive efforts and more conducive to their growth and competence;

5. empowering parents and redefining them as resources in their own behalf as well as their children's;

6. redefining the relationships between parents and foster parents or other substitute caretakers such as child care staff members, to emphasize their complementary contributions;

7. redefining the primary role of social workers as catalysts or enabling agents who help clients to identify or create and use necessary resources.

## CONCLUSION

The focus on parents of children in foster care has once again drawn our attention to a variety of recurring issues, many of which are discussed in subsequent sections of this volume. These include:

1. complex legal questions about definition of the rights of parents, children, and foster parents; state intervention into the family; termination of parental rights; and psychological versus biological parents;

2. economic issues, as reflected in society's reluctance to provide truly adequate resources that would enable parents to keep children in their own homes, in contrast to its funding more expensive out-of-home placement;

3. sociocultural aspects, such as recognition and acceptance of the unique needs, qualities, and strengths of different ethnic groups;

4. provision of adequate services for minority children and their families, including agency structures adapted to their particular needs and coping styles;

5. prevention of placement, particularly with regard to minority children, who are disproportionately represented in the foster care population.

To deal forcefully with these issues and provide effective services to parents that contribute to the goal of permanent planning for each child, concerted, skilled, and multifaceted intervention with parents before, during, and following placement is essential. Working with parents has too often been viewed as a hopeless task. They have been labeled as unmotivated, untreatable, unresponsive, or hard-to-reach. In the reality of practice, working with many of these parents can indeed be discouraging and time-consuming—but it is not hopeless or impossible. It is a task that requires the highest of professional skills, the best of agency services, and extensive community support:

> Only through a total commitment to working with parents can we expect to be truly helpful to them; without this, we are in actuality leaving them to rehabilitate themselves in what we at times expect to be "a self-healing process." (Maluccio, 1966: 5)

## REFERENCES

Benas, Evelyn. "Residential Care of the Child-Mother and Her Infant: An Extended Family Concept," Child Welfare LIV, 4 (April 1975): 290–294.

Bryce, Marvin E. and Ehlert, Roger C. "144 Foster Children," Child Welfare, L, 9 (November 1971): 499–503.

Children's Defense Fund, Children Without Homes. Washington, D.C.: Children's Defense Fund, 1978.

Claburn, W.E.; Magura, S.; and Chizeck, S. "Case Reopening: An Emerging Issue in Child Welfare Services," Child Welfare, LVI, 10 (December 1977): 655–663.

Emlen, A., et al. *Overcoming Barriers to Planning for Children in Foster Care.* Portland, Oreg. Regional Research Institute for Human Services, 1977.

Fanshel, David and Shinn, Eugene B. *Children in Foster Care—A Longitudinal Investigation.* New York: Columbia University Press, 1978.

Fein, Edith; Davies, Linda; and Knight, Gerrie. "Placement Stability in Foster Care," Social Work, 24, 2 (March 1979): 156–157.

Germain, Carel B. and Gitterman, Alex. *The Life Model of Social Work Practice.* New York: Columbia University Press, 1980.

Goldstein, Joseph; Freud, Anna; and Solnit, Albert J. *Beyond the Best Interests of the Child.* New York: Free Press, 1973.

Gruber, A.R. *Children in Foster Care.* New York: Human Sciences Press, 1978.

Jenkins, Shirley and Norman, Elaine. *Filial Deprivation and Foster Care.* New York: Columbia University Press, 1972.

Jenkins, Shirley and Norman, Elaine. *Beyond Placement: Mothers View Foster Care.* New York: Columbia University Press, 1975.

Jones, Mary Ann; Neuman, Renee; and Shyne, Ann. *A Second Chance for Families.* New York: Child Welfare League of America, 1976.

Keith-Lucas, A. and Sanford, C.W. *Group Child Care as a Family Service.* Chapel Hill, N.C.: University of North Carolina Press, 1977.

Lahti, Janet, et al. *A Follow-up Study of the Oregon Project.* Portland, Oreg. Regional Research Institute for Human Services, 1978.

Laird, Joan. "An Ecological Approach to Child Welfare: Issues of Family Identity and Continuity," in Germain, Carel, Editor. Social Work Practice: People and Environments. New York: Columbia University Press, 1979: 174–209.

Maas, Henry S. and Engler, Richard E., Jr. *Children in Need of Parents*. New York: Columbia University Press, 1959.

Maluccio, Anthony N. "Casework with Parents of Children in Foster Care," Catholic Charities Review, 50, 7 (September 1966): 4–12.

Maluccio, Anthony N. "Community-Based Child Placement Services: Current Issues and Trends," Child and Youth Services, 1, 6 (November-December 1977): 1–12.

Maluccio, Anthony N. "An Ecological Perspective on Practice with Parents of Children in Foster Care," in Maluccio, Anthony N. and Sinanoglu, Paula A., Editors, *The Challenge of Partnership: Working with Parents of Children in Foster Care*. New York: Child Welfare League of America, 1981a.

Maluccio, Anthony N. "Promoting Client and Worker Competence in Child Welfare," in *Social Welfare Forum, 1980*. New York: Columbia University Press, 1981b.

Maluccio, Anthony N., et al. "Beyond Permanency Planning," Child Welfare, LIX, 9 (November 1980): 515–530.

Maluccio, Anthony N. and Sinanoglu, Paula A., Editors, *The Challenge of Partnership: Working with Parents of Children in Foster Care*. New York: Child Welfare League of America, 1981.

Nayman, Louis and Witkin, Stanley L. "Parent/Child Foster Placement: An Alternate Approach in Child Abuse and Neglect," Child Welfare, LVII, 4 (April 1978): 249–258.

Simmons, G.; Gumpert, J.; and Rothman, B. "Natural Parents as Partners in Child Care Placement," Social Casework, 54, 4 (April 1973): 224–232.

Taylor, Delores and Alpert, Stuart S. *Continuity and Support Following Residential Treatment*. New York: Child Welfare League of America, 1973.

Wiltse, Kermit T. and Gambrill, Eileen. "Foster Care, 1973: A Reappraisal," Public Welfare, 32, 4 (Winter 1974): 7–15.

Zigler, Edward and Hunsinger, Susan. "Our Neglected Children." Yale Alumni Magazine, 41, 6 (February 1978).

# 2

# Casework with Parents of Children in Foster Care

ANTHONY N. MALUCCIO

Casework with natural parents of children in foster care (foster home or institutional placements) constitutes an integral part of the services given by child welfare agencies. The necessity for providing this service in a qualitative as well as a quantitative fashion has been increasingly recognized, as the field has gained greater awareness and understanding of the multiple and complex problems typical of families whose children move into foster care.

The purpose of this paper is to clarify the role of the caseworker in working with parents of placed children by considering such aspects as the meaning of placement for the family and the child, the caseworker's attitudes toward placement, and some of the generic principles necessary to provide an effective service.

Who are the children needing placement today, and where do they come from? The answers to these questions are in an extensive study conducted by Maas and Engler a few years ago; their findings suggest that a great majority of the nearly 300,000 children in foster care in the United States come from

---

Reprinted with permission from *Catholic Charities Review*, Vol. 50, No. 7 (September 1966), pp. 4–12. 

disorganzied families, show symptoms of emotional disturbance, and seem destined to remain in foster care indefinitely without any prospect of reunion with their parents [1].

The current experiences of agencies throughout the country confirms the findings of Maas and Engler. If we exclude babies awaiting adoption (who present a special situation) and concentrate on older children, we find that a majority suffer from some degree of emotional disturbance. As succinctly expressed in the Child Welfare League of America's *Standards for Foster Family Care Service*, "Children who require placement . . . today tend to come largely from families where social disorganization or personality disorders of parents are so severe as to affect their ability to provide adequate parental care" [2]. Parents who may be going through a crisis, but who have certain strengths, can be helped to keep the children at home through aid from various public welfare programs, counseling in clinics or family agencies, homemaker services, or day care services.

In contrast, the parents of placed children are increasingly those who have variously been labeled as "untreatable," "multi-problem," "inaccessible," "unresponsive," or "hard-to-reach." Often these are parents who have overwhelming reality problems in such areas as health, employment, and housing; who have been traumatized by their own separation experiences and deprivation in early childhood; and who are fearful of any relationship and distrustful of social workers [3]. Their children are not placed voluntarily and carefully, but on an emergency basis as a result of a court-ordered removal, family disintegration, or the development of a gross character disorder or borderline psychosis in the child or the parent. The placement itself is frequently a drastic and traumatic experience for parents as well as children. In addition, child welfare agencies in general, and child welfare workers in particular, experience a sense of frustration and confusion in the face of such an apparently hopeless task.

## IS WORKING WITH PARENTS A "HOPELESS" TASK?

But need this be a "hopeless" task? Should all of these parents be summarily dismissed as being hopeless, untreatable, unresponsive, etc? We think not. These are indeed parents who are burdened by a variety of complex reality problems, psychological conflicts, and inter-personal difficulties. Working with them can be discouraging and time-consuming—in certain cases perhaps even overwhelming—but it is not hopeless or impossible. This is a task requiring the highest of professional skills, the best of agency services, and the greatest of community support.

Only through a total commitment to working with parents can we expect to be truly helpful to them; without this, we are in actuality leaving them to rehabilitate themselves in what we at times expect to be "a self-healing process" [4]. Such a commitment involves the development of an agency philosophy which views help to parents and children as one integrated whole, the conviction that these clients can and should be helped, and the willingness to use professional skills and knowledge in a truly flexible and creative fashion.

## MEANING OF PLACEMENT FOR FAMILY AND CHILD

Placement has tremendous significance for the child as well as his parents and siblings, depending, of course, on such factors as the child's developmental level and the family's circumstances. In one placement after another, we see how physical separation from the parents can threaten the child's sense of identity and self-worth; his feelings of worthlessness, helplessness, and anger can be accentuated by the very act of placement as well as the events leading to it, with consequently adverse effects on his capacity to trust other human beings, to relate to substitute parents, and to grow. Dr. Ner Littner has vividly described the potential effects of separation, particularly on the young child, and the resulting reactive defensive patterns which the child develops [5]. Even though physical separation occurs with a placement, and even though in some cases there is limited if any ongoing contact with the parents, they continue to play an important role in the child's fantasy world.

Similarly, the trauma of separation has a significant impact on the parents. For the mother, in our society, placement connotes a serious social stigma, since it highlights her inability to discharge her maternal functions [6]. With all of our clients, the act of placement reveals their inadequacy as parents and their lack of worth as human beings; it represents another failure which serves to intensify their feelings about previous failures and concomitant doubts about themselves.

While the parents through the placement may experience some temporary relief of their intense anxiety, their negative feelings are more durable and pervasive. Their guilt and anger toward the child are reinforced by their rejection of the child through the placement, thus increasing their overall anxiety. If the child's behavior should improve following placement in a foster home or institution, the improvement often serves to confirm the parents' sense of failure, helplessness and inadequacy. The parents' feelings are directly or indirectly communicated to the child in placement, while the child may further upset his parents through his reactions of anger or indifference or withdrawal.

Without elaborating any further, it is apparent that the biological and psychological bond uniting parents with child endures throughout placement and inevitably affects them in their struggles toward ego growth and reality adaptation. As Draza Kline points out, "there is cumulative evidence that the frequency, nature, and duration of the placed child's contacts with his parents, subsequent to placement, may play a critical role in determining his future development" [7].

While in general we recognize the impact of placement upon the child and his parents, at times we tend to overlook its effect on the child's siblings. Particularly as more children are placed as a result of personality problems and defects in the parent-child relationship, it is not uncommon to have a child placed while leaving behind in the home one or more siblings. As suggested by our knowledge of family interaction, the removal of a significant member from the home tends to upset the often delicate family balance. At times we see that, following one child's placement, another child becomes the focus of parental anxiety and hostility and develops maladaptive symptoms. In other cases, the parents' marital interaction is threatened, further affecting the remaining child as well as the parents. At any rate, in addition to understanding and working with the parents of the placed child, it is important to be aware of the potential effect of the placement on any siblings and to provide appropriate help on a preventive as well as corrective basis.

## THE CASEWORKER'S ATTITUDES

Having considered the impact of a child's foster care placement on the child and his family, we turn to the main focus of this paper—namely, the caseworker's role with natural parents. To begin with, we need to examine the caseworker's attitudes regarding such parents. In an article on countertransference in the residential treatment of children, Rudolph Ekstein, et al., discuss the negative feelings which are aroused in members of the residential staff and which interfere with their relationship with natural parents; Ekstein, et al., indicate that "generally children who have endured a particularly unhappy life experience, or whose condition calls forth immediate pity, are more likely to evoke these fantasies and feelings in total staff with extraordinary swiftness and intensity" [8].

Basically, the above can apply in varying degrees to all caseworkers in child welfare; our concern for the child, coupled with residual childhood conflicts which we may have, may lead to over-identification with the child and rejection of the parents. Thus, we may experience wishes to punish the parents or "rescue" fantasies leading us to see our "mission in life as rescuing helpless children from their wicked parents and becoming the good parents ourselves" [9]. The arousing of our own feelings is compounded by the fact that working with these children is an exacting situation for caseworkers, in view of the need to relate to the complex and multiple set of demands presented by the child, his parents, and substitute caretakers such as foster parents. Often, in this process, the parents become the focus of the caseworker's frustration and anxiety.

Our perception of the parents as bad, inadequate and worthless is easily conveyed to the child as well as the natural parents and substitute parents, thus seriously affecting our relationship with each of them and our efforts to be of help. Our negative view of the parents is in fact reflected in the low concept which they have of themselves. It is therefore worth emphasizing, although perhaps too obvious, that the extent to which we can help a child and his parents is dependent upon the degree to which we can understand our own feelings and learn to accept the parents through the development of mature and objective attitudes.

In contrast to our over-identification with the child, at other times we may become over-involved with the parents, resulting in a tendency to blame the child for his own difficulties or to view the parents as the victims of a disturbed or delinquent child. In either case, the effect is essentially the same: our over-identification with the child or the parents influences our ability to perceive them clearly and objectively, and diagnostic and treatment formulations may then be based on our subjective reactions rather than on the reality of each situation.

## WORKING WITH PARENTS IN THE PRE-PLACEMENT PERIOD

We turn now to our direct work with parents. Although we are at this time primarily concerned with working with the parents following placement, we need to go back to the pre-placement period and the point of referral. Any treatment plan with the child and his parents should be based on a thorough diagnostic evaluation of the child and his total family situation. Our involvement of the parents from the beginning is crucial not only in reaching a decision regarding the advisability of placement, but also in establishing a firm foundation for our ongoing work with the parents and the child.

It is true that there are some situations in which an emergency placement is necessary, thus precluding the implementation of a thorough and careful intake study. On the other hand, there are few "true" emergencies, but many situations in which, with appropriate conviction and strength, we could tolerate the parents' acute anxiety, while also helping them to tolerate their stress long enough to allow us to make a careful study and to determine with the parents the best course of action. As suggested by Draza Kline, in addition to a full understanding of the child, such a study should include an assessment of the following: "(1) The parent's early history, with special emphasis on his separation experiences and his reaction to them; (2) the parent's patterns of relating to his children; and (3) the current patterns of his relationship with adults—his parents, parent substitutes, and the caseworker" [10].

Armed with such an understanding of the child and his parents and their strengths and weaknesses, we are better able to predict the parents' potential reactions to the placement and possible areas of difficulty for them; thus, we can formulate appropriate treatment plans through which to help the parents to cope with the stress created by the placement.

## WORKING WITH PARENTS DURING PLACEMENT

While casework with parents should be based on a differential diagnosis of each situation [11], there are certain considerations which can serve as guidelines in our work with them. First of all, it is important to see the parent as a major client and to make it administratively feasible for the caseworker to concentrate on the parent. Placement thus should be viewed as one aspect of a total service to the parent.

Furthermore, it is crucial that very early in our contact with the parents we obtain a thorough assessment of their strengths and potential as parents, keeping in mind that at the time of placement these are human beings who are at their worst and who expose their weaknesses more than their strengths. This assessment is extremely important since, as Florence Silverblatt indicates, "we must consider the strengthening of parental capacities during the period of placement to be an essential task of our child welfare agencies" [12]. In order to achieve this goal, we need to place emphasis on holding the parents to their responsibilities toward the child as much as possible and helping them to sustain and carry whatever responsibility they can. In effect, our conviction about parental rights should be accompanied by an equal conviction about their responsibilities and appropriate focus on how much of a parent they want or are able to be [13].

While alleviating the parents' guilt is important, we should not go to the extreme of absolving them of total responsibility for the child and his problems and thus encouraging their physical or psychological abandonment of the child. In this regard, it is pertinent to note that too many parents of children in foster care today have for all intents and purposes disappeared from the child's life; in some cases, the parents' whereabouts are unknown to the child or the agency. We must therefore ask ourselves whether more effective services to the parents at the point of referral and early in the placement could not have prevented such total abandonment, with its inherent and often indelible damage to the child as well as the parents. Whenever we have been able to give appropriate help to the parents, we have found that, following removal of the day-to-day pressure of living with the child, some parents can be helped to learn or relearn more adequate ways of discharging their functions.

Involvement of the parents begins long before the act of placement and in the preparation for placement itself. Unless the parents participate actively in placement plans and convey some measure of consent, the child is not able to make constructive use of the experience, regardless of the quality and quantity of services provided to him. In addition, just as the child is helped to face separation, we need to work with the parents in order to help them to understand the meaning of separation and placement, to express the feelings which are aroused in them, and to deal with their attitudes toward the child and placement. The placement inevitably arouses the parents' own unresolved conflicts and experiences with their own parents; reactivation of their feelings colors their relationship with the agency, the caseworker and the child, as well as substitute parents. The parents, as much as the child, have a right to receive help with these feelings and reactions.

Following placement, the parents should be helped to maintain their relationship with the child, as indicated by individual circumstances. As noted earlier, parents remain important in the child's adjustment following the placement just as they were important in the development of his problems. They can be helped, in varying degrees, to allow the child to use the placement constructively. Even if termination of the parent-child relationship should eventually be indicated, maintaining this relationship for a while can have therapeutic value for the child as well as parents; for example, the child can be helped to take on substitute parents more effectively as he sees the reality of his inadequate parents and as he works through his fantasies about them. In order to be of utmost value, visiting between the child and his family should be individually determined and carefully utilized [14].

Since these are usually parents who have weak or defective ego structures and who are very needy themselves, they can best be helped through a total therapeutic approach involving ego-building procedures and aid with immediate practical problems as well as with their emotional difficulties. Kline points out that "a further consideration in offering a total therapeutic service is that, for the client with serious ego-defects, the caseworker must become the integrating force, the source of a corrective emotional and educational experience and, if possible, the new ego ideal [15]. With these parents, it is rarely possible to focus on the resolution of inner conflicts; as a matter of fact, the existence of inner conflicts is often minimal [16]. But we can help them through the conscious use of the relationship, through consistent giving, setting limits, and providing active guidance. As the parents themselves receive some emotional nourishment, they can hopefully be enabled to provide greater gratification for their children.

Although the consistent use of the casework relationship with parents on a long-term basis can be meaningful and helpful, it should be emphasized that families of children in foster care have numerous needs in such areas as health, education, housing, employment, and financial assistance. An important function of the child welfare worker therefore is to help the parents in identifying their central needs and in finding the services required to fulfill them [17].

With many parents of children in foster care, the concepts and techniques of "assertive casework" or working with the "hard-to-reach" and "multi-problem" families can be quite pertinent and effective [18]. In addition we should constantly strive to develop new or more effective methods of working with these parents—methods through which to supplement or complement traditional casework efforts. As an example, certain institutions have introduced some forms of group therapy as an extension of their services to parents [19]. As another example, in a unique experiment described in a recent issue of *The Catholic Charities Review*, a small child-care institution in the country established an office in a rented apartment in the heart of one of the poorest areas of New York City; since many of the children placed in the institution come from this area, the office enabled the casework staff to establish a closer relationship with their families and to adapt casework services to their culture in a truly creative and impressive way [20].

Finally, while recognizing that many parents of placed children are disorganized and disturbed, we should not view all of them in such a stereotyped fashion. We know that there are parents who have certain strengths and who can be helped to resolve their problems sufficiently to result in improvement of the parent-child relationship, enhancement of their potential for parental functioning, and perhaps successful reunion of the child with the parents.

## CLARIFICATION OF LONG-TERM PLANNING

It is of the utmost importance that a child's placement in a foster home or institution not be allowed to continue indefinitely without a clear determination of the long-term plan. Parents and child should be meaningfully involved in the definition and implementation of such a plan. Our experience shows that some parents can be helped to re-establish a home for their child; in a few other cases, the parents can be helped to release a child for adoption and the child can be placed in an adoptive home; but in a majority of cases, neither of these alternatives is feasible or desirable and the child needs to remain in long-term foster care [21]. If so, this fact must be faced by us and our knowledge and skills must be utilized in order to make the most adequate long-term plan and to help both the child and the parents with the reality of their extended separation.

Often it is difficult to reach a decision as to which would be the best of these alternatives; our decision is complicated by the difficulties inherent in each case, the pressure of large caseloads, the lack of resources, and our ambivalence toward the parents and the child. At times, the child is consequently left "dangling" and "drifting" from year to year without clarity or direction. He remains on an unplanned basis in a situation in which he exists rather than lives, a situation which has not been clearly defined for him and which therefore adds to his already confused identity and his disturbed development. As long as we allow this to happen, we are not helping either parents or children, but contributing to their personal and family pathology.

## CONCLUDING COMMENTS

Casework with natural parents of placed children should be based on a deep conviction that parents can be helped and that they have a right to receive help not only for their child's sake, but also for themselves, as human beings with personal worth, feelings, and needs. The specific methods, form, and extent of help which can be provided for parents should be determined through a careful evaluation of their total situation. Other intrinsically important factors in the provision of this help are: (1) the community's support of services to parents; (2) the agency's commitment to work with parents as an integral part of its functions; and (3) the caseworker's creative and flexible use of his professional skills and knowledge.

While eventual reunion of the child with his parents is the ideal goal, in practice this is not feasible in numerous placements, particularly as placed children are coming more and more from families marked by chronic disorganization, severely disturbed relationships, and serious personal problems. The caseworker should face the family situation as realistically as possible and recognize the limitations as well as potentialities of child and parents. Although the goal of reunion between parents and child cannot always be achieved, this does not necessarily represent a failure on the part of the caseworker or the agency; on the contrary, with proper conviction and support, the caseworker can still play a meaningful role by helping parents and child to grow and to live more satisfactorily, although apart from each other.

## REFERENCES

1. Henry S. Maas and Richard E. Engler, Jr., *Children in Need of Parents* (New York: Columbia University Press, 1959), pp. 378–382.
2. *Standards for Foster Family Care Service* (New York: Child Welfare League of America, 1959) p. 3.
3. Draza Kline, "Service to Parents of Placed Children: Some Changing Problems and Goals," in *Changing Needs and Practices in Child Welfare* (New York: Child Welfare League of America, 1960), pp. 37–40.
4. Henry S. Maas, "Highlights of the Foster Care Project: Introduction," *Child Welfare* (July 1959), p. 5.
5. Ner Littner, *Some Traumatic Effects of Separation and Placement* (New York: Child Welfare League of America, 1956).
6. Jeanne C. Pollock, "The Meaning of Parents to the Placed Child," *Child Welfare* (April 1957), p. 10.
7. Kline, *op cit.*, p. 36.
8. Rudolph Ekstein *et al.*, "Countertransference in the Residential Treatment of Children," in *Psychoanalytic Study of the Child*, Vol. 14 (New York: International Universities Press, 1959), p. 189.
9. Pollock, *op cit.*, p. 11.

10. Kline, *op cit.*, p. 46.

11. Esther Glickman, *Child Placement Through Clinically Oriented Casework* (New York: Columbia University Press, 1957), chapters 2 and 7.

12. Florence Silverblatt, "The Child Welfare Agency's Services to Own Parents," in *Today's Child and Foster Care* (New York: Child Welfare League of America, 1963), p. 21.

13. Alan Keith-Lucas, "More, Not Less, Emphasis on Parents' Rights," *Child Welfare* (September 1961), pp. 21–23.

14. Sylvester Adessa and Audrey Laatsch, "Therapeutic Use of Visiting in Residential Treatment," *Child Welfare* (May 1965), pp. 245–251.

15. Kline, *op cit.*, p. 44.

16. Berta Fantl, "Integrating Psychological, Social and Cultural Factors in Assertive Casework," *Smith College Studies in Social Work* (June 1964), p. 199.

17. Kate B. Helms, "Essential Components in a Foster Care Program," in *Today's Child and Foster Care* (New York: Child Welfare League of America, 1963), pp. 53–54.

18. See, for example, Charles J. Birt, "Family-centered Project of St. Paul," *Social Work* (October 1956); Berta Fantl, "Casework in Lower Class Districts," *Mental Hygiene* (July 1961); Berta Fantl, "Preventive Intervention," *Social Work* (July 1962).

19. Alvin E. Winder *et al.*, "Group Therapy with Parents of Children in a Residential Treatment Center," *Child Welfare* (May 1965), pp. 266–271.

20. Sister Mary Christella, F.M.M., "Adapting Service to Culture," *The Catholic Charities Review* (January 1966), pp. 11–15.

21. Draza Kline, "The Validity of Long-term Foster Family Care Services," *Child Welfare* (April 1965), pp. 185–195.

# Part II
# Early Professional Perspectives

# Part II

## Early Professional Perspectives

Although attention to the parents of children in placement has grown over the last decade, it is not new to the profession. As early as four decades ago, authors were alert to the need for a focus on work with parents. This section brings together selections from the writings of three leading pioneers in the field of child welfare: Gordon (1941), Hutchinson (1944), and Jolowicz (1947). Their articles are still vital today because they draw attention to recurring and significant issues.

In Chapter 3, Gordon reviews the shifting emphasis, historically, toward and away from parents. She states that in the late 1800s the entire duration of childhood was the accepted period of care for the child, and the agency's role was that of total parental responsibility. Parents were excluded from agency concern. However, in 1919 there was a "radical change in thinking": the task of the child welfare agency shifted from total responsibility to helping parents with problems and home conditions that led to the child's placement. Gordon laments the fact that, although this philosophical change was well articulated, in practice children in care continued to be surrounded by a "forever" attitude. She therefore advocates early planning for discharge, the use of time-limited care with return home as a goal, the need for client participation in planning and during placement. Gordon regards the request for placement on the part of parents as a recognition of their parental responsibility as well as a desire to do something about a problem that is interfering with their parental functioning.

In Chapter 4, Hutchinson alludes to the child welfare worker as a "baby snatcher" and takes note of the countermovement that almost prohibited separation of parent and child. She states that crucial skills of the worker include knowing when separation is needed and possible and being able to effect the separation. Hutchinson warns of the harm to the client who becomes the target of a worker's unconscious hostility and biases. To be effective, the worker must be aware that a "request for placement is as individual as people are individuals."

Jolowicz's eloquence about the need for children in foster care to maintain ties with their parents is well known in child welfare. Chapter 5 is a condensation of her classic presentation at the 1946 New York State Conference of Social Welfare. Jolowicz addresses the fallacy that removing a child from a bad environment to a good one will make him a respectable citizen. She emphasizes the powerful influence that the absent parent has over the child's internal life, since conflicting feelings about the parents usually remain present in the child. The strength and influence of these feelings are amplified by their being "hidden." The best way of dealing with these feelings, Jolowicz argues, is by continuing to discuss the parents with the child as well as maintaining parent-child contact. Failure to counter the child's "fantasy of the parent" with the "reality of the parent" will probably amplify the usual turmoils of adolescent identity, to the bewilderment of everyone: "But s/he was such a nice little girl/boy!" Emphasizing the importance of work with the parents, Jolowicz ponders: "Good placement is neither easy nor cheap, and one is often led to wonder if as good results could not have been achieved if an equal amount of thought, effort, and time went into working with the child's parents before placement was considered."

The issues brought up by these authors have a familiar ring. Many of them are the issues that child welfare practitioners continue to grapple with today: time-limited placement; early decision making concerning permanent plans for the child; the profound significance of the parents for the child, even from a distance; the importance of parent participation and involvement in placement; and the need to work with the parents as well as the child.

In reading these earlier articles, one is at first pleased by the harmony of thought and the link between decades that these common ideas provide. However, after reflecting, one is also sobered: Why, if these questions were raised long ago, has there been so little change? Why do the issues of yesterday continue to be the issues of today? Reviewing earlier professional perspectives has the value of allowing us to learn from history. As we consider these articles, one of the key questions to bear in mind is: What were the barriers to implementation? The answer may lead us to better understanding and practice with parents.

## SUGGESTIONS FOR FURTHER READING

Clement, Priscilla Ferguson, "Families and Foster Care: Philadelphia in the Late Nineteenth Century," *Social Service Review*, 53: 3 (September 1979): 407–420.

Hanford, Jeannette, "Child Placement as Viewed by the Family Agency," *Social Service Review*, 15: 4 (December 1944): 706–720.

Hutchinson, Dorothy, "The Placement Worker and the Child's Own Parents," *Social Casework*, 35: 7 (July 1954): 292–296.

Jolowicz, Almeda R., "The Hidden Parent." in *Sourcebook of Teaching Materials on the Welfare of Children*. New York: Council on Social Work Education, 1969, 105–110. (Originally presented by the author at the 1946 New York State Conference of Social Welfare.)

Laufer, Marie L., "Casework with Parents: Our Obligation to Their Adolescents in Placement," *Child Welfare*, 32: 9 (November 1953): 3–7.

Philbrick, Norma, "The Interrelation of Parents and Agency in Child Placement," *Journal of Social Work Process*, 3: 1 (December 1939): 17–28.

Radinsky, Elizabeth K., "The Parent's Role in Long Time Care," *Child Welfare*, 29: 2 (February 1950): 8–12.

Smith, Barbara, "Helping Neglectful Parents to Become Responsible," *The Child*, 14: 3 (September 1949): 36–46.

Watkins, Elizabeth G., "So That Children May Remain in Their Own Homes," *The Child*, 18: 2 (October 1953): 25–29.

Weisenberger, Ruth, "Direct Casework with the Child in Foster Home Placement," *Child Welfare*, 30: 4 (April 1951): 3–6.

# 3

# Discharge: An Integral Aspect of the Placement Process

HENRIETTA L. GORDON

As long as it was assumed that discharge simply marked the end of a period of placement, child-placing agencies questioned the value of a discussion confined to the final aspect of their very complicated job. There are so many pressing problems around the period of care—for instance, how to help parents and children bear the terrifying experience of separation, how to help a child, often such a distorted and twisted little being, grow in this artificial soil. But workers in after-care departments can testify to the growing concern with this subject of discharge and its inherent problems.

Two definitions of the word "discharge" are quite illuminating. Discharge means release from a charge or responsibility, the end. It also means performance of a duty or service. Performance is related to purpose or function of that service and the way in which the service is made available to the client. For a clarification of the subject of discharge a clarification of case work goals and procedure is imperative. The many cases marked "case closed—client uncooperative" give mute evidence that our practices often contradict our accepted theory; our functions and procedures are at times at cross purposes with themselves. If an agency is to be clear about the practice of discharge, it must be clear about its function and process.

---

Reprinted by permission of Family Service Association of America, publisher, from *The Family*, Vol. XXII, No. 2 (March 1941), pp. 35–42.

It fell to the family field, historically the first of the social services, to be first confronted with the necessity of re-examining its purpose. The upheaval in our economic life that brought public relief into being has been forcing the family agencies to a more conscious scrutiny of their activities. Since public agencies have taken over responsibility for maintenance, a few family agencies have already come to such thinking as this: A client comes to us because he is faced with a problem in his living with which he feels he must have some help. We can help him if, working with him, we can find a way in which he can use our services effectively, so that when we step out he will be better able to cope with the difficulties that brought him to us. This must of necessity involve a consideration with the client as to what brings him for help, what the agency has to offer, and the terms on which the help can be given. One of the terms naturally will be "For how long the service?" Discharge then becomes a consideration from the point of intake.

In the dependent children's field, pressures toward change have been less precipitous, although the placement service with its problems around intake, the period of care and discharge, has been under philosophical scrutiny. In 1889, the Hebrew Sheltering Guardian Society, in its tenth annual report expressed the following "benevolent purpose"—"that inmates are to be prepared to go forth into the world educated to go into the ranks of society by honest industry and moral work." As long as fifty years ago the principle of discharge was clearly related to purpose and understood so at intake, the period of care was accepted as all of childhood, and the agency assumed its case work responsibility to be the total responsibility of parent to child, the rearing of children. The parent was excluded. In 1919, a radical change in thinking resulted in the Jewish Children's Clearing Bureau's stating as a goal: "To stimulate the discharge of children from institutions and boarding homes as soon as home conditions and welfare of the child permit." The case work goal shifted from complete parental responsibility to responsibility for help with the problems that brought parents to ask for placement—home conditions and the child's resulting behavior. Interestingly for us, this newer concept of case work goal is stated, through implication, in terms of conditions for considering discharge. In 1932, at a tri-city conference held in New York to review child care practices, it was recommended that "preparation for discharge should begin at intake." This was reiterated in 1937 by a committee studying child care needs in anticipation of a merger of the Jewish Child Care Agencies in New York City.

## DISCHARGE BEGINS AT INTAKE

Not only should discharge be an integral part of the placement process but concern with it should begin at intake. Yet records of the period of intake and admission show little recognition with parent, child, and in foster home care with foster parents, that the service of the agency will end. There is little indication of planning for how long the service will continue, or under what circumstances someone else will take over the responsibility assumed by the agency. In actual practice we continue to see children in placement surrounded by a "forever" attitude so that discharges are frequently precipitated by children or parents as unprepared for this experience as they were for placement. This necessitates a long period of after-care. So separate has discharge been seen from the placement experience that after-care departments as distinct units have been the common structure in more consciously functioning agencies.

What does the recommendation that preparation for discharge should begin at intake mean? We have noted in the definition of the term that discharge is an integral part of the purpose of the services and that change in thinking regarding discharge implied change in case work goals. What help is being asked of the child-placing agency? What is the placement function? What is its basic philosophy?

## THE RESPONSIBILITY OF THE PARENT

The placement service begins at a point when the normal life process, that is, the child's growth and development in his own home, in relationship with his own parents, is being severed. This breaking up of a child's natural connections is a traumatic experience for him, despite its very positive values and the real fact that there may be no alternative. In our valid enthusiasm over the vast improvement in child care methods, that is, the actual care that children are now receiving in contrast to earlier institutional and farming methods, and in our appreciation of how much nearer a foster home approximates a real home, we tend to overlook the fact that at best foster care is only a substitute and carries such differences from the natural child-parent relationship as to have quite different, never altogether acceptable, psychological values for child, parent, or foster parent. For the parent, giving up a child for placement means recognizing a problem in relation to rearing his child for which he must ask help. He must ask the agency to take over at least a part of his parental responsibility. Concern with parental responsibility at a point when a parent must ask for placement may sound theoretical but actually it is a cardinal factor in the placement problem. Dr. Thurston says, "There has always been present in the problem of the care of the dependent child this question as to his relationship to his own parents" [1]. It is quite generally accepted that in our culture a child's physical and emotional development is dependent on its relationship with its parents. That is why placement must mean the severing of a normal life process.

Actually in our community the parent is responsible for his child. The primary right and responsibility of parent to child is a law that prevails in all the states of the union. While the state admits a protective obligation to children, rare indeed is the situation in which a community will step in to take over parental responsibility. In New York City, even when the court has removed a child for improper guardianship, that court takes little responsibility for seeing that the child continues away from the parent. Only in the most flagrant violations of our community standards will the S.P.C.C. bestir itself to assume authority over children. For example, a mother who had spent four or five periods in a hospital because of a manic depressive psychosis, whose children came for care in so deplorable a condition that they required two months' hospitalization, took her children home at the end of the second week of her release though she was still on parole and though the doctor advised her that she was not fit to give them care. Here is unsound social practice.

## THE RESPONSIBILITY OF THE WORKER

The concept of primary parental right is at cross purposes with the concept of community obligation for the protection of children, and may be a source of conflict for the case worker. What is her professional responsibility? In the example given, it was to help the mother to some recognition of what responsibility she was able to assume, what help she needed, in the best interests of herself and her children, and to help sustain what capacity she had to meet these responsibilities. Further, because of this mother's particular difficulty in accepting her need for help in bringing up her children, the case worker had to call on such community aids as the hospital social service and such protection for the children as the S.P.C.C. might offer. When case work cannot reach the mother and the community still allows her the right to keep her children, what is our further responsibility? As a case worker, it seems clear to me that I cannot represent the placement function and simultaneously carry responsibility for the community's protective function. A situation may arouse my sense of obligation for social action in relation to basic human needs, but while this sense of obligation may grow out of my professional experience, I must find another avenue of expression for this purpose. I cannot confuse it with my professional responsibility in carrying out my agency's function.

The primary right of the parent to his child is in essence the right of the parent to determine the ultimate solution to the conflict in his relationship to his child. Practice under this philosophy accepts the client as a responsible human being who is asking for help with a problem in his living and recognizes that he must be free to solve that problem to his own satisfaction if he is to live with that solution. The authoritative reformist role of the case worker gives way to the concept of self-determination of the client. But, you may ask, what is the case worker's responsibility? Is it not to diagnose the parent's ability to function for his child, to recognize the period when even a most disturbed parent may be capable of constructive relationship with his child as against those times when the child may need protection from the parent, in order that we can know how to help the parent? Earlier we mentioned briefly the community's obligation to protect the child and the case worker's part in calling in such help. We certainly must understand the meaning of a parent's behavior in relation to his child, if we are to help him with the problem that brought him to us, his conflict about his responsibility for rearing his child. He and we ultimately must know whether he does or does not want to assume his parental responsibility and to what extent. In testing this out it is helpful to recognize that although emotional ill health underlies the difficulties in the child-parent relationship, it is insight and determination to help himself that motivate the parent's coming to us. We must respect and challenge that determination.

Psychiatrists hold that in emotional disturbances insight is the most important indication of the degree of health still left in any person, and this, together with the willingness and ability to come to the doctor, constitutes the most important sign of a favorable prognosis. In fact, their therapy consists in building up this insight and in supporting and challenging the will to do something about the ailment. We who call ourselves social doctors, who have tended to take liberally from the psychiatric philosophy, theory, and technique, seem to have overlooked this principle which is basic to therapy in emotional disturbance. We subscribe to the theory that being able to take help is a sign of health, yet when a parent brings us his child for placement, our way of giving help betrays our feeling that by his coming the parent shows he is too sick to carry his responsibility. We tend, therefore, to take over not a part but the total parental responsibility.

Agency paternalism as against self-determination of the client has persistently characterized foster care. It has its roots deep in the history of the care of dependent children. The very first child-care institution, the New York Orphan Asylum Society, established in 1789, revealed in its charter its total parental role, even to the extent of complete surrender by all relatives as a condition for acceptance of a child for care. Psychologically, too, it is natural for children's workers to assume a parental role, first, because the dependence of childhood engenders a feeling of deep concern and calls out in us this strongest of instincts, the parental instinct. It is as though the child in each of us tends to identify with the dependent child and wants to be to him what we each have wanted for ourself, a protective parent. Second, the parental role is natural because actually at least a part of the parental responsibility is delegated to the agency at placement.

Under the philosophy of self-determination of the client, practice must therefore be rooted in an unshakable conviction of the validity of the principle; it must spring from respect for the essential dignity of human beings; it must be based on the belief that even a more or less bewildered client has the right to determine his own destiny with what case work help we have to offer; and it must have faith in his ability to bear the consequences of that right.

We can see that the attempt of the case worker to be consistent meets with two essential difficulties. The first arises from the difficulties that a human being has in separating her own experiences and her own needs from those with which her client is struggling. It takes long years of experience (besides a conviction in the rights and abilities of human beings to determine their own destinies) for the most professionally developed person to be able to say: "This is not my child. I cannot carry responsibility for his total life problem. The help I can give is defined by the amount of responsibility the community takes for dependent children, and described more specifically by the function of the agency I represent." The second difficulty arises when the agency's function and the philosophy on which it is based are not too clearly defined. Their clarification can be a bulwark of support not only to the client, as he struggles to determine for himself what he really wants when he comes for help and whether he can bear to take it, but also to the case worker.

## HELPING THE PARENT AND THE CHILD

If we accept the parent's coming for help as a sign of his insight, his essential strength, and desire to solve his problem, and accept as our working philosophy the right of self-determination and the parent's primary right to his child, then we shall see as our responsibility not the client's total problem, whether rooted in his personality or in his environment, but the role allotted to us by the service we represent. In child placement it means to help the parent know what placement will really mean to him and to his child, to leave the decision to him while we hold him to the realities involved, so that he does not continue through evasion of the truth to remain enmeshed in his conflict. In other words we must so clearly present to him the terms on which the services of the agency can be offered that he can know whether he wants the service on these terms. Only thus can the client decide whether this is the

the help he wants and whether he can use it toward solving the problem that brought him seeking for help. After placement it includes, besides actual care needed by the child, a relationship with the parent that leaves him still responsible for having placed his child and for the choice as to the ultimate solution of the problem of responsibility for rearing that child. Placement is seen now as one way through which a parent may find the solution to his problem. That problem is only fully solved when the client can take back the responsibility he asked us to assume or when he surrenders his claim to sharing it.

In the placement situation the question, "Who is the client?" has been a source of controversy. The child in placement is in need of vital help and is receiving it. He is experiencing difficulties with which we are often ill equipped to help him. If, however, we accept the philosophy of self-determination and the primary right of parent to child, then, even after placement, the relation of parent to child remains the focus of attention; for in it we see rooted the child's old and new problems of adjustment. Since public relief and aid to dependent children have made it possible for more parents and relatives to care for their own children, it has been increasingly evident that except where there is actually no home, children are brought to placement largely because of a problem in the child-parent relationship. Thus, the parent is the client, his relation to his child the central problem.

## CASE ILLUSTRATIONS

With such a definition of function, discharge must begin at intake, for from the beginning the case worker is concerned with whether and how the parent can use the period of placement in the solution of his problem. Can he or can he not be a parent to his child? When he takes back his responsibility, or gives it up, then for him the problem is settled. The worker ultimately came to this realization in the case of Mrs. C, who had asked for the placement of her 9-year-old son.

> Mrs. C had been having marital difficulty. Her husband had never maintained her or their son, David, adequately. Soon the family had to apply for relief. Mrs. C separated from her husband. Her dissatisfaction mounted until finally she decided that for her the solution lay in the placement of her child and a job for herself. Her ambivalence was clear at intake. She would find it difficult to see her child in the care of another mother. It was arranged therefore that she would not visit in the foster home for the first six

months. Soon she was working as a practical nurse and was much happier. David, however, was finding it difficult to take to the foster home. He seemed happy there but in the semi-monthly visits with his mother at the office he was asking her when she would take him home. The placement worker in her interviews with the mother was supporting her in the decision to leave the child in placement, through reviewing with her the difficulties she had experienced before his placement. At the end of the six months, the child was replaced in a permanent home, and the mother permitted to visit. She soon complained about the distance to the foster home, that the foster mother was not motherly enough and her children were unfriendly, and insisted on replacement. In several interviews she cried about the boy's begging her to take him home, and about her guilt in not doing it. When the boy questioned both mother and worker as to how long he would be placed, the worker was at a loss as to what to tell him, and the mother would say, "For a little while."

Mrs. C's criticism of the foster home and the requests for replacement made it clear to the case worker that the problem lay in the mother's feeling of responsibility for the rearing of her child, but since the "diagnosis" had been that she could function best with her child away and since that seemed to be borne out by her very happy adjustment in her work, the worker decided to try to let the mother have some share in the rearing of her child through discussion as to what kind of home she thought her child would be happy in. Mrs. C's prompt reply was, "I can't tell you; that's your job." She seemed clear that whereas her difficulty was around her feeling of responsibility for rearing her child, she could not solve that by taking over part of the agency function, decisions about placement. She must decide whether she would take her child or would temporarily or permanently surrender claim to rearing him. It became clear to the worker that the job was a solution to part of the mother's problem, but that the problem that led her to placing David was in her relationship with him; that her conflict was being projected on the question of type of home and the length of placement. Now the worker was able to help Mrs. C face it more clearly. Mrs. C kept insisting that the child be moved to see if he could be happier elsewhere and stated that in the meantime she had applied for relief, adding laughing, "I'll never get it on the terms I'm insisting upon." When the worker could accept that the mother was wanting and yet not

> wanting placement, and that it was all right for her to decide either way, she could then be firm that no other plan could be made for the boy until Mrs. C decided for how long she would want this service. Mrs. C soon agreed that that would have to be done, that her confusion was upsetting David, so that he could not really use the foster home. Finally she came to the decision that, having found work so satisfying, she would have to find a way of living with her boy that would allow her to go on with the job. This she did within a month and the boy was discharged for a two months' trial period. At the end of that period, Mrs. C reported how happy she and David were and how much more grown up David had become.

No foster home is perfect because no home is perfect. Yet many a child has been subjected to replacement after replacement to satisfy a complaining parent who was projecting his confusion about whether he really wanted the service and for how long he would need it. In the placement of David C the case work service was to help Mrs. C assume responsibility for the placement and what use she could make of it. It is clear that the question of discharge was an integral part of the placement service. The case work services were based on a recognition of Mrs. C's essential health and her right to make a decision, and included a challenge to the impulse to do something about the problem, which had made it possible for her to ask for help.

This is not to imply that a child can or need be discharged at the end of a year or two or three, for that will depend upon circumstances. Nor does it imply that foster home care cannot be given to children whose parents will be interested and visiting in the home. It does mean that from the beginning both the parent and the agency will know that the service will end and that the when and how are essential realities in the ultimate solution. It does mean that, before we settle into a pattern of care, the child and the parent will be clearer about what placement will mean to them and whether they can use it. It means, too, that the worker will be freer to recognize when the parent needs help to hold to his own plan, as in the case of Eve K.

> Eve K, aged 9, had been in foster care since her second birthday, just after her mother's death. Her father's devotion and interest in eventually having a home for her were unquestionable. He visited fairly regularly and took her to visit his family during the holiday season. Eve was quite devoted to him. During the past year he had been seeing the child less regularly and less frequently. At times he had brought along a woman friend and Eve had confided to the worker and to the foster family that she

didn't like "her." The child became disturbed by the father's growing neglect of her and his apparent interest in the woman. Her troubled feelings were manifested in quarrels with friends, insatiable demands on the foster mother, and restlessness at school. Then the foster mother became ill and replacement was necessary. Mr. K came in to discuss the pending change of home. He was upset and talked about wishing he could take Eve home. The worker asked about his plans, indicating that Eve seemed to be wanting more than he felt free to give. Replacement in a permanent home was presented as a possibility. Mr. K said no, he had not wanted the child to call the foster mother "mother," and he would be wanting to take her home some day. The worker said she knew he was thinking that, but what did he mean by some day? Mr. K said he had no way of knowing. He hoped to get married and establish a home for the child. He talked of her excessive demands and his fear that no stepmother could satisfy them. The worker accepted that as a real problem for him and wondered whether he would be wanting to leave her in a foster home till she grew up. He questioned whether the city would allow that and was told that he might have to pay for her care now that he was earning money. He asked that she be placed nearer to him so he could visit more frequently. We discussed how his plans would affect our plans for her continued placement. She would have to know whether and when there would be a chance of going home so that she could make an adjustment to placement.

Several weeks later Mr. K came in to say that he did not want a permanent home for his child; he really wanted her. The question of how much longer he thought placement would be necessary was raised and he said six months to a year. He then added that he had remarried a few weeks ago and his wife was continuing to work so that they could furnish a home. We discussed the possibility of postponing discharge for one year, two, or three, and the purpose that would be served for them and for Eve.

The following week Mr. and Mrs. K were seen and told there was a home for the child where she could remain for the school period, nine months. They both thought that would be just right. During this time they would be visiting Eve but would not be talking to her about going home until the end of that period for they feared disturbing her. It was recognized that though they wanted her they had some reservations about being able to carry

> out that responsibility. We discussed Eve's part in making this new adjustment and they came to the decision that they would tell her their plans.
>
> On invitation, Mrs. K came in twice during the first six months, talked about never having had any children, wanting to be a mother to Eve and fear of Eve's over-activity. We considered how it would be if she did not assume this responsibility. A month before school closed, on being contacted, Mrs. K said that they had no apartment yet and wondered what would happen. Worker again questioned whether they were able to take Eve. She made clear what would be involved for them and for the child in a more permanent placement.
>
> Two weeks later the K's advised that they had an apartment and were busy furnishing it. On the last day of school Eve went to camp. Mrs. K was in the office and we talked about Eve's difficulties. At the end of the camp period Mrs. K met Eve at the train and took her home directly. Two weeks later Mrs. K called to find out how to get some of Eve's belongings which were still in the foster home. She added that she "certainly had thought it would be much harder."

This is, indeed, a cursory picture of what took place. It omits Eve's activity altogether. For example, at one point she indicated her fear of going home, although she wanted to, by saying "I ain't going to call her mama. She's nice, but I don't know her long enough." It does indicate how these perplexed parents were helped to know what was involved for them in the various possible solutions, so that they could know which decision they could live with. Often, in an attempt to protect adult and child from the fear and pain involved in a readjustment, we fail to help them know more clearly what is involved in the decision they are making. Then they must and do put upon the case worker the responsibility for making the decision.

Finally, we must consider the discharge problem of the child without parents. Now the child becomes the client and his relationship to the foster family the problem. Frequently the child must first be helped to find what use he can make of the placement situation, on what terms he can give himself to the relationship before he and the foster family together can accept that our service will end, and how at that time they will carry the further responsibility. When there are no interested parents, discharge seems to be even more difficult to contemplate. Here foster care would indeed seem to be forever. Again we must look to our purpose.

Every child needs a parental relationship for his growth. Where there are no parents, substitute parents need to be found among foster parents who want to assume a responsibility for the rearing of the child and who are prepared to help the child feel that within the limits of their capacity the family is taking him on. Child and foster parents will need to know what that will mean to them, what obligations it places on them. A foster family may be willing to take this responsibility and yet need our help in holding to this purpose. Sometimes it is money that befogs the issue and sometimes our very concern about the child's security interferes with the way in which it is to be achieved, as, for instance, in the case of Harry F.

> When Harry, a bright, attractive youngster, was placed at the age of ten it was clear that he would need foster care "forever," since he had no parents and was not eligible for adoption. The home chosen was that of a family financially comfortable. The foster parents both expressed a desire for a child who could become a member of their family. They had only two sons and had always wanted a larger family. Soon the foster mother was telling with pride that Harry was taken for one of her children; there was such a close relationship. The foster parents both talked about how gladly they would help through college should he be interested. The foster mother made demands on the agency for all the boy's special needs, while she was supplying him with many luxuries of her own. Fearing the boy might feel deprived or discriminated against, the agency continued for seven years to carry full responsibility. Distressed about its implications, but because of her feeling for the boy, the worker, whenever possible, met all requests for additional clothing, carfare, and incidentals. Naturally Harry knew of all these discussions. How he felt about them can only be conjectured. He knew also of the foster mother's deep concern about him. As he grew older, she would not let him work summers; he needed a vacation, she thought, as did her children. When the boy was approaching his eighteenth birthday, the foster mother was told there would be no more funds for Harry, except for a partial scholarship for a short period. This was the first attempt to clarify what obligations are imposed in taking a child on such a basis. Experience had taught the foster mother that persistence was fruitful but the worker stood firmly on the reality that there was no money. Harry expressed some concern about how the foster mother felt about the matter though he knew he would in any event remain in the home. Soon the foster mother realized her persistence was of no avail. Her whole attitude changed and her husband confirmed her feeling. Of

> course this boy was a part of her family, no matter what the partial scholarship would amount to. There was no question about it; Harry would continue his schooling. For the first time it was made clear to the boy, too, what he really meant to the family.

In this case there was an evasion of the problem of the child's relationship to the foster family, through kindly intent to protect him. The worker failed to see the foster mother's own ambivalence projected on minor money matters. Through not clarifying with the foster mother her real interest in the boy, she interfered with a solution of the boy's problem—finding foster parents who could frankly affirm their willingness to be substitute parents with what obligation was within their power to assume. Had the foster mother been helped to know what obligations she was imposing on herself by taking this boy on as a member of her family, not only she but also the boy would have had a happier time of it.

Discharge emerging as the very purpose of placement, beginning at intake, brings us back to some consideration of the structure of the agency. Although that is really not within the scope of this paper, it does make me pause to wonder whether intake and discharge services can be so separate and distinct from the placement unit as they often are today.

## CONCLUSION

We have re-examined our purpose and philosophy in order to be able to understand better the function that we are asked to serve. I do not mean to minimize the complexity of placement. To me it becomes clear, however, that the case work service to children in placement can under no circumstances be an ultimate solution of their problems. Children belong first and foremost to their parents and need to belong to them. If we accept the parents' coming to ask for placement as indicating not only recognition of a difficulty in being parents—a recognition of their responsibility—but also a desire to do something about the conflict which is interfering with their functioning as parents, the ultimate purpose of placement becomes clear: to help the parent in his efforts to determine when, if ever, he will be able to resume that obligation. If, with our case work help, the parent cannot assume responsibility for placing his child and yet cannot relinquish the claim to that responsibility, our service can be of little use to him or to his child. Where there is no parent, the purpose of placement is to help the child and the foster parents determine how much responsibility they can take together for their relationship. It includes their knowing early that the agency service will end and what obligations this fact will place on them. When an agency sees its function as serving these purposes, it can take seriously the recommendations that discharge be an integral part of placement beginning at intake. It will be nothing more or less than applying the Biblical precept, "Whatever thou thinkest to do remember the end and thou canst not go amiss."

## REFERENCE

1. Henry W. Thurston: *The Dependent Child*. Columbia University Press, New York, 1930, p. 9.

# 4

# The Request for Placement Has Meaning

DOROTHY HUTCHINSON

It is characteristic of social workers that they want to do a better job. They do not remain satisfied for long. The relentless pressure from people in trouble impels them toward a perpetual examination of their work. Frustrations and failures serve as incentives to deeper self-scrutiny and supply the wish for greater achievement. The foreground of the war and the prospect of rehabilitation add a further stimulus to the study of old practices. The child-placing worker today is attempting to appraise and to reappraise her workmanship, to understand placement more accurately, and to bring greater skill to her practice. It is the purpose of this paper to re-examine some of the implications of child placement and to review these as they bear on the parent, on the child, and on the worker.

The request for placement is merely the threshold to a family situation. Many times it signifies the culmination of unbearable conditions, a near breaking point of conflicting forces within the parent and his attempt at a solution to his predicament. Sometimes it denotes an inability to fulfill and a running away from the pressing responsibilities of parenthood. In the majority of cases it involves a large degree of repudiation of the child, whether this is openly expressed or disguised beneath a mixture of guilt, of martyrdom,

---

Reprinted by permission of Family Service Association of America, publisher, from *The Family*, Vol. XXV, No. 4 (June 1944), pp. 128–132.

and/or of indulgence. Most parents are driven to great lengths before they can ask for placement and practically all have to be helped with a decision that so violently contradicts their own code of behavior and that of society. Placing one's child even with the best and most benevolent of reasons is injurious to one's self-esteem and a blow to the conscience. However desirable, the great dilemma of placement is its abnormality, as compared to customary family life, and it is this very abnormality that throws upon the worker a responsibility for helping the parent with it.

> Mrs. Y's new baby, Agnes, is illegitimate. She becomes a guilty intruder in a family of six legitimate children. She preys on her mother's mind. Mrs. Y anxiously points out her difference from the other children. Mr. Y will not speak to the child and tortures his wife with constant reminders of her indiscretion. After 20 years of marriage to an abusive husband Mrs. Y is still irrevocably bound to him and insists on being mistreated. When the child is 4 years old Mrs. Y seeks a children's agency, demanding placement for Agnes who is, by now, suffering greatly. The child symbolizes Mrs. Y's sin and her uppermost desire is to blot out all reminders of this. The case worker's study of the situation confirms the need to place Agnes for whatever peace of mind is possible for both mother and child. However, as plans for a foster home develop and the time for placement is at hand, Mrs. Y begins to withdraw and to be doubtful of her decision. Her conflict at what she is about to do paralyzes her ability to act on her original decision. The case worker does not leave this mother to decide by herself but draws out her worry and actively throws her weight in favor of placement. She deliberately gives Mrs. Y sufficient approval and support so she is able to feel that she not only has a right to place her child but also is doing a good and approved thing for both herself and Agnes. In this case the worker does not wait for the mother to make up her mind but, because she sees the significance of Mrs. Y's request for both herself and Agnes, takes an active responsibility for encouraging placement and thereby helps both mother and child.

The request for placement frequently involves the parent who can no longer stand the strains pressing on him from without and from within. His desire to place his child may be the only sign of dissatisfaction with himself, an unwillingness to go on, and a wish to break the vicious circle in which he finds himself. If at this point he meets with too great obstruction or disapproval, he may give up and retreat into his vicious circle. Placement for him is always an active step and action, particularly of this nature, requires great courage. In the case of Agnes' mother the worker's skill consists not only in diagnostically understanding what she is dealing with but also in allying herself with the spark of courage she discovers in Mrs. Y.

The request for placement can also mean for the parent a denial of his difficulties, his sins, and his failures. He chooses to deny and to repudiate these by removing from his immediate gaze "all evidence of the crime." Many young unmarried mothers who give up their babies for adoption are above all concerned with hiding and covering up their "unhappy tracks" as soon as possible. Their request for placement is a request for cancellation of the deed itself. The case worker who understands what she is dealing with can (depending on the individual case and the worker) help a mother face her predicament and in so doing give up her child without denying it. An unmarried mother cannot really give up her baby if she refuses to acknowledge the baby. She can in many instances be helpfully led to face it and to surrender the child with more peace of mind and with the assurance that she is doing something beneficial.

Some parents seek a child-placing agency as a kind of super-conscience which gives them permission to go ahead with a decision they have already made, where this permission is needed as parental sanction. The act of placement for other parents may be a vindictive measure directed at the child, at the marital partner, or at himself, that is, the perpetuation and living out of long-held grudges.

The above examples illustrating various types of the placement request are, of course, oversimplified. The majority of such requests are mixtures of various motives, psychologies, strivings, and practical factors growing out of individual situations. In the midst of these is the great need for *diagnostic understanding*. To *know what* we are dealing with is the best guarantee of service as well as an insurance against damage to parents and children. Above all, every request for placement grows out of a family situation involving a man, a woman, and a child. We cannot select foster homes for children, we cannot help children to be placed and parents to place them, unless we see some meaning in the life of the person making the request. The child-placing worker at intake is faced with a highly emotional situation back of which lie the story and the forces that have brought to pass the request itself. To understand this is imperative to real helping.

Not many parents who come to child-placing agencies want to change or to be changed. The very fact that the parent seeks a solution to his predicament by means of a children's agency is evidence of this. The problem in most instances lies within the parent first and then becomes manifest in the child.

> Mrs. B is an immature and sickly person who suffers acutely from competition with her 6-year-old-son George. She speaks openly of her hatred for him and is actively cruel and punishing with him. George, at 6, is a highly anxious child who vacillates between depressions and destructive activity of a terrorizing nature. Day after day becomes a battle of wills and an outwitting of each other on the part of mother and son. Mrs. B asks for placement as the only way of keeping her sanity and as the means by which her suffering can be mitigated.
>
> She is fairly intelligent, is able to acknowledge her hatred of George and her feeling of competition with him. To the case worker she speaks of wanting to feel happier and to become different and she sees this as essential before the child can ever be returned to her. Mr. B, 20 years older than his wife, is fond of George and is willing to place him in order to have peace at home. Through the efforts of the case worker Mrs. B voluntarily seeks the services of a psychiatrist for herself and seems eager for the forthcoming help. However, after a few interviews she refuses to continue, preferring her misery. She makes herself more and more sick so she will surely not have to take the child back home. To do so would mean giving up her competition with George and, back of this, her possessive love for her husband. Her desire to change "falls short." It was only possible on her own terms, those of an unconditional love from her husband. He must love no one but herself, not even their child.

Not all parents are as difficult and as immature as Mrs. B. There are those, in contrast, whose response to the case worker's interest in them and recognition of them as real people is remarkable. Although their outward request for placement is put in terms of the child, they are close to wanting some help directly for themselves. There are many placement situations where the major case work focus needs to be on the parent and, indeed, where it is the only assurance that both the child and his parent can beneficially use the service. Although more than half the case work in child-placing agencies is with adults, the children's field still suffers from a reputation of working only with and for children. Placement in most instances is both futile and barren without a case work relationship with the child's own parents. "Family case work" is not the monopoly of any one field, just as the factor of separation is not the exclusive possession of the children's field. The request for placement can validly begin in either family or children's agencies, although it comes more frequently to the latter. The same diagnostic skill is needed in both settings, as well as a willingness to renounce possessiveness of cases in favor of joint and mutual working together, on the one hand or, on the other, giving up the case to the appropriate agency, when indicated. Where such professional relationships obtain we may hope to avoid those twin pitfalls, namely, the family worker using placement as a hasty first resort and the children's worker only at long last.

To the child old enough to understand, the request for his placement is usually a frightening and disillusioning experience, coming as it so frequently does on the heels of his parents' rejection. In many instances the child actually and emotionally has *already* been separated from them. His present placement or replacement comes as further repudiation of his desirableness and seems to him now the final proof of his badness. To say that he feels unwanted is not enough; that he needs love, insufficient. Certain children who are placed not only feel that they are unwanted but also that behind this lies the fact that they are defective and *therefore* unwanted. For years placed children have been described as feeling "atypical" and "different" from other children. Depending on the individual situation, what the child actually feels is something stronger and more disturbing than "being different." From his own inner point of view, perhaps, he regards himself as downright "queer." To feel that he is defective is worse than to feel he is bad. Many children, the necessity for whose placement comes about because of the parent's commitment to a state hospital, need a great deal of help with their feelings not only concerning their parents but also concerning themselves.

It is very easy for many children to look on placement as punishment, not just because of what they have done but because of the kinds of thoughts they have had about their parents. Children are afraid of their thoughts as well as of their actions. The placement experience now becomes proof to them of those bad thoughts; to some children it means that God or their parents are now actively bringing retaliation to bear against them.

To know the particular set of feelings and ideas that individual children bring to placement requires a *diagnostic understanding of their past relationships.* Placement itself is frequently only the re-creation of older life situations in which the child felt uncherished, confused, and betrayed. It is what the child brings to placement that necessitates giving him a large measure of help with it. To expect a child to live alone through the trauma of separation is to deny his need and his suffering and to evade case work responsibility. The child is prepared for the future by supporting him in the present. His need is for a person who really understands his fears and confusions and who is able to talk to him in a realistic way about them. It is easier to do this where the reasons for separation lie in the practical areas of the parent's life—for example, where a mother must work or a father gets sick. It is more difficult when the deplorable behavior of the parent or of the child is obviously a major cause. To avoid talking with a child about his troubles is to deny them. Although at first a child may be unable to discuss these troubles of his own accord it is reassuring to have a worker express what is happening to him in a realistic, matter-of-fact, and accepting manner. He gains assurance when the worker says that she knows he did not get along at home, that things didn't go well, and that what seemed to happen there to him really *did* happen. To leave the child alone with his feelings about what has taken place or to avoid them by just building up a rosy future is to miss the child's real suffering and to lose out on a critical opportunity for forestalling the dangers of denial, fantasy, and repression.

The worker herself plays a major role in the sequence of events around placement. She is confronted with disturbing facts, circumstances, and responsibilities. The constant exposure to separation of parents and children is likely to arouse her own tender feelings about the subject. Awareness of how the placement process can affect her and her own feelings leads to greater control on the worker's part and this, in turn, to greater skill. Case workers are human beings. They are also instruments by which other human beings seek to work out their desires, their conflicts, their enmities, and their bad wishes. The case worker in child placement frequently encounters situations that touch off her own sensitivities in regard to parent-child relationships and relations between men and women. Child placement frequently has to do with men who hate women and women who hate men. It is often face to face with cold, unrelenting wives, with husbands who shun responsibility, with philanderers, with bad women, with the eccentric, with those who hold grudges, and with all manner of people whose lives exemplify sickness, immaturity, and irregularity. Child placement is a constant witness to the child who is being exploited emotionally at the expense of deficient and unhappy parents. Such a background for everyday work calls for a high degree of objectivity and control of one's feelings. The worker herself needs to be unconflicted about highly disquieting subjects—sex, marital relations, incest, adultery, rivalries, jealousies, exploitations, and separation of children from parents. A worker who compulsively believes in the child's own family at all costs and under any circumstances will have difficulty in seeing when separation is beneficial. She will also find it impossible to help a parent with separation when this is necessary.

The worker who consciously or unconsciously feels she is "stealing babies" from parents cannot help an unmarried mother give up her child for adoption. There was a time when the worker in the children's field was called a "baby snatcher." This was expressive of a too ready willingness to take children away from their own homes. This was followed by a countermovement which almost prohibited her from separating children and parents at all or made her feel guilty when she did so. The skill of the present consists, first, in the worker's knowing when separation is needed and possible and, second, in feeling free and unconflicted in handling this with both child and parent. The case worker's expertness is more than a body of knowledge and more than a mastery of method. It involves having come to terms with the less civilized aspects of life and a comfortable acceptance of all manner of transgressions. The case worker has to be able to talk easily on many subjects which, although they may be distasteful to her personally, must be discussed by the client if he is to have eventual peace of mind. The request for placement of one's child almost always involves new and old anxieties for parents. It is fraught with ambivalences and defenses. The case worker who is able and free to talk about these anxieties with parents, who does not avoid them or sacrifice them to the practical exigencies of placement, comes closer to being truly helpful. The greatest harm likely to be done to the client lies in those situations where he becomes the victim of the unconscious hostilities and biases of a worker who has no insight into her own feelings. Not only does the worker need to know what she is doing but she must also *believe in* what she is doing. She must feel she has a right to place children and have confidence in the soundness and in the goodness of a well-conducted child-placement program.

The request for placement also has significant meaning to foster parents, but it is not the purpose of this paper to cover this area in any detail. Although the foster mother lives with the child and, in boarding situations, frequently sees the parent also, her relation to both is different from that of the case worker. In order to give the child her mothering and care, the foster mother must certainly become involved closely in his life. She loves, judges, disciplines, and is personal, whereas the case worker is professional and unentangled at the same time that she is sincere and warm with the child. Her contribution does not compete with that of the foster mother but supplements it. The case worker is likely to be the only person in a child's life able to talk objectively with him about his worries, to see his present troubles in relation to past experiences, and to face with him difficult and necessary facts without becoming his enemy. The child is inclined, if not impelled, to reproduce with the foster mother old attitudes and feelings held toward his own parents. By contrast the case worker can refuse to allow him to do this at the same time that she gives him her support and understanding.

The request for placement is as individual as people are individual. Behind this request lies the life story of men, women, and children. To understand the implications of placement, to read its meaning in each case, is the responsibility of the case worker as well as her opportunity for more effective helping. The gist of separation and of placement is psychological and emotional. A recognition of this fact is the first step in being able to do anything about it, for we cannot treat problems we do not see, nor can we help people we do not understand. Child placement always has to do with people in need. Surely they have a right to a worker's best diagnostic understanding, for out of this comes the key to helping them.

# 5

# A Foster Child Needs His Own Parents

ALMEDA R. JOLOWICZ

Every experienced child welfare worker is sometimes tormented by doubts of the efficacy of foster home care for a child who must be cared for away from his own home. In fact, a worker viewing the end result of years of foster care for a child will sometimes remark that the child could not have been much worse off if he had remained in the home from which he was removed.

It is true that many children in foster homes have grown up happy and well adjusted; these help to preserve our faith in what we are trying to do. And some are never able to adjust at all.

There are other children, however, who for some years after going into a foster home seem to be well adjusted to it until adolescence. At about that time the boy or girl becomes more than normally moody, irritable, and defiant. Often such a youngster, who for years had had only a desultory contact with his own kinfolk, or none at all, will suddenly go to great lengths to look them up, and sometimes will even begin to act like one of his parents.

One such child is Mary, who was placed in a boarding home at the age of 4. Her father had left home some time before, and no one knew what became of him. Her mother, a promiscuous woman, had often entertained men at home even before her husband left her. This continued afterward, and there is no doubt that the child knew much of her mother's intimate affairs.

---

Reprinted from *The Child*, Vol. 12, No. 2 (August 1947), pp. 18–21. Condensed from a paper given at the New York State Conference of Social Welfare, New York City, November 1946.

Mary adjusted fairly well to her foster home, was sweet, obedient, never a real problem. To everyone's relief the mother visited her only rarely. The child seldom, if ever, asked about her mother. The social worker rarely mentioned the mother to the little girl, and the foster mother did so only when she expressed her disapproval of the mother's visiting.

At 14 this well-behaved, sweet child became "boy crazy" to a rather alarming degree, and when the foster mother finally discovered some notes written by the girl which in her opinion were vulgar and seductive, the comfortable years in the foster home came to an abrupt end. Because the girl's behavior seemed to be patterned on her mother's, no one will ever convince the foster mother that blood is not thicker than water or that her years of care were not wasted.

Another example is John. Born out of wedlock, John lived in several successive foster homes during his first 3 years. Then he became settled with foster parents, who lived on a farm, and there he remained throughout childhood. The foster parents did not adopt him. In all these years his mother never visited him, and the boy never asked about her, though he knew the foster parents were not his own, and no one mentioned the mother to him.

When John reached adolescence, behavior difficulties appeared, which did not seem important, but which gradually grew more serious. He refused to do his chores and would leave the farm for absences during which no one knew where he was. He said that he did not have to obey his foster mother, toward whom he had previously been affectionate, and he began to ask many questions about his own mother, whom he could not remember having ever seen. Finally, the foster parents asked the agency to remove him, and a series of unsuccessful placements in wage and work homes followed.

## CHILD INFLUENCED BY ABSENT PARENT

Such stories make one stop and think. Could a mother who apparently had been forgotten by her daughter have more effect on the daughter's life than the foster home? Could a boy who had never known his own mother be so influenced by her that after a dozen years with kind and loving foster parents he entirely rejected them? Is there something in the parent-child relationship that gives a parent control over the child even in absence?

To answer these questions we have to go back to a misconception upon which some—perhaps many—foster home placements have been made. That is the mistaken idea that one has only to remove a child from a bad environment and place him in a good one to make him into a respectable citizen. This concept of the child's being a pliable piece of material, which can be molded into a desirable finished product by proper training and environment, is part of the historical development of the philosophy of child care programs.

In this philosophy behavior was the result of habit, and habit the result of training. That a child already had tendencies that would direct his behavior, that a child had an inner life that might be far more important in the development of his character than his outer life, were concepts far in advance of the early workers.

We know now that every child coming into foster care must be regarded as an individual needing help, and that there should be no place in our thinking for generalities about good and bad environments.

## GOOD ENVIRONMENT NOT ENOUGH

We now know that a child may be placed in a good environment and not be affected by it. Nowhere is the expression, "you may lead a horse to water but you cannot make him drink" more apt than in relation to a child who is picked up from one setting and dropped into another.

The reasons why foster-home placements sometimes fail are many. To cover them all one would have to touch upon the way the foster home is studied by the agency, the matching of the home and the child, the preparation of the home for the child. One would have to consider the parent who never will be able to accept with good grace the placement of her child in foster care, also the many aspects of the inner life of the child. This paper deals only with that part of the child's inner life that has to do with his relationship with his parents.

If placement is to be more than just transferring a child into a good environment, we must realize that the child does have an inner life, in which he maintains a parent-child relationship. Secondly, we must accept the evidence of numerous cases that physical separation of parent and child does not necessarily interfere with the parent's influence upon the child. On the contrary, the separation may lead to the child's idealizing the parent. This may become clearer if we go back to our two stories.

Let's begin with Mary. Psychiatrists tell us that it is in the preschool period that little girls really become feminine. It is not at all uncommon to hear an adult say of a 5- or 6-year-old girl, "What a little flirt she is" or "she's already a little woman." We know also that a little girl gets her concept of womanhood from her mother. The child's growth in the direction of becoming like her mother is marked by two-way feelings, of love and hatred.

The little girl admires the mother and is jealous because she has characteristics now denied the little daughter.

These conflicting feelings cause tensions in the little girl which may be eased if she remains under the loving care of her mother. However, if the little girl is removed from her mother, the child still loves her, and the yearning to be loved by her continues. But with this is a natural resentment, for she feels that the mother did not love her enough to want to keep her.

## CHILD IS LOYAL TO OWN MOTHER

In the foster home the little girl finds another mother who is kind and loving, and the child accepts this substitute love and appears to adjust well to this new home. But what about the real mother? Whenever she makes one of her infrequent appearances, or whenever the question of the little girl's going home for Christmas or a weekend arises, the foster mother shows, directly or indirectly, her disapproval and her unmistakable opinion that the mother is a decidedly poor influence.

In the meantime, what has the social worker been doing? She has been skirting the subject of the child's mother, which is as bad as the open criticism by the foster mother. This action probably arises from the fact that we should like children to have ideal parents, and when we find a most un-ideal lot and see the grief they cause their children, we cannot bear it. We avoid the subject of the disreputable mother to save our own feelings, and we overlook the fact that if we talked to the child about her we should be talking about something that the child knows more about than we do.

And so the little girl gets the impression that everyone thinks she should not love her mother. However, her yearning to love and be loved by her mother continues. She condemns her own resentment and is aware only of her loyalty and of a strong need to defend her mother. Love and hatred then are both repressed, which simply means that they have gone underground, where, unknown both to the child and to the people around her, they continue to be active in forming her personality. The little girl, as she grows up, seems to get her mother back by becoming like her. At adolescence, boy-crazy behavior shows up, and now everyone says, "Isn't it too bad, she's become just like her mother. And after all we've done for her!"

But we find that one important item was missing from the "all we've done." That was giving the little girl a chance to talk about her mother. Mary should have been not only allowed to ask questions but even encouraged to do so.

Someone should have acknowledged to her that of course she loved her mother. Almost everyone loves his mother; there's something wrong if you don't, not if you do. Once the child learned that no one would condemn her for loving her mother, and that she no longer had to defend her against criticism, she should have been encouraged to talk freely, even to tell of her resentment and anger that her mother had let her down, had failed to be the kind of mother that she should have been. Talking would have released some of the child's tensions and left her freer to pattern her life after that of the foster mother's.

Now take John, who had never known his mother. Did she influence his life so much that he lost the only home he ever had? Can you imagine that a child can grow up in a home that he knows is not his own, and never, never wonder about who he is? Who were his mother and father? What did they look like? Does he look like them? What kind of people were they? Why didn't they keep him? Why do they never come to see him?

Is it not logical to think that at adolescence John's normal drive to be free of the restrictions set by adults was stepped up by his resentment because these people were not his own? Why should he obey them? They weren't his own parents. After all, what did he owe them? That may not be logical reasoning, because maybe he owed them a lot, but on whom else can he get rid of the resentment that comes not only of not having parents but of not even knowing anything about them?

Barring the rather obvious point that maybe this boy needed to be adopted instead of being kept at loose ends in boarding care, would it not have been better for the social worker to have talked with him from time to time, explaining that his mother had not been able to care for him, that she had wanted him to have a good home with a father and mother, that she had asked the social worker to find one for him, and that these parents were like real parents to him? With some of his longing to know about his own parents fulfilled, his wish to belong, his loyalties, and his feelings of love might have been securely moored to his foster home.

What can we learn from these two stories? First, they reaffirm what we already know, that the child continues to maintain some kind of relationship with his parents long after being separated from them. This relationship may be one that exists entirely in the child's inner life, with no counterpart in reality. In it may mingle love, anger, disappointment. Whatever these feelings are, part of their power over the child comes from the fact that they are hidden. Feelings that have no outlet have a strong effect upon personality.

To this point we have been developing three ideas: (1) Elimination of a parent from the life of the child does not necessarily eliminate that parent's influence upon the child. (2) Strong conflicting feelings about the parent may be present in the child. (3) The strength and influence of these feelings are increased by their concealment.

## HOW SOCIAL WORKER CAN HELP

Now what meaning do these facts have for the everyday practice of a social worker? First of all, social workers should take the initiative in helping children work out some of these conflicts about their own parents. What Anna Freud calls "the images of the parents" must be kept clear in the child's mind, even if a parent is dead, or committed for life to a hospital for the insane, or if of the parent's own volition he is completely out of the child's life, as in the story of John.

Only in this way will the feelings attached to his curiosity lose some of their strength; only in this way will some of the sting be taken away; only in this way can the longing for his own people be satisfied in some measure and his longing to be loved directed toward the foster parents.

There are three ways by which the social worker may help the child in this.

First is talking with the child about the parents. This is not easy. But the difficulties lie solely within ourselves, and most of them center around fear. We are afraid to hear children speak ill or disrespectfully of their fathers and mothers. Criticism of parents not only goes against our upbringing but arouses in us the fear that if we let the child criticize his parents openly, we are teaching him that he may be critical of any authority. This might mean he could react in the same manner toward the foster parents, and ultimately toward all law and authority.

These fears are groundless. On the contrary, if a child has resentments and disillusionments because adults have neglected him or pushed him around, it is reassuring to find in the social worker a person who agrees openly with him that his life has been hard and who lets him know that she doesn't blame him for feeling as he does. Such a person can help reestablish his faith in adults.

Strange to say, we sometimes fear the child's love for a delinquent parent. We are afraid of this love because we all know that a child often becomes like the person he loves. On the surface it seems that if we tell a child that of course he should love his mother or father, we are telling him to become like the parent. Again this need not be so.

Another reason why it is not easy to talk to these children about their parents is that we are afraid to talk about the parents' behavior. Think of the sex offenses committed by some parents. Think of their laziness; think of their filth; think of their alcoholism.

We could have greater peace of mind about the parents' behavior if we could see beyond the behavior to the person, and realize that his behavior represents his fumbling attempts to be happy. In this respect he is no different from ourselves.

## CHILD IS NOT DECEIVED

Only if the social worker sees beyond behavior to the person, only if her feelings about the child's parents are warm and friendly, will she be able to talk with this child about them. If she attempts to sound broad-minded while she is really sitting in judgment, if she is afraid of the parent or of his influence, if she attempts to cover critical feelings with a veneer of tolerance, the child will know it. In that case, he will simply add her conflicts to his own.

It is this "how" of talking to a child that is hardest. It must be a matter-of-fact "how," in which liking for the parent and acceptance of the child's two-way feelings are implicit.

Once we have mastered the "how," the "what" becomes easier. First, we must tell the truth. A child can stand the truth when *with it* goes the worker's sincere interest in the child's happiness, her warm regard for his parents, and her recognition of his hardships. What we tell him will depend also upon what the child tells or asks us, provided our manner encourages him to ask questions.

Though it seems to be a paradox, a child can give up the past more easily if he can keep part of it with him in the sense that he is free to talk about it. He can loosen his bond with his parents more easily if he is not called upon to abandon them entirely.

The "when" of talking to a foster child about his parents, the timing of our telling, is particularly important. One cannot avoid talking about the parents at the time the child is placed in the foster home, when the reasons for placement are being explained, but one should give only as much information then as the child can digest. As the child becomes more secure in the new home, more details about his parents can be given him. Age is another factor to be considered; what one would tell a 5-year-old would be very different from what one would tell the same child at 15. And we cannot tell a 5-year-old about the mother or daddy who went away and then drop the subject forever after. We must keep it open and help the child to formulate his own questions, which change as he matures.

In addition to helping the child ask questions about his parents, the worker can help him feel that his parents are not shut out of his foster home by seeing that he has photographs of them and mementoes of home. Why don't foster children have large, framed pictures of their parents in their rooms? Many have snapshots, but why shouldn't the parents have a place of honor on the child's dresser?

Mementoes of home would also help the child. I wonder why, when we are preparing a child for placement, we don't suggest that he take some favorite object along that will always remind him of home. The picture and the memento could then be mentioned casually from time to time.

Foster parents should be helped to see that casual conversation with the child about his parents is desirable. If the little girl's pretty hair is just like her mother's, why not say so, just as the foster mother might remark that her own daughter looks more and more like grandma? Why couldn't we say casually to a child that daddy has a birthday next month? Let's see, how old would he be now? It is through such discussions about the details of family life, through the jokes about grandfather's mustache cup, through comments about whom one resembles, through remembrances of birthdays, that we come to have a sense of belonging. Through such little things do we feel that we have roots in the past. There is a place for some of this in the life of a child in foster care. By these devices foster parents keep open the subject of the child's own parents.

Of course, we shall have a difficult time getting foster parents to do these things. However, let's not forget that foster homes are to serve children, and the support and guidance we give foster parents must always be in that direction.

The third thing a social worker can do to help the child with his relationship to his parents lies in the realm of work with the parents. Admittedly the steps suggested here require careful, time-consuming work. Good child placement is neither easy nor cheap, and one is often led to wonder if as good results could not have been achieved if an equal amount of thought, effort, and time went into working with the child's parents before placement was considered.

When it seems as if placement of the child is necessary, whether because of circumstances beyond the parent's control, or because the parent really cannot cope with the responsibility of keeping the child, we must help this father or mother to play a modified role in the child's life. The manner in which he or she adapts to this new role will be influenced by the kind of treatment received from the social worker and the agency she represents.

Sometimes after a parent has ceased to visit the child and has therefore lost contact with him, it seems as if this may have happened because no one ever made the parent feel important. Defeated as a parent, faced by this defeat at every visit to the foster home and at every request not to bring so much candy, not to stay so long, not to upset the child to such an extent, many a parent finally gives up.

Only when we recognize why the parent brings too much candy and stays too long, only when we catch some insight into a father's or mother's life, and feelings, and needs, only when we feel with and for this person as a human being, apart from being a parent, can we help him see that he has not wholly given up responsibility for the child.

Children need to have parents visit. Anna Freud points out that we have been wrong even in asking parents to wait for a few weeks until the child seems to be settled in foster care. It is better for the child to have the parent visit soon after placement, even though these visits seem to increase the child's homesickness and grief. And visiting is not the only way parents can help in a child's adjustment: some children are helped by knowing that the parent is paying for the care.

There is one implied but final conclusion in all this. The more we recognize the importance of the parent in the life of the placed child, and the more we come to know and to like the parent, and the more we come to respect him or her as a human being, the less often shall we place a child too hastily and without making every effort to preserve for him his own niche in this universe, which is simply his place in his own home.

# Part III
# Ecological Perspective

# Part III

## Ecological Perspective

In a field as complex and unwieldy as child welfare, an organizing conceptual framework is essential, particularly in regard to work with parents of the child in placement. The ecological perspective is uniquely suited to this task because it is a model dealing with the impact of physical, social, and economic factors in the environment on the functioning of human beings. It focuses on the transactions between people and their environments.

The ecological perspective stresses the development of people's adaptive capacities and the improvement of environments for those who function within them. It emphasizes a sensitive awareness of the multiplicity of factors that contribute to the problems encountered by children and their parents. It underlines availability, continuity, and interdisciplinary collaboration in the delivery of services; and, through its focus on the interrelated nature of causal factors in the etiology of problems, it considers preventive services as important as rehabilitative services. Furthermore, particularly in relationship to parents, "an inescapable consequence of an ecological perspective in child welfare is a newly articulated imperative for sustaining connectedness to the natural family."[1]

The authors of the three articles in this section support the ecological approach from a variety of viewpoints. In Chapter 6, Maas highlights the impact of the environment on the child and implications for policy, particularly for preventive intervention. Minuchin, in Chapter 7, cautions us against the use of the pathological model. Finally, in Chapter 8 by Laird, the importance of the biological tie with its concomitant sense of human connectedness is underscored.

[1] Germain, Carel B., Editor, *Social Work Practice: People and Environments*. New York: Columbia University Press, 1979: pp. 174–175.

Maas gears his discussion of the ecological perspective to its relevance to child welfare policy. The relationship between children and their environments is explored, with implications for policy formulation and practice. Preventive programs are proposed as a means of ameliorating the effects of poverty and other stressful environmental factors. Child welfare policy should ideally create, in UNICEF's terms, "a better social environment" in which normal family life for children is supported and enriched.

Minuchin observes that interventions are derived from assessments or diagnoses that stem from particular conceptual frameworks: "Our diagnostic systems have been organized to determine normality or pathology in a middle-class framework that does not correspond to the life styles of the poor family." He therefore urges that social agencies shift their approach from a pathological model to an ecological approach in order to be more effective in their work with the poor. Social interventions deriving from the pathological model have tended to fragment families; in contrast, viewing the family as part of an ecosystem can elicit and utilize the supportive resources in the environment and help hold it together. He concludes that the adoption of an ecological approach could lead to more "truly change-producing and helpful" interventions in support of families and their children, poor or otherwise.

Looking at the full spectrum of child welfare practice from an ecological perspective, Laird focuses on the value of the biological tie of children to their parents, a tie so basic and so compelling that there is no substitute. Reechoing and further developing Jolowicz's earlier plea for recognition of the importance of the parents for the child's sense of identity, Laird emphasizes ways of attending to, nurturing, and supporting the family and presents specific applications of the ecological perspective to practice situations.

After reviewing current child welfare policy, Laird proposes drastic alterations to make it more supportive of children in their own families. In this process, she raises challenging and sometimes frightening questions, such as: "Are we indeed guilty, in the name of 'child-saving,' of brokering children from poor to rich families just as we found poor city children to act as farm labor in the 19th century?" Noting that the concept of the "psychological parent" is an oversimplification of a very complex human situation, Laird maintains that the guiding conviction in child welfare practice should be the fundamental importance of the biological family.

## SUGGESTIONS FOR FURTHER READING

Becker, Jerome, "Ecological Foundations of Practice in Child and Youth Services," *Child and Youth Services*, 1: 2 (March–April 1977): 1–7.

Bronfenbrenner, Urie. *The Ecology of Human Development*. Cambridge, Mass.: Harvard University Press, 1979.

Gelles, Richard J., "Child Abuse as Psychopathology: A Sociological Critique and Reformulation," *American Journal of Orthopsychiatry*, 43: 4 (July 1973): 611–621.

Maluccio, Anthony N., "An Ecological Perspective on Practice with Parents of Children in Foster Care," in Maluccio, Anthony N. and Sinanoglu, Paula A., Editors, *The Challenge of Partnership: Working with Parents of Children in Foster Care*. New York: Child Welfare League of America, 1981.

Stephens, Douglas, "In-Home Family Support Services: An Ecological Systems Approach," in Maybanks, Sheila and Bryce, Marvin, Editors, *Home Based Services for Children and Families*. Springfield, Ill.: Charles C Thomas 1979: 283–295.

Torczyner, J. and Pare, Arleen, "The Influence of Environmental Factors on Foster Care," *Social Service Review*, 53: 3 (September 1979): 358–377.

# 6

# Children's Environments and Child Welfare

HENRY S. MAAS

Where children are concerned, the primary aims of the social services are:

> To preserve and strengthen the protection afforded the child by the basic unit of his social environment, the family. To provide special protection for the abandoned, neglected, or malnourished child.
>
> As part of broader, long-range objectives, to promote a better social environment for the child and adolescent, both in the city and rural areas. [1]

In child welfare, however, the term "social environment" denotes a rather ill-defined area surrounding the child. The purpose of this article is to propose clarifying perspectives on children's environments, with implications for child welfare policy, program, and practice.

The Canadian Conference on Children has echoed UNICEF's statement of child welfare's primary aims—to reinforce, support, and supplement normal family life for children [2]. In effect, though, the secondary aims of compensatory, substitutive, and treatment services preoccupy the field and have become the most prestigious of child welfare services. It is possible that the dominance of clinical orientations in North

---

Reprinted from *Child Welfare*, Vol. L, No. 3 (March 1971): 132–142.

American child welfare and our inability to examine children's environments in much more than structural terms—bearing, for example, on the size and composition of children's living units—have too narrowly limited child welfare's concerns. With a keener sense of the usefulness of interactional and ecological perspectives on children's environments, together with clinical and structural viewpoints, we might attend more actively to, for example, what Jenkins describes as the separation experience of parents whose children are in foster care [3]. We might learn how to interrupt constructively the cycle of environmental (including medical) nonrecognition of the familial and anomic community situations of battered children [4]. We should be able to act upon the bureaucratization of child welfare agencies and the rapid turnover of staff [5] and to work at a neighborhood level to help integrate otherwise anomic families into mutual self-help services. We should develop economic plans and other social policy proposals for governmental action. For the social environments of a child are far broader and more complex than the influence upon him of his immediate caretaker.

This paper deals with three matters: (1) general ideas about environment, (2) specific ideas about children's environments conceived in ecological and social interactional terms, and (3) implications for child welfare.

## 1. GENERAL CONCEPTIONS OF ENVIRONMENT

The environment of children is simplistically conceived when it is seen to be *the* shaper of the child's development and behavior. Much of child welfare's efforts devoted to "matching" is based in this simple assumption. The notion of environment as the shaper of the child ignores the influences of the child's genetic potentials; different children's different ways of perceiving, interpreting, and experiencing the same environment; and different children's varying capacities to influence or act upon and control their environments.

We should recall a fundamental biological assumption: "There is a boundary, though not a precise one, between organism and environment" [6]. This imprecise boundary varies in permeability from organism to organism. The permeability varies also from time to time or situation to situation involving the same organism. Thus the mutual influences of child upon environment and environment upon child differ when a child is fatigued and hungry or when the same child is rested and well fed. To try to "match" in any way beyond the lowest limits of parental tolerances and the most potentially intolerable behavior of a given child is to give more weight to statics than a dynamic conception of child-environment interaction suggests is necessary—to predict in realms that are too complex and multivariate for such foresight. Children can change their caretakers—and vice versa—unpredictably.

The complexity of organism-environment interaction is further compounded by the constant changes that both organism and environment are naturally and simultaneously engaged in. Commenting on "the psychological implications of social or cultural changes," anthropologist Hughes notes diametrically opposed conclusions about the effects of rapid environmental change. He alludes to behavioral scientists "basing their arguments on the 'function of the similar' in . . . life (who) emphasize . . . the disruptive effects of changes through heightened anxiety and stress, especially if the change is rapid. Others, however, point to the psychological beneficence of change and stress the advantages of rapidity in the turnover of an entire way of life. The evidence, to say the least, is mixed . . ." [7]. Clearly, on the issue of environmental change for the young child, child welfare has been on the side of those who argue for maintenance of the familiar. On the pace of change, we have been for the gradual and accommodative rather than the rapid—but I'm not sure what beyond hunch has convinced us that this is uniformly best, or whether we have thought differently about children for whom rapid change might be better than the gradual, when we have genuine choice.

Finally, environments are effective at different levels or distances in relation to children. For child welfare purposes, it is useful to distinguish between immediate (or 'proximal') environments and more remote (or 'distal') environments [8]. The latter include, for example, social class and the culture of poverty. These distal environments may be somewhat, but never completely, mediated by a child's family or caretakers. For example, research indicates that children's "imaginative capacity" is most likely to be developed when the child is engaged in "interaction with a variety of physical objects and toys, as well as with meaningful contacts with adults" [9]. In describing one *vecinidad* of 83 persons composing 14 families, as part of his long-term study of the culture of poverty, Lewis observes, "Only half of the families in the tenement were able to invest in any toys for their children" [10]. Furthermore, in view of the overcrowded living quarters of these families, averaging six persons sleeping and eating in each one-room shack, we note with dismay that "imaginative capacity" flourishes in an environment that provides also "some opportunities for solitary play or privacy. . . . There is evidence that firstborn or only children, or children with relatively few siblings, are likely to have the time and privacy for practice and the greater contact with adults to permit full development of fantasy play" [11]. Clearly remote environments expand or limit the opportunities for children's development.

In general, then, environments should be seen as changing and variously responsive to children, who can more or less effectively act upon and control their surroundings. An interactional framework amplifies this point of view. In addition, ecological perspectives elaborate relationships between proximal and distal environments—as they ultimately affect and are affected by such living organisms as the young.

## 2. SOME ECOLOGICAL PERSPECTIVES

By contrast with structural perspectives, which lead to analysis of relationships among component parts in fragmentary ways, the ecological approach uses a wide-angled lens to encompass the interplay between living organisms and their proximal and distal environments. Ecology, with its biological and social perspectives, provides evidence that every living organism has "in addition to minimum requirements of things such as food, minimal requirements of living space and distance from others of its own species" [12]. Cognizant of the great variety of genetic potentials in man, Dubos says our environments must offer diversity or the availability of a "wide range of experiences" [13]. Regarding food, he writes:

> Nutritional deprivations or imbalances occurring early in life (prenatal or postnatal) will interfere with the normal development of the brain and of learning ability. Furthermore, bad dietary habits acquired early in life tend to persist throughout the whole life span. . . . People born and raised in an environment where food intake is quantitatively or qualitatively inadequate achieve a certain form of physiological and behavioral adaptation to low food intake. They tend to restrict their physical and mental activity and thereby to reduce their nutritional needs; in other words, they become adjusted to undernutrition by living less intensely . . . Physical and mental apathy and other forms of indolence . . . (result) . . . especially when nutritional scarcity has occurred during very early life. [14]

Regarding population density or crowding, Dubos generalizes from experiments with various animal species that "as the population pressure increases . . . varieties of abnormal behavior" appear, of a kind that reflects "social unawareness" of others. "Behavior is asocial rather than antisocial." He continues:

> The humanness of man is not innate; it is a product of socialization. Some of the peculiarly "human" traits disappear

> under conditions of extreme crowding, probably because man achieves his humanness only through contact with human beings *under the proper conditions* (my italics, HSM). [15]

Ecological perspectives direct our attention to more than basic needs for proper diet and for spatial and population arrangements that allow for balances in togetherness and separateness, conducive to optimal human growth and development. One British ecologist complains, "There are too many variables, and it requires very extensive work for long periods of time, at the end of which you have only unraveled one corner of the situation," pursuing such questions as, "What impact did the rabbit have on the environment and vegetation?" [16]. Increasingly in child welfare we must ask the analogous questions about the child: What impact does this child have on this or that environment? Answers to this question—provided that we have a useful view of relevant environmental parameters—can tell us as much that is practically fruitful as the traditional child welfare question: How does (or, more precariously, how will) this environment influence this child?

## 3. SOME INTERACTIONAL PERSPECTIVES

By contrast with the fundamentally intrapersonal focus of clinical perspectives, the interactional approach is primarily interpersonal. Although the clinical tends to be concerned with internal constancies, the interactional deals more with the changing flow and continual feedback and patterning of human communication. The clinical effort is highly inferential, involving judgments about such only indirect observables as motives and defenses. The interactional stays closer to observed behavior and its configurations, or patterns and sequences, or stages.

Within this framework, the ecologically oriented biologist and the interactionally oriented psychologist start their observations with complementary premises. Writes Dubos, "Environmental information becomes formative only when it evokes a creative response from the organism" [17]. Writes child psychologist J.L. Gewirtz, ". . . our key assumption [is] that the infant's behavior is not simply a function of evoking stimuli in the environment, but a function also of whether and how the environment responds to his behavior" [18]. The interactional approach postulates neither merely a shaping environment nor a shaped person. Rather, both environment and person variously, if complexly and at times innovatively and thus unpredictably, respond to one another. And with interactional perspectives, nonresponse is a response too.

Consider Kagan's hypothetical descriptions of the experiences of a lower-middle-class infant and an upper-middle-class infant:

> The upper-middle-class child is lying in her crib in her bedroom on the second floor of a suburban home. She wakes, the room is quiet, her mother is downstairs baking. The infant studies the crib and her fingers. Suddenly the quiet is broken as the mother enters and speaks to the child. The auditory intrusion is maximally distinctive and likely to orient the infant to her mother and to the vocalization. If the child responds vocally, the mother is apt to continue the dialogue. Contrast this set of events with those that occur to an infant girl in Harlem lying on a couch in a two-room apartment with the television going and siblings peering into her face. The child lies in a sea of sound, but like the sea, it is homogeneous. The mother approaches the child and says something to her. The communication, however, is minimally distinctive from background noise and as such, is not likely to recruit the infant's attention. Many of the infant's vocalizations during the day are not likely to be heard nor are they likely to elicit a special response. The fundamental theme of this argument seeks to minimize the importance of absolute amount of stimulation the child receives and spotlights instead the distinctiveness of that stimulation. [19]

So concludes Kagan, talking like an ecologist about noise levels and related phenomena in two infants' proximal environments. The key differentiating environmental process is, however, the suburban infant's control over her environment. She has a power, in time internalizable as a sense of competence, potentially missing from the slum child's interaction with her environment.

An environment upon which the infant or young child can act in ways which make it do things, under his controlling behavior, is very different from an environment that is nonresponsive. Psychologist John S. Watson has recently been experimenting with colorful mobiles, hung over an infant's crib and rotating as the infant learns to activate them himself. Watson finds learning and social-emotional responses in his experimental infants that do not occur among his control infants [20]. The infant enjoys a reciprocal interaction with an environment, to which he becomes increasingly attentive and responsive as it seems attentive and responsive to him. He can recreate his environment.

This human-responsiveness component—or psychological aspect of environments—is sometimes overlooked in social interaction research that contrasts caretaking settings. Described in terms of the intentions of caretakers—for example, as monitoring, guidance, support, and integration [21]—social environments take on differential forms, but another set of categories is needed to define the crucial difference such environments make to children and youth. If the boundary between organism and environment is not a precise one, and the critical difference in child welfare environments is the child's "creative response," then interactional configurations [22] should be defined in terms that include the degree of their modifiability by the young [23]. Though Watson cautiously questions the long-term effects of infants' activation of mobiles [24], for older children, and most clearly for adults, environments which give evidence that one is heard are markedly different psychologically from those in which one is not.

Finally, interactional perspectives upset other ways of "seeing." In his study of social functioning as a social work concept, Alary argues that "interactional determinants" are "in contradistinction (to the view of) personal needs and capacities as internal determinants and environmental demands and opportunities as external determinants" [25]. His argument cannot be pursued here, but what he alludes to as a split between "external" and "internal" seems still today to permeate child welfare thinking and practice. The child welfare worker who thinks of a child's needs and capacities and a foster or adoptive home's demands and opportunities may be doing her very best to "match" yesterday's family with a child as of yesterday. Tomorrow, placed together, or after a longer period of interaction, neither child nor environment may look the same as the opportunities/demands and capacities/needs that had been so carefully "matched," unless a pathological stereotypy binds all persons involved.

## 4. IMPLICATIONS FOR CHILD WELFARE

Four sets of proposals for child welfare can be derived from the ideas and observations sketched in the foregoing.

(1) Child welfare should both expand and reallocate its existing resources for a more concerted effort in preventive programs. Prevention means keeping more and more children out of child placement even temporarily or for short-term care. Every relevant study I know indicates that at least some children are placed who need never have been if . . . if . . . and if. We must get to work on these "ifs"—though it means that professional personnel now engaged in adoptive and foster home activities redirect their efforts to the kinds of preventive program to be cited later. We have at present no evidence—in Ripple's followup study of adoptions [26] or elsewhere [27]—that the time

invested in "matching" pays off for children or their substitute parents. Why continue it, if our primary concern is the welfare of children?

First, we do know that the vast majority of children cared for by child welfare agencies are poor children in or removed from poor families. Adequate amounts of money for poor families are not a panacea; money alone does not cure all. But money, available at the right time in the family cycle of otherwise poor families, provides opportunities. Money contributes to the prevention of interpersonal and psychic strains and stresses that result in family breakdown and the ostensible need to place children. We need a Family Starting Allowance for the reasons that follow.

An interactional approach to familial environments calls for the conceptualization of stages or phases through which families pass, from one interactional context to another. There are a few such conceptual sequences proposed by students of family life. All give some focus to the new or starting family, on through variously conceived subsequent phases, to the empty nest stage of family life, and finally to the aging parental dyad or widowhood. Schorr describes a four-or-five-stage poor family's cycle in relation to income development. Using demographic data, he writes of stage 1, Initial Marriage and Child Rearing; stage 2, Occupational Choice; stage 3, The Family Cycle Squeeze; and stage 4, Family Breakdown. The culmination for many such poor families is breakdown, in part because of the squeeze between aspirations and always drastically limiting amounts of money. His appended stage 5 involves the children in these families, the next generation, who emerge from family breakdown to repeat the same cycle of a family entrapped in poverty [28].

How does the poor family cycle develop? A combination of factors, beginning with too-early marriage, often before age 18, leads to the following, in Schorr's research-based statements [29]:

> ". . . low income is likely to be a continual experience for those who marry before 18."
>
> ". . . earlier marriages tend to be less stable."
>
> ". . . young marriage is associated with less education for the husband," and "a poor first job, a chaotic work history. . ."
>
> "When a couple starts out together early, they are not only likely to have their first child earlier than usual; they are likely to have more children."
>
> "They are more than ordinarily likely to suffer separation or divorce."
>
> "Mothers in broken families are likely to have more children than those in stable families." There is a high "prevalence of

> poverty among families headed by women; obviously mothers who start out without a husband are no better off."
>
> "The path that opens before (any such) . . . family is a sequence of marriages or liaisons in which the notion of a stable, intact marriage, if it was ever present, becomes fainter."

The poor family cycle Schorr describes is a familiar and well-documented one. Out of such families come a large proportion of the children thrust into placement. The provision of a Family Starting Allowance, granted to such families when the cycle is just beginning, might do much to set the family's interaction-sequence on a different course. It should help to keep out of placement many children who travel the long-term foster care path. And most of the children in long-term foster care are the poorest of the poor children in foster care [30].

Child welfare workers can document from thick case files how poverty contributes directly and indirectly to current child placement caseloads. Child welfare workers can provide evidence of the rising costs of expanding substitute care programs. Child welfare workers can consult with knowledgeable co-professionals on the economics of income supplementation programs. Child welfare workers can assess the pros and cons of various possible alternative plans, for poor families, of some kind of Family Starting Allowance. Child welfare workers can shepherd their proposal through to the appropriate governmental authorities, and stay with their proposal until it becomes reality. Not a simple series of steps at all—but one that has an ultimate outcome of great promise. That is one kind of preventive child welfare program.

(2) We now know a good deal about the psychosocial conditions of familial environments from which children are catapulted into foster care. Long-term foster care involves primarily families who neglect their children or who contribute to the children's development of serious emotional problems. By contrast, children who are brief care charges (under 3 months) come mostly from homes in which mother's illness or confinement precipitates the children's placement. I am primarily concerned here with this latter group, brief-termers, who may so easily become long-termers. A Scottish study that tells us much about these families is useful in preventive work aimed at keeping children from ever entering care. The Schaffers contrasted 100 such families who placed their children in care during mother's confinement with 100 families who made other arrangements [31]. The child-placing families were essentially alienated families, isolated from their extended families and from neighbors. Compared with nonplacing families, the child-placing families were more likely to live in electoral wards

with higher rates of population turnover and a higher population density—e.g., more persons per room. They moved more frequently, and more often lived in redevelopment areas or postwar housing estates. Though both groups of families had the same number of relatives and the same number living within the same city, fewer relatives of child-placing families lived within a 10-minute walk, and there was less contact with relatives, as well as with church and political activities or with neighborhood mutual self-help services. Only medical facilities were more extensively used by the child-placing family.

Within the family, dissociation prevailed—e.g., far fewer of the parents in these families ever went out together and far fewer of the fathers ever helped in the home. Though the Schaffers nowhere make this explicit in their study report, judging by the age distributions of grandparents (more younger ones in the child-placing families) and of the children (more children under age 4), I estimate that these were younger families, much of the kind Schorr describes, very much in need of some kind of Family Starting Allowance, but, in addition, also in need of professional services aimed at family social integration, both intrafamilially and extrafamilially.

I cannot specify in any detail what the intervention strategies and social work practice methods should be, but the goals are definable. They involve increasing the meaningful social interaction of these parents so that they become more integrated and less alienated members of their neighborhoods. For those who would leap in with clinical strategies—such as family therapy programs—I propose that working through the neighborhood environment to engage these families in self-help services, for example, around the development or expansion of parent-staffed child care facilities in their housing units, may be a complementary if not equally effective alternative strategy. Knowledgeable and skillful neighborhood workers, keenly aware of family life and its possible enrichment through mutual neighborhood aid, may induce alienated families to participate in local enterprises. Social workers may support them on a casework basis through their initial efforts to engage in meaningful interaction with neighbors. Social workers may use group work skills and community organization techniques as needed, providing these young families, at an early and critical point in their family cycle, with what may be for them a completely new kind of human experience. For child welfare workers who think first in terms of psychopathology—of possible character disorders, affective deprivation, or the ego impoverishment of these adults—I remind them of therapeutic milieu or therapeutic community approaches. Community mental health programs aim to keep persons from entering—or to bring patients back from—distant governmental hospitals, to live and be cared for in their home communities. As "sick" as these parents may be, they may, like others, rediscover health in a neighborhood milieu that evidences concern for them. More specifically, the professional worker who helps to launch a day care neighbor service, of the kind with which Emlen has been concerned in Portland [32], may be serving many neighborhood needs, and at the same time be providing a crucial preventive family service.

Most of the child-placing parents in the Scottish study never went out together. But such parents could be informed of and encouraged to participate in a neighborhood child care group, which, long before an emergency or crisis situation arises, might provide a few hours every other week or so for a couple to get away from their children. Relevant here are the previously cited ecological observations on the effects of overcrowding and the need for periods of distance from others, as well as closeness.

(3) The theoretical perspectives outlined here suggest some "should nots" as well as "shoulds" for child welfare workers. I raised questions earlier about the dominance of the clinical approach in present-day child placement. In their review of the literature on foster parenting, Taylor and Starr conclude, "While specific emphases are attached by different authors to various aspects of the home study, the model for the study is the diagnostic assessment process as utilized in a child guidance or family agency setting. This model is based on an untested assumption that such an assessment is necessary for the appropriate placement of foster children" [33]. So far as the assumption has been tested, the answer is essentially negative. For example, in his study of 101 foster families, Fanshel observes, "The capacities foster parents display when they first apply to an agency . . . must . . . be seen as potentialities . . . (and) parental capacity must be seen as a variable performance" [34], since different children evoke different foster parent behavior.

Clinical assessments have questionable payoff not only in foster care but in adoption. In a properly cautious summary following his review of research on adoptions, Kadushin concludes, "Research indicates that the assessments of parents' motivation for adoption are of questionable significance as a predictor of successful adoptive parenting, as are attitudes toward infertility . . ." [35]. Ripple concludes from her followup study of adopted children, "None of the factors believed to be important to realistic integration of the adopted child into the family—'matching' and handling the facts of adoption—showed the expected association with favorable outcome" [36].

In regard to day care services, the picture is somewhat clearer. "It is small wonder that agency family day care programs have remained small in scope, considering the elaborate formal requirements of professionally supervised family day care," writes Emlen, ". . . family day care is presented to the community as a social agency service based on diagnostic assessment of a family problem. . . . Ruderman and Mayer have pointed to the problem-oriented character of the services offered as unattractive to the general consumer" [37]. In short, perspectives developed out of efforts to understand psychopathology may, when applied in child placement situations, communicate to parents an unacceptable, and seemingly irrelevant set of questions about their own possible sickness.

Even the clinical approach to family as the context for childhood disturbance has shaky empirical referents. At least, psychological research has been unable to give us any consistent findings about the influence of family dynamics on the development of psychopathology in children. One recent review of the literature on parental deprivation and the etiology of psychiatric illness points only to the contradictory or conflicting nature of the existing evidence [38]. In another, the author concludes, "No factors were found in the parent-child interaction of schizophrenics, neurotics, or those with behavior disorders which could be identified as unique to them or could distinguish one group from another, or any of the groups from the families of the controls" [39]. Until we know much more than we do now about such matters, child welfare workers might well consider whether their time is not better invested in other than clinical procedures in their home-finding and placement activities.

I am not putting down clinical orientations and procedures for those parts of the child welfare enterprise that are concerned with the treatment of disturbed children or their troubled parents. I am questioning, however, the relevance of clinical approaches in such activities as home finding and related services that are not typically aimed at psychotherapy.

(4) Finally, I suggest that an ecological approach seems more promising for child welfare than a structural approach to children's environments. We have thus far had only a relatively small yield of useful structural formulations from research. For example, regarding the composition of living groups for children, Wolins' findings on the SOS Kinderdorf [40] and my research on preadolescent peer relations [41] give some support to the placement of school-age children in group-care living units patterned on family-like sibships, mixed by sex and age—rather than sex-divided and strictly age-graded. Benson's review of the research literature on fatherlessness and the conflicting evidence regarding the effects on children of father-absence, concludes, "We could very well give more thought to changing legislation to allow the placement of children in one-parent homes" [42]. In a structural framework, child-development research has examined the effects on children's cognitive or social-emotional development of birth order and the sex composition of sibships, but as yet there is little practical guidance for child welfare workers in such research on family structure.

With an ecological framework, however, the world of child and family life widens to larger vistas. For example, there is some ecologically based research on the effects of social isolation. One such inquiry is a study of Norwegian farm families, living miles apart from one another in Norway's mountain country. Drs. Anna von der Lippe and Ernest A. Haggard have been assessing the psychological effects of such isolated living [43]. In briefest terms, they find that these mountain farm families tend to be composed of affectively nonexpressive and cognitively deprived children. If overcrowding in urban neighborhoods makes for a chaotic and overwhelming environment, isolated families apparently experience another kind of sensory deprivation, in an environment that also inhibits optimal human development.

Earlier, using ecological and social interactional frameworks, I alluded to the desirability of helping to integrate anomic families into their neighborhood's services. Richard Titmuss, in his collection of essays entitled *Commitment to Welfare*, remarks that the unifying aim of the social services is social integration and, conversely, the discouragement of alienation [44]. Perhaps child welfare needs to reconsider not only its conceptual views of children's environments, but the extent to which its services promote a constructive bringing together of children, parents, and in UNICEF's terms, "a better social environment . . . both in the city and rural areas." At a distal level, this better social environment excludes extremes of poverty and both social isolation and high density "living," for only in their absence do optimal human growth and development begin.

## NOTES AND REFERENCES

1. UNICEF, *Children of the Developing Countries* (Cleveland and New York: World Publishing Co., 1963), 89.
2. Ray Godfrey and B. Schlesinger, *Child Welfare Services: Winding Paths to Maturity* (Toronto: Canadian Conference on Children, 1969), 179.
3. Shirley Jenkins, "Separation Experience of Parents Whose Children Are in Foster Care," *Child Welfare*, XLVIII, No. 6 (1969), 334–340.
4. Angela E. Skinner and Raymond L. Castle, *Seventy-Eight Battered Children: A Retrospective Study* (London: National Society for the Prevention of Cruelty to Children, 1969).
5. Harry Wasserman, "Early Careers of Professional Social Workers in a Public Child Welfare Agency," *Social Work*, XV, No. 3 (1970), 93–101.
6. C.F.A. Pantin, "Organism and Environment," *Psychological Issues*, IV, No. 2., Monograph 22 (1969), 114.

7. Charles C. Hughes, "Psychocultural Dimensions of Social Change," in Joseph C. Finney, ed., *Cultural Change, Mental Health, and Poverty* (Lexington: University of Kentucky Press, 1969), 179.
8. *Perspectives on Human Deprivation: Biological, Psychological, and Sociological* (Washington, D.C.: National Institute of Child Health and Human Development, U.S. Public Health Service, 1968).
9. *Ibid.*, 10.
10. Oscar Lewis, "The Possessions of the Poor," *Scientific American*, CCXXI (Oct. 1969), 123.
11. *Perspectives on Human Deprivation*, *op. cit.*
12. Roman Mykytowycz, "Territorial Marking by Rabbits," *Scientific American*, CCXVIII (May 1968), 126.
13. Rene Dubos, "Environmental Determinants of Human Life," in D.C. Glass, ed., *Environmental Influences* (New York: Rockefeller University Press and Russell Sage Foundation, 1968), 139.
14. *Ibid.*, 144–145.
15. *Ibid.*, 146.
16. Anne Chisholm, "Nature's Doctors," *Manchester Guardian Weekly*, CII, No. 14 (1970), 16.
17. Dubos, *op. cit.*, 150.
18. H.B. Gewirtz and J.L. Gewirtz, "Caretaker Settings, Background, and Events and Behavior Differences in Four Israeli Child-Rearing Environments: Some Preliminary Trends," in B.M. Foss, ed., *Determinants in Infant Behavior*, IV (London: Methuen & Co., 1969), 247.
19. Jerome Kagan, "On Cultural Deprivation," in *Environmental Influences*, *op. cit.*, 238–239.
20. John S. Watson, "Cognitive-Perceptual Developments in Infancy: Setting for the Seventies," paper presented at the Merrill-Palmer Conference on Research and Teaching of Infant Development, Detroit, 1970; also, John S. Watson and Craig T. Ramey, "Reactions to Response-Contingent Stimulation in Early Infancy," paper read, in part, at meeting of the Society for Research in Child Development, California, 1969, and in part at the Institute of Human Development Symposium, University of California, Berkeley, 1969.
21. Howard W. Polsky and Daniel B. Claster, *The Dynamics of Residential Treatment: A Social System Analysis* (Chapel Hill: University of North Carolina Press, 1968), 12–20.
22. Henry L. Lennard and Arnold Bernstein, *Patterns in Human Interaction* (San Francisco: Jossey-Bass, 1969).
23. H.B. and J.L. Gewirtz, *op. cit.*

24. Watson, *op. cit.*

25. J.O. Jacques Alary, "A Meaning Analysis of the Expression 'Social Functioning' as a Social Work Concept," doctoral dissertation, School of Social Work, Tulane University, New Orleans, 1967, 32.

26. Lilian Ripple, "A Follow-up Study of Adopted Children," *Social Service Review*, XLII, No. 4 (1968), 496.

27. Alfred Kadushin, "Child Welfare," in Henry S. Maas, ed., *Research in the Social Services: A Five-Year Review* (New York: National Association of Social Workers, 1970).

28. Alvin L. Schorr, *Poor Kids: A Report on Children in Poverty* (New York: Basic Books, 1966).

29. *Ibid.*, 26–43.

30. Henry S. Maas, "Children in Long-Term Foster Care," *Child Welfare*, XLVIII, No. 6 (1969), 321–333, 347.

31. H.R. Schaffer and Evelyn B. Schaffer, *Child Care and the Family: A Study of Short-Term Admissions to Care* (London: Bell and Sons, 1968). See also findings on rootlessness of families in high-risk child-placement regions in Jean Packman, *Child Care Needs and Numbers* (London: Allen and Unwin, 1968).

32. Arthur C. Emlen, "Realistic Planning for the Day Care Consumer," paper presented at the National Conference of Social Welfare, Chicago, 1970: also, Alice H. Collins and Eunice L. Watson, *The Day Care Neighbor Service: A Handbook for the Organization and Operation of a New Approach to Family Day Care* (Portland, Ore.: School of Social Work, Portland State University, 1969).

33. Delores A. Taylor and Philip Starr, "Foster Parenting: An Integrative Review of the Literature," *Child Welfare*, XLVI, No. 7 (1967), 374.

34. David Fanshel, *Foster Parenthood: A Role Analysis* (Minneapolis: University of Minnesota Press, 1966), 155, 162.

35. Kadushin, *op. cit.*

36. Ripple, *op. cit.*

37. Emlen, *op. cit.*

38. Alistair Munroe, "The Theoretical Importance of Parental Deprivation in the Aetiology of Psychiatric Illness," *Applied Social Studies*, I (June 1969), 81–92.

39. G.H. Frank, "The Role of the Family in the Development of Psychopathology," *Psychological Bulletin* (1965), 191.

40. Martin Wolins, "Group Care: Friend or Foe," *Social Work*, XIV, No. 1 (1969), 35–53.

41. Henry S. Maas, "Preadolescent Peer Relations and Adult Intimacy," *Psychiatry: Journal for the Study of Interpersonal Processes*, XXXI (May 1968), 161–172.

42. Leonard Benson, *Fatherhood: A Sociological Perspective* (New York: Random House, 1968), 267.
43. Ernest A. Haggard and Anna von der Lippe, "Isolated Families in the Mountains of Norway," in E. James Anthony and Cyrille Koupernik, eds., *The Child in His Family* (New York: Wiley-Interscience, 1970), 465–488.
44. Richard Titmuss, *Commitment to Welfare* (London: Allen and Unwin, 1968), 22.

# 7

# The Plight of the Poverty-Stricken Family in the United States

SALVADOR MINUCHIN

The title of this paper is not merely a title; it is also a diagnosis. The "poverty-stricken family" has become a target for intervention by mental health professionals, and because we are presumably change-agents, our target logically must be something that needs change-producing help. The poverty-stricken family (a term that covers about 20 million people, whose strengths and problems are bewilderingly diverse) is conceptualized as an entity that must be sick. The poverty-stricken family is seen as a locus of pathology.

This paper deals with the misuse of this kind of undifferentiated diagnosis, with the impossibilities of the task that faces mental health interveners who enter this broad social arena with an inadequate psychological armamentarium, and with the way social agencies have inadvertently rendered ineffective, and sometimes harmful, their own services for the poor. Our interventions with the poor have been the product of genuine concern. Unfortunately, we have been hampered by ignorance of the field, by a set of ill-defined assumptions about the "poor," and by a predominantly middle-class set of values. The institutions that affect

Reprinted from *Child Welfare* XLIX (March 1970): 124–130.

poverty-stricken families have been organized according to a philosophy of delivery of services that sees the recipient, or client, as a sick patient. Our diagnostic systems have been organized to determine normality or pathology in a middle-class framework that does not correspond to the life styles of the poor family. Variations from the modes and mores of the mainstream society, such as the intact nuclear family, are seen as abnormal and injurious.

In general, our concepts of problems and services have been related to those of dynamic psychiatry, which has conceptualized pathology as existing within the individual and has paid little or no attention to the ways in which the systems surrounding the individual maintain or program his responses. The same tendency has been carried over into our work with families. Because we do not take into account the family's ecological systems, family problems and pathology are seen as arising from within the family. Therefore, our interventions are designed to impinge upon the family.

## THE ECOLOGICAL APPROACH

Though the mental health field has always recognized that the child can be understood only as an organism within its environment, particularly the family, the field has been less accepting of the general concept of the importance of the ecosystem; that is, the framework of systems surrounding and interacting with the individual, including the family, school, job, and so on. But lately, mental health theories have been enriched by the "ecological systems approach." The family is conceptualized as a group of people involved in constant mutual impingement. If one member of the family changes, this change affects the rest of the system. If we remove one member of the family by sending him to a residential institution for juvenile delinquents, for instance, we affect not only him, but his siblings and parents. The family system itself is seen as an entity in constant interaction with larger systems, such as the neighborhood, a racial group, and society in general.

With this view, pathology is no longer seen as a predominantly internal phenomenon. It can also be seen in, and as a product of, transactions between the individual and other systems and between the family and other systems. We do not lack conceptual knowledge of the importance of the life circumstances of our clients. But our armamentarium of interventions has failed to change in response to our broadening conceptualizations.

A major problem blocking the development of new interventions is our lack of knowledge about normal development and normal reactions to different contexts. Researchers have tended to concentrate on the observation of people we have labeled schizophrenic, phobic, delinquent, antisocial, or poor, and observations are tinged with suspicion that every part of their life styles represents part of the pathological syndrome. More knowledge of normal people's interactions with contexts would allow us to differentiate the parts of a syndrome that actually are pathological, and the parts that are a reaction to contexts and can change if the context changes. Knowledge of normality would provide a field-ground structure we badly need. This is especially true in the study of the poverty-stricken family. In research at the Wiltwyck School for Boys, for instance, my coworkers and I found definite consequences traceable to our index patients' socialization in disorganized families. We reported our data in a book we entitled *Families of the Slums* [1]. The material for this book was gathered specifically from unstable, disorganized, low socioeconomic families, mostly in clinical surroundings. But we gave the book a title that implied it encompassed the whole heterogenous group living in the slums, in all contexts. When we finished that book and began to study similar families in their natural social surroundings, we were impressed by how much we had not seen. Certain aspects of disorganized families, such as the extended family structure, which we had labeled pathological, could be seen in the larger context as significant systems of support. But social agencies, accepting the model of the nuclear family as correct, willingly or not penalized other structural types.

In general, our interventions have not been ameliorative. Welfare, as Moynihan points out [2], was originally designed to tide people over until better times. The existence of "third generation welfare" families shows that some families crystallize in the welfare position. I need not elaborate this problem; what I am interested in elaborating is the nonchange-producing aspects of interventions that were designed to help and change the family. Perhaps the best way to do this is to present a composite poverty-stricken family, with familiar characteristics and problems, and discuss the effects of interventions on it.

## THE COMPOSITE FAMILY

This family consists of a mother and her six illegitimate children, the oldest of whom is 12. The mother was born in the South, the youngest of seven children. When she was 16, she came North to live with her married sister. A year after her arrival, her first child was born. The sisters rented a crumbling brownstone and pooled their money and work. The older sister lived on the top floor with her two children, and the younger sister and her children lived below. The women made out fairly well until the need to take care of her children made the younger go on relief. At this point she became homebound, caring for her children and her sister's, while the sister worked as a maid.

After several years of trying, the older sister was admitted to a low-income housing project. She and her children moved, and at that time the younger sister bore her sixth child. She began to drink and became promiscuous. The older sister visited the family as often as possible, doing the laundry, and so forth, but the main responsibility for the children fell on the oldest daughter, 12. The mother became more and more depressed; the children's situation deteriorated. The oldest girl was responsible but subdued. She was doing well enough in school, but the teachers were worried about her tendency to withdraw. The oldest boy, 11, was a truant; he stole and otherwise acted out. The younger children showed no symptoms of pathology yet.

At the urging of the caseworker, the mother consented to have the children placed. After court procedures, the children were put in a shelter. From there, the oldest daughter went to a foster home, the oldest son was placed in a residential institution for delinquent youths, and the 9- and 8-year-olds were placed in different foster homes. The 8-year-old lived in three different foster homes during this period. The 5-year-old spent some months in the shelter because of hyperactive behavior that suggested minimal brain dysfunction. He was finally placed in an institution. The baby remained with his mother, whose caseworker continued to work with her.

It is difficult to calculate the cost to the children of this separation from their mother and each other. But the financial cost is staggering [3].

The mother was eager to get her children back. Finally, the caseworker helped her petition the department of welfare and the children in foster care were returned to her. The family was referred for treatment to a child guidance clinic, since childrearing problems remained. When a clinic social worker visited the home, he found all the children dressed up waiting to greet him. The mother put the children through rehearsed routines to show that they minded her and that she could take care of them. She said to him: "I love my kids and I want them. But if that judge takes them away again—well, I'm 34 now. That gives me about 10 years. If they take these away from me, I'll have 10 more."

## NATURE OF THE INTERVENTIONS

The social interventions for this family were designed in good faith to assist them and, theoretically, to help them change. But the effect of the interventions was to fragment the family and increase their difficulties. Let us look at these interventions before we consider how to organize services according to a conceptual framework that sees the family as a whole system and takes into account the effect interventions with individual members have upon the family. First, the mother received welfare checks for years. These helped feed, shelter, and clothe the children, but this was only maintenance. Payments were made to the mother; in effect, the state was paying her to babysit. No attempt was made to help the family change or to change their circumstances. The main concern was the well-being of the children, and as long as the sisters lived together, the children received satisfactory care. The mother was given no employment counseling, and if she had been, her sense of ineffectiveness would have made the counseling futile. In any case, someone had to look after the children, and even if she had been able to hold a job, the lack of adequate day care facilities would have made it impossible for her and her sister to keep their children together. Birth control information was not made available to her. The caseworker did not mention it, and the mother never sought it. She did not know where to go to get family planning advice, and had only a vague idea of the function of social agencies; furthermore, she felt that no man would accept her use of a birth control device. The department of welfare intervened only when the mother's deterioration threatened her children. That intervention took the form of breaking up the family for 2 years.

The older sister's departure to the housing project is also illustrative. She was a widow with two children, a good candidate for low-income housing. Her application was approved, though it took a year because of an overload of applications. But the younger sister, mother of more than two illegitimate children, was never considered as a possible candidate. If she had been, her oldest son's record of truancy and stealing would have labeled her family ineligible. Thus, a system of interdependence and support between the two families was shattered, and nothing was supplied to take its place.

## SYSTEMS OF SUPPORT

We know from studies of the low socioeconomic population that many systems of support exist within the neighborhood, including churches, social groups, and "social networks." We also know that the various forms of the extended family can be important systems of support. But this knowledge is not carried over into interventive techniques. Cases such as that of our composite family are not uncommon. It never occurred to the social worker to try to help repair the loss of support represented by the breakup of the joint family; the only intervention was to break up the family still more.

What would be more helpful to a family like our composite? For such a family an ecologically oriented intervener would first study the ecology of the family, to pick out the supportive systems and the harmful components, particularly those that tended to keep the family dependent. He would determine the relevant kinds of intervention, deciding whether to concentrate on the nuclear family or younger sister and her children, subunits of this group, the extended family, the neighborhood, the school, or a variety of targets. He would decide who should intervene—a social worker, a teacher, a counselor, or a community worker. He would then plan goals for family change and plot interventions directed toward those goals, based on the realization that the true family unit was the joint family. The smallest effective target of intervention would be the younger sister and her children, but the operant nuclear target would be the two sisters and their children.

The therapist would also consider three other sisters who were living in the immediate area. He would take into account two fathers of the younger sister's children, still in the area, not stable members of the family unit, but in contact with their children. Also part of the family's ecosystem would be the children's teachers and the school guidance counselor, the department of welfare caseworker, the minister of the neighborhood storefront church, the personnel of the medical clinic the children attended, two staff members of the child guidance clinic with whom the children had formed relationships, and other unmapped contacts.

Interventions to help the composite family could take various forms. Some would require the expertise of a mental health practitioner and some would require the work of an educator. The help of the area committee woman might be needed. The mental health intervener would have to coordinate these steps carefully, so that the interventions did not add to the chaotic impingement of life upon this family.

## A COURSE OF TREATMENT

Here's a hypothetical course of treatment.:

The clinician would conduct family therapy sessions in the clinic and the home. From the family's interactions, he might conclude that the family fell in the category designated as the disorganized family [4,5]. As such, they would have a particular style of communicating. They would tend to focus on the end product of behavior, rather than on content. They would be oriented toward externalization and projection, and be unskilled in readings of interpersonal causality. They would be untrained in self-observation, and therefore unavailable for traditional therapeutic techniques. Family conflicts would be expressed in a global way, rendering them unavailable for problem-solving. The children, reared in an environment of impermanence and unpredictability, would have difficulty defining themselves in relation to the world. Such rules as were set would be largely the responsibility of the parental child. The mother would alternately defer to her and try to wrest some of her power back. All of the children, handicapped by the random and erratic rules, would look to adult responses for cues as to behavior, instead of depending on internalized rules [6].

At the same time, there would be good features in the family that could be utilized. Immediately obvious would be the warmth and love within the family, and the mother's determination to keep her children. The availability of the older sister for support could be utilized. A neighbor who made a pet of the youngest boy could be enlisted as a babysitter so the mother could go to a "slimnastics" class she has been wanting to take at the YWCA.

A community worker could join clinic sessions designed to help the mother establish rules for the children and to offer guidance instead of the excessive control she had adopted after the children's return. The medical clinic would aid the youngest boy, 7, whose hyperactivity might cause great problems in school. Dexadrine might be prescribed, and the school counselor and teacher would consult with the combined medical and mental health team. Through a community worker, the mother might become a member of a neighborhood social club [7]. If the group had a speaker to discuss job training programs, she might enroll in a training course for sewing machine operators. At this point, if in the judgment of the clinicians the family had attained a certain degree of change and autonomy, they might enter a period of discontinuous treatment. The community worker would keep in close touch with the family, and the clinic would always be available in any crisis, but the family would be seen in the clinic only once every 6 weeks or so. This type of service relates to that of a family medical practitioner, who establishes a base of health and then remains available for crises.

The emphasis throughout would be not on exploring pathology, but on finding, enhancing, and rewarding competence. People change not only through the lifting of inhibitions, as in traditional psychoanalytic theory, but through the development of competences. The family would be hooked into therapy rapidly because they would perceive the therapist as responsive to their needs. The impact of the interventions would be multiplied by the use of natural systems of support within the family and community. The therapist would have to be supersensitive to the danger that his interventions would further rob the mother of her executive power and increase her dependency on social agencies, but this danger could be avoided. The intervention with this family would not be short term. But the redoubled nature of the interventions and the possibility of discontinuous clinical interventions would make the work effective and thrifty.

## DEALING WITH THE TOTAL FAMILY

Family services oriented toward the total family within its ecosystem are becoming more and more the treatment of choice for a wide range of mental health and social problem families, not just members of the low socioeconomic groups. But the response of social agencies in general is still to break up the family. The records of improvement in foster care and residential treatment are not encouraging, and the costs of these approaches are discouraging, but there still has not been an organized, overall conceptualization of the delivery of services to families in this country. The family is studied and respected as a viable socialization unit when it is working; when trouble arises, the response is to split it.

This is part of the American philosophy of individualism; we are oriented toward the individual child and his rights. But this does seem to have been carried to extremes. In most countries, the function performed here by the ADC is fulfilled by family allowances, but in the United States, support goes through the mother to the child. This is an antifamilial force even without the concomitant problems of "man-in-the-house" rules.

Only recently are we beginning to develop a concept of services to the child in his ecological systems—the family, the school, the neighborhood, and so on. Within this new concept, what are the changes we should sponsor in ourselves and push for on larger levels [8]? At the level of intervention with specific family units, we must change our goals. Instead of discovering and inadvertently maintaining pathology, we must discover and enhance competence. We must change the locality of our change-producing interventions, moving into the home and community in order to study and develop goals for change in the particular family in its day-by-day life and interactions with its surrounding systems. In doing so, we will discover the natural systems of support that exist in the community and be able to work with them to enhance their supportive function.

In moving away from clinic-centered interventions into the actual life of a family, we find many new ways to help and to change the family. Auerswald [9] found that some multiproblem families were in contact with seven or more agencies, all impinging upon one part of the family's life. A family might be dealing with the school counselor and truant officer, the court's parole officer and probation officer, the social workers of a residential school for delinquents, and the caseworker of the department of welfare. It is helpful to bring all the interveners and the family together to discuss overall goals and plans.

Looking at people as they interact with their environment and social institutions, we cease to consider the intervener the only major variable in the development of change. We will become more concerned with allowing natural systems of support to function more effectively. Studying the feedback processes between the family and its surroundings, we will change the delivery of our services. To make the total family the focus of integrated services, we have to reconceptualize, and realize that we are delivering services to people with rights, people who are responding to an ecosystem of which we are part.

We are beginning to understand the importance of ecological systems and the way they affect health and mental health. Slowly, we are beginning to incorporate this understanding in the development of services. In the measure in which this concept is taken into account in our planning and execution of interventions, those interventions will become truly change-producing and helpful.

## NOTES AND REFERENCES

1. Salvador Minuchin, Braulio Montalvo, *et al.* (New York: Basic Books, 1967).
2. Daniel Patrick Moynihan and Paul Barton, *The Negro Family: The Case for National Action* (Washington D.C.: U.S. Department of Labor, 1965).
3. The Children's Aid Society of Pennsylvania estimates the average yearly cost of keeping a child in residential treatment is $7975. For keeping an older child in foster care, the average cost is $2304. Thus the cost of keeping three children in foster care and two children in institutional care for 2 years would exceed $40,000.
4. Eleanor Pavenstedt, "A Comparison of the Childrearing Environment of Upper-Lower and Very Low-Lower Class Families," *American Journal of Orthopsychiatry*, XXXV, No. 1 (1965), 89 ff.
5. Minuchin, *op. cit.*
6. For a more thorough discussion, see Minuchin, *op. cit.*
7. Richard Taber, "A Systems Approach to the Delivery of Mental Health Services to Children in a Low Socioeconomic Black Community: Work with Two Natural Groups," presented to the American Orthopsychiatric Association, March 1969. Mimeo.
8. See E.H. Auerswald, "Cognitive Development and Psychopathology in the Urban Environment," in P.S. Graubard, ed., *Children Against Schools* (Chicago: Follett Educational Corporation, 1969); Lynn Hoffman and Lawrence Long, "A Systems Dilemma," mimeo; Ross V. Speck, "Psychotherapy and the Social Network of a Schizophrenic Family," *Family Process*, VI, (1967); and Taber, *op. cit.*
9. E.H. Auerswald, "Interdisciplinary Versus Ecological Approach," *Family Process*, VII, No. 2 (1968).

# 8

# An Ecological Approach to Child Welfare: Issues of Family Identity and Continuity

JOAN LAIRD

Change in today's world occurs at such rapid rates that human beings' adaptive abilities are strained to their very limits. On the other hand, in some areas change or progress seems painfully slow. On a societal level we have only recently become alarmed enough about the destruction of our natural environment to seriously examine the impact of social, economic, and political planning and decision-making on the systems upon which we must depend for future survival.

Social workers, in spite of their historical focus on human beings in relation to their social environments, have also often been slow to recognize the far-reaching destructive effects that policies, programs, and service delivery approaches may have on delicate but vital human systems. A case in point is the undermining effect some kinds of practice have had on that most important natural human system, the family. Perhaps nowhere has resistance

---

Reprinted from *Social Work Practice: People and Environments*, Edited by Carel B. Germain. New York: Columbia University Press, 1979, pp. 174–209. By permission of the author, editor, and publisher.

to change, resistance to take account of, support, and protect natural systems been more troublesome or more paradoxical than in the field of family and childrens' services, that area of practice known, interestingly enough, as "child welfare."

The metaphorical use of principles from ecology focusses attention on the extent to which people are dependent upon and immersed in their social, physical, cultural, and emotional environments.

What are the implications of an ecological orientation for practice in child welfare? In this chapter we will describe what current child welfare practice seems to look like and how an ecological perspective would alter it. We will explore some of the resistances and obstacles that may stand in the way of change. Finally, we will describe some applications of ecological practice principles in specific practice situations.

## THE BIOLOGICAL FAMILY

This presentation takes as its starting point the conviction that human beings are profoundly affected by the family system of which they are a part. Kin ties are powerful and compelling and the individual's sense of identity and continuity is formed not only by the significant attachments in his intimate environment but also is deeply rooted in the biological family—in the genetic link that reaches back into the past and ahead into the future.

This view of the significance of kin ties runs deep in American culture and is expressed by such sayings as "blood is thicker than water." Whether this deep sense of kinship connection is biologically based [1] or is a cultural "artifact" [2] is hotly disputed. No matter which explanation one favors, the felt experience of the importance of kin ties does exist, whether it is a part of our genetic heritage or a part of our cultural heritage. And although there are many other sources of identity, continuity, and attachment, the importance of the biological family cannot be ignored.

Ecologically oriented child welfare practice attends to, nurtures, and supports the biological family. Further, when it is necessary to substitute for the biological family, such practice dictates that every effort be made to preserve and protect important kinship ties. Intervening in families must be done with great care to avoid actions which could weaken the natural family system, sap its vitality and strength, or force it to make difficult, costly adjustments.

Although this position is based on the importance of individuals' connection with their family systems, there are other considerations which lead to such a conception of ecological child welfare practice. The most important of these is the demonstrated fact that it is difficult, expensive, and wasteful of valuable resources to locate and support substitute forms of care. Consider the cost in human and material resources of maintaining a single child in institutional care. Consider the cost of foster home care in terms of professional services and financial support, to say nothing of the psychological cost to children and foster parents of the frequent replacements which continue to typify the foster care experience.

## CURRENT CHILD WELFARE PRACTICE

Although one should be careful of generalizing, and certainly we can point to many outstanding exceptions to general trends, our largest social, economic, and professional investment continues to lie in obtaining and maintaining substitute care arrangements for children, and in the treatment of emotionally damaged children. As Salvador Minuchin so bluntly phrases it, even though we have conceptual knowledge which enables us to understand family difficulties in an ecological framework, as products of transactions between the family and its surrounding life space,

> Our armamentarium of interventions has failed to change in response to our broadening conceptualizations . . . . [3] (The) response of social agencies in general is still to break up the family. The records of improvement in foster care and residential treatment are not encouraging, and the costs of these approaches is discouraging, but there still has not been an organized, overall conceptualization of the delivery of services to families in this country. The family is studied and respected as a viable socialization unit when it is working; when trouble arises, the response is to split it. [4]

The typical child welfare case looks something like this:

> Janet Roberts calls the police, reporting that her sister-in-law Denise Jackson is at the local bar with a boyfriend, having left her four children ranging in age from 3 to 11 alone. The oldest daughter, age 14, is in a foster home. The police remove the children to an emergency "temporary" foster home. The following day a Protective Services worker visits Mrs. Jackson, finding her alternately angry and tearful, worrying whether the children have enough clothing, and accusing her sister-in-law of "trying to get my children." The worker learns that Mr. Jackson is

> in jail, having stolen from his employer. The house is disorderly. From the case record, the worker is already familiar with a family history reflecting several years of multiple problems, unemployment and underemployment, marital stress, and conflict with both maternal and paternal extended families. The protective worker, hoping to reunite the family, spends considerable time with Mrs. Jackson, counseling, cajoling, advising, insisting that she clean up the house, supervise and discipline the children more consistently, and initiate therapy at the local mental health clinic. Mrs. Jackson, although she makes many promises and some ineffectual attempts, does not follow through, and a petition of neglect is adjudicated. The case is then transferred from the Protective Services Unit to Foster Care. The foster care worker's efforts center on helping the children with separation difficulties and adjustment to a new environment, and working with the foster family around a variety of parenting issues and related concerns. The visiting of the natural parent(s) often becomes the most potentially flammable issue, the one requiring the most sensitive work: Mrs. Jackson begins to fade as a central part of the case, her visits taper off, she seems disinterested . . . .

What was visualized originally as a temporary foster placement, a stop on a circular path to the reunion and rehabilitation of the natural family, has instead become a straight and narrow road toward substitute care. This can mean permanent placement or, as is often the case, a dismal succession of repeated separations and placements in foster homes and institutions sometimes interspersed, when resources are exhausted, with temporary and unsuccessful trips home.

Some of the more blatant examples of current policy and/or practice which belie our publicly stated goal of supporting and strengthening natural family systems should be mentioned:

1. Native American and other concerned professionals are descrying what they describe as the destruction of the American Indian family, as it is alleged that some 25 to 35 percent of Indian children are being placed in foster or adoptive care. Surely widespread removal out of race, culture, and family heritage is an illogical and destructive approach to the enhancement of healthy development for Indian children! [5]

2. Public agency protective and other family service units continue to be plagued with high caseloads, inadequate human and financial resources, and heavy paper and reporting

responsibilities which may be needed but which interfere with direct service potential. [6]

3. While funds for services to families are limited, we seem willing to invest $10,000 to $20,000 per year to care for one child in a residential treatment center.

4. We seem to believe, in this society, that an AFDC mother deserves less and can support her child on less income than can a foster mother.

The most ironic note is the troubling question of whether our investments are successful, whether, in our public and professional roles as substitute parents we are doing a better job than natural families might have done if left to their own devices, let alone given similar time and investment. How do we explain the statistics on the numbers of repeated, unsuccessful placements, the number of children in limbo, without permanent planning? How do we continue to justify the return of children who were removed because of neglect to families who are no more economically, physically, socially, or emotionally equipped to give adequate care than they were when their children were placed? How often are these decisions made on the basis of lack of agency and community resources but described as appropriate treatment plans?

How do we explain the return home of children from residential treatment facilities to families who have not been involved in the treatment effort? How can we expect the returning child to shoulder the burden of adjusting to or even changing a stressful family system which itself has perhaps accommodated to the child's absence? How long will it be before the child has been recast into his or her traditional role, whether it be scapegoat, delinquent, or some other type of family symptom bearer?

Such practices are not only "unecological" but paradoxically "antifamily" in their effects. If an ecological approach to child welfare means the preservation of the natural family wherever possible, we clearly need to scrutinize our seeming inability to shift direction.

## OBSTACLES TO AN ECOLOGICAL APPROACH

Why have we not put our stated beliefs about family life into practice? This is an exceedingly complex question that defies any simple "cause and effect" answer. Economic, political, cultural, and professional forces combine to inhibit change in child welfare, thus the emphasis on substitute care and the failure to "think" or "act" family persist.

Perhaps the most striking obstacle is the lack of consistent philosophical agreement in the United States as to the role of government in relation to the family. We have no "family policy" as such, for example, one which supports or guarantees universal basic income or service levels for all families. Only recently has interest developed in the notion of examining the "impact" on the family of political and economic planning and decison-making. Our national ambivalence is surfaced as we promote policies and programs which pressure AFDC mothers of young children to seek employment, yet fail to provide an adequate day care system for fear of usurping the traditional family role of child-rearing.

Not only do we lack commitment to a uniform family policy, but we also continue to struggle with the sometimes conflicting interests of parents and children and to debate the issue of whose rights take precedence. Clear definitions of "minimal standards of child care" and "neglect" continue to elude us, as social, moral, economic, and racial factors influence our thinking. Some social critics state that in our society, abuse and neglect are inevitable in an economic environment in which children continue to be viewed as commodities or property and thus exploited [7]. The abuse and neglect of children in public and private institutions continues and confusion about the nature of abuse is expressed in the Supreme Court's refusal to rule against corporal punishment in the schools [8]. Cynical and uncomfortably provocative questions are raised concerning the latent role of child welfare programs. One prominent analyst recently attacked the myth that "child care facilities and agencies are sanctioned and supported by the community primarily out of concern for children and what is best for the child," suggesting that our real function may be that of removing "embarrassing debris from visibility," the "social control" role social workers have often unwittingly performed [9]. Even more challenging is the suggestion that social workers not only perform social control functions but are acting as brokers of a very valuable and increasingly scarce commodity, young children. The practice of transracial and transcultural adoption, for example, has been under angry attack as professionals are accused of exploiting poor and minority families in meeting the "demand" for babies in a market whose character has changed drastically as a result of increased birth control, legality and availability of abortion, and fewer surrenders on the part of unmarried parents. Are we indeed guilty, in the name of "child-saving," of brokering children from poor to rich families just as we found poor city children to act as farm labor in the 19th century? Such questions are frightening and challenging, but exceedingly necessary.

At the program level child welfare suffers from lack of clarity concerning program objectives. Even when overall objectives are clearly defined, successful coordination of a variety of services and interests is difficult [10]. And finally, child welfare is plagued by the same criticisms all human services face, a dearth of tested methods for evaluating the outcome of our efforts, the achievement of objectives [11].

In addition to these political, social, and economic variables, there are other powerful forces which influence current child welfare practice. One major handicap is our lack of understanding of family systems. Historically, our knowledge and training were shaped by psychoanalytic and child development theories, and were largely confined to the understanding of individuals. We have been trained, albeit often inadequately, to monitor child development, to construct models for healthy physical, social, and emotional development, and to attempt to understand and diagnose a variety of adult and child pathologies. The bulk of the child abuse literature, for example, centers on the psychological profile of the abusing parent [12]. Understandably then, the choice of intervention often leads us to removal of children and referral to mental health facilities, and to treatment of individual family members. Child welfare workers are often frustrated as parents seem "uncooperative," "unmotivated," do not follow through with treatment plans, and the treatment of the emotionally damaged child becomes a long expensive process with what often seem limited gains.

This is not to suggest that knowledge of individual psychological development and functioning is not valuable or essential, but only to say that new ways of understanding family systems in space, in relation to their complex environments, and as they develop over time are now available as well and should be used by child welfare workers. Concepts from family system theorists, from ecological and general systems theory, and from communication theory, are aids to understanding and assessing the transactional relationships among family members and between the family and its environment.

Ironically, social work can be proud of the fact it was the first profession to "think" and "act" family, and has a tradition of being the profession concerned with the total person-situation complex. Other disciplines have only recently discovered, for example, the assessment and intervention potentials of home visits! In the last 25 years, however, while child welfare has largely clung to older "medical model" approaches, the family therapy field, dominated by psychologists and psychiatrists, has been characterized by an exciting development of new frameworks or models for understanding and intervening in complex family relationships [13]. It is time now for child welfare to examine and integrate new thinking about families in their world.

All workers must deal with the impact of their own personal and familial experiences on their professional development. Young workers, called upon to make decisions affecting the future lives of families, parents, and children alike, are often themselves in the height of their own efforts to separate and differentiate from their families of origin. It may well be that this conflict strengthens their wish to rescue children from their families.

Issues of adulthood, of identity consolidation, never totally resolved for anyone, profoundly affect how we view and work with client families. A group of child welfare trainees, presented with a living family sculpture which demonstrated the family emotional system, were asked to resculpt the family as they would like it to be, or as they would want it to change with family intervention. The trainees were surprised and amused to discover that each had his own ideas on the subject. These ideas, which were argued enthusiastically, seemed to reflect either their real or idealized images of their own families.

In another family sculpture experience, a child welfare worker in her 40s, herself a parent, found she was the only person in the room feeling empathetic with the parents in the presented family, while most of the younger workers were more identified with the children. How much conviction, how much hope we have about the family, is deeply related to our own family relationships and experiences. Some workers, perhaps having had painful experiences with their own parents, view their roles as obtaining "better" parents for children. Young workers, testing out and not yet acclimated to their own new roles as adults with power and authority may find it easier to identify with and to work with children than to plunge with conviction into family work with adults who may be angry, attacking, and involved in a seemingly hopeless, tangled procession of psychological, marital, social, economic, and other difficulties.

The preceding attempt to search out some explanations for our reluctance to move toward a clear family emphasis in child welfare is intended to raise questions which need to be addressed. There may be no easy solutions, but the first step surely must be to critically examine the issues, dilemmas, and myths which shape our practice.

## ISSUES OF PARENTING AND IDENTITY

A particularly profound, persistent, and troubling challenge in child placement is to understand and ameliorate the traumatic effects on children of both temporary and permanent separations from their families of origin or other primary caretakers. The child welfare worker is also faced with the task of helping children cope with threats to healthy identity formation and consolidation provoked by physical and emotional cutoffs from their biological roots [14].

Although we share a common knowledge base [15], social workers in general seem vulnerable to dichotomies which, in their extreme form, tend to retard progress. Just as we have in the past separated ourselves into the caseworkers and the social changemakers, arguing about which is best and which is the "real" social work, so today we find ourselves debating with renewed vigor an enduring controversy in the child welfare area. We might call this the "case of the biological parent vs. the psychological parent," as if one had to rule finally that one or the other were the "real" parent.

The family itself, variously described in recent years as outmoded, overwhelmed, functionless, or breaking down, is making a comeback. Whatever the reasons, people seem to be fighting to preserve the family as a meaningful and viable institution. There is, for example, a new surge of interest in genealogy and in family reunions, predating but also stimulated by Alex Haley's *Roots* [16]. In the mental health field, the interdisciplinary family therapy movement, now some 25 years old, attracts increasing numbers of trainees, as new ways of thinking about and working with families are generated.

At the same time that we are experiencing the renewed interest in the family and particularly the biological family, Anna Freud, Albert J. Solnit, and Joseph Goldstein take a strong position in defense of the concept of the psychological parent [17]. Few would argue against their efforts to better define that nebulous term, the "best interests of the child," or would contest their basic premise that the guideline of "continuity," of "the need of every child for unbroken continuity of affectionate and stimulating relationships with an adult" is paramount in child welfare [18].

It is the next step the authors take which the writer finds illogical if not potentially damaging to progress in child welfare. The position, never explicitly clarified, is most dramatically implied in the following excerpt concerning parental visitation and custody issues in divorce situations:

> Children have difficulty in relating positively to, profiting from, and maintaining the contact with two psychological parents who are not in positive contact with each other. Loyalty conflicts are common and normal under such conditions and may have devastating consequences by destroying the child's positive relationships to both parents. A "visiting" or "visited" parent has little chance to serve as a true object for love, trust, and identification, since this role is based on his being available on an uninterrupted day-to-day basis.
>
> Once it is determined who will be the custodial parent, it is that parent, not the court, who must decide under what conditions he or she wishes to raise the child. Thus, the

> noncustodial parent should have no legally enforceable right to visit the child, and the custodial parent should have the right to decide whether it is desirable for the child to have such visits. [19]

To argue that a child's psychological parent, and thus the source of his own psychological identity, is determined solely from his nurturing, caretaking experiences seems an oversimplification of a very complex human situation. Children identify both positively and negatively with many real and fantasy figures other than their full-time caretakers, from the loving weekend and summer vacation daddy to the deserting father "who kicked my mother in the stomach when she was pregnant with me" [20]. Most child welfare workers have experienced the pain, frustration, and feeling of failure when, in spite of dedicated efforts to provide a supportive environment for a child, a foster child acts out destructively in a way which reflects the few facts he may have about his hidden or lost parents, or even worse, on the basis of his fantasies about the lost object. Family systems therapists understand that family secrets, physical and emotional cutoffs from family, and family myths can contribute as powerfully if not more powerfully to individual dysfunction as those family conflicts and crises which can be openly identified and thus tackled.

In recent years we have witnessed a growing interest on the part of adult adoptees in searching out their origins and in some cases in meeting their natural parents or extended biological families. Accounts of these difficult and often emotionally draining adventures have portrayed human beings' deep psychological needs for rootedness. The following comments are illustrative of the experiences many of them share.

One writer, a psychologist and family therapist who was raised in foster care and as an adult embarked on an "identity trip," tells of the impact on him of seeing for the first time a picture of his deceased mother. The experience of seeing oneself reflected in another human being is described as "a stunning experience!" [21].

A foster child, David, was recently reintroduced to his long lost extended family through the determined efforts of his worker, who traced his family while she was on vacation to the east coast. He expressed his relief this way:

> I told my caseworker . . . after seeing my grandparents and aunts, uncles, cousins, etc. and knowing now that I have them . . . before I never felt that I belonged anywhere or if for that matter, (it) mattered if I had anyone. The reason I say belonged anywhere is because of my other grandparents dying when I was 13, and then going through a number of different foster homes. . . . After seeing my grandparents, I feel as though I belong now, and that I

> am somebody, and that is the best feeling anyone could have in this situation. [22]

Many adoptees are not necessarily interested in reunion, but in knowing their biological histories [23]. Such information "provides a frame for their lives, and a continuity with their pasts. It confirms and solidifies their images of themselves" in a search to achieve a unity and persistence of personality [24].

This need for "rootedness" has at times been characterized by professionals as neurotic or is said to exist only in those unhappy, unfulfilled persons who have had inadequate alternate family experiences. Psychiatrist Robert Jay Lifton, in contrast to the view developed by Freud and her colleagues describes "the duality of all involvement—*immediate* psychological struggles around connection and separation, integrity and disintegration, and movement and stasis; and *ultimate* struggles with forces beyond the self, with meanings around historical and biological continuity" [23]. Lifton stresses that identity formation is not simply a matter of one's immediate life experiences and relationships but is also strongly influenced by one's larger sense of heritage [26]. The adopted child and the foster child, however reluctant we may be to admit it, each has two families. It is a major life task to understand and integrate the meanings and experiences from both families, to incorporate his or her historical and biological heritage into the foster or other family experience. It is our responsibility to help the child achieve this bio-psycho-social integration.

We have often encouraged children to estrange themselves from and to repress painful family experiences. In doing so, we robbed them of their rights to their own histories and of opportunities to gain freedom from the emotional "stucktogetherness" which can inhibit functioning. We have recognized that adults need the opportunity to experience and master the developmental and situational crises of death, of separation, and divorce. Cannot we offer the same opportunity to children?

The second implication of the view expressed by Freud and her colleagues is that loyalty conflicts, whether between divorced parents or between biological and foster parents, are more harmful to a child than what amounts to a possible repudiation of a major part of self. One writer points out that the authors' view lacks any basis in empirical research, and in fact cites several studies which support the belief that those children who fare best after divorce are those who are free to develop relationships with both parents. "Children are not only deeply pained by . . . [a parent's] . . . absence but they interpret it as abandonment; as a consequence they feel devalued and guilty, and yet they find they have few ways to express their anger and confusion" [27].

Just as we cannot decide that one biological parent is to own the psychological parent role, we cannot separate biological and psychological identity as if they were two opposing and isolated parts of human personality. Nor should we ask that children make such choices. Instead we need to help children come to terms with and maintain their biological realities in whatever ways may be possible. Certainly the integration of potentially compelling and conflicting forces, whether maternal and paternal, biological or adoptive family, fostering or visiting parent, are difficult for everyone concerned—for the child, the adults, and the professional. The solution, however, lies not in obliterating one side of the competition but in reexamining our biases and enhancing our knowledge and skills so that we may better help our clients master these life challenges.

## AN ECOLOGICAL APPROACH TO CHILD WELFARE

The most effective way to preserve natural family ties is to strengthen and preserve the family itself. While it is beyond the parameters of this chapter to discuss working with natural families in any depth, a few comments should be made.

The first step in moving toward ecological practice mandates a serious reexamination and clarification of our goals and priorities, coupled with a willingness not only to advocate for new programs and funding but to shift a large portion of our energies and funds from a placement to a natural family focus.

We have the conceptual framework which enables us to better understand the complex relationships between families and their ecological environments, to identify those interfaces where there is stress, conflict, or insufficient exchange across family-environment boundaries, and to plan interventions which can most quickly and economically promote major improvement in family functioning. Such practice models encourage both workers and families to mobilize and utilize potentially enriching natural support networks [28]. This knowledge is seeping into child welfare practice, but a model of ecological family-centered practice must be developed and refined for child welfare, and all workers must have training in work with families.

Family-centered practice is an empty concept, however, if we are unable to provide families with the institutional supports and services needed to prevent family dysfunction and enrich family life. For example, on a larger scale, this country has yet to commit itself to an adequate family income program, equal educational opportunities for all children, meaningful employment opportunities for all who are able to work, or universally available health and medical care. In the last fifteen years the introduction of homemaker and day care services has provided an important resource in the preserving of family life, but often even these services are extremely limited and the eligibility requirements narrow and prohibitive for many families. We need to broaden the availability of such programs and services and to expand opportunities for family education and self-fulfillment.

Where priorities have been reexamined and efforts made to sanction and support work with natural families through provision of special training and expansion or reallocation of resources, results are encouraging. Recently, in a New York State demonstration project, worker caseloads were limited to ten families, and project agencies were required to meet client needs for homemaker, day care, vocational, and educational services [29]. It was found that fewer children in the experimental group, who received "intensive" services, entered placement than in the control group, who received "usual" service. Additionally, those children who did enter placement remained for shorter periods of time, and a larger percentage of them had been returned home by the end of the evaluation period.

In Michigan, the Temporary Foster Care Project is designed to encourage foster care workers to widen the unit of attention to include intensive work with natural families. Workers are given several days of training in family assessment and intervention, they are introduced to newly developed family intervention tools and provided with follow-up consultation. The training emphasizes assessment and intervention in the interface between family and ecological environment, although workers are also introduced to family systems frameworks for assessing the internal family system. Workers are asked to identify specific goals and tasks and taught to develop time-limited contracts between family and worker. The project's stated goal is to "move children from the uncertain and temporary status of foster care to a more permanent and hopefully stable situation, preferably a return to the biological family" [30]. At the end of the first project year, the percentage of placed children returned to their biological families within six months of placement more than doubled over the previous year in all four of the pilot counties [31]. Workers are also better able to move confidently toward permanent planning and termination of parental rights in those cases where families will not be able to resume care of their children. Project leaders hope to spread the family orientation and training opportunities to other counties and service units through the use of peer trainers.

## PRESERVING FAMILY TIES IN PLACEMENT

Even if a major shift toward family-centered practice is accomplished, there will continue to be some children who will need temporary or permanent substitute care. Family assessment and intervention knowledge and techniques backed by careful court review and monitoring are not only helpful in making more intelligent decisions about placement and termination of parental rights but in helping families and children master the separation and relinquishment process. Further, a family systems perspective is extremely valuable in improving our potential for making more accurate, dynamic, predictive assessments of potential foster and adoptive families.

An ecological approach in child welfare suggests that those placement systems closest to the natural system promise the least disruption for child and family and should be explored first. This maxim has been accepted as we have preferred foster care over institutional placement in order to approximate the natural family relationships. The obvious implication here is that every effort should be made to utilize the extended family as a placement resource.

This implication is frequently given short shrift. For one thing, many workers assume that if one member of a family has abused or neglected a child, other members will do the same. This point of view is given considerable support in the child welfare literature. Blair and Rita Justice state:

> Breaking the multigenerational cycle of child abuse, then, is of paramount importance. Accomplishing this often means that children must be kept out of the hands of their grandparents and the abusing parents must be helped to break away from their families of origin. [32]

I believe this position is based on a serious misinterpretation of Bowen family theory. The authors confuse the concepts of "differentiation" and "separation" as used by Bowen and other family theorists. Those individuals who are poorly differentiated, according to family systems theory, have more intense unresolved emotional attachments to their parents than most, they are more fused or emotionally "stuck together" [33]. Some practitioners assume that dysfunctional family relationships are best handled by withdrawing, putting physical distance between individuals and their families. Thus they view abusing families as families from which children should be encouraged to physically and emotionally separate. However, in the family therapy field there is widespread conviction that physical and emotional distancing promotes rather than weakens psychological dependency. In situations where the physical and emotional cutoffs become intense, as in prolonged placements, the child may be even more prone to duplicate destructive family patterns in his or her own adult interpersonal and family relationships.

Certainly we see evidence of this phenomenon, as many emotionally damaged children repeat the dysfunctional marital and parenting patterns of their parents in spite of adequate placement experiences and supportive service. We need to help children instead come to terms with their families, to renegotiate their family relationships, whether they remain in their own families or, for protective reasons, are placed.

A child may represent different meanings for grandparents or other relatives than he does for his parents. And relatives themselves may not relate to him in the same way they do to the child's parents. We know that particular children are selected out for scapegoating in order to maintain family homeostasis. Similarly, in Bowen's theory, the "triangled" child refers to the child who is the main focus of the family projection process [34]. Which child is selected depends on many factors such as personal characteristics, sex, or sibling position. Another issue to consider is that the abusing parent, who may have been the abused, scapegoated, or triangled child in his or her generation of siblings, may be functioning at a lower level of differentiation than either grandparents or other relatives. Negative assumptions about the child-caring potential of relatives must therefore be carefully questioned, and family dynamics assessed on an individual basis, in order to make intelligent decisions about the potential of particular relatives for assuming care of children.

Practitioners are further influenced toward placement outside of the family by a welfare structure which is reluctant to provide relatives with the same financial resources available to strangers. This bias, which in effect results in shifting children from poor to more economically secure environments, reflects the idea that "if they really cared, they would make the necessary sacrifices." The fact is, there are many families who might want to care for a sister's or a nephew's child but cannot absorb the financial burdens presented by the addition of another child [35].

A third reason workers sometimes avoid placement with relatives has to do with their own anxieties about and inadequate preparation for helping families deal with emotionally charged issues of possessiveness, competitiveness, and loyalty which may arise. It is somewhat easier to avoid these particular conflicts if children are placed with strangers. Yet, from the child's point of view, the separation may be far less painful, the physical and emotional cutoffs less severe or psychologically damaging if the child remains with relatives. The child's sense of belonging, of biological identity, is more easily maintained. The following example illustrates one worker's approach:

> Jeffrey Marino, aged 6 months, was soon to be released from the hospital after surviving severe burns from scalding at the age of 4 months. Although Mrs. Marino claimed the baby had accidentally turned hot tap water on himself while left alone in his bath for a moment, the worker, supervisor, and doctor believed

> the mother, under extreme stress as a result of her husband leaving her for another woman the week before Jeffrey's birth, and lacking family or other environmental supports, had displaced her hurt and anger onto the child. Jeffrey would need extensive physical therapy at home and frequent doctor visits. It was felt that Mrs. Marino could not cope with these demands nor was she emotionally ready to resume care of her child without extensive psychological and environmental intervention.

In exploring potential resources for Jeffrey's care, the worker felt that the paternal grandparents were in the best position to meet this child's need for intensive, loving, physical and emotional care. The supervisor recommended against placement with relatives since she feared the worker and the agency would become involved in heated family rivalries and conflicts. Agency concerns and potential sources of conflict and difficulty were discussed with the mother, both sets of in-laws, and with Jeffrey's father, who had returned to the area. Ultimately, Mrs. Marino chose to place Jeffrey with her in-laws.

In assessing the results, the worker and agency believed the decision to keep Jeffrey in the family had been justified. Family rivalries, jealousies, and open conflicts occurred frequently throughout the placement, straining the worker's mediating skills and agency patience. Jeffrey's progress, however, surpassed everyone's expectations. It had originally been feared he might not walk, but by his first birthday he was taking his first steps. The placement had unanticipated consequences for Mrs. Marino's adaptation to the dissolution of the marriage and her own emotional adjustment. Neglected and emotionally deprived in her own disturbed family of origin, her relationship with her in-laws had been extremely important during her marriage, and she saw the elder Mrs. Marino as a positive maternal figure. The abandonment by her husband represented a double loss, as she felt betrayed again by parental figures.

A key element in the placement was the younger Mrs. Marino's right to visit, and the understanding that if possible she would resume care of Jeffrey over a period of time. This process was not without its crises and conflicts, but its positive results were significant. Much of Mrs. Marino's bitterness dissipated as she was able, on somewhat changed terms, to establish a workable relationship with her in-laws, and to take a more adult stance in relation to her own parents, who kept threatening her with isolation if she had any contact with the in-laws. She was gradually able to understand her own role in the marital conflict and family triangles. She could accept Jeffrey's need to have a connection with his father.

It is important to mention that, in addition to and simultaneously with intensive work with the extended family system many other interventions were made in the family life space. They were designed to build an ongoing supportive network for the mother in order to decrease her social isolation.

If placement with relatives is not feasible, the next system closest to the natural family system is that of neighborhood. Often a neglected resource, temporary placement of children with neighborhood families has obvious advantages. Children are not forced to adjust to separation from family *and* social milieu and thus can maintain family, peer, neighborhood, and school relationships more easily. Some agencies are developing group home placements for troubled youths located in their own neighborhoods [36]. The following vignette is more typical of child welfare practice:

> The protective worker received an emergency call at 7 P.M., learning that a Mrs. Ramirez had died in the hospital that day, following complications after surgery, leaving a family of 11 children. The supervisor had already lined up emergency placement homes. The small ghetto house was dirty and chaotic, and the neighbors who had gathered were like the Ramirez family, Puerto Rican and Spanish-speaking. The worker, well-intentioned but overwhelmed by the crisis and the confusion, lacked familiarity with the community. Unable to provide a homemaker she spent the night placing all 11 children in four agency foster homes ranging from five to sixty miles from the community. The following day the worker learned that several neighbors were willing to take in the children at least until permanent plans could be made, there were two aunts living in the neighborhood who might, with financial help, care for the children, and further, Mrs. Ramirez's common-law husband, father to the three youngest children, might have managed to keep the family together.

In the above example, the children need not have been so abruptly severed from family, neighborhood, and culture. Social workers in general are members of urban, individualistic, middle-class nuclear families that are usually small, independent, and "semi-closed." Thus a worker may overlook the possibility that certain client families have the kind of "openness" and deep ties to extended family and neighborhood which are more characteristic of folk societies [37].

The Ramirez vignette exposes another possibility often ignored, the potential of the male single parent for maintaining the family. If he receives adequate services as needed, including financial assistance, homemaker-teacher aid, chore service, day care, counseling and family life education, placement can often be prevented altogether or children in placement returned to their natural environments.

If none of the alternatives is feasible, temporary foster care or small group home placement may become necessary. It still may be possible to place in the same neighborhood, parish, or school district. The tragedy of child welfare, however, is that the intended "revolving door" between foster home care and natural family all too often becomes a door that is closed, locking the child into an uncertain future as a foster child. This unintended consequence is understandable, given the inherent difficulties and financial costs of rehabilitation compared to prevention. Not only must workers possess the knowledge and skills necessary to effect change in a complicated, expanded client system which now includes natural family, foster parents, and foster child, but they must also have available the organizational supports and resources necessary to promote the rehabilitation and reuniting of natural families. The latter is frequently lacking as most child welfare structures support the maintenance of children in foster care.

As mentioned earlier, in those projects where permanent planning for children was stressed and supported with financial and service resources, the numbers of children returned annually to their own families greatly increased. In another approach—court monitoring—Festinger found that periodic court review of all cases of children in voluntary placement served as a catalyst in stimulating agencies to make "permanent" decisions—to return children to their biological families, to continue foster care, or to free them for adoptive placement. When the court slackened its monitoring function, agencies tended to drift again and delayed decision-making [38].

While children are in substitute care, whether temporary or permanent, the issues of biological family identity and maintenance of familiy ties can be crucial to the emotional growth of the child. However, we are usually more protective of foster parents' feelings and privacy than of the natural parents' rights, feelings, and concerns about their children, or of the child's right to family contacts and his need to "belong."

Several factors may support this tendency. Just as the triangle is seen as the basic building block of the family emotional system, so the socio-emotional system of natural family, foster family, and foster child may be viewed as a triangular relationship. As tension mounts between two corners of the triangle, for example, between natural and foster parent, efforts are made by one or both to triangulate the third member, the child, into an emotional alliance. The child and foster family, for example, may achieve some feeling of togetherness and comfort by pushing the natural parent to the "outsider" position. Similarly, the worker may be pulled into interlocking triangular relationships, frequently occupying the same corner as the child, caught in the middle of the tension between the two sets of parents. The worker's increasing discomfort can lead to an attempt to detriangulate by extruding one member, usually the natural parent.

Another reason the natural parents may be shut out arises from an understandable need on the part of the worker to avoid pain, the worker's own and that of the child. Just as parents were sometimes discouraged from visiting their hospitalized children because the children would cry when they left, making it more difficult for staff physically and emotionally, parental visits are said to upset children and to make foster home adjustment more difficult. In this instance the avoidance of emotional pain becomes more important than the opportunity to master the separation and conflict.

Lack of natural parent involvement is also influenced by the workers' anxiety around preserving tenuous foster home placements, particularly in urban areas where foster home resources may be seriously limited. Foster home placements, even if less than desirable, are sometimes maintained at the expense of parent-child contact in order to mollify burdened and critical foster parents.

Foster parents themselves are in a difficult and paradoxical position. They have been asked to love and care for a child as if he were their own, but at the same time they must be ready to relinquish him at short notice for return home or adoption. Additionally they are expected to show tolerance for parents who may seem neglectful, hostile, repulsive, or deviant to them. Insecure, fragile, conditional relationships between foster parent and child are frequently the result of trying to balance these difficult involvements, as foster parents dare not risk the deep emotional hurts which accompany separating from a loved child.

One difficulty in managing productive visiting is related to confusion about and lack of preparation for the foster parent role. The gradual professionalization (in the positive sense) of the foster parent role through foster parent training, more adequate remuneration, and redefinition and clarification of the place of the natural family in the child's life may enable foster parents with worker help to reconceptualize their role as that of serving child *and* family.

There are many ways in which workers with a family orientation and a conviction about biological connectedness not only can help a child integrate his biological and psychological identities, but help insure that the foster home is generally used for temporary substitute care. The most important prerequisite for both connectedness and potential return home is personal contact and sharing of life experiences between biological parents and children. Many parents of children in placement, after early efforts to maintain contact, tend to drift away, to terminate visitation, and are finally accused of lacking interest in their children. The visiting rights of others are reduced or terminated as a result of intense conflict between foster and natural parent or because it is concluded that visiting has deleterious effects on the child.

While some parents will not be able to maintain personal contact, very often the lack of sensitivity to the difficult position of the parent in the life of the child is a crucial element in discouraging visitation. Phyllis McAdams writes of her shattered self-esteem and of feeling excluded from the lives of her children as she painfully tried to maintain a relationship with her children in foster care. She questions the fact that neither workers nor foster parents seem to feel that parents can or should participate in such seemingly minor but emotionally important considerations as whether a child should have a new hair style, whether she should have swimming lessons, needs a winter coat this year, or how she can get along better with a particular teacher [39]. Couldn't children be allowed to telephone their parents or relatives more frequently to share their happy and sad experiences? Must even temporary foster care often result in an almost total termination of parental involvement in the child's life? Unfortunately these emotional cutoffs lead to alienation and loss on the part of both family and child which militate against eventual reuniting.

We need to consider and test new approaches to shared parenting, to support and encourage parental visiting with both emotional and concrete help. The child's extended family can also often serve as a positive resource for nourishment of family identity, in addition to or in place of the parents. Where parents are judged to be too destructive or are deceased, as in the case of David cited earlier, workers should carefully explore the possibility that other relatives might provide a meaningful family connection for a foster child, and sustain his/her sense of belonging.

In addition to or in lieu of visitation, natural family ties can be enriched and connectedness preserved through the use of family history, pictures, mementos, and possessions. The genogram is another tool used by more and more protective, foster care, and adoptive workers. . . . Some child welfare workers who use the genogram report feeling far less critical of abusing and neglecting parents. The genogram helps them develop a dynamic understanding of the parents' family environments and family history. The genogram also helps preserve family environments and biological history for children who are separated from their families. In a sense it is a road map of one's family heritage and biological rootedness. Its usefulness in exposing powerful intergenerational family patterns, strong identifications, losses, and so on may prove valuable not only in helping the placed child understand and differentiate from dysfunctional family patterns but in connecting him with strengths and sources of pride [40].

As workers become more sensitive to the importance of preserving family ties, they themselves develop creative techniques. Some child welfare workers report they are actively engaged in convincing foster parents to allow children to bring in other cherished possessions. One group of workers created an ecological pictorial map of the foster child's life space, including own family, foster family, and other significant systems which the child could color and talk about with the worker. This helps the child master the placement experience [41]. The worker-child-family construction of "life books" or family scrapbooks, which include genealogical information and accounts of significant experiences in the life of child and family are of increasing interest.

These techniques, simple to learn and use, are valuable in helping parents and children master the placement experience, and in helping to alleviate the deep feelings of loss and rootlessness.

The same issues exist and the same techniques can be employed for emotionally disturbed, physically handicapped, delinquent, or other children whose special needs require placement in institutional settings for brief to extended periods of time. Some institutions, primarily custodial and/or disciplinary, offer little or no treatment to either child or family. Those institutions or residential centers which are treatment oriented, focus chiefly on psychological or social-psychological treatment of the child. Often highly identified with the child, practitioners become, if not angry with parents, discouraged by what seems regressions in the child's adjustment after weekend and vacation visits home. Families are sometimes seen for diagnostic purposes and progress-reporting sessions, but relatively few centers involve the family in the total treatment plan.

The lack of family participation can have serious repercussions. First of all, the more the child is emotionally and physically distanced, the more the family system forms a new homeostatic balance without his presence. If and when the child returns, he may find the family has adapted to his absence in a variety of ways which may be experienced as further rejection and isolation. Whittaker assumes that success in treating childhood disorders varies according to the ability of the helping person to involve parents "as full and equal participants in the helping process" [42]. He suggests ways for agencies to help parents maintain contact and meaningful involvement with their institutionalized children.

Before turning to identity issues and family ties in adoption practice, it is important to consider briefly the changing status of the single parent. Harsh attitudes toward illegitimacy are slowly easing and more unmarried parents are opting to raise their children. Agencies must be ready with a variety of supports for single parents who make this decision. One adoptive agency, in shifting its priority from obtaining and placing children to supporting "familiness," established a residence for unmarried mothers and their infants. It provides a supportive environment where young mothers learn parenting skills and are provided with a variety of concrete services and employment and educational opportunities to help parent and child prepare for community living. Putative fathers, whom agencies have traditionally disregarded or avoided except for issues of child support and legitimacy, are encouraged to visit the residence [43]. Such a setting encourages the involvement of both biological parents in the life of the child, laying the groundwork for the preservation of biological family ties in whatever ways may be possible.

Finally, no matter how extended our resource system or how skillful our interventive measures, there are and will continue to be children for whom a permanent family must be found, through adoption.

Adoption practice is currently undergoing reevaluation and change. Two major developments are having a far-reaching impact on the field of adoption and are presenting new challenges and shaping new models of practice. These are open adoption and the changed character of the "adoption market." Growing concern for continuity of identity and family ties has led to a questioning of closed adoption files and secrecy about origins, and has pointed to the consideration of other kinds of adoption models, "open adoption," and a range of forms of shared parenting.

While advocates of these models recognize that sensitive issues need to be confronted which carry the potential for rejection, hurt, and disappointment to all three parties in the adoption triangle, nevertheless conviction is growing that children have the right and should have the opportunity to know who they are, that "it is time to reconsider the strange legal policy of the sealing of records and the equally strange role of adoptive agencies in perpetuating the whole constellation of deception and illusion" [44]. While thinking historically and from a cross-cultural perspective, others maintain we need "a wider range of options for parents who can neither raise their own children nor face the finality of the traditional relinquishment and adoptive placement process" [45].

Early adoption practices in the United States permitted adoptive records to be open to all who wished to examine them and diligent efforts were made to preserve biological and historical information for adoptive parents to impart later to their adoptive children. But in more recent times adoptive practice placed more emphasis on secrecy [46]. Betty Jean Lifton suggests that secrecy has been rationalized as a way of protecting the child from the shame of illegitimacy while, in actuality, secrecy sanctions the adoptive family's "emotional need to live *as if* they had produced offspring of their own" [47]. Agency efforts to "match physical characteristics and religious background perpetuate the delusion" [48]. Lifton sums up the adoption dilemma:

> The adoption experience cannot be free of dislocated human arrangements. For the most part our society handles the dislocation by offering a substitute family, but at a price. That

> price is the suppression of the adoptee's life story—the psychological and practical exclusion of his or her personal history and biological connectedness. What has been excised is replaced by fantasy—the adoptee's, the adoptive parents', and society's. The fantasy . . . begins with the falsification of the birth certificate and extends indefinitely around most of the adoptee's life process. [49]

In other societies and cultures, the importance of one's original family membership and the continuity of the genealogical line is stressed [50]. In our own country, our ambivalence in relation to the preservation of natural family identity or contacts means that adoptive parents have often received little or no help in helping children come to terms with troubling identity issues nor in resolving the disappointment of their own infertility.

New thinking about adoption calls into question old practices which allowed only two acceptable but extreme options for a parent: surrender or keep. For parents who may not have the desire or the psychological resources to raise a child themselves, there is a pressing need for "a new kind of adoptive placement in which they can actively participate" [51]. In this arrangement parents who have previously been reluctant to surrender their children for adoption but may not be in a position to raise them can have the security of knowing they have provided their child with opportunities for a healthy loving environment, without giving up the possibility of knowing their child's fate and without abandoning the hope of maintaining some ties. An "open adoption" is defined as "one in which the birth parents participate in the separation and placement process, relinquish all legal, moral, and nurturing rights to the child, but retain the right to continuing contact and a knowledge of the child's whereabouts and welfare" [52]. Natural parents, as their part of the contract, provide as complete a family history as possible and agree to keep the agency informed of their whereabouts. Before surrendering they are prepared for and agree that the child may someday choose to know about them or may even wish to meet them.

The advantages to the child are obvious, as he or she can have the opportunity to come to terms with fantasies and those uncompleted, unknown parts of identity. Adoptive parents can be educated to understand the child's psychological needs, indeed his right, to know his roots from the beginning of the adoptive relationship.

The "open adoption" contract thus leads to a self-selection process in the sense that those adoptive parents who cannot relinquish the "as if" fantasy and who are unwilling or unable to accept the child's need for knowledge about and perhaps even eventual contact with his biological family will choose not to adopt.

Still, several difficult questions are raised. Most families with adopted children have been assured that birth records will remain sealed and parents who relinquished their children have been assured of anonymity. Is it fair to those adults to change the rules? While this writer believes the evils we know and have opportunity to exorcize are usually less destructive than those which are hidden or repressed, some children enter adoption from extremely troubled situations. Examples include children born of incestuous relationships or children severely and sadistically abused as infants. What if the natural parent is psychotic, a criminal, an addict? Would it not be better for the child to cling to his fantasies, whatever they are, than to know the hurtful reality? What information would be given? What withheld? At what age are children able to assimilate genealogical information? What is the role of the adoptive parent here? Of the agency? What if the natural parent turns away from or rejects the child? Should older adopted children be encouraged to forget and repress earlier experiences which may have been painful and unhappy? Lifton, who searches for, finds, and finally meets her natural mother, and must abandon any hope of nurturing the relationship because of her mother's need for secrecy and inability to acknowledge her existence in her current life, suggests that "just as one must have the courage to find one's natural parents, one must have the courage to say goodbye, if necessary. To let go" [53].

As child welfare administrators and adoption workers reconsider and redefine their practice goals, new roles and new techniques emerge. Some workers and some agencies have already begun to help individual adoptees and self-help organizations such as ALMA in their searches. Others tackle the role of mediator among all three parties to the adoption triangle where one or more seek information or even reunion. Many adoptees have taken matters into their own hands, initiating searches, petitioning courts, cajoling agencies to produce records, and forming self-help organizations to assist other searchers. One agency at least, as part of its research efforts, has held adoptee, adoptive parent, and natural parent forums to air attitudes and feelings [54].

The need for such help emphasizes the importance of developing and helping families make use of postadoption services. The lack of such services again illustrates denial on the part of families and professionals that adoption is different from biological parenting and that parents and children have special tasks to perform and may need some expert help in dealing with these special tasks. Postadoption services should not only be available, they should be offered as developmental and educational rather than remedial services. Adoptive families should be able to find consultation around their special tasks without being defined as problematic.

As we move to more open forms of adoption, adoptive families and their children may well need to use consultation at various crucial points in the child's life. This can help them help the child deal with his or her special status, with identity issues, and with information about or contact with their biological families. These issues emerge differently at different points in the child's development; particularly in latency when the concept of being an adopted child begins to have meaning, in adolescence when issues of identity and differentiation surface with such intensity, and again at marriage as the adopted person moves toward becoming a parent.

A second major factor altering adoptive practice is the rapidly changing nature of the "adoption market." The availability and legality of abortion, widespread knowledge about and use of birth control devices, and the increasing number of single parents who elect to keep their babies have led to a marked decrease in the number of infants available for adoption, especially white infants who once constituted a major portion of those adopted.

An early response to the growing shortage was the move to transracial and international adoption. This practice generated concern and criticism as well as efforts to defend and justify it [55]. American blacks and other racial minority groups and the governments of many poor countries question both the morality and the effects on children of such adoptions. Particular concern is focussed upon just the issue addressed in this discussion, namely the issue of identity formation and consolidation. "In a system of gross economic inequality, they say, is it right that weaker groups should be systematically deprived, first of their ability to make a living and then of the children they are unable to support?" [56]. But are we to abandon children who are victims of war, poverty, and abuse while we wait for society-wide solutions to massive social problems? On the other hand, how much will it postpone needed social and economic changes if we continue to temporize with second best or ad hoc solutions?

A second response to the changing adoption market, reinforced by the child advocacy movement, is a major redefinition of the adoptable child. Gone are the days of the study home where infants and children stayed until the agency was able to assure a potential adoptive couple that a child was healthy and "normal" in every way. Every child is now considered potentially adoptable, including the physically or mentally handicapped, the older child, the child who has suffered emotional damage, and the child of mixed or uncertain heritage, many of whom once grew up in foster care or in institutions. The adoption field has redefined its major task from finding babies for childless couples to finding families for children in need of permanent homes. Many of these children are older and remember biological family members and experiences. Many have been removed from their biological families because of irreversible patterns of abuse and neglect and remember those experiences. There has been a tendency to help such children deal with painful pasts by totally cutting them off from their biological families. Such cutoffs do not really sever the emotional bonds. Recently, one public child-caring agency discovered that many of the older children whose parents' rights had been terminated years earlier had, on their own and unbeknownst to the agency, kept up regular contact with their parents or other members of their biological families.

In the case of older children, the concept of "closed adoption" is a fiction. In fact, concern around potential adoptive families being troubled by members of the old child's biological family has sometimes led to such children being defined as unadoptable. As we move such children into adoptive homes, the need for postadoptive services to help families and children deal with the complexities inherent in the adoption of an older child is once again highlighted.

## SUMMARY

An ecological perspective in child welfare takes as its starting point the importance of the biological family. In considering a range of practice from supportive through substitutive care services, this conviction remains central.

Every effort is thus made to support the family, to enhance its functioning, and to avoid separation and placement. When separation is necessary, the importance of the family continues to be recognized through active efforts to maintain family ties, to support shared parenting by biological and foster parents, and to work, wherever possible, toward reuniting the family. In adoption practice, this perspective suggests a consideration of open adoption and a range of pre- and postadoption services which help all of the parties in this complex human situation accept rather than deny the fact that an adopted person has two families.

## NOTES AND REFERENCES

1. Richard Dawkins, *The Selfish Gene* (New York: Oxford University Press, 1976) and Edward O. Wilson, *Sociobiology* (Cambridge, Mass.: Harvard University Press, 1975), pp 106–29.
2. David Schneider, *American Kinship: A Cultural Account* (Englewood Cliffs, N.J.: Prentice-Hall, 1968), p. 116.

3. Salvador Minuchin, "The Plight of the Poverty-Stricken Family in the United States," *Child Welfare* 49, no. 3 (March 1970), p. 125.
4. Ibid., p. 129.
5. Editorial Notes, "Destruction of American Indian Families." *Social Casework* 58, no. 5 (May 1977) pp. 312–14. Also see Charles E. Farris and Lorene S. Farris, "Indian Children: The Struggle for Survival," *Social Work* 21, no. 5 (September 1976) pp. 386–94.
6. Douglas J. Besharov, "Putting Central Registers to Work," *Children Today* 6, no. 5 (September–October 1977) pp. 9–13.
7. David G. Gil, "Unraveling Child Abuse," *American Journal of Orthopsychiatry* 45, no. 3 (April 1975) pp. 346–56.
8. Karen Schaar, "Corporal Punishment Foes Strike Out," *Children Today* 6, no. 5 (September–October 1977), pp. 16–23.
9. Alfred Kadushin, "Myths and Dilemmas in Child Welfare," *Child Welfare* 56, no. 3 (March 1977), p. 143.
10. Marvin Rosenberg and Ralph Brody, *Systems Serving People: A Breakthrough in Service Delivery* (Cleveland, Ohio: School of Applied Social Sciences, Case Western Reserve University, 1974).
11. Ann W. Shyne, "Evaluation in Child Welfare," *Child Welfare* 55, no. 1 (January 1976), pp. 5–18.
12. Srinika Jayaratne, "Psychological Characteristics of Parents Who Abuse Their Children" (unpublished paper presented at the 1977 Annual Program Meeting, Council on Social Work Education, Phoenix, Ariz., March 2, 1977).
13. For an excellent compilation of the approaches of leading family theorists, see Philip J. Guerin (ed.), *Family Therapy: Theory and Practice* (New York: Gardner Press, 1976).
14. These dilemmas have periodically been explored in the mental health literature, and some of the earlier classics from the child welfare field may still provide us with the most sensitive descriptions available of the meaning of separation and the importance of the natural family to children's sense of identity. See, in particular, Alameda R. Jolowicz, "The Hidden Parent: Some Effects of the Concealment of the Parent's Life Upon the Child's Use of a Foster Home" (unpublished paper presented at the New York State Conference of Social Welfare, New York, November 1946); and Ner Littner, *Some Traumatic Effects of Separation and Placement* (New York: Child Welfare League of America, October 1956).
15. Most child welfare workers are familiar with the work of Erikson on identity and on the interaction of biological, social, and psychological factors in human growth and development. See, for example, Erik H. Erikson, "Identity and the Life Cycle," *Psychological Issues*, Monograph I (New York: International Universities Press, 1959), and *Identity: Youth and Crisis* (New York: W.W.

Norton, 1968). The work of Bowlby and others on attachment, separation, and loss and on the need for continuity of nurturing is also familiar to most child welfare workers. See, for example, John Bowlby, *Attachment and Loss (Vol. 1: Attachment: Vol. II: Separation)* (New York: Basic Books, 1973). R.A. Spitz, "Anaclitic Depression," *Psychoanalytic Study of the Child* 2 (1946) pp. 313–42.

16. Alex Haley, *Roots* (Garden City, N.Y.: Doubleday & Co., 1976).

17. Joseph Goldstein, Anna Freud, and Albert J. Solnit, *Beyond the Best Interests of the Child* (New York: The Free Press, 1973).

18. Ibid., p. 6.

19. Ibid., p. 38.

20. The writer was told this by a 16-year-old young man in residential care whose goal, as soon as he was discharged, was to find the father who had abandoned the family before he was born.

21. Fernando Colon, "In Search of One's Past: An Identity Trip," *Family Process* 12, no. 4 (December 1973), p. 433. Adoptee Florence Fisher describes a similar feeling when she met her natural mother for the first time—a sense of wonderment and joy at discovering one's genetic reality. See Florence Fisher, *The Search for Anna Fisher* (Greenwich, Conn.: Fawcett Publications, 1973).

22. Quoted from a letter from David to his social worker.

23. For a discussion of the Scottish experience, see Rita Dukette, "Perspectives for Agency Response to the Adoption-Record Controversy," *Child Welfare* 54, no. 8 (September–October 1975), pp. 545–54.

24. Florence Fisher, p. 10.

25. Robert Jay Lifton, "Foreword: On the Adoption Experience," in Mary Kathleen Benet, *The Politics of Adoption* (New York: The Free Press, 1976).

26. Ibid., p. 3.

27. Melvin Roman, "The Disposable Parent" (unpublished paper presented at the Association of Family Conciliation Courts, Minneapolis, Minn., May 1977), p. 14.

28. For ecological or systems approaches to social work practice, see Alice H. Collins and Diane L. Pancoast, *Natural Helping Networks: A Strategy for Prevention* (Washington, D.C.: National Association of Social Workers, 1976); Beulah Compton and Burt Galaway, *Social Work Processes* (Homewood, Ill.: The Dorsey Press, 1975); Alex Gitterman and Carel B. Germain, "Social Work Practice: A Life Model," *Social Service Review* 50, no. 4 (December 1976), pp. 601–10; Ann Hartman, "The Generic Stance and the Family Agency," *Social Casework* 56, no. 4 (April 1975), pp. 199–208; and Carol H. Meyer, *Social Work Practice: The Changing Landscape*, 2d ed. (New York: The Free Press, 1976).

29. Mary Ann Jones, Renee Neumann, and Ann W. Shyne, *A Second Chance for Families: Evaluation of a Program to Reduce Foster Care* (New York: Child Welfare League of America, 1976).

30. Gloria Thomas, "Temporary Foster Care Project: The First Year (Michigan State Department of Social Services, November 1977), p. 2. Report of a research project, mimeographed.
31. Ibid., p. 6.
32. Blair and Rita Justice, *The Abusing Family* (New York: Human Sciences Press, 1976), p. 68. Other authorities are quoted by the authors to support the thesis that placing abused children in the homes of grandparents or other relatives is bad practice.
33. For a discussion of the concept of differentiation, see Murray Bowen. "Theory in the Practice of Psychotherapy," in Philip J. Guerin (ed.), *Family Therapy*, pp. 65–70.
34. Ibid., p. 84.
35. For a provocative discussion of the preservation of family ties, see Fernando Colon, "Family Ties and Child Placement" (unpublished paper, May 1976). Dr. Colon mentions he discovered, as an adult, at least six branches of his extended family who, given the opportunity would have taken him in, thus eliminating the need for permanent foster care.
36. Michael Garber, "Neighborhood-Based Child Welfare," *Child Welfare* 54, no. 2 (February 1975), pp. 73–81.
37. David Fanshel, *Foster Parenthood* (Minneapolis: University of Minnesota Press, 1966), p. 15.
38. Trudy Bradley Festinger, "The Impact of the New York Court Review of Children in Foster Care: A Followup Report," *Child Welfare* 55, no. 8 (October 1976), pp. 51–55.
39. Phyllis Johnson McAdams, "The Parent in the Shadows," *Child Welfare* 51, no. 1 (January 1972), pp. 51–55.
40. The genogram is also particularly valuable in guiding foster and adoptive home studies, as the worker is able to quickly gain a sense of family patterns, forces, relationships, losses, and myths.
41. The writer is indebted to Jean Felton, Sherry Miller, and Doris Stagg of the Branch County Department of Social Services, Michigan, for sharing their ideas and experiences.
42. James K. Whittaker, "Causes of Childhood Disorders: New Findings," *Social Work* 21, no. 2 (March 1976), pp. 91–96.
43. Florence Kreech, "A Residence for Mothers and Their Babies," *Child Welfare* 54, no. 8 (September–October 1975), pp. 581–92.
44. Robert Jay Lifton, "Foreword," p. 6.
45. Annette Baran, Reuben Pannor, and Arthur D. Sorosky, "Open Adoption," *Social Work* 21, no. 2, p. 97.
46. Rita Dukette, "Perspectives for Agency Response."

47. Betty Jean Lifton, *Twice Born: Memoirs of an Adopted Daughter* (New York: Penguin Books, 1977), p. 13.
48. Ibid.
49. Robert J. Lifton, "Foreword," p. 1.
50. Baran et al., "Open Adoption," p. 97.
51. Ibid.
52. Ibid.
53. Betty Jean Lifton, *Twice Born*, p. 247.
54. Annette Baran, Reuben Pannor and Arthur D. Sorosky, "Adoptive Parents and the Sealed Record Controversy," *Social Casework* 55, no. 8 (November 1974), pp. 531–36.
55. See, for example, Amuzie Chimezie, "Transracial Adoption of Black Children," *Social Work* 20, no. 4 (July 1975), pp. 296–301; Amuzie Chimezie, "Bold but Irrelevant; Grow and Shapiro on Transracial Adoption," *Child Welfare* 56, no. 2 (February 1977), pp. 75–86; Deborah Shapiro and Lucille J. Grow, "Not So Bold and Not So Irrelevant: A Reply to Chimuzie," ibid., pp. 86–91; Dong Soo Kim, "How They Fared in American Homes: A Follow-up Study of Adopted Korean Children," *Children Today* 6, no. 2 (March–April 1977), pp. 2–6 and 36.
56. Mary Kathleen Benet, *The Politics of Adoption*, p. 20.

# Part IV
# Sociocultural Perspectives

# Part IV

## Sociocultural Perspectives

Examining how different cultural groups deal with common human problems can reduce rigid ethnocentricities and biases and, by providing a fresh perspective, lend creativity to problem solving and interventions. A cross-cultural perspective may increase acceptance of—and sensitivity to—norms and mores different from one's own: in child welfare, sensitivity to different ways of parenting is especially crucial to prevent unnecessary removal of the child.

Within the United States, diverse groups continue to maintain extended families by a kinship system. Children of minorities such as blacks, Puerto Ricans, American Indians, and Chinese are still often cared for by kin. The term "informal adoption" is used to describe the provision of continuity of care within the kinship system for black children whose parents may not be available to them. This wide-ranging kinship system may explain why 15% of all black children are taken in by siblings, aunts, uncles or grandparents.[1]

This section includes three articles examining child welfare practice, particularly with parents, from the black, native American, and cross-cultural perspectives. Although we had hoped to include selections on other minority perspectives, we were not able to locate suitable articles.

In Chapter 9, Walker concentrates on cultural and ethnic issues involved in working with black families in the child welfare system in the United States. She argues that child welfare, by failing to understand black culture, traditionally has brought about estrangement between the agency and the client and unnecessary separation of children from their homes. Pointing to the rich variety of strengths and adaptive patterns developed by black families

[1]Spanier, Graham B., "Outsiders Looking In," *The Wilson Quarterly*, Vol. IV, No. 3 (Summer 1980): 131.

in response to discrimination and poverty, Walker offers guidelines for practice with parents. Above all, she advocates prevention of agency placement by seeking resources within kinship and extended networks, provision of supportive services to parents, and creation of alternative community structures combining informal helping resources with formal systems.

In Chapter 10, Ishisaka reports on a program to prevent placement of American Indian children. Removal of children from their families has often resulted from workers' being ill-equipped to make placement decisions because of their lack of knowledge of the accepted behavior of American Indians, particularly with regard to child rearing. Parents may look deficient in one culture and adequate in another. A specific example is the use of silence; an uninformed worker may evaluate silence as rejection, whereas silence is an appropriate response in certain American Indian groups. As Ishisaka points out, uprooting children on questionable grounds from their cultural and familial underpinnings can have serious implications for their identity. In addition to having serious repercussions for the individual child, the process of uprooting has also been described as cultural genocide.

Baran, Pannor, and Sorosky, in Chapter 11, use cultural comparisons to argue that the time has come for open adoption to be accepted as an alternative. They demonstrate that other societies view parents more comfortably than we do in the United States. Our Puritan heritage has saddled us with a legacy of regarding the poor as "bad" and illegitimacy as "sinful." As an example these authors note that if an Eskimo or Hawaiian child has to leave home for any reason, the tie to the biological parents is kept alive, even if the child is given up for adoption. The child can belong to "two families openly and proudly: the family that gave him his birthright and the family that nurtured and protected him." Baran, Pannor and Sorosky conclude that perhaps other societies are more realistic in their expectations of human behavior and do not expect the family to be what one American scholar calls the "paradox of perfection."[2] As a result, the failed family is not dealt with as punitively.

[2]Skolnick, Arlene, "The Paradox of Perfection," *The Wilson Quarterly*, Vol. IV, No. 3 (Summer 1980): 113–121.

## SUGGESTIONS FOR FURTHER READING

Billingsley, Andrew and Giovannoni, Jeanne M., *Children of the Storm: Black Children and Child Welfare*. New York: Harcourt Brace Jovanovich, 1972.

Chestang, Leon W., "The Delivery of Child Welfare Services to Minority Group Children and Their Families," in *Child Welfare Strategy in the Coming Years*. DHEW Publication No. (OHDS) 78-30158. Washington, D.C.: U.S. Department of Health, Education and Welfare, 1978: 169–194.

Dodge, Mary K., "Swedish Programs for Children: A Comprehensive Approach to Family Needs," *Child Care Quarterly*, 8: 4 (Winter 1979): 254–265.

Ellis, June, "The Fostering of West African Children in England," *Social Work Today*, 2: 5 (June 1971): 21–24.

Madison, Bernice, "Social Services for Families and Children in the Soviet Union Since 1967," *Child Welfare*, 53: 7 (July 1974): 423–434.

Valentin, John M., "Responding to Ethnic Dimensions in Child Care," in D.J. Curren and others, Editors, *Proceedings of Puerto Rican Conferences on Human Services*. Washington, D.C.: National Coalition of Spanish-Speaking Mental Health Organizations, 1975.

Veillard-Cybulska, Henryka, "The Legal Welfare of Children in a Disturbed Family Situation" (Part I), *International Child Welfare Review*, 25 (May 1975): 34–48.

# 9

# Cultural and Ethnic Issues in Working with Black Families in the Child Welfare System

FLORENCE C. WALKER

Growing concern about the number of children in the foster care system, the negative psychological effects of long-term, indefinite care, and the high costs involved have led to a serious reappraisal of the foster care system with particular attention to work with families, since a major goal of foster care is to help families resume responsibility for their children as quickly as possible [9]. This has special relevance for black families whose children: 1) are disproportionately overrepresented in the population of placed children; 2) remain in foster care longer than children from other ethnic groups; and 3) are disproportionately underrepresented in the population of children who achieve permanence through formal adoption.

The purpose of this chapter is to identify some of the cultural and ethnic issues that affect the lives of black families and address the issues raised in practice with black families, particularly in relation to foster care.

## FOSTER CARE SYSTEM AND BLACK FAMILIES

My personal recollection of the caseworker's experience of "working with" biological families toward discharge many years ago is twofold: workers

---

An original article prepared for this volume.

were not trained to work with families nor were they ever trained to take into account the critical significance of the black experience. Regular contacts were seldom sustained because other responsibilities made drastic inroads on the worker's limited time and seeing parents usually meant making special arrangements. Child welfare services were centralized and it was not easy for many parents to come to the office. One had to see them miles away at their place of employment, perhaps trying to synchronize one's schedule with their lunch or coffee break in some crowded public place. Home visits neither guaranteed a semblance of privacy nor the sense of personal comfort and security that encouraged the worker's willingness to work with parents in a consistent, ongoing way. Special efforts to see the parents were usually initiated, however, in relation to visiting the child in care. These discussions often reflected the foster parents' complaints about being inconvenienced by the parents.

At almost every contact, a dutiful inquiry would be made about how the parents were progressing in prerequisites to having their child returned home. Certainly efforts were made to understand the family's problems, to empathize with the parents' own backgrounds of deprivation, pain and disappointment, and to offer suggestions about where to get needed services. Relationships did develop between worker and parents and contact with the children was usually encouraged; at times this even involved visiting arrangements in which the worker transported children at great distances to and from the meeting place. Yet, under the best circumstances of worker-client cooperation and obvious affectional bonds between parents and child, few discharges were made. Invariably, progress in meeting goals or prerequisites was slow; often what was achieved was not stabilized long enough to plan seriously for discharge. The one notable exception to this, of course, occurred when the child in placement was not working out satisfactorily in the foster home and had exhausted the supply of available placements.

This encapsulated version is undoubtedly an oversimplification of the self-maintaining aspects of the foster care system, but it does lend itself to dramatizing how goals based on lack of understanding of black families in particular often brought about estrangement between the agency and the client. Basically, the approach was child-oriented rather than family-oriented, with demands being placed on the family to provide things for the child in placement that most black families could not. This dead-end situation persisted for many families because there was a lack of options available to them.

## Cultural Misperceptions

As for all families, the foster care system has offered alternative living arrangements for black children whose parents' coping abilities have deteriorated under stress, resulting in mental and/or physical illness, imprisonment, abandonment, neglect, or abuse of their children. The foster care system has also subjected children to unnecessary placements because of discrepancies occasioned by a system of myths and misconceptions about black families and their culture, stemming from a failure to understand the social conditions under which black people live and the cultural forms they have developed as a means of coping with these conditions [2:169–194]. This has resulted in viewing the black family as deviant and disorganized and fails to take into account that much of the black family's dysfunction is rooted in poverty.

Requiring parents to find larger quarters or a better neighborhood as a condition for discharge is not a ready option for families of children in placement, just as it is not an option for the great majority of black families in the urban cities. Requiring parents to achieve steady employment is also largely out of the control of black families. The standard of living available to families on public assistance perpetuates the unsatisfactory living conditions that ostensibly foster care "rescued" the child from originally and certainly discourages the child's return to a situation where nothing has changed. Much of the effort then is directed at involving the families in work on problems associated with their "deviant" life style.

Since these parents are often employed in tenuous, marginal jobs, their need to hold the job as long as it lasts is frequently in conflict with agency practices. For example, if visits are scheduled during the five-day work week and within the worker's scheduled hours of work, parents will surely fall into the 45% category of black mothers who do not visit at least once a month, as reported by Fanshel and Shinn [4].

One insidious by-product of viewing the family as disorganized and inferior is reflected in the inequitable treatment of children in the foster care system. More black children are placed in detention facilities, training schools, marginal foster home placements, etc., than in residential treatment centers, boarding schools, group care facilities, and quality foster homes. These are by-products of the same manifestations of racism that are evident in working with the families of these children [2:169–194].

Finally, there have been few consistent efforts on the part of the child welfare system to change the system to meet the needs of black children and families through increased services to families before, during, and after placement that hold promise of real changes in their lives [3].

## UNDERSTANDING BLACK FAMILIES

Although not representative of black families as a whole [1], the children who come to the attention of child welfare agencies are from poverty or near-poverty families living in large cities and who, for the most part, represent the first or second generation of blacks who migrated from the South.

Originally the great majority of blacks made their living off the land; however, between 1910 and 1920 over a million were propelled out of the countryside into urban areas of the North and South. Factors leading to this migration were natural disasters, mechanization of agriculture, and the demands created by World War I for labor and industrial expansion in the North. Between the end of World War II and 1970, over four million blacks moved out of the South and the proportion of black population in cities increased from 44% to 58% [12:2–10]. The waves of migration to the city to find work are in keeping with the strong work orientation of blacks, described by Hill [6].

### Difficulties Facing Black Families

Besides gross economic problems, the urban black family faces many difficulties. Not only is the urban school system openly acknowledged to be of poor quality, but the health, housing and sanitation services are inadequate. Black and other minority males are four times more likely to contract tuberculosis than their white counterparts; black and other minority mothers are three times more likely to die in childbirth than their white counterparts; and black and other minority infants are more likely to die than white babies [2].

Crime is a major problem in urban areas, with many of the perpetrators of violent crime being young blacks in the inner city. In this group the real rate of unemployment is estimated at 75%. Crime has accelerated as unemployment and poorly paid employment have increased. Other than government employment, service jobs are increasingly all that are left for urban blacks. In 1975, the average annual earnings of service industry workers exceeded the federal government's official poverty line by only $850. The correlation between unemployment of blacks and crime may be seen in federal statistics, which indicate that of the 400,000 or more men and women in prison in America, more than 300,000 are black [10:484–487]. Further, studies have made clear that equal protection before the courts depends to a large degree on the financial resources that can be mobilized. The relationship of poverty to jail sentences can be seen readily in the lack of resources rather than in the seriousness of the crime, since comparable crimes do not result in jail sentences for those with greater resources.

The concentration of blacks in the poorest sections of the cities is also maintained through continual discrimination in the sale or rental of housing. Relocation is thereby horizontal—from one poor section to another—with evictions a common practice because of fires, abandonment of buildings by landlords, moves to extend middle-class housing into other areas, and so on. In fact, blacks represented 20% of all movers in 1975, mostly to meet housing needs (U.S. Bureau of Census, Part D, Housing Characteristics of Recent Movers for the U.S. and Regions, 1975. Series H-150 75D, U.S. Government Printing Office, Washington, D.C., 1976).

## The Strengths of Black Families

This grim reality for urban black families has required the development of considerable adaptive and coping mechanisms [6:4]. Hill has identified five characteristics that serve as adaptations necessary for survival and advancement in a hostile environment and labels these traits as key black family strengths: 1) strong kinship bonds; 2) strong work orientation; 3) adaptability of family roles; 4) strong achievement orientation; and 5) strong religious orientation.

**Kinship Bonds.** According to Hill [6:5], black families take relatives into their households more frequently than white families and, in most cases, these additional relatives are likely to be children rather than adults. In husband-wife families, only 3% of white families compared to 13% of black families took in relatives under 18. In 41% of families headed by black women, compared to 7% of similarly situated white women, relatives under 18 were living with them. Families headed by elderly black women took in the highest proportion of children (48%). This explains, in part, a common course of action among mothers who have migrated from the South who are unfamiliar with or averse to placing their children in the child welfare system. They frequently transport their infants or young children "back home" where they will zealously canvass extended kin such as great aunts or second and third elderly cousins to care for their children if their own parents or grandparents are not available. From their earnings, they send money for their children's support and fully anticipate making a home for them at some future time when they have accumulated enough resources.

In some instances, children return to their mother's homes in adolescence or earlier, but a great many children are informally adopted or absorbed permanently into the homes of relatives. In 1969, for example, 160,000 babies were provided such homes in contrast to the 7% who were formally adopted [6:7]. Hill makes the point that this self-help among black families is remarkable when one realizes their precarious economic position; the bonds between relatives in black families must be tight and the value placed upon children very high for such a rate of absorption of additional children to occur so regularly among these families.

In urban areas where the extended family has often eroded, the city-born mother will frequently develop kinship ties among friends who may not be related at all. These are designated as aunts, cousins, or godparents. In contrast to white families where such titles might also indicate affectional attachments, these nonrelated kin frequently informally adopt children by bringing them into their homes and raising them. According to one research study, black nonrelated kin who informally adopted children outranked the legally adopted by a ratio of 10 to 1 by 1972 [5:68].

Inasmuch as both blood and nonblood-related kin provide an important support network for the black family, parents of children in the child welfare system often find it difficult to understand the inferences, attitudes, and behaviors of some child welfare workers. An example is this account of an agency visit told to the child welfare supervisor of a private agency.

> The worker—boy, she seemed mad when she saw me at the agency. My cousin was with me and the baby's godmother. At first she [the worker] didn't say anything. She just looked angry but later she asked me if I was afraid to see the baby alone. I told her "no" but that I wasn't the only one who wanted to see the baby. She asked me who the people were who were with me and I told her. Before we left she told me if I ever brought anyone with me again to make sure they were "real family." Isn't the baby's godmother real family? She is to me.

In another instance a puzzled young mother reported to the assistant director of another private agency:

> Workers sure are funny—no, they're weird! After my last visit, she asked a lot of questions about how I *really* feel about my daughter. I didn't know what she was getting at but I told her I love my daughter. She kept asking questions about my plans and my real feelings. Then she finally told me that it seemed to her

> that I was rejecting Sharma. You know what gave her that idea? My mother was with me and when the worker brought Sharma in, I gave her to my mother. It had almost been a year since my mother had seen her and I knew she wanted to hold her on her lap.

In the first instance, the kinship tie was soon validated, as the godmother's family made room for the young mother and her infant. Even if this had not been possible, the young mother perceived her friend as kin and relied on her for support. The worker's values, interpretation, or need to control caused a dissonance in the relationship that was not forgotten.

In the second instance, the predilection for focusing on pathology in the mother-infant relationship clearly outweighed any consideration of other possible dynamics. It is not uncommon in the literature on the unmarried mother, for example, to link the pregnancy with a wish to get close to the maternal grandmother through the child. In this situation, however, there was nothing to suggest that anything more was operating than a simple act of generosity in giving grandma first chance to enjoy her grandchild.

The importance of the family is not always challenged circuitously or with any semblance of subtlety. In a public agency hearing, a young woman reported that her worker explained the need to re-place her child because of the illness of the foster mother. When she commented in response that her mother (the child's grandmother) had mentioned that her active toddler would benefit from a placement with young foster parents, the worker interrupted angrily and suggested that perhaps the maternal grandmother could pay for boarding care and could then make her own arrangements. This, of course, put the client on the defensive. She later made the observation that "when you are poor, you have no say about your own child . . . in fact, they do everything to make you feel it isn't your child."

Finally, there are times when parents and placed adolescents have reached such an impasse that, in combination with the variety of foster home placements for this age group, the workers begin to think of emancipated minor status. For some adolescents, this is helpful, but it is not always necessary when the family functions within the cultural framework of the extended family. Usually a place can be found where protection and nurturing can be provided on a temporary or even permanent basis. One adolescent selected her own placement resource; the caseworker records this account of the potential foster mother's willingness to keep her, as described in a home visit:

> I knew this child when I lived in the same building she did. I know her mother and I knew her father before he died. I wasn't

> surprised when she told me she and her mother couldn't get along. They haven't been able to since she was 10 or 11. I told her mother that rather than put her away or having her live alone in some rattrap, let her come and stay with me. We get along real fine. She understands my rules and she's no trouble at all. We really look out for each other. Since my kids got grown and moved on their own, I've been here alone.

**Work Orientation.** The strong work orientation and ambition of black families has proved to be another adaptation in the interest of survival. Three-fifths of the black poor work, compared to about half of the white poor, even though the median income of blacks is less than two-thirds than that of whites, and blacks are three times as likely as white to be poor [6:9]. Black employment rates remain at recession levels, even during periods of prosperity.

According to Hill [6:9], three-fifths of women heading black families work (most of them full-time), although over 60% of them are poor. About half of them receive welfare assistance. The majority are therefore not completely dependent on welfare. In husband-wife families, two-thirds of the wives work compared to only half of the wives in white families.

**Adaptability of Family Roles.** A given in the life style of many poor black families, which is often in conflict with workers' views on childhood, is the expectation that all family members work. Children are acculturated to this quite early, with "knee babies" often being dressed and looked after by siblings, who are not much older. Usually this replicates the mother's own life experience. While this appears to the mother, then, to be a reasonable expectation, the worker's observation of this practice sometimes leads to the automatic assumption that the mother is neglectful and rejecting.

Ladner [7] has pointed out that the majority of black children have never been able to have a childhood free from responsibilities. If the majority of black children are raised in poverty or near-poverty, it could hardly be different. To help the family survive, children are expected to care for younger siblings and to perform a substantial amount of the household chores whether they are boys or girls. The children are given to understand that the parents must work (usually on more than one job) to meet the needs of the family and they must help at home. While there are obvious disadvantages in this practice, children are often compensated for carrying out their tasks responsibly. Warm approval is given by family members, the minister, other church members and neighbors—all of whom are part of the family's reference group. The strong religious orientation of many black families makes the approval of the church community much treasured, and it complements the pride of the immediate family.

The term "parental child" usually carries a pejorative connotation in the professional literature, which fails to take into account its adaptive function in the life style of poor black families. It is clearly perceived by blacks as preparation for the real world and, in a sense, is a "rite of passage." One mother reflected on this as she commented to a community poverty agency worker on the adjustment of her children following a period of foster care.

> Things are gradually working out. At first Louise and Johnny didn't do anything but make up their beds and wash dishes. They acted like I hadn't trained them. I was coming home from work, cooking the meals and cleaning the house. Every Saturday I was at the laundromat and then back home to iron. Finally I decided these were my kids in my home. Maybe they played all the time in the foster home but they weren't going to be able to play all of their lives. What if something happens to me? I told them no more babysitters for the younger ones. They had to look out for their brothers and sisters. I gave everybody something to do when they get home from school. I have to work and they have to help. They may not like it now, but they'll be glad later on.

The nondiscrimination of tasks according to sex is also listed as one of the strengths of black families. According to Hill [6:17], "such role flexibility helps to stabilize the family in the event of an unanticipated separation (because of death, divorce, separation or a sustained illness) of the husband, wife, or other key family members, for example. In most black families, there is much sharing of decisions and tasks." Contrary to the belief that black families are matriarchal, most empirical data suggest that "an egalitarian pattern is characteristic of most black families" [6:18].

**Achievement Orientation.** The high achievement orientation of black families can be seen in their aspirations for their children. Like other minority groups, blacks have equated better jobs and a less stressful way of life with education. However, blacks recognize that, unlike most other minorities, there are powerful constraints to their achieving more than relative stability and status because of the deep-seated and long-standing assumption that color is synonymous with inferiority. American blacks suffer the disadvantage of their beginnings in America along with their inability to blend into the larger population because of their high visibility. In spite of this and other deterrents, education has been pursued by black families of all social strata.

According to Hill [6], the overwhelming majority of black college students come from lower and working-class families. He suggests that these students not only internalize the educational aspirations of their families but actively pursue the acquisition of a college degree.

One of the ways in which both black biological families and foster families determine the credibility of the social worker is by the measure of what is perceived as his or her degree of racism. What is perceived as premature closure to higher education for black children in foster care is particularly critical. In a foster parent training course, one foster mother described it this way:

> Sometimes the workers act like those guidance counselors. They [guidance counselors] are always trying to show you that all black kids are too dumb to go to college. They did it with my own kids. They were no help in recommending schools for my children. I had to find them myself and then I had to sit in that high school to make certain they sent the forms out . . . the worker tried to discourage me about Billy's going to college but I know he wants to go and I know when he makes up his mind about something, he does a good job. He brought his grades way up this year. It seems to me if a college is willing to take a chance on Billy, I don't understand why the worker wants to talk him out of it. I told Billy if he wants to go, we'll find a way. Never mind the worker!

This foster mother later described the expressions of gratitude on the part of Billy's mother, who felt less able to express her concern about the worker's attitude.

On the other hand, aspirations should be supported by some evidence that there is realistic potential for achievement of one's goals; without such evidence, the worker's misplaced support for and acceptance of a plan for higher education can only result in a self-fulfilling prophecy of failure—and failure, with knowledge aforethought, makes the worker equally suspect as a racist for permitting it to happen.

Like the foster mother quoted above, many more examples are given by parents of workers' active efforts to foreclose on opportunities for higher education of black youth based on a very narrow assessment of potential. In spite of considerable debate and massive amounts of supporting data that place the validity of I.Q. scores and achievement tests in great question as indicators of intellectual potential among minority groups in particular, the scores often serve as the worker's undisputed source of evidence and justification for discouraging the family and child's aspirations for college education.

It is the literal use of this "objective" evidence by nonblack social workers that many black families perceive as a way to mask racism through professionalism. Such a narrow definition does not take into account the oppression of the black experience, the emotional and attendant intellectual flattening occasioned by familial disruptions, including out-of-home placements, and the strong motivation of the child and his family for achievement. Perhaps the really "gifted" child is the one who is functioning on or close to grade level in the poverty areas and ghettos of our communities and who sustains and/or improves performance in spite of environmental, social and emotional stress.

It is no secret to blacks that many nonblack families of greater affluence bolster their children's academic performance through the use of good public and private schools, individual tutoring, academic camp experiences, and other programs of enrichment. Perhaps less well known is that in similar programs utilized for foster children remarkable elevations in school performance and achievement have been reported, including those children designated as emotionally disturbed and receiving psychiatric treatment.

**Religious Orientation.** The strong religious orientation of black families has been identified as another strength. Blacks have been adept at using religion as a mechanism for survival and advancement throughout their history in America. During slavery, religion served as a stimulus for hundreds of rebellions and was a major source of strength during the civil rights movement of the 50s and 60s. It was through the church, one of the most independent institutions in the black community, that blacks learned to use religion as a survival mechanism. Black ministers frequently used their sermons to transmit coded messages to the congregation. Negro spirituals were often used for similar purposes, particularly in assisting runaway slaves [6].

The black church continues to give meaningful institutional support to many poor and working class families, and represents stability and constancy. To families whose lives are characterized by instability and uncertainty, the church often represents the most organized part of their lives. Children and youth are particularly valued. In addition to being provided moral training, they are encouraged in their aspirations and accomplishments and are helped to develop pride and self-esteem. Baptism and other religious practices promote the idea of family bonds and church fellowship.

The minister of the black church is sometimes a religious evangelist whose major interest and emphasis are the spiritual awakening of the members of the congregation. Some ministers are both religious and social leaders who address political and social concerns of the members. Speaking of the strengths and stresses of the black experience, their focus is on what Hill terms the social gospel [6]. Whatever kind of approach the religious leader takes, the members of the congregation also look to him for advice and counsel for a variety of family problems and as their spokesman when difficulties arise with other systems such as courts and school.

Church services often act as a catharsis for the release of many pent-up and repressed feelings of the congregation. Participation is evident in verbalized responses to the minister's sermon, clapping and moving to the spirit of the music in joyous fashion.

Although it is expected that foster parents have some religious affiliation which is documented in the homefinding process, social workers have not been trained to recognize the value of the foster parents' participation in the black church or the foster child's participation. Since the church is open to all, foster children are warmly accepted by the congregation and do not suffer the discrimination and differentiation they do in other settings. It is sometimes the only place where the child can freely demonstrate his or her emerging talents, secure support and recognition from peers and adults, and receive stimulation, acceptance, and support from others outside the foster family.

The way in which social workers transmit their lack of understanding of the significance of this experience is demonstrated by the following excerpt from a public child welfare worker's recording.

> Mrs. Jones was beaming today and told me with some excitement about a youth program of some kind at the church the previous day. All three foster children participated. Velma read the scripture lesson, Virgil sang a solo, and Dwayne ushered people to their seats. Mrs. Jones received many compliments on the children's performance. I asked her if Virgil was in the school chorus and she said he wasn't. I also asked if Velma's reading scores had improved. We then focused on their school performance and Mrs. Jones was able to give me information about their current functioning.

In this instance the foster mother quickly responded to the worker's cue, that value was afforded to school, not church, performance.

It would seem appropriate for workers to recognize the values that foster parents share and the benefits which the child may receive from participation in the black church. Sharing the foster child's church activities with his or her birth parents may function as a possible social support when the child returns home.

## WORKING WITH BLACK FAMILIES

The practice implications for child welfare workers who view working with black families as a major priority in the interest of permanence emphasize above all the maintenance of black children in their own homes through efforts to eliminate or reduce the crippling effects of poverty. The cost effectiveness of providing each family with $4,000 to $5,000 a year more would surely be borne out in view of present-day costs for substitute care. Elimination of the effects of poverty may be made possible through increases in income maintenance allowances to meet full financial needs, greater employment opportunities, and assisting families to realize all the help that can be made available by present service providers.

### Adapting Services for Black Families

Recognizing that black parents are not and do not feel an equal part of the larger community and therefore often do not know of or venture to seek help from a community system from which they feel excluded, workers will be participants in helping the clients receive services. Accompanying them when necessary, they will broker for medical services, housing, legal services, education, day care, and employment. Not only can such activities result in tangible evidences of help, but a worker's willingness to be a part of the frustration and endless red tape that bureaucratic structures invariably engender speaks in a powerful way to the respect one feels for the client and his or her right to service. The presence of the worker often helps also to dilute the unresponsiveness or seeming hostility that parents experience from overburdened or indifferent workers in large bureaucracies.

Priority should be given to seeking resources within kinship and extended networks to get children out of agency placement or to prevent placement. Hill [6:8] has documented that extended families have demonstrated a capacity to absorb placed children and that innovative placement procedures, such as income subsidies to poor families and families headed by women, should be greatly expanded. Case reviews should document fully that agency placements are absolutely necessary in view of objective evidence that neither the family nor extended networks can provide the child a home.

Advocacy can be extended to many other components of programs as well, particularly as we emphasize preventive services to families and children. Homemaker service, for example, has not been used extensively to assist overburdened black mothers. Used imaginatively and flexibly, it can provide educational as well as supportive help. Young mothers, in particular, can benefit from the role models and skills of the homemakers in parenting, shopping, and household care. The criteria for the use of homemakers are often so constricted that they fail to take into account the needs and deficits in resources of many black mothers and the genuine benefits that can be realized in a fairly short period of time.

The increasing use of home aides or home management specialists is a promising new resource for families, since concrete benefits result for both parents and children [11:43–51]. Parents have shown that marked increases in self-esteem have led to their assuming more competent authority roles with their children, higher educational achievement for themselves, and better living conditions for their families. These home aides have also been able to overcome many of the barriers of mistrust that black families have for some white agency caseworkers, which suggests that home aides serving blacks should be black.

Flexible office hours and offices nearer to families are essential for black families if they are to participate in visits with their children and with the worker in the interest of discharge.

Black professional staff needs to be increased in child welfare agencies, to serve black families and to train other workers to become sensitive to ethnic and cultural patterns, nuances of behavior and attitudes, and to support the identified strengths of black families.

## Use of Alternative Service Structures

All of the foregoing presumes that child welfare services will continue to be provided under the auspices of the present network of child-caring agencies. It may be that this is an excellent time to consider alternative structures to meet the needs of black families.

An impressive range of preventive and rehabilitative services to black families are already being provided by the "nonprofessional" agencies best known under the rubric of community poverty agencies. They not only supplement the services of the longstanding, traditional agencies but serve as the primary resource to families in the community. An outstanding example is Harlem Teams for Self-Help, Inc., located in central Harlem. Community residents use this agency for basic, concrete services, for example, housing; employment; legal services; remedial workshops for children in mathematics, English, and other academic areas; education for high school dropouts; consumer information; and education regarding substance abuse. Families are provided with the concrete services they seek and then are encouraged to make use of a variety of other services, including family counseling. A prevention focus is evident in approaches such as requiring counselors to see that every child (about 300) receives an annual physical examination and followup of recommended health measures; quarterly school visits are also made in behalf of each child. A small staff of professional and paraprofessional social workers provide intensive family counseling in two to three home and office visits per week to a caseload of about 30 to 40 children and their parents. Although referrals are occasionally made to specialized agencies, community-based personnel are able to meet most, if not all, of the needs of its residents. Expanded counseling services could be made available to many more families if staff could be increased.

## CONCLUSION

The majority of black children in foster care are from families in which poverty and racism are most deeply experienced. The child welfare system with its current focus on working with families toward permanence for children [8:515–530] must make concerted efforts to understand cultural and ethnic issues that affect the lives of black families, seek to bring about changes in society and the agency that adversely affect black families, and narrow the gap between the promise of foster care and its fulfillment. Toward this goal, it is especially crucial to use informal helping systems within the community as well as promote alternative community structures that provide intensive services to families.

## REFERENCES

1. Billingsley, Andrew. *Black Families in White America.* Englewood Cliffs, N.J.: Prentice-Hall, 1968.
2. Chestang, Leon W. "The Delivery of Child Welfare Services to Minority Group Children and Their Families," in *Child Welfare Strategy in the Coming Years*, by Alfred Kadushin et al. Washington, D.C.: U.S. Department of Health, Education and Welfare, Children's Bureau, 1978 Publication No. (OHDS) 78-30158.
3. Children's Defense Fund. *Children Without Homes: An Examination of Public Responsibility*. Washington, D.C.: Children's Defense Fund, 1978.
4. Fanshel, David and Shinn, Eugene. *Children in Foster Care: A Longitudinal Investigation*. New York: Columbia University Press, 1978.
5. Grant, Maye H. "Perspective on Adoption: Black into White," *Black World* 22 (November 1972).

6. Hill, Robert B. *The Strengths of Black Families.* New York: Emerson Hall Publishers, 1971.

7. Ladner, Joyce. *Tomorrow's Tomorrow: The Black Woman*. Garden City, N.Y.: Doubleday, 1971.

8. Maluccio, Anthony N. et al. "Beyond Permanency Planning," *Child Welfare* LIX (November 1980).

9. Maluccio, Anthony N. and Sinanoglu, Paula A. *The Challenge of Partnership: Working with Parents of Children in Foster Care*. New York: Child Welfare League of America, 1981.

10. Savitz, Leonard, "Black Crime," in *Comparative Studies of Blacks and Whites in the United States*, edited by K. Miller and R. Drager. New York: Seminar Press, 1973.

11. Spinelli, Lauren A., and Barton, Karen S. "Home Management Services for Families with Emotionally Disturbed Children," *Child Welfare* LIX (January 1980).

12. Staples, Robert. "Land of Promise, Cities of Despair: Blacks in Urban America," *The Black Scholar* 10 (October 1978).

# 10

# American Indians and Foster Care: Cultural Factors and Separation

HIDEKI ISHISAKA

Concern regarding the child welfare system in the U.S., specifically in the area of foster care, has been growing [7:340–341; 18:321–333; 19:132–142]. It has been estimated that there are 220,000 children living in foster care homes that receive state funds [6:219–223]. Although this is a national problem involving children and families from all sectors of the population, the threat of child separation may be disproportionately greater for families of underprivileged ethnic-minority groups [24;23:15–17, 22].

Neave and Matheson surveyed families involved in child separation in British Columbia, Canada, to ascertain patterns of child separation and factors associated with those patterns [23]. The authors used a two-part typology to analyze causes; norm-violative separations were due to physical abuse, neglect, desertion/abandonment of children and sexual deviation or imprisonment of parents; non-norm-violative separations were due to family problems or needs that could be helped or met by placement of the child outside of the home.

Neave and Matheson suggest that for families involved in non-norm-violative separations, existing services may be adequate, but for families

---

Reprinted from *Child Welfare*, Vol. LVII, No. 5 (May 1978): 299–308.

involved in norm-violative separations, additional services may be necessary. Families involved in norm-violative separations tended to evidence characteristics that resulted in social marginality.

The information regarding American Indian families involved with foster care presented in this paper supports Neave and Matheson's general finding. Additional information from this study suggests that life-style patterns and/or cultural differences in behavior play a critical role in the separation of Indian children from their parents. The data are derived from a 2½-year research and demonstration project funded by the Office of Child Development, Department of Health, Education and Welfare. The project had as its major goal the development of procedures by which American Indian families could be assisted to avert child separation. A residential facility was located. American Indian program staff were hired and trained, and families were admitted into the project. The project, called the Alternative to Foster Care Program (ATFCP), was the first program of its kind in the United States. The ATFCP provided families with apartment units in its residential facility. Services available through project staff included child care, child management counseling, dietary counseling, employment and social service advocacy and other case management services. When indicated, referrals were made to treatment services available in the locale for difficulties with alcohol and other problems in personal functioning.

Data contained in this study represent a majority of the 26 families who have been in residence. The families were admitted to the ATFCP program on the basis of need for service, with no attempt to select a representative sample. Following the typology developed by Neave and Matheson, the families were sorted according to the reason for separation or the threat of separation. The results are shown in Table 1.

**TABLE 1**
**Reason for Referral**

| **Norm-Violative** | | **Non-Norm-Violative** | |
|---|---|---|---|
| Abandonment | 11 cases | Escape from abusive partner | 4 |
| Abandonment and physical abuse | 1 | Illness of parent | 1 |
| Abandonment/neglect | 1 | Psychiatric problem of parent | 1 |
| Physical abuse | 2 | Extreme youth and indigent status of mother | 2 |
| Neglect | 2 | | |
| Parent sexual deviation | 1 | | |
| | 18 (69%) | | 8 (31%) |

## SUMMARY OF DESCRIPTIVE DATA

The families had varied child placement histories, ranging from no previous child separations to 16 individual child separations for one family. Nineteen families (73%) had had prior separations. The majority of the families were headed by women (85%), with only four couples intact. Family heads were economically marginal (92%) and were largely dependent on public welfare. Family heads' formal education ranged from 3 to 13 years, with 10 years as both a mean and median. In only five families was the head of the household a skilled worker. The rest reported little, if any, employment history. The majority were making the rural-urban move. Seventeen defined themselves as reservation families. Yet even among those heads of household who identified their families as urban, ignorance of available social programs, transportation systems and medical services, to name but a few examples, indicated that there was an urban adjustment problem for all the families. This problem may be related to the large number of family heads (N =23) who requested assistance with alcohol management. The most common alcohol use pattern among the family heads was so-called "binge" drinking. In only one instance was there evidence of chronic alcohol abuse. In the majority of cases of alcohol use, it was part of the rationale for child separation provided by referring caseworkers or other agency personnel. The most frequent complaint about the families was abandonment associated with alcohol abuse by the parent(s). Abuse-neglect as separate categories were sometimes confounded, due to problems of definition. Neglect resulting from abandonment is an example of the overlapping of norm-violative categories used by referring personnel. Because of the large number of recidivist families, including many who had children separated at the time of admission to the ATFCP, reconstitution of the family unit was a goal for 65% of all families in residence. In most cases the ATFCP staff were able to help family heads regain custody of their children.

## CRITICISM OF PRACTICES

Reexamination of child welfare policies and agency procedures in regard to Indians may be necessary. Criticism of existing foster care practices is made on two levels, one general, the other specific to cultural minorities.

First, the foster care system fails to make adequate efforts to avoid initial placement [25:3–9; 3:499–503]. In the absence of established and standardized definitions that inform caseworkers as to when children should be removed or returned to their parents, decision making tends to be highly subjective [21:13–17].

Another problem is the use of the family pathology model for decision making in regard to separation. Maas has suggested that the use of questionable indicators of family pathology be deemphasized, in the absence of validated associations between family pathology and subsequent childhood disorders [19:132–142]. Mech has pointed to the problem of decision making in foster care placement [20:26–51]. Procedures for making decisions do not always include all available options, nor is there adequate documentation after separation that placement was the best choice. A final general problem is the ubiquitous use of the terms abandonment, neglect and abuse as proffered reasons for the separation of children from their parents. There is a great need for more precise definitions of such widely used terms [21:13–17; 5:432–443]. Distinctions must be made between cases in which documented parental behaviors can be related to harm or potential harm to children and cases in which the decision to separate is based on inferred potential threat, given subjective indicators.

These issues are relevant to all groups in the child care system; for ethnic minority groups, other considerations play a role in the placement decision. The characteristics of families involved in the ATFCP were consistent with the concept of a multiproblem family. The ATFCP families were highly vulnerable to child separations involving alleged norm-violative conduct by the parents. As mentioned, abandonment accounted for a majority of the separations, and in many cases assumed norm-violative conduct was associated with alcohol problems. But over the course of the ATFCP operation, staff noted few instances of neglectful or abusive behavior on the part of parents toward their children. The most frequent pattern among the family heads who did drink and for whom drinking was a self-defined problem was the tendency to leave children in the care of older siblings or on their own when parents were drinking. Through interviews with the parents, it became clear that for the majority, such behavior was not seen as faulty parenting or as grounds for child separation.

Among Indian cultures, different conceptions of childhood competence may be related to presumed norm-violative conduct by parents [22:165]. Cultures vary in regard to the responsibilities deemed appropriate to children of different ages. That younger children are sometimes left under the care of older children does not necessarily constitute grounds for child separation. Adequate care is an empirical issue that must be addressed case by case. In several instances over the course of the ATFCP operation, young children were left under the care of older brothers and sisters who were also young (for example, 8 years old). Yet, the younger children appeared to be well cared for, and there were other adults in the vicinity in case of emergencies. A source of misunderstanding may be related to differences in norms of parental conduct. Parenting customs may be brought to the urban environment from cultural settings in which they are common practice, but in the city such practices are viewed by social agents as deviant and evidence of faulty parenting. Jayaratne has raised serious issues relevant to sociocultural differences and their potential role in the misperception of parenting behaviors on the part of social agents [15:5–9].

## SILENCE AS A RESPONSE

An example of a cultural difference reported in the literature on American Indians is a case in point. Among the Western Apache, silence plays an important role in cultural functioning [2:213 ff.]. Silence is considered an appropriate response at times of role ambiguity. A child returning from a boarding school may be greeted with silence on the part of the parents because it is unknown what changes in the child may have occurred in the child's absence from home. With time, silence is broken as parents and child become reacquainted through nonverbal signs. Such a cultural pattern invites cultural misunderstanding. An outsider witnessing what would be an occasion for embraces and verbal intimacy among Anglo people might misperceive the Western Apache cultural pattern as an indication of coldness of parents toward their child, or make other culturally biased inferences.

Another example has been described by Good Tracks—a pattern of noninterference among certain Indian groups [11:30–34]. Noninterference is a standard of conduct derived from the traditional value placed on individual rights and prerogatives that extend to children as well as adults. The rights of a child include the expectation that his or her autonomy will be respected by others. The child learns early not to interfere with others. The parents may ignore intrusive or interfering youngsters, and may be seen as uncaring or uninvolved, rather than evidencing a pattern of parenting different from that of the majority society.

Among the families at the ATFCP there were few examples of inadequate parenting judged by their own cultural standards. The common perception of family functioning by staff members was of harmonious and warm relationships between parents and children. Parents tended to be permissive, seldom insisting that the children comply with parental wishes. But where children violated standards of behavior consistent with their Indian cultural backgrounds, the parents assumed a direct and forceful role in guidance. As Locklear contends, the role of the parent in traditional Indian cultures as an authority figure must be understood [17:202–207]. The role can include corporal punishment when deemed necessary. In a time of increasing disapproval of corporal punishment, such punishment can be misinterpreted as abuse or evidence of potential abuse.

Misperceptions of behavior and unfounded inferences regarding motives can play a significant role in the decision to separate Indian children from their parents. The experiences of the ATFCP staff indicate either an unwillingness or an inability of some caseworkers and other agency personnel involved with Indian families to consider cultural factors in regard to problem identification and in service provision.

## CULTURAL GENOCIDE?

Yet, problems associated with the placement decision are only a small part of the general dilemma of Indians in the foster care system. Incalculable damage to many Indian children may be the result of repeated or permanent separation from parents. The potential deculturative effect of such dispositions lends support to Farris and Farris' accusation that such policies amount to cultural genocide [9:386–389]. Some data suggest that removal of Indian children from their homes with relocation to culturally alien environments has serious implications for identity development. Identity confusion has been demonstrated to be a result of the removal of children from their natural parents and cultural contexts for educational purposes [14:7–17; 16:94–103; 10:85–92].

For the ATFCP families, use of alcohol was not necessarily seen as the cause of parenting deficiencies. The high rate of alcohol use may be associated with the pressures of urban adjustment. In addition to the stress engendered by leaving family and other social supports, adults had to deal with unemployment, social marginality, discrimination and prejudice [4:359–369]. Value conflicts, loneliness and unfamiliarity with aspects of life in a heavily populated area may all increase stress and the likelihood of use of alcohol [26:398–403; 13:35–38; 1:199–205].

As mentioned, the pattern most evident in the ATFCP group was "binge drinking." There was only one case of chronic alcohol use. In that sense the ATFCP sample's use of alcohol supports Price's observation that physical addiction to alcohol may be low among Indians and alcohol use could be lessened if the predisposing conditions for binge drinking were remediated [24:17–26]. Among the ATFCP clients, drinking patterns suggested that for some, drinking was a means of escape from a punishing day-to-day life, and to relieve a sense of personal failure and inadequacy [12:306–321; 8:72–87]. But drinking also appeared to serve a social purpose. Deprived of close friends and relatives by the relocation to the urban environment, many of the clients seemed to use drinking as a means of socializing with other Indians. It is unlikely that any one explanation covers the variety of drinking patterns in this heterogeneous population [24:17–26].

In view of the possible cultural biases influencing the decision to separate, every attempt should be made to keep Indian children in their homes. Neave and Matheson suggest that new types of service delivery be made available to the societally marginal families frequently associated with norm-violative child separations [23]. Alcohol use should be treated when parents request treatment, but assumed alcohol abuse should not be construed as grounds for child separation unless there is clear evidence that alcohol use creates a situation dangerous to the child.

Day care centers would permit parents time out from parenting. An opportunity to engage in other activities would benefit many, especially single-parent families lacking resources for child care. Classes to familiarize new arrivals from reservation areas with urban resources and services would help them to cope in an alien environment.

Finally, in those cases in which separation is unavoidable, work with parents toward early return of children to their homes should be an integral part of the initial treatment plan. Every attempt should be made to strengthen the Indian family through resources and supports. Only in this way can progress be made toward preventing many Indian children from becoming drifters in the child welfare system.

In the long run, the focus on individual difficulties, e.g., alcohol, may be dysfunctional. For the majority of the ATFCP clients, the obstacles to personal achievement and adjustment were external. There is a great need to make new opportunities available to Indians. The removal of children from their parents due to family poverty or misperceptions of parenting behavior because of differing cultural standards is not an adequate response. Chronic unemployment, educational underachievement and residence in substandard housing all constitute social problems of enormous consequence to American Indians. Educational programs agreeable to Indians, job training and increased availability of adequate housing are basic changes that must occur if Indian families in both rural and urban areas are to be freed from problems arising from poverty. These problems are all too often seen as originating from within the Indian community itself, and not as the legacy of centuries of restricted opportunities, genocide and forced assimilation.

## REFERENCES

1. Ablon, J. "Cultural Conflict in Urban Indians," Mental Hygiene, LV (1971).
2. Basso, K.H. "To Give Up on Words: Silence in Western Apache Culture," Southwestern Journal of Anthropology, XXVI, 3 (Autumn 1970).

3. Bryce, M.E., and Ehlert, R.C. "144 Foster Children," Child Welfare, L, 9 (November 1971).
4. Chadwick, B.A., and Stauss, J.H. "The Assimilation of American Indians into Urban Society: The Seattle Case." Human Organization, XXXIV, 4 (Winter 1975).
5. Cohen, S.J., and Sussman, A. "The Incidence of Child Abuse in the U.S.," Child Welfare, LIV, 6 (June 1975).
6. Culley, J.E., et al. "Public Payments for Foster Care," Social Work, XXII, 3 (May 1977).
7. Donadello, G. "Commentary," Child Welfare, XLVIII, 6 (June 1969).
8. Dozier, E.O. "Problem Drinking Among American Indians," Quarterly Journal of Studies on Alcohol, XXVII (March 1966).
9. Farris, C.E., and Farris, L.S. "Indian Children: The Struggle for Survival," Social Work, XXI, 5 (September 1976).
10. Goldstein, G.S. "The Model Dormitory," Psychiatric Annals, IV, 9 (November 1974).
11. Good Tracks, J.G. "Native American Non-Interference," Social Work, XVIII, 6 (November 1973).
12. Graves, T.D. "Acculturation, Access and Alcohol in a Tri-Ethnic Community," American Anthropology, LXIX (April 1967).
13. Hamer, J. "Acculturation Stress and the Function of Alcohol Among the Forest Potawatomi," Quarterly Journal of Studies on Alcohol, XXX (1969).
14. Hobart, C.W. "Some Consequences of Residential Schooling," Journal of American Indian Education, VII, 2 (January 1968).
15. Jayaratne, S. "Child Abusers as Parents and Children: A Review," Social Work, XXII, 1 (January 1977).
16. Krush, T. and Bjork, J. "Mental Health Factors in an Indian Boarding School," Mental Hygiene, XL (1963).
17. Locklear, H.H. "American Indian Alcoholism: Program for Treatment," Social Work, XXII, 3 (May 1977).
18. Maas, H.S. "Children in Long-Term Foster Care," Child Welfare, XLVIII, 6 (June 1969).
19. ———. "Children's Environments and Child Welfare," Child Welfare, L, 3 (March 1971).
20. Mech, E.V. "Decision Analysis in Foster Care Practice," in H.D. Stone, ed., Foster Care in Question. New York: Child Welfare League of America, 1970.
21. Nagi, S.Z. "Child Abuse and Neglect Programs: A National Overview," Children Today, IV 3 (May–June 1975).

22. National Action for Foster Children: A Survey of Activities Based on Reports Submitted by States and Communities, October 1973–October 1974, U.S. Department of Health, Education and Welfare, Office of Human Development, Office of Child Development, Washington, D.C.

23. Neave, D.C., and Matheson, D.K. "Directions in Research Questions About Policies and Practice in Parent–Child Separation," Canadian Welfare, XLVI, 6 (November–December 1970).

24. Price, J.A. "An Applied Analysis of North American Indian Drinking Patterns," Human Organization, XXXIV, 1 (Spring 1975).

25. Shapiro, D. "Agency Investment in Foster Care: A Followup," Social Work, XVII, 6 (November 1973).

26. Westermeyer, J. "Opinions Regarding Alcohol Use Among the Chippewa," American Journal of Orthopsychiatry, XLII (1972).

EDITOR'S NOTE: *In this addendum to his paper, the author comments on the relationship between the problems he has described and the Indian Child Welfare Act.*

The Indian Child Welfare Act has passed the Senate and is likely to undergo further changes. The act, important as it is, would be in its present form only a beginning toward improving the dilemma of American Indian families caught in the foster care bind. The legislation—S.1214—has some perhaps unavoidable limitations. It is understandably biased in favor of existing American Indian groups that maintain federally recognized tribal status, and that remain on the land. The law's language is quite clear concerning the mechanisms whereby American Indian children in reservation settings, or those closely affiliated with reservation-based groups, are to be handled in regard to separation from their parents or guardians. The basic problem remains, since a large number of American Indians are no longer on the land. The number of urban Indians recently passed the number remaining on or near reservations. Children of families who are from tribes that have been dispersed, or who have lost meaningful contact with the tribe of origin, or children of parents of different tribal origins whose registration may be problematic, do not seem to be covered by the act. The language dealing with Indian families off the reservations raises difficulties. Protection of Indian children from prejudicial action in separation cases is transferred to Indian organizations existing in the urban area. Such jurisdictional transfer presupposes that any such organizations have the personnel and skill resources to act as alternative service providers.

S.1214, like the Title IV regulations regarding Indian education, is a great step forward, but no panacea. As with Title IV regulation, large numbers of Indian children are not covered by the act. Many Indian children will slip through the cracks in the legislation, and for them the issues raised in the foregoing article remain valid. Many instances of child separation will continue to occur among Indian communities, especially in urban areas, that will be based on the judgments of caseworkers unfamiliar with the issues involved. Finally, the shift of jurisdiction, even in those cases clearly covered by the articles in S.1214, presents many problems for landed tribes. Many tribes do not maintain tribal courts and will have to develop such institutions before the act will be meaningful for them. For urban Indian communities the problem is even greater. The skills necessary to provide culturally sensitive alternative services for Indians in urban areas cannot be assumed to be available. It will take many years before the problems inherent in the implementation of the law can be worked out in a fashion that will help prevent the breakup of Indian families.

# 11

# Open Adoption

ANNETTE BARAN,
REUBEN PANNOR,
AND ARTHUR D. SOROSKY

When the adoption of a child is legally consummated, the original birth record is sealed and replaced with an amended birth certificate. Access to the original record is subsequently denied except through a court order issued for good cause. An increasing number of adult adoptees have begun to challenge this procedure, feeling they have a right to such information. Because of this situation the authors have been studying the problems associated with sealed records in adoptions for the past two years. This inquiry has led into many areas, including the reevaluation of past practices and the consideration of new approaches for the present and future [1].

In addition to a new appraisal of the concepts of anonymity and confidentiality as epitomized by the sealed record, there is also a need to develop a wider range of options for parents who can neither raise their own children nor face the finality of the traditional relinquishment and adoptive placement process. The concept of open adoption should be considered as an alternative that can meet the needs of some children. An open adoption is one in which the birth parents meet the adoptive parents, participate in the separation and placement process, relinquish all legal, moral, and nurturing rights to the child, but retain the right to continuing contact and to knowledge of the child's whereabouts and welfare.

---

There is nothing new about the institution of adoption. It has been practiced since people grouped together and formed the most primitive societies. Bronowski maintains that the first socialization step taken within groups, tribes, or bands was the acceptance of collective responsibility for orphaned children [2]. Adoption, then, began as a means of protecting young children who lacked parents to nurture them. However, adoption has also come to perform another important function. It fulfills childless couples' lives and gives them a tight family unit that conceals their infertility and denies the existence of another set of parents. What was originally seen as a great need for the child is now viewed, perhaps, as a greater need for the parents.

As the competition for perfect babies grew among childless couples, the rewards for being perfect adoptive parents increased. These rewards took the form of increased guarantees of anonymity and confidentiality. The shift toward closed adoptions occurred in a gradual, continuing pattern without critical evaluation of the changes. There was no attempt to assess the psychological burden of secrecy imposed upon adoptive parents and adoptees, nor were the feelings of loss and mourning by the birth parents carefully considered. It is difficult to know why a process as final and irreversible as the traditional relinquishment and adoption was so little questioned by professionals in the field.

## CULTURAL COMPARISON

Other societies do not seek to give adults artificial parenthood by denying a child his birthright. This is perhaps because they place greater emphasis on the meaning of one's original family membership and on the continuity of the genealogical line.

An excellent example of this, because it has been studied and documented, is the method of adoption practiced in the Hawaiian culture for centuries. *Ohana*, or family clan, is a most important concept to Hawaiians. It is certainly more important than the question of legitimacy. To lack original family membership or to lose it is more shameful than to be born out of wedlock. In the old Hawaiian culture adoption, or *hanai*, was neither uncommon nor secret. If a child could not be reared by his own parents or grandparents, another family would *hanai* the child. As Handy and Pukui point out:

> Children could not be adopted without the full consent of both true parents, lest some misfortune befall the child, and when consent had been given the child was handed to the adopting parents by the true parents with the saying, *Ke haawi aku nei maua i ke keiki ia olua, kukae a na'au* ("We give the child to you,

> excrement, intestines and all"). This was as binding as any law made in our modern courts. The child became the child of the adopting or "feeding parents," and only under rare circumstance did the biological parents attempt to take the child back unless the adoptive parents died.
>
> If a disagreement did arise between the adopting and biological parents, so that the biological parents tried to recover their child, it was believed that the child would fall prey to a sickness that might result in death. Such a disagreement between the two sets of parents was called *hukihuki* ("pulling back and forth"). So it was well for adopting parents and biological parents to keep on good terms with each other for the sake of the child.
>
> Unlike the modern way of concealing the true parentage of an adopted child, he was told who his biological parents were and all about them, so there was no shock and weeping at finding out that he was adopted and not an "own" child. If possible, the child was taken to his true parents to become well acquainted with them and with his brothers and sisters if there were any, and he was always welcomed there. [3]

The child, in essence, belonged to two families openly and proudly; the family that gave him his birthright, and the family that nurtured and protected him. Many well-known Hawaiians have been raised in the *hanai* system and they speak openly of their dual identity. Their loyalty appears to be with their adoptive families, but they also take pride in the connection with their birth families.

American-style adoptions are now becoming predominant in Hawaii, and as Pukui, Haertig, and Lee indicate, this is causing conflict among old Hawaiian families:

> Hawaiian grandparents and other relatives feel strongly that even the child of unwed parents should know his family background, and object to legal adoption because it blots out the past. The Hawaiian couple who want to adopt a child feel much the same. They are not at all concerned if the child is illegitimate. What they are worried about is taking a child whose parentage is concealed. [4]

In the Eskimo culture a type of open adoption is also practiced; Chance describes it as follows:

> . . . the child's origin never is concealed and in many instances he is considered as belonging to both families. He may call the two sets of parents by the same names and maintain strong bonds with his real parents and siblings. In undertaking genealogical

> studies, anthropologists often have become confused about the biological parents of an adopted child since both sets claim him. It is evident that, whatever the reasons for adoption, the parents usually treat an adoptive child with as much warmth and affection as they do their own. [5]

In the United States, indications are that past adoption practices were more open. There has been a tendency to deny the value of these practices and to consider them as irregular and unprofessional, but they worked well and deserve reconsideration. It was not unusual before World War II for a couple to take in a pregnant unwed woman, care for her through the pregnancy and delivery, and then adopt her child. A close connection developed between the couple and the unwed mother, which permitted the mother to relinquish her baby confidently, knowing she was providing the child with a home she approved of and felt a part of.

There is no evidence that this practice caused any later problems for either the birth or adoptive parents. Neither is there evidence that birth parents came back to harass the adoptive families. The adoptive parents could tell the child of its birth heritage convincingly and with first-hand knowledge and understanding. There was an openness in such situations, and a good feeling was transmitted to the adoptee. This approach expressed the principle that a mother had the right to choose the substitute parents for her child, and that their caring for her was an indication of how they would care for her child. Such a principle is still recognized in the many states that have laws distinguishing between agency and independent adoptions. Independent adoptions are predicated on the belief that birth parents have the right to choose those who will raise their children.

There are a number of possible reasons why a closed and secretive approach to adoptions has developed in the United States. To the Puritan settlers, illegitimacy was considered a sin of overwhelming proportions, to be hidden at any cost. Subsequent immigration created a melting-pot nation in which genealogical lines became indistinct, and mobility and change were important. Pride was not based on family name and position, but on the achievement of success and wealth. People denied their origins rather than remain within a rigid social structure. They took on new names, new positions, and new responsibilities, and their attitudes toward adoption reflected these changes.

## OPEN ADOPTIONS

Today the adoption picture has totally changed, but thinking on the subject has not. The emphasis is still on keeping records sealed, protecting parents, matching babies, and resolving ambivalence for pregnant girls, when in reality that world no longer exists. Such approaches are out of phase with current needs and do not encourage creative solutions to meet those needs.

During the past five or six years thousands of unwed mothers all over the United States have chosen to keep their children rather than offer them for adoption. Although the stigma surrounding single unwed parenthood has lessened sufficiently to give those women the courage to keep their children, the problems of coping with the situation have not decreased, but have perhaps increased. The numbers of such children on the welfare rolls, in and out of foster home placement, or under protective services, is increasing continuously.

The young single mothers who have an emotional attachment—whether positive or negative—to their children desperately need a new kind of adoptive placement in which they can actively participate. They want the security of knowing they have helped provide their children with a loving, secure existence and yet have not denied themselves the possibility of knowing them in the future.

Recently one of the authors met with a group of young unwed mothers whose children ranged from one to five years of age. The women talked of their struggles, frustrations, and feelings of bitterness and anger. They regretted their inability to offer their children the kind of loving care they had expected to give them. Regarding adoption, the women felt that although they were failing to provide adequately, they could not face the possibility of a final and total separation from their children. They felt that any of the alternatives they faced would bring them intense feelings of guilt. It was untenable to keep their children with them under existing conditions, but it was impossible to cut themselves off completely. They equated relinquishment with amputation of a part of their bodies, or with the loss of a close relative through death. When they were asked how they would feel about an open adoption, their attitudes were totally different. They thought they could face and even welcome adoption for their children if they could meet the adoptive parents, help in the separation and the move to the new home, and then maintain some contact with the children.

Another of the authors helped initiate an open adoption. It was an experiment that seemed to be the best solution to the situation faced by an unwed mother in her early twenties. She knew she could not adequately care for her three-year-old son, who was beginning to show signs of emotional deprivation. Despite that, the mother could not bring herself to relinquish the boy to the agency. She began to search for families who would take the child and whom she could meet and know personally. However, she was unable to find an appropriate family.

At the same time, the agency was studying a family that already included one adopted child. In the course of the study, it was learned that the family had known the parents of their adopted child and felt the experience was meaningful to them. They were eager to have a second child and were even considering the role of foster parents. They were asked whether they would consider an open adoption. Without fear, but with thoughtfulness, they agreed to meet the mother and child and discuss the possibility. Given this opportunity, both the birth parent and adoptive parents showed new resources and strengths. They succeeded in understanding each other's needs with the focus on mutual care for the boy.

The adoptive placement was made in a way that gave the child as much honest comprehension of the process as possible. The postplacement period saw the complete transfer of parental responsibility to the new family, with the birth mother furnishing a meaningful emotional tie through occasional visits. Continued counseling services were produced to help maintain and enrich the child's new status without creating a threat to either birth or adoptive parents. The social worker summarized the experience in the record as follows:

> Both Gar [the boy] and the Blakes [the adoptive couple] have had an ongoing relationship and contact with the natural mother. Sandy, the natural mother, will call about once a month and arrange her visit to the Blakes's home. The visits occur in the early evening and last from two to four hours. Both Sandy and the Blakes say that the visits are comfortable. Sandy usually stays after Gar goes to sleep. He greets her warmly and separates easily. Gar now calls her Sandy, and Mrs. Blake, mother.
>
> Although the Blakes have some feelings that they would just as soon Sandy spaced her visits less frequently, they have accepted the situation. They are concerned about Gar's reaction as he grows older, but feel they can cope by explaining the actual circumstances, which are less rejecting than if he had no contact with his natural mother. . . . The Blakes say that the community response to Sandy's visits continues to be negative and nonunderstanding. Their friends' reactions do bother them more than Sandy's visits by far. . . .
>
> Sandy says she feels good about the placement. . . . On occasion she at first felt some anger over the Blakes's ways, in areas where their ideas deviated from her way of handling a situation. . . . She has never expressed her differences of opinion to the Blakes, as she has consciously given them the full responsibility for raising Gar. . . .

> Gar's progress and adjustment speak loudly and clearly that this has been a smooth course to follow. I feel that the placement in the adoptive home has been a most natural event for Gar and he is responding beautifully. . . .
>
> The Blakes and Sandy have been able to work out a reasonable relationship. This relationship has necessarily been somewhat monitored by my suggestions. It is in an area where too much intimacy might encourage situations of rivalry between the natural and adoptive parents, which would confuse the adoptee. . . . One of the most exciting feelings about this placement for me is to be able to see how genuinely satisfied all of the involved parties seem to be. The Blakes, Gar, and Sandy are having their individual needs met. No one is excluded, and no one has to be excluded or rejected in the future because of agency or environmental prerogatives.

## CONCLUSIONS

Is this a unique case? The authors believe there are many families throughout this country who would consider such open adoptions. The type of adoption they currently know and seek is the one adoption agencies have perpetuated. Families have never been offered alternatives. Agencies have learned during the past decade that many "unthinkable" things are thinkable, and that many "unattainable" goals can be attained.

Children who used to be considered "unadoptable" were really in that category because adoption workers felt that each family needed a "perfect" child. When families were asked whether they would consider adopting physically handicapped, congenitally deformed, or mentally retarded children, it was found there were indeed families who were willing to accept such children. When the baby population dwindled, adoption agencies had time to take a look at the older children and sibling groups who had been considered too hard to place. Families were found who would accept children who had a knowledge of their own past and who maintained emotional ties with relatives or foster parents. For some older children, single-parent adoptions were arranged, and instead of being only an expedient, such adoptions were found to be preferable for older children who could not accept a close family unit.

Agencies even broke one of their oldest taboos. They accepted and encouraged the idea of foster parents adopting the children under their care.

And here again, when older children were involved, the legalizing and making permanent of a good relationship added another dimension of security to all parties concerned. Even foster parents who knew the natural parents were willing to adopt the children.

Partially open adoptions have been accepted as appropriate for children in the latency and teenage periods. Openness has been encouraged by showing such children albums of family pictures while telling them about their relatives and foster parents. When sibling groups must be separated, arrangements are made for future meetings. The idea that these children may one day seek a reunion with one another and with their parents has been accepted.

An obvious benefit of open adoption is that children who would otherwise be deprived can have a permanent home and reliable parental care. However, there are also less obvious emotional benefits for the child and for the birth and adoptive parents. The child's tendency to feel rejected by the birth parent can be decreased considerably through continuing, even if minimal, contact with her. As the child matures, he is more likely to gain a realistic understanding of the problems that led to his adoption. The birth parent is less subject to overwhelming feelings of mourning and loss, and her feelings of guilt become less destructive. She can build a new, more satisfying life for herself once the problems of parenthood are solved, and this can have a positive effect on her new relationship with the child. For adoptive parents, acquaintanceship with the birth parents can help them avoid fears and fantasies and make their relationship to the child more natural and honest.

Open adoption is not a panacea and should not be considered a suitable procedure for all birth or adoptive parents. It is, however, a viable approach in specific situations and can offer an acceptable solution to an otherwise insoluble problem. If open adoption is to be mutually satisfactory and beneficial, adoption agencies must be willing to expend greater efforts over longer periods of time. The professional skills available are more than equal to the task. However, what is currently lacking in the profession is the willingness to consider adoption that allows the birth mother a continuing role in her child's life. Perhaps the clear definition of this need will lead to the consideration of open adoption as an alternative.

## REFERENCES

1. *See* Annette Baran, Arthur Sorosky, and Reuben Pannor, "Adoptive Parents and the Sealed Record Controversy," *Social Casework*, 55 (November 1974), pp. 531–536; Pannor, Sorosky, and Baran, "Opening the Sealed Records in

Adoption—The Human Need for Continuity," *Jewish Community Service*, 51 (December 1974), pp. 188–196; Sorosky, Baran, and Pannor, "The Reunion of Adoptees and Birth Relatives," *Journal of Youth and Adolescence*, 3 (January 1974), pp. 195–206; and Sorosky, Baran, and Pannor, "Identity Conflicts in Adoptees," *American Journal of Orthopsychiatry*, 45 (January 1975), pp. 18–25.

2. J. Bronowski, *The Ascent of Man* (Boston: Little, Brown & Co., 1973).

3. Craighill Handy and Mary Pukui, *The Polynesian Family System in Ka-U-Hawaii* (Wellington, New Zealand: The Polynesian Society, Inc., 1958).

4. Mary Pukui, Elizabeth Haertig, and Charles Lee, *Look to the Source* (Honolulu: Hui Hanai, 1972).

5. Norman A. Chance, *The Eskimo of North Alaska* (New York: Holt, Rinehart & Winston, 1966).

# Part V
# Legal Issues

# Part V

## Legal Issues

"Limbo" and "drift," words so often used to describe the vicissitudes of parents and their children involved in the foster care system, are also applicable to their involvement in the legal system. Standards and statutes for the removal of a child from his or her parents are broad, vague, and inconsistent. There are no clear definitions of "neglected" children and "fit" or "unfit" parents. Hence, parents, children, and foster parents are subject to a rule of wide discretion and subjective determination. By this failure of definition, the statutes create an atmosphere of inaction and delay, neither facilitating the prompt return of the child to the parents nor ensuring that the child will be promptly freed for adoption.[1]

Central to a discussion of the law's effect on parents and their children in care is consideration of the degree to which the state has the right to intrude in the domain of the home. The Fourteenth Amendment with its due process and equal protection clauses has led the Supreme Court to opinions upholding parents' "immediate right to the care, custody, management and companionship of . . . minor children," referring to parental custody of a child as "rights more precious than property rights."[2] Despite this assurance, scholars see the power of the government to protect children by removing them from their parents to be as deeply rooted in American history. The Tenth Amendment reserves to the states the area of domestic relations law. Today, every state has a statute allowing a court to intervene into the family to protect a child.

[1]"In the Child's Best Interests: Rights of the Natural Parents in Child Placement Proceedings," *New York University Law Review*, Vol. 51, No. 3 (June 1976): 458.

[2]May vs. Anderson, 1953. From Derdeyn, Andre P., "Child Abuse and Neglect: The Rights of Parents and the Needs of Their Children," *American Journal of Orthopsychiatry*, Vol. 47, No. 3 (July 1977): 377–387.

As a consequence of government intervention into the familial arena, there has been increased attention to the definitions of the rights of parents, children, and foster parents. These definitions have not been clearly ascertained and continue to be debated without resolution. Within the last decade, the Supreme Court has been called upon to distinguish between the interests of parent and children (Wyman vs. James, 1972) and will probably continue to do so. Other areas of conflict include the question of mandatory representation for the child or the parents or both. Courts often act against the parent by failing to mandate rehabilitation as well.

Related to the rights of children are the concepts of the "bests interests of the child" and "the least detrimental alternative." Both of these, in being determined, take into consideration the psychological or *de facto* parent, as opposed to the biological parent. Emphasizing continuity of care and attachment for the child, Goldstein, Freud, and Solnit support the concept of the psychological parent, and that of the "least detrimental alternative."[3]

These are among the legal issues examined in the two chapters in this section. In Chapter 12, Goldstein analyzes a New York case, Rothman vs. Jewish Child Care Association, in which custody of a child was awarded to the mother, despite the fact that she was psychiatrically hospitalized over a seven-year period and the child was in foster care during that entire period. Goldstein objects to this ruling and uses this case illustration to argue the concept of the "psychological parent"; this concept can be perceived as the "least detrimental among available alternatives for the child," a criterion seen as more suited to child placement decisions than the more traditional "in the best interests of the child."

In Chapter 13, Mnookin reviews the legal problems of the foster care system and makes recommendations for improvement. In the context of a comprehensive presentation of current legal criteria for removing children and the process of intervention, Mnookin asks two basic questions: "First, what legal standards should govern the judicial decision to remove a child over parental objections and place the child in foster care? And second, how can the law ensure developmental continuity and stability for children who must be so removed?" Mnookin questions whether there might not be something better than the "best interests of the child" standard and proposes that law reform rest on three basic principles:

1. Removal should take place only when the child cannot be protected within the home.

[3]Goldstein, Joseph; Freud, Anna; and Solnit, Albert, *Beyond the Best Interests of the Child*, New Edition with Epilogue. New York: The Free Press, 1979. *See also* Goldstein, Joseph; Freud, Anna; and Solnit, Albert, *Before the Best Interests of the Child*. New York: The Free Press, 1979.

2. To the extent possible, the decision to require foster care placement should be based on legal standards that can be applied in a consistent and even-handed way.

3. The state should make every possible effort to provide children who must be removed with as much continuity and stability as possible.

## SUGGESTIONS FOR FURTHER READING

Burt, Robert A., "Forcing Protection on Children and Their Parents: The Impact of Wyman v. James," *Michigan Law Review*, 69: 7 (June 1971): 1259–1310.

Campbell, Lee H., "The Birthparent's Right to Know," *Public Welfare*, 37: 3 (Summer 1979): 22–27.

Columbia Journal of Law and Social Problems, "Representation in Child Neglect Cases: Are Parents Neglected?" *Colombia Journal of Law and Social Problems*, 4: 2 (July 1968): 230–254.

Connecticut Law Journal, "In Re: Juvenile Appeal (Anonymous) v. Commissioner of Children and Youth Services," *Connecticut Law Journal*, 40–50 (June 12, 1979): 1–10.

Derdeyn, Andre P., "Child Abuse and Neglect: The Rights of Parents and the Needs of Their Children," *American Journal of Orthopsychiatry*, 47: 3 (July 1977): 377–387.

Derdeyn, Andre P. and Wadlington, W. J. III, "Adoption: The Rights of Parents versus the Best Interests of Their Children," *Journal of the American Academy of Child Psychiatry*, 16: 2 (1977): 238–255.

Goldstein, Joseph; Freud, Anna; and Solnit, Albert J., *Beyond the Best Interests of the Child*. New York: The Free Press, 1973.

Goldstein, Joseph; Freud, Anna; and Solnit, Albert J., *Before the Best Interests of the Child*. New York: The Free Press, 1979.

"In the Child's Best Interests: Rights of the Natural Parents in Child Placement Proceedings," *New York University Law Review*, 51: 3 (June 1976): 446–477.

Sorosky, Arthur D.; Baran, Annette; and Pannor, Reuben, "The Effects of the Sealed Record in Adoption," *American Journal of Psychiatry*, 133: 8 (August 1976): 900–904.

Sussman, Alan and Guggenheim, Martin, *The Rights of Parents*. New York: American Civil Liberties Union, 1980.

Wald, Michael, "State Intervention on Behalf of 'Neglected' Children: A Search for Realistic Standards," *Stanford Law Review*, 27: 4 (April 1975): 985–1040.

# 12

# Finding the Least Detrimental Alternative: The Problem for the Law of Child Placement

JOSEPH GOLDSTEIN

For this essay I have selected for examination a not uncommon court decision involving the placement of a "foster" child. This material is drawn from a book which I am writing with Anna Freud and Albert J. Solnit. The book, on which Seymour Lustman was to collaborate and which he helped plan, is to be entitled *Beyond the Best Interests of the Child*. In it, we seek to develop psychoanalytic guides which will (1) provide a basis for critically evaluating individual case decisions as well as the varied legal procedures concerned with determining who is or should be assigned the opportunity and the task of being "parent" to a child; and (2) constitute a theoretical and conceptual framework, not only for identifying and criticizing unsound precedents, but also for understanding and making secure many sound, but frequently

---

Reprinted from *The Psychoanalytic Study of the Child*, Vol. 27, edited by Ruth S. Eissler, Anna Freud, Marianne Kris, and Albert J. Solnit. New York: Quadrangle Books, 1972, pp. 626–641. By permission of Times Books, Inc.

unfollowed precedents—many of which were intuitively developed long before psychoanalysis.

I have chosen to evaluate a New York case, *Rothman v. Jewish Child Care Association*, decided in 1971 by Justice Nadel [1]. This evaluation is presented in the form of an opinion written by a fictitious Judge Analjo. Analjo's opinion is what might have been written had Justice Nadel, the actual trial judge, applied guides from psychoanalysis about child development in determining whom Stacey, age 8 and a "foster" child, should have as parents.

My minutes of one of five meetings held for planning the book during the Spring of 1970 between Drs. Freud, Lustman, Solnit and myself at Yale's Davenport College record that Dr. Lustman set in motion a discussion which led to the observation that a psychological bond frequently develops between child and foster parents despite a child care agency's purpose and the law's interest in providing no more than a "temporary" custodial relationship for the child. He was thinking about a 1959 New York appellate court decision involving the very same Jewish Child Care Association but concerned with another child, Laura [2]. In that case the Association, at the request of the natural mother, placed Laura, an infant of 1 year, in the "temporary" custody of foster parents. Four and a half years later, when the foster parents indicated that they wished to adopt Laura, the Association, in the name of "the child's best interests," thwarted their efforts and convinced the court that Laura should be returned to the custody of her biological mother. Further discussion of this decision, which wrenched Laura from her psychological parents led, as the minutes of April 15, 1970, record, "to the idea that we should develop a set of guides for foster parents. . . . From there, Dr. Lustman turned our attention to another lesson from the Laura case, which is that child agencies ought not to be so specialized that there is one for adoption and another one for foster care, but that agencies should be multifunctional so that staff can consider as many alternatives as might be made available in selecting a placement that is least likely to disserve the interests of the particular child involved." Thus, he argued that there should be agencies of general child placement rather than agencies exclusively concerned with either adoption or foster care.

Interestingly, it appears from the *Rothman* case that the Jewish Child Care Association, sometime since its 1959 "victory," may have modified its policy regarding such cases as Laura's [3]. Unfortunately, the same cannot be said for the court, as Justice Nadel's decision, which is first reproduced in full, demonstrates.

# I

## *Rothman v. Jewish Child Care Ass'n.*

Supreme Ct. New York County
166 N.Y. *Law Journal*, p. 17, Col. I (Nov. 5, 1971)

Justice Nadel

In this proceeding the natural mother seeks a judgment for the return of her eight-year-old daughter, Stacey. Petitioner gave her daughter to respondents for temporary care in December, 1964, when she voluntarily entered a hospital for treatment of a mental illness. Petitioner left the hospital for a period of time and then was readmitted. In December, 1969, the petitioner was released from the hospital and has not been hospitalized since. She is living with her parents, is employed as an executive secretary, and earns $140 per week.

The petitioner has never surrendered the child for adoption. The respondent, Jewish Child Care Association, opposes giving custody to the natural mother on the ground that she is unfit to care for the child by reason of her vast mental illness. However, on the trial they failed to produce any evidence upon which the court could make a finding that the petitioner is unfit to have custody of the child. The burden is upon the non-parent respondent to prove that petitioner is unfit to care for her daughter, and that the child's well-being requires separation from her mother. The Court of Appeals has ruled that absent abandonment of the child, statutory surrender of the child or the established unfitness of the mother, a court is without power to deprive the mother of custody *(Spence-Chapin Adoption Service v. Polk, N.Y.L.J., Sept. 27, 1971, p. 1, col. 1)*. At best, respondents have shown that the relationship between mother and daughter is not as good as it should be. That this is so is primarily the fault of the Jewish Child Care Association. Its extra-judicial determination that the child should not be returned, its hindrance of visitation and its failure to encourage the parental relationship were, to a great extent, responsible for the lack of a better relationship. It has been established in the Family Court that the said Association failed to make any real efforts to encourage and strengthen the parental relationship. The petitioner had to commence court proceedings for visitation and custody of her child, which were denied her by the Association.

Not only have respondents failed to sustain their burden of proof, but the evidence submitted amply demonstrates petitioner's fitness to have custody of her child. It was in the interest of the welfare of her daughter that the petitioner gave respondents temporary custody when she was hospitalized and unable to care for the child.

In the period of nearly two years preceding this trial, petitioner has been gainfully employed and she has been active in community, charitable and religious affairs. During the trying period of her hospitalization and separation from her child, petitioner appears to have successfully rehabilitated herself.

The court has observed petitioner during the course of her testimony. After hearing and observing the petitioner, the court finds that she is sincere in her desire to care for her daughter, and that she is able to do so. Petitioner is residing with her parents, and they will be able to care for their grandchild in the interim between the child's return from school and the time when the petitioner comes home from work. Their presence adds two persons to aid petitioner in the care of her daughter.

The request by the attorneys for the respondent Association to reargue the motion to refer this case to the Family Counseling Service is denied. Similar relief was denied respondent by several justices of this court. In any event, there has been a trial of the issues involved, and the court finds no valid reason for any further delay in returning the child to her natural mother.

The petitioner indicated that she realizes that the attitude of her daughter may require a transitional period before acquiring full custody. The parties shall, therefore, confer and shall submit in the judgment to be settled herein, a program for visitation and transfer of custody. Should the parties fail to agree, the court will determine such provisions, giving due consideration to their suggestions.

Settle judgment. Exhibits are with the clerk of the part.

## II

Judge Analjo reaches his decision using only the data relied upon by Justice Nadel. Since it is realistic to assume that no more adequate data about the child or the competing adults are generally available to a court, Judge Analjo, to compensate for the data deficiency, develops for general application a number of new legal concepts and presumptions sensitive to our knowledge of a child's developmental needs. Beyond this, Judge Analjo, in order to keep Stacey and her interests in focus, has, in restating the facts, refrained from using such emotionally freighted and conclusion-tending words and phrases as "natural mother" or "mother" in describing Ms. Rothman. In accord with the sound legal tradition of using such neutralizing, not dehumanizing, words as "petitioner" and "respondent" rather than continuously repeating the real names of the parties to the proceeding, Judge Analjo identifies Ms. Rothman only as an adult who gave birth to a female child named Stacey. Enough by way of introduction to the Analjo decision:

*Rothman v. Jewish Child Care Ass'n.*

Supreme Ct. Hampstead-Haven County
1 *New World Law Journal* p. 1, col. 1 (Nov. 5, 1971)

Justice Analjo

In this proceeding, the petitioner, an adult woman, seeks our judgment to award to her for custody and care an 8-year-old female child named Stacey. To support her claim, she established the following uncontested facts:

> 1. In December of 1963 petitioner gave birth to Stacey and, in accord with custom, practice, and the law, was initially and automatically assigned parental responsibility for the custody and care of the infant.
>
> 2. Seven years ago petitioner entered the hospital for the treatment of a mental illness. At the same time, she gave Stacey, then 1 year old, to the Jewish Child Care Association, the respondent, with the intention that she be cared for temporarily.
>
> 3. Two years ago, petitioner was released from the hospital and has not been hospitalized since. She is now living with her parents, is employed as an executive secretary, and earns $140 per week.
>
> 4. Petitioner is sincere in her request to care for Stacey, and her parents are prepared to assist in this while she is at work.
>
> 5. The respondent has refused to disturb Stacey's present relationship with her adult custodians. It has hindered petitioner's efforts to visit Stacey and to establish a parental relationship.

The respondent, on Stacey's behalf, opposed giving custody to petitioner. Because of her prior illness, it asserts that she is unfit to care for the child, to serve as a parent. So far as this case is concerned, petitioner is, as is any other adult, initially presumed in law to be fit to be a parent. We need not and do not reach that question.

The real question is: does Stacey need to have a parent assigned to her by the court. The presumption that petitioner is fit could have become subject to challenge only had it first been established that Stacey is currently an unwanted child in need of a parent. Not until then could the court admit evidence concerning the petitioner either to overcome the presumption or, preferably, to inform the court about petitioner and others in terms of determining whose custody, among available alternatives, would serve Stacey's best interests by providing the least detrimental opportunity for meeting her needs.

What is strangely missing from the evidence is any material on Stacey's needs. In the absence of such evidence the law must and does presume that Stacey is a *wanted child* and that her present custody ought not to be disturbed. It is presumed, therefore, that she is receiving affection and nourishment on a continuing basis from at least one adult and that she feels that she is valued by those who take care of her [4]. The burden is on the petitioner (assuming she had standing to invoke this proceeding) to overcome the presumption that the adult or adults who currently are responsible for Stacey are fit to remain her parents; and to overcome the presumption that Stacey (after living from infancy for such an extended period of time with her foster parents) is a wanted child—not merely in the sense of "want" as expressed by the competing adults, but additionally in her feeling of being wanted by those who have become a continuing source of affection, nourishment and well-being [5]. Another facet of these presumptions is that the relinquishing "parent," here the petitioner, after such a lapse of time, has, from the child's psychological vantage point, abandoned her. The burden then is on petitioner to establish that there is a necessity for altering the now long-standing ongoing relationship between Stacey and whoever may have become her "common-law" parent or parents, as well as between her and whoever may have become her "common-law" siblings, if there be any. The burden in short is to show that Stacey is an *unwanted child* in her present home. If petitioner were to meet the burden (and her attempts to do so do not give her license to invade the privacy of Stacey's "common-law" family [6]), she would not then have to prove her fitness to be a parent. Rather, she would have to establish that among the interested adults, all of whom are presumed fit to be parents, her taking custody would be *least detrimental* (Goldstein and Katz, 1965, p. 4, n. 57) to Stacey's healthy growth and development and to her physical and psychological well-being.

Though not directly in issue here, it is appropriate to digress momentarily in order to suggest that the legislature, in addition to giving statutory recognition to the "right to be a wanted child," consider establishing in its guides to child placement a new standard, "that which is least detrimental among available alternatives for the child" as a substitute for the now traditional "that which is in the best interests of the child." Under such a legislative mandate to use "least detrimental" rather than "best interest," courts as well as child care agencies are more likely to confront the detriments inherent in each child placement decision without getting enmeshed in the hope and magic associated with "best" in a way which often misleads decision makers into believing they have more power for "good" than for "bad" in what they may decide.

Introducing the idea of "available alternatives" should force into focus from the child's vantage point consideration of the advantages and disadvantages of the actual real options to be measured in terms of that which is least likely to preclude the chances of the child becoming "wanted." The proposed standard is less awesome, more realistic, and thus more amenable to relevant data gathering than "best interest." No magic is to be attributed to the new formulation, but there is in any new set of guiding words an opportunity at least for courts and agencies to re-examine their tasks and thus possibly to force into view factors of low visibility which seem frequently to have resulted in decisions actually in conflict with "the best interests of the child."

Further, it is not beyond the capacity of the court, were the legislature not inclined to accept the suggestion, to construe the statutory guide of "in the best interests of the child" to require the court or agency to select that placement which is "the least detrimental available alternative." In any event, whether by legislative or judicial decision, the new standard might permit going beyond the best interest of the child by enhancing the opportunities for each child to have made secure his or her right to be and feel wanted.

Petitioner further argues, returning now to the specific claims in this case, that she never lost custody-in-law of Stacey. She established that she has always considered herself responsible for Stacey's care, that she had made "temporary" arrangements for her with the respondent, that from the outset it was understood that they were to be temporary, and that she had always intended, once her health was restored, to care personally for Stacey. At no time during the last 7 years, she asserts, has she *abandoned* Stacey; has she ever ceased being her "mother." If anyone is at fault, it is, she claims, the respondent Association. It has prevented her from maintaining, or, at least, establishing a parental relationship with Stacey.

These arguments, and the supporting facts reflect an understandable, but still mistaken notion of the law [7], its limits and limitations. Like the wanted child concept, abandonment of a child by an adult, at least for the purpose of determining who is parent, rests, not on the intentions of the adult, but rather on the impact such a leave-taking has on the child. In the absence of specific evidence to the contrary, a child of 1 year, who has been left in "temporary" care for as many years as have elapsed since Stacey had continuous, affectionate, and otherwise nurturing contact with petitioner, must be presumed in law to be wanted by petitioner and to have been *abandoned* for purposes of custody and care. If nothing else, from Stacey's vantage point, there has been a critical break in whatever psychological tie had begun to develop between herself and petitioner. Painful as it must be for this well-meaning woman, her intentions alone are not enough to prevent such psychological abandonment. Those intentions would have had to be accompanied by a carefully designed program with respondent, and then only for a relatively short time span, which did, in fact, maintain petitioner as the primary adult source for Stacey of affection, stimulation, and, most importantly, of a sense of continuity essential to securing healthy growth and development [8].

So far as Stacey's interests are concerned, it matters not that the implementation of those intentions may have actually been thwarted by the actions of the respondent, or by anyone else, nor does it matter, for purposes of determining custody, whether petitioner's intentions were defeated through her kindness, her misunderstanding, or her ignorance. Whatever the cause, whoever may feel responsible, the psychological fact, which the law must recognize, is that Stacey does not now have in petitioner a parent.

It is impossible to locate precisely the moment in time when a parent's "temporary" relinquishment of a child to the custody of another becomes abandonment for that child. To put it more affirmatively and, hopefully, realistically, it is not possible to determine just when a new parent-child relationship has formed which deserves the recognition and protection of the law. That new relationship, which in the absence of contrary evidence must be presumed to have developed over the past 7 years, may be perceived, not unlike a common-law marriage, as one of *common-law parenthood* or *common-law adoption*. While the process through which a new child-parent status emerges is too complex and subject to too many individual variations for the law to know just when "abandonment" may have occurred, the law can generally verify that the biological tie never matured into an affirmative psychological tie for the child or that a developing psychological tie has been broken or damaged and whether a promising new relationship has developed and is being formed. The law presumes, barring extraordinary efforts to maintain the continuity of a "temporarily interrupted" relationship, that the younger the child, the shorter the period of relinquishment before a developing psychological tie is broken and a new relationship begins—a relationship which must not be put in jeopardy if the primary goal of the state is to safeguard the health and well-being of the child.

The court is mindful that a parent (an adult with primary responsibility for the continuous care of a child) may entrust a child to others for short periods of time (with the length of time amenable to extension for older children) and may make arrangements for maintaining the continuity of existing ties without necessarily jeopardizing the child's health and well-being. But there comes a point, whatever the declared or conscious intent of the "parent" and whatever the nature of the arrangement for assuring continuity, when temporary arrangements are no longer temporary, when separations are so prolonged that the force of the law must be available to protect, not break, already established or even newly developing parent-child relationships. The abandoned child has, hopefully, begun to establish a new tie with an adult or adults who for all purposes are then becoming his or her psychological parents [9]. And such persons are in law recognized as parents by a process we would call *common-law adoption*. Such an adoption carries with it all the legal protections generally available to nurture and secure healthy ties between parent and child. Were the state to intervene, as it often has following "abandonment" and before the hoped-for new tie has begun to develop, the "abandoning" parent, if he or she wished, might be given a preference based on the expectation that the residue of the former relationship would facilitate renewal of the earlier tie and thus provide the least detrimental alternative.

This decision is not and must not be read to require the assigning of fault to any person or to any child placement agency [10]. By shifting the focus of decision to the problem of meeting the needs of the child, the intent of the leave-taking adult or of the administrative agency is no longer of relevance. The law moves as it should, away from making moral judgments about fitness to be a parent; away from assigning blame; and away from looking at the child and the award or denial of custody as reward or punishment. It becomes unimportant then whether the parent-child relationship grew out of circumstances within or beyond the "control" of an adult claimant.

Though obvious once said, when left unsaid, the limitations of law often go unacknowledged in cases such as this. There is attributed to the law a magical power, a capacity to do what is far beyond its means. While the law may claim the power to establish relationships, it can, in fact, do little more than acknowledge them and give them recognition. It may be able to destroy human relationships, but it cannot compel them to develop. It has taken the law a long time to recognize that the power to deny divorce cannot establish a healthy marriage, preclude the parties from separating, or prevent new "married" relationships from maturing [11]. While the impact of a court decision concerning adult-child relationship is not necessarily quite so limited as with adult-adult relationships in divorce proceedings, the court still does not have the power to establish meaningful relationships. Here it can destroy or protect such relationships and can facilitate their growth. But it cannot compel them, even though the child, unlike the adult in the denial-of-divorce situation, has less freedom to establish new relationships on his own. The child is far more vulnerable to exploitation by the adult who is recognized in law as parent or custodian. By decreeing that Stacey be returned to her biological "mother," no court could establish a real relationship between them. Yet such a decision cannot be assumed to be a hollow or meaningless one for either of them or for the adopting foster parents. It would have greater potential for damage and pain for all than for the health and well-being of any of them.

There will, of course, as in all human situations, be the hard case. But more than likely the law can resolve such cases, if it has clarified for itself and the participants the function and purpose of the proceeding and the limitations of the legal process. In so doing, it is less likely to obscure the problem by a mistaken concern for the person whose only special claim to the child rests on a biological tie. Such a tie deserves and receives an initial acknowledgment in law by making it the basis for determining who will first be "parent." But the status of parent, once a child has left the chemical exchange of the womb for the social exchange, where law has a role to play, rests on maintaining a continuous nurturing, affectionate, and stimulating relationship essential to the physical and psychological health and development of the child.

Though the status of parent is not easily lost in law, it can exist only so long as it is real in terms of the health and well-being of the child. It is a relationship from birth, whether legitimate or illegitimate, or from adoption, whether statutory or common-law, which requires a continuing interaction between adult and child to survive. It can be broken by the adult parent by "chance," by the establishment of a new adult-child relationship, which we call common-law adoption, or by "choice," through a more formal legal process we have come to call adoption.

It must be realized that the tie of adoption is no more nor less significant than the biological tie. It is the real tie—the reality of an ongoing relationship—that is crucial to this court's decision and that demands the protection of the state through law. The court must not, despite its sympathetic concern for the petitioner, become a party to tearing Stacey away from the only affectionate parents she knows. Stacey must be presumed to be, in her present surroundings, a wanted child.

Finally, it must be observed that this decision does not constitute a break with the past. Rather, the past is future. There is in law, as psychoanalysis teaches that there is in man, a rich residue which each generation preserves from the past, modifies for the now, and in turn leaves for the future. Law, is, after all, a continuous process for meeting society's need for stability by providing authority and precedent and, at the same time, meeting its need for flexibility and change by providing for each authority a counterauthority and for each precedent a counterprecedent. The living law thus seeks to secure an environment conducive to society's healthy growth and development.

That this decision is not incompatible with legal decisions of the last century will come as no surprise then, either to students of law who constructively resist sharp breaks with the past or to students of child development who have made us understand man's need for continuity. In 1824, for example, the distinguished American jurist and justice of the United States Supreme Court, Joseph Story, had no psychoanalytic theory of child development to draw upon, yet acting as circuit judge he could write in *U.S. v. Green* (3 Mason 482 Fed. Cas. No. 15256 [1824]):

> As to the question of the right of the father to have the custody of his infant child, in a general sense it is true. But this is not on account of any absolute right of the father, but for the benefit of the infant, the law presuming it to be for its interests to be under the nurture and care of his natural protector, both for maintenance and education. When, therefore, the court is asked to lend its aid to put the infant into the custody of the father, and to withdraw him from other persons, it will look into all the circumstances, and ascertain whether it will be for the real, permanent interests of the infant and if the infant be of sufficient discretion, it will also consult its personal wishes.

Far less vague and in language often sounding psychoanalytic, yet written more than a decade before Freud published *The Interpretation of Dreams*, are the words of Justice Brewer speaking for the Supreme Court of Kansas in 1889 in the child placement case of *Chapsky v. Wood* (26 Kan. Reports, pp. 650–658 [2nd ed. annotated, 1889]):

> [When a] child has been left for years in the care and custody of others, who have discharged all the obligations of support and care which naturally rest upon the parent, then, whether the courts will enforce the father's right to the custody of the child, will depend mainly upon the question whether such custody will promote the welfare and interest of such child. This distinction must be recognized. If, immediately after [giving up the child] reclamation be sought, and the father is not what may be called an unfit person by reason of immorality, etc., the courts will pay little attention to any mere speculation as to the probability of benefit to the child by leaving or returning it. In other words, they will consider that the law of nature which declares the strength of a father's love is more to be considered than any mere speculation whatever as to the advantages which possible wealth and social position might otherwise bestow. But, on the other hand, when

reclamation is not sought until a lapse of years, when new ties have been formed and a certain current given to the child's life and thought, much attention should be paid to the probabilities of a benefit to the child from the change. *It is an obvious fact that ties of blood weaken, and ties of companionship strengthen, by lapse of time; and the prosperity and welfare of the child depend on the number and strength of these ties, as well as on the ability to do all which the promptings of these ties compel* [my italics].

[T]hey who have for years filled the place of the parent, have discharged all the obligations of care and support, and especially when they have discharged these duties during those years of infancy when the burden is especially heavy, when the labor and care are of a kind whose value cannot be expressed in money—when all these labors have been performed and the child has bloomed into bright and happy girlhood, it is but fair and proper that their previous faithfulness, and the interest and affection which these labors have created in them, should be respected. Above all things, the paramount consideration is, what will promote the welfare of the child? These, I think, are about all the rules of law applicable to a case of this kind.

. . . What the future of the child will be is a question of probability. No one is wise enough to forecast or determine absolutely what would or what would not be best for it; yet we have to act upon these probabilities from the testimony before us, guided by the ordinary laws of human experience. . . .

[T]he child has had, and has today, all that a mother's love and care can give. The affection which a mother may have and does have, springing from the fact that a child is her offspring, is an affection which perhaps no other one can really possess; but so far as it is possible, springing from years of patient care of a little, helpless babe, from association, and as an outgrowth from those little cares and motherly attentions bestowed upon it, an affection for the child is seen in Mrs. Wood that can be found nowhere else. And it is apparent, that so far as a mother's love can be equaled, its foster-mother has that love, and will continue to have it.

On the other hand, if she goes to the house of her father's family, the female inmates are an aunt, just ripening into womanhood, and a grandmother; they have never seen the child; they have no affection for it springing from years of companionship. . . .

> Human impulses are such that doubtless they would form an affection for the child—it is hardly possible to believe otherwise; but to that deep, strong, patient love which springs from either motherhood, or from a patient care during years of helpless babyhood, they will be strangers.

In acknowledging Stacey's adoption by affirming the respondent Association's assertion of her right to remain with her "foster" but real parents of the past 8 years, the court takes the position of Justice Brewer in the *Chapsky* case:

> It is a serious question, always to be considered, whether a change should be advised. "Let well enough alone" is an axiom founded on abundant experience [at p. 656].

So ordered.

## REFERENCES

1. 166 N.Y. *Law J.*, p. 17, col. 1 (Nov. 4, 1971).
2. *In Re* Jewish Child Care Association 5 N.Y. 2nd 222, 156 N.E., 2d 700 (1959).
3. But see, *New York ex rel: Jewish Child Care Association v. Cahn* Sup. Ct. Nassau County Special Term Part V (April 28, 1972) in which the court upholds the Association's efforts to remove a 9-year-old child from "foster" parents with whom she had been placed for more than 9 years in order to return her to her "natural" parents.
4. On the right to be a wanted child and some of its implications for law, see Goldstein and Provence (1970).
5. See, e.g., Anna Freud (1965), "According to the psychoanalyst's experience, the best interests of an infant are safeguarded under the condition that three needs are fulfilled: the need for *affection* (for the unfolding and centering of the infant's own feelings); the need for *stimulation* (to elicit inherent functions and potentialities); and the need for *unbroken continuity* (to prevent damage done to the personality by the loss of function and destruction of capacities which follow invariably on the emotional upheavals brought about by separation from, death or disappearance of, the child's first love-objects)" (p. 1053).
6. The law, seeking to safeguard the privacy of family relationships and the private ordering of one's life, has adopted a policy of minimum state intervention consistent, of course, with the state's goal of safeguarding the well-being of children, protecting them from exploitation by adults (Goldstein and Gitter, 1969, p. 82).

7. Courts have consistently held that for a child to be considered abandoned the natural parents must have a "settled intent to renounce the parental relationship" (*Winnans v. Luppie* 47 N.J. Eq. 302, 305 [1890]) and see, e.g., *In re* Adoption of Branzley 122 So. 2d 423 (Fla. 1960) (abandonment is a "settled purpose to permanently forgo all parental rights"). The problem has generally not been conceptualized, as the original Rothman case demonstrates, in terms of the child's sense of abandonment.

8. See A. Freud's and D. Burlingham's Monthly Reports of the activities of the Hampstead War Nurseries for descriptions of a variety of efforts to maintain alive the image of the parent during separations (A. Freud, 1973).

9. Art Buchwald, the distinguished humorist, who 50 years ago was a foster child, recalled in a speech celebrating the 150th Anniversary of the Jewish Child Care Association in April, 1972:

   "The status of a foster child, particularly *for* the foster child, is a strange one. He's part of no-man's land.

   ". . . The child knows instinctively that there is nothing permanent about the setup, and he is, so to speak, on loan to the family he is residing with. If it doesn't work out, he can be swooped up and put in another home.

   "It's pretty hard to ask a child or foster parent to make a large emotional commitment under these conditions, and so I think I was about seven years old, when confused, lonely and terribly insecure I said to myself, 'The hell with it. I think I'll become a humorist.'

   "From then on I turned everything into a joke. Starting as the class clown, I graduated to making fun of all authority figures from the principal of the school to the social service worker who visited every month. When a person is grown up and he attacks authority, society pays him large sums of money. But when he's a kid and he makes fun of authority, they beat his brains in.

   "Having chosen this dangerous pastime of getting attention by poking fun at everything, I found I could survive. I had my bag of laughs and I had my fantasies, which I must say were really great. Would you believe that I dreamed I was really the son of a Rothschild, and I was kidnapped by gypsies when I was six months old, and sold to a couple who were going to America?

   "If you believe that, would you believe the Rothschilds had hired France's foremost detective to find me and that it was only a matter of time when he would trace me to the foster home in Hollis, Long Island, and would you believe that once my true identity had been established, I would prevail on my Rothschild father to drop all charges against the people that had kidnapped me, and give them a substantial pension.

   "That's the kind of kid my social worker had to deal with."

10. Of course, an agency may lose its license or be liable for damages if it is negligent in carrying out responsibilities it undertakes. What is important here is that the child not become the award for damages.

11. See generally Goldstein and Gitter (1969).

## BIBLIOGRAPHY

Buchwald, A. (1972), Speech to Jewish Child Care Association (Pierre Hotel, New York, April 19; unpublished).

Freud, A. (1965), Cindy. In: *The Family and the Law* by J. Goldstein & J. Katz. New York: Free Press, pp. 1051–1053.

———& Burlingham, D. (1973), Monthly Reports (of the Activities of the Hampstead War Nurseries). In: *The Writings of Anna Freud*, Vol. III. New York: International Universities Press (in press).

Goldstein, J. (1968), Psychoanalysis and Jurisprudence. *This Annual*, 23:459–478.

———& Gitter, M. (1969). On the Abolition of Grounds for Divorce: A Model Statute and Commentary. *Family Law Quart.*, 3:75–99.

———&Katz, J. (1965), *The Family and the Law*, New York: Free Press.

———& Provence, S. (1970), The Rights of Children. *Memorandum Prepared for Forum 22 of the White House Conference on Children* (unpublished).

# 13

# Foster Care
# In Whose Best Interest?

ROBERT H. MNOOKIN

Most American parents raise their children free of intrusive legal constraints or major governmental intervention. Although compulsory education and child labor laws indicate there are some conspicuous legal limitations on parents, it is the family, not the state, which has primary responsibility for child rearing [1]. Despite this predominant pattern, there are about 285,000 children under eighteen [2] among the nation's nearly 70 million [3] for whom the state has assumed primary responsibility. These children live in state sponsored foster care, a term used in this paper to include foster family homes, group homes, and child welfare institutions. For a number of the children in foster care, the state has assumed responsibility because no one else is available. Some children are orphans; others have been voluntarily given up by a family no longer willing or able to care for them. A significant number of children, however, are placed in foster care because the state has intervened and coercively removed the child from parental custody.

---

Reprinted from *Harvard Educational Review*, Vol. 43, No. 4 (November 1973), pp. 599–638. 

Research for this article was supported by grants to the Childhood and Government Project, University of California, Berkeley, from the Ford Foundation and the Carnegie Corporation of New York. A revised version of this article, with greater emphasis on law, will appear in the May 1974 issue of the *California Law Review*.

No national statistics are available to indicate what proportion of the children in foster care have been removed because of state coercion. When parents oppose foster care placement, a court can nevertheless order removal after a judicial proceeding if the state can demonstrate parental abuse or neglect. But if parents consent to foster care placement, no judicial action is necessary. Many foster care placements, perhaps one-half or more, are arranged by state social welfare departments without any court involvement. In California, for example, the State Social Welfare Board estimated recently that one-half of the children in state-sponsored foster care were "voluntary" placements where the parent(s) consented to relinquish custody without a formal court proceeding [4]. A study in New York City found that 58 percent of the natural parents of foster children had agreed to foster care placement [5].

A substantial degree of state coercion may be involved in many so-called voluntary placements, making the distinction between voluntary and coercive placement illusory. Many social welfare departments routinely ask parents to agree to give up their children before initiating neglect proceedings in court. Some parents who would have been willing to keep their children may consent to placement to avoid a court proceeding against them. If one were to use the legal standards of voluntariness and informed consent applied in the criminal law to confessions [6] and to the waiver of important legal rights [7], many cases of relinquishment after state intervention might not be considered voluntary. On the other hand, not all court-ordered foster care placements involve coercion of the parents. Some take place with their full concurrence. In some cases State welfare agencies require even parents who desire to place their children in foster care to go through a court proceeding. There is a financial incentive for the State to do this because under the Social Security Act, a state can be partially reimbursed by the federal government only if a court orders placement [8].

Although it is unrealistic to make precise estimates given the complexities just outlined, I would judge that at least 100,000 children

I wish gratefully to acknowledge the research assistance of Susan Waisbren, graduate student, Department of Psychology, University of California, and Kate Bartlett, a second year student at the School of Law, University of California, Berkeley. Many of my colleagues at Berkeley made helpful comments on an earlier draft. In particular, I wish to thank Jessica Pers, Raymond Marks, Randall McCathren, Arlene Skolnick, Louis Freedberg of the Childhood and Government Project, and Professors Jerome Skolnick, Paul Mishkin, Herma Hill Kay, Caleb Foote, John Coons, Stephen Sugarman, David Kirp, and Kermit Wiltse. Finally, I have benefited considerably from conversations with Robert Walker, Esq., of the Youth Law Center, San Francisco.

around the country are now in foster care because of coercive state intervention. Whatever their exact number, the state's role in placing them in foster care suggests a significant social responsibility. Even though state coercion can occur outside of court, judges usually have been responsible for deciding whether or not to remove children over parental objection. Law provides the principal framework to inform and constrain judicial action. This paper therefore addresses two basic questions. First, what legal standards should govern the judicial decision to remove a child over parental objections and place the child in foster care? And second, how can the law ensure developmental continuity and stability for children who must be so removed?

As background, the present legal standards for removing children, the process of intervention, and what is known about foster children and the foster care system are briefly described. I think three principles, currently violated, should govern its operation:

1. Removal should be a last resort, used only when the child cannot be protected within the home.

2. The decision to require foster care placement should be based on legal standards that can be applied in a consistent and even-handed way, and not be profoundly influenced by the values of the particular deciding judge.

3. If removal is necessary, the state should actively seek, when possible, to help the child's parents overcome the problems that led to removal so that the child can be returned home as soon as possible. In cases where the child cannot be returned home in a reasonable time, despite efforts by the state, the state should find a stable alternative arrangement such as adoption for the child. A child should not be left in foster care for an indefinite period of time.

Current legal standards for removal, under which courts increasingly purport to make individualized determinations of what is in the best interests of the child, contribute significantly to the failings of the present foster care system. My criticism is not that present standards fail to give adequate weight to parental interests, as compared to the child's interests; indeed, the focus of social concern probably should be on the child. Nor do I believe that it is always inappropriate to remove a child from parental custody for placement in foster care; in some circumstances nothing less drastic will protect a child from abusing or neglectful parents. Instead, what is wrong with the existing legal standards is that they call for individualized determinations based on discretionary assessments of the best interests of the child, and these determinations cannot be made consistently and fairly. They result in the unnecessary placement of children in foster care and do little to protect children against remaining in foster care for too long. Accordingly, substantial changes in the legal standards are needed, designed to make it more difficult to remove children initially and to provide more continuity and stability for children if removal is necessary. These changes will entail more than added procedural safeguards.

## HOW THE STATE REMOVES CHILDREN FROM THEIR PARENTS

### Source of the Power

The power of government to protect children by removing them from parental custody has roots deep in American history. And in colonial times just as today, the children of the poor were the most affected. Seventeenth century laws of Massachusetts, Connecticut, and Virginia, for example, specifically authorized magistrates to "bind out" or indenture children *of the poor* over parental objections [9]. Although it is unclear how frequently this power was exercised, the records of Watertown, Massachusetts, for instance, show that in 1671 Edward Sanderson's two oldest children were bound out as apprentices "where they may be educated and brought up in the knowledge of God and some honest calling." The reason given: poverty [10].

By the early nineteenth century, the *parens patriae* power of the state, i.e., the sovereign's ultimate responsibility to guard the interests of children and others who lacked legal capacity, was thought sufficient to empower courts to remove a child from parental custody. Significantly, the reinforcement of public morality, and not simply the protection of children from cruelty, was seen as sufficient justification for the exercise of this power. Joseph Story, the renowned Massachusetts legal scholar who sat on the Supreme Court from 1811 to 1845, stated in his treatise on equity courts:

> Although, in general, parents are intrusted with the custody of the persons, and the education of their children, yet this is done upon the natural presumption, that the children will be properly taken care of, and will be brought up with a due education in literature, and morals, and religion; and that they will be treated with kindness and affection. But, whenever this presumption is removed; whenever (for example,) it is found, that a father is guilty of gross ill-treatment or cruelty towards his infant children; or that he is in constant habits of drunkenness and blasphemy, or low and gross debauchery; or that he professes atheistical or irreligious principles; or that his domestic associations are such as tend to the corruption and contamination of his children; or that he otherwise acts in a manner injurious to the morals and interests

> of his children; in every such case, the Court of Chancery will interfere, and deprive him of the custody of his children, and appoint a suitable person to act as guardian, and to take care of them, and to superintend their education. [11]

Today, every state has a statute allowing a court to intervene into the family to protect a child; this authority is usually conferred on the juvenile or family court [12]. Apart from situations where the child has engaged in wrongful behavior of some sort, the statutes in most states allow the court to intrude into the child's life if, for whatever reason, he or she lacks a parent or guardian (dependent or abandoned children), if the parent has neglected properly to care for or to support him or her (neglected children), or if the parent has willfully injured the child (abused children). Frequently the terms "dependent" and "neglected" are used to describe all children subject to a juvenile court's jurisdiction who have not engaged in any wrongful behavior. In this paper, the term "neglected" is so used, and is meant to include dependent and abused children as well.

In several respects present-day legislative standards defining the circumstances where a court may intervene into the family bear a remarkable similarity to Story's nineteenth century characterization. They are vague and open-ended, they require highly subjective determinations, and they permit intervention not only when the child has been demonstrably harmed or is physically endangered but also when parental habits or attitudes are adverse to the inculcation of proper moral values. Typical statutory provisions allow court intrusion to protect a child who is not receiving "proper parental care" [13], "proper attention" [14], "whose home is an unfit place for him by reason of neglect, cruelty, depravity, or physical abuse" [15], or whose parents neglect to provide the "care necessary for his health, morals or well being" [16]. The Minnesota statute explicitly specifies that emotional neglect of the child is relevant to intervention [17].

## The Process of Removal

While the legal standards for court intervention are scarcely more precise today than 100 years ago, far more complex administrative processes are involved [18]. In Story's time, social workers and probation departments did not exist. Today a case usually reaches court after weaving through a complicated social welfare bureaucracy where numerous officials including social workers, probation officers, and court personnel, may have had contact with the family.

Unfortunately, very little is known about how the discretion of these various administrative officers is exercised before a case reaches court. The process is usually initiated by a report from a social worker or the police, or less frequently from a neighbor, medical professional, or school staff member [19]. Although practices vary, a member of a special unit of the social welfare or probation department is usually responsible for an initial investigation of the report. Customarily this investigation is not extensive; often it will only involve a visit to the home and a telephone conversation with the person who turned in the report. The investigator, sometimes together with a supervisor, then must decide whether to close the case, to suggest that the welfare agency informally (and non-coercively) provide services or supervision, or to file a petition in court.

Filing a petition initiates a judicial inquiry that usually has two stages. First, the court must determine whether it has jurisdiction over the child. This involves deciding on the basis of exceedingly broad and ill-defined statutory provisions whether the parents have failed to live up to acceptable social standards for child rearing. If it is determined that they have, then such jurisdiction empowers the court to intervene into the family. In the words of one juvenile court judge, "It is the ultimate finding of neglect which releases the court's wide discretionary powers of disposition, a discretion beholden to and circumscribed by the law's most challenging aphorism, 'the best interests of the child' " [20]. The second stage involves a dispositional hearing, where the judge decides the manner of intervention. Removal from the home is by no means mandatory. The court can instead require supervision within the child's own home, psychological counseling for the parents and/or the child, or periodic home visits by a social worker, probation officer, or homemaker.

No national data are available, but it appears that children are removed from parental custody in a significant percentage of the cases when the juvenile court assumes jurisdiction. In 1972, for example, the Los Angeles juvenile courts ordered removal in 1,028 out of 1,656 of the cases where jurisdiction was assumed—62 percent [21]. For San Francisco in the same year, 65 percent were ordered removed (262 out of 402) [22]. Although some of these children were placed with relatives, over 80 percent of those removed were placed in foster care. Likewise, a study of dispositions in New York State during the years 1957–60 showed that the probability of removal from the home was as great as that of supervision by the probation department—each occurred in slightly over 30 percent of the neglect petitions adjudicated by the court [23]. More recently, Professor Peter Straus has estimated that in New York the child is taken from its home "in about half" of the cases of abuse or neglect [24].

## CHILDREN IN FOSTER CARE:

### The Characteristics of Foster Children—The Reasons for Removal

The social welfare literature provides some information about the age and economic circumstances of the children placed in foster care. Most of the children are quite young at the time of removal; a majority are probably six years of age or younger [25]. Their families are usually very poor, often on welfare [26]. A disproportionate number are from single parent families [27].

Unfortunately there is very little systematic information about the circumstances that result in foster care placement over parental objections. Although some social welfare research attempts to analyze why children are placed in foster care, these studies are based on samples where many parents agreed to placement or sought it. There is no reason to assume that the circumstances leading a family to wish to give up a child are the same as those leading professionals to decide the state should compel removal. The most extensive work on reasons for foster placement has been done by Shirley Jenkins and her associates at Columbia University, published in 1966. Jenkins and Sauber analyzed 425 families whose children were placed in foster care in New York City. Using five major categories, they describe the "main reason for placement" as follows:

> (1) physical illness or incapacity of child-caring person, including confinement, 29 percent; (2) mental illness of the mother, 11 percent; (3) child personality or emotional problems, 17 percent; (4) severe neglect or abuse, 10 percent; (5) "family problems," 33 percent. The last group includes cases of unwillingness or inability to continue care on the part of an adult other than a parent, children left or deserted, parental incompetence, and conflicts or arrests [28].

A later study published in 1972 by Jenkins and Norman found the following distribution of families according to reason for placement [29]. (See Table 1.)

Neither study is particularly helpful for analyzing antecedents of the legal decision to place children in foster homes. In the first study, parents were known to have objected to placement in only ten percent of the sample cases, and the percentage distribution of reasons for placement among this subgroup is not given. While it is suggested that the "severe abuse or neglect" category included most of the objecting parents, that category, as its label shows, is no more helpful in describing the reason for the decision than the underlying

TABLE 1

Distribution of Families According to Reason for Placement

| Reason for Placement | Number of Families | Percent Distribution |
|---|---|---|
| Mental illness | 86 | 22 |
| Child behavior | 63 | 16 |
| Neglect or abuse | 54 | 14 |
| Physical illness | 44 | 11 |
| Unwillingness or inability to continue care | 41 | 11 |
| Family dysfunction | 36 | 9 |
| Unwillingness or inability to assume care | 30 | 8 |
| Abandonment or desertion | 30 | 8 |
| Other problems | 6 | 1 |
| Total | 390 | 100 |

statute. The later study is also based on samples that include voluntary and non-voluntary placements. It too uses descriptive categories lacking definitional clarity and combining situations where parents no longer want child care responsibility with those where a professional has decided the parent is not competent. Finally, as these researchers realized, more than one reason frequently can be identified for foster care placement, making the selection of a single reason difficult or inappropriate. Other social welfare research has sought to analyze the factors influencing a social worker's preference for placement outside the home as opposed to provision of services in the child's own home [30]. None, however, focuses primarily on judicial determinations.

Nor do judicial opinions or legal scholarship provide a solid basis for generalizations about the circumstances leading courts to remove children over parental objections. Legal scholarship usually is based on reported cases. It cannot be assumed these are reliable guides to the circumstances leading to removal, for two reasons. First, juvenile and family court judges rarely dispose of cases with written opinions at all, much less reported ones. Second, although appealed cases often result in reported opinions, very few neglect cases are appealed. I estimate during the past six years that only about one in every thousand cases where a California court has ordered foster care placement has resulted in a reported appellate opinion [31]. There is no basis for assuming these cases are representative.

Despite the paucity of data, it appears that removal over parental objections takes place most often where the court determines the parents' supervision and guidance of the child are inadequate, where the mother is thought to be emotionally ill, or where the child has behavior problems [32].

Although highly publicized, cases involving child battery, where a parent has intentionally abused or injured a child, are in a distinct minority [33].

## Where the Children Go

After a court decides to remove a child from home, a public agency, often the social welfare or probation department, is assigned responsibility for placing the child. In 1933 about half of the nation's neglected children were in large institutions, and a large proportion were supervised by some religiously sponsored voluntary agency [34]. In 1970 only 42,200 children lived in foster care under the auspices of voluntary agencies, while over 284,000 were under the supervision of state social service agencies. Of the state-supervised children, 243,600 lived in foster family homes, 3,600 in group homes, and only 37,300 in child welfare institutions [35].

Foster family homes are usually licensed by the state, with regulations regarding aspects such as the size of the home, number of children, and age of foster parents. Under a contract, foster parents are paid a monthly fee for each child in their care [36]. Most foster parents, it appears, are middle- or lower-middle-class and are forty years old or older [37]. Although foster parents are responsible for the day-to-day care of the children, the contract between the agency and the foster parents usually requires the foster parents to acknowledge that "the legal responsibility for the foster child remains with the Agency," and to "accept and comply with any plans the Agency makes for the child," including "the right to determine when and how the child leaves" the foster home [38].

## How Long Do Children Remain in Foster Care?

In theory, "the distinguishing aspect of foster care is that it is designed to be a temporary arrangement. The family is broken up only so that it can be put together again in a way that will be less problematic for the child" [39]. It would be reassuring to know that children who enter foster care remain there only a short time, then either return to their parents or are adopted by some other family. Some children indeed do remain in foster care only a short period, but the evidence suggests that this pattern is the exception rather than the rule. Foster care is not typically short-term. On the basis of their analysis, Maas and Engler predicted that "better than half" of the more than 4,000 children they studied would be"living a major part of their childhood in foster families and institutions" [40]. Similarly, in a study of 624 children under twelve who entered foster care during 1966 and were there at least 90 days, Fanshel found that 46 percent were still in foster care three and one-half years later [41]. Wiltse and Gambrill recently examined a sample composed of 772 San Francisco foster children, about one-half of that city's entire caseload. They found that 62 percent of these children were expected to remain in foster care until maturity; the average length of time in care for all the children in their sample was nearly five years [42]. One juvenile judge has written about his surprise at the beginning of his term when he found that many of the neglected children under his jurisdiction had been in "temporary" foster care for five to six years [43].

One way the state might minimize the length of time children remain in foster care is to work intensively with the natural parents to correct the deficiency which led to coercive removal. However, natural parents are rarely offered rehabilitative services after the children are removed. In examining foster care in nine communities, Maas and Engler found that:

> More than 70 percent of the fathers and mothers of the children in this study either had no relationship with the agencies responsible for the care of their children or their relationship was erratic or untrusting. In many instances the agencies' resources were such that their staff's time was entirely consumed with the day-to-day job of caring for the children. They had no time for the kind of continuous work with the parents of the children which could effect the rehabilitation of the home. Frequently agencies fail to appreciate the dynamics of intrafamily relationships as a whole and work only with the child. [44]

Interviews for the last six months with a number of social workers in Northern California suggest that after removal, caseworkers focus attention almost exclusively on the child and the foster parents, spending little if any time with the natural parents. This may reflect lack of clarity about the parental default which must be corrected, or absence of available techniques or resources to correct the deficiencies, or both.

Whether or not rehabilitative services would help, the present reality is such that for "only a fraction of children now in foster care is there a possibility of return to their own homes" [45]. Wiltse and Gambrill found in their San Francisco study that return to home was expected in only fifteen percent of the cases [46]; Maas and Engler concluded on the basis of their study of 4,281 children in nine communities that for "no more than twenty-five percent" was it probable that the foster child would return home [47].

Although many foster children never return to their natural parents, long-term plans that would provide these children with a sense of security and stability are seldom made and rarely implemented. One study concluded that "for nearly two-thirds (sixty-four percent) of the children in foster care the public agencies reported that the only plan was continuation in foster care" [48]. Moreover, because neither the foster parents nor the agency is under an obligation to keep the child where originally placed, children are often moved from one foster home to another [49]. Adoption probably provides the best chance for stability and continuity. It creates the same legal relationship between child and adult in terms of custody, support, discipline, and inheritance as exists between a parent and a biologically-related, legitimate child. But very few foster children are ever adopted. In one study of foster children supervised by public agencies, only thirteen percent of the children were considered likely to be adopted [50]. Social welfare agencies are frequently reluctant to place foster children for adoption because this requires final termination of the natural parents' legal rights, an act that necessitates a separate legal proceeding often involving more stringent standards than those used for the initial removal. Wishing to avoid anything drastic, and uncertain of their legal ability to act, these agencies do nothing, and, as more time goes by, adoption becomes less possible [51]. Indeed, it appears that after a child has been in foster care for more than eighteen months, the chance of either returning home or being adopted is remote [52].

In summary, children removed by the state from the home of their parents are often destined to remain in limbo until adulthood, the wards of a largely indifferent state. On the one hand, they frequently are unable to return to their natural parents, who are offered little rehabilitative help. On the other hand, they are usually placed with a foster family and cautioned not to become too attached. These children thus grow up without a permanent and secure home.

## WHAT IS WRONG WITH THE BEST INTERESTS STANDARD?

We now turn to a close examination of the "bests interests of the child" test, the legal standard usually employed by courts to decide whether a child should be removed from parental custody in the dispositional stage of neglect proceedings. This standard has long been used to decide matters of child custody, particularly in disputes between parents. In an opinion written nearly fifty years ago, Benjamin Cardozo described as follows the role of the judge in any child custody proceeding brought before a court of equity:

> He acts as *parens patriae* to do what is best for the interest of the child. He is to put himself in the position of a "wise, affectionate,

> and careful parent" . . . and make provision for the child accordingly. He may act at the intervention of a kinsman, if so the petition comes before him, but equally he may act at the instance or on the motion of any one else. He is not adjudicating a controversy between adversary parties, to compare their private differences. He is not determining rights "as between a parent and a child"; or as between one parent and another . . . He "interferes for the protection of infants, *qua* infants, by virtue of the prerogative which belongs to the Crown as *parens patriae*." [53]

Cardozo's description appears in a decision involving a dispute between estranged parents over who should have custody of the children. Today some version of the best interests standard is incorporated in the divorce legislation of nearly every state [54]. But Cardozo's expansive language makes it easy to understand how the test could be applied not only in disputes between parents, but also in neglect proceedings. Presently, the best interests test is widely used to decide what should be done for a child over whom a juvenile court has assumed jurisdiction [55], indeed it is sometimes used to decide whether jurisdiction should be assumed [56].

For the dispositional decision in neglect cases, the best interests test would appear to have much to commend it. It focuses principally on the child rather than on arbitrary legal rights of parents. It implicitly recognizes that each child is unique, and that parental conduct and home environments may have substantially different effects on different children. It also seems to require that the judge find out as much as possible about the child, the child's circumstances, the parents, and the available alternative arrangements. In fact, the best interests standard embodies what David Matza has described as a basic precept of juvenile court philosophy: the principle of "individualized justice." This principle requires each dispositional decision, in Matza's words, "to be guided by a *full understanding* of the client's personal and social characteristics and by his 'individual needs' " [57].

Nonetheless, a careful analysis reveals serious deficiencies in the best interests test when it is used to decide whether the state should remove a child from parental custody and place the child in foster care. I will discuss some of the test's shortcomings as it is applied in foster care cases.

## Conceptual Problems with the Test

One obvious objection to the best interests of the child test is that by its very terms it ignores completely the interests of the parents. Obviously a child's parents have important interests at stake when the state seeks to intervene; a parent can derive important satisfactions and pleasures from a relationship with a child, and the destruction of this relationship can have an enormous effect on the parent quite apart from benefits or losses to the child. I doubt whether courts ignore the effects of judicial action on parents, but the best interests of the child test disallows explicit consideration of parental interests, making the process more high-sounding, perhaps, but less honest.

But even if we assume that it is appropriate to focus attention exclusively on the child's interests, there remain conceptual difficulties with the best interests test. Its application assumes the judge will compare the probable consequences for the child of remaining in the home with the probable consequences of removal. How might a judge make this comparison? He or she would need considerable information and predictive ability. The information would include knowledge of how the parents had behaved in the past, the effect of this parental behavior on the child, and the child's present condition. Then the judge would need to predict the probable future behavior of the parents if the child were to remain in the home and to gauge the probable effects of his behavior on the child. Obviously, more than one outcome is possible, so the judge would have to assess the probability of various outcomes and evaluate the seriousness of possible benefits and harms associated with each. Next, the judge would have to compare this set of possible consequences with those if the child were placed in a foster home. This would require predicting the effect of removing the child from home, school, friends, and familiar surroundings, as well as predicting the child's experience while in the foster care system. Such predictions involve estimates of the child's future relationship with the foster parents, the child's future contact with natural parents and siblings, the number of foster homes in which the child ultimately will have to be placed, the length of time spent in foster care, the potential for acquiring a stable home, and myriad other factors.

Obviously one can question whether a judge has the necessary information. In many instances he or she lacks adequate information even about a child's life with his or her parents. Moreover, at the time of the dispositional hearing, the judge typically has *no* information about where the child will be placed if removal is ordered; he or she usually knows nothing about the characteristics of the foster family, or how long that family will want or be able to keep the child. In deciding who should raise a particular child, the court in a neglect proceeding is comparing an existing family with a largely unknown alternative. In this regard, the dispositional phase of a neglect proceeding stands in sharp contrast with a divorce custody dispute, where the best interests test is also widely employed. In a divorce custody contest, the judge is settling a dispute between two adults, usually both before the court, each of whom had a prior relationship with the child and each of whom wishes to assume full parental authority [58]. In a neglect case, the judge is deciding in a state-initiated proceeding whether to remove a child from parental custody and have the state assume responsibility by placing the child in a state-sponsored home about which the judge knows few, if any, particulars.

Even if the judge had substantial information about both the child's existing home life and the foster care alternatives, our knowledge about human behavior provides no basis for the predictions called for by the best interest standard. No consensus exists about a theory of human behavior, and no theory is widely considered capable of generating reliable predictions about the psychological and behavioral consequences of alternative dispositions. This does not imply a criticism of the behavioral sciences. Indeed, Anna Freud, who has devoted her life to the study of the child and who plainly believes that theory can be a useful guide to treatment, has warned that theory alone does not provide a reliable guide for prediction: "In spite of . . . advances," she suggests, "there remain factors which make clinical foresight, i.e., prediction, difficult and hazardous," not the least of which is that "the environmental happenings in a child's life will always remain unpredictable since they are not governed by any known laws . . . " [59].

The limitations of psychological theory in generating verifiable predictions is suggested by the numerous studies which have attempted to trace effects of various child-rearing techniques and parental attitudes on adult personality traits. Under Sigmund Freud's influence, many psychologists have assumed the importance of a child's early years, searching for the importance of timing and techniques of nursing, weaning, toilet training, and the like. But in Sibylle Escalona's words:

> The net result of a great many studies can be compressed into a single sentence: When child-rearing techniques of this order are treated as the independent variable, no significant relationship can be shown to exist between child-rearing techniques and later personality characteristics. Some parental attitudes do relate to child characteristics at school age and in adolescence, but no significant relationships have been demonstrated between parental attitudes towards a child during the first three or four years of life and the child's later characteristics. [60]

Studies that have attempted to trace personality development to specific antecedent variables have assumed that a particular practice would have the same effect on different children. This assumption is now widely questioned by experimental psychologists such as H.R. Schaffer. Schaffer and others think that infants experience in individual ways [61]. The implication of this for prediction is described very well by Arlene Skolnick: ". . . if the child selectively interprets situations and events, we cannot confidently predict behavior from knowledge of the situation alone" [62].

The difficulty of making accurate predictions is shown clearly by a study undertaken by Joan Macfarlane and her associates in Berkeley, California [63]. Using various tests and interviews, the Berkeley group studied during a thirty-year period a group of 166 infants born in 1929. Their objective was to observe the growth—emotional, mental, and physical—of normal people. As Skolnick observed:

> Over the years this study has generated several significant research findings, but the most surprising of all was the difficulty of predicting what thirty-year-old adults would be like even after the most sophisticated data had been gathered on them as children. . . . the researchers experienced shock after shock as they saw the people they had last seen at age eighteen. It turned out that the predictions they had made about the subjects were wrong in about two-thirds of the cases! How could a group of competent psychologists have been so mistaken?
>
> Foremost, the researchers had tended to overestimate the damaging effects of early troubles of various kinds. Most personality theory had been derived from observations of troubled people in therapy. The pathology of adult neurotics and psychotics was traced back to disturbances early in childhood—poor parent-child relations, chronic school difficulties, and so forth. Consequently, theories of personality based on clinical observation tended to define adult psychological problems as socialization failures. But the psychiatrist sees only disturbed people; he does not encounter "normal" individuals who may experience childhood difficulties but who do not grow into troubled adults. The Berkeley method, however, called for studying such people. Data on the experience of these subjects demonstrated the error of assuming that similar childhood conditions affect every child the same way. Indeed, many instances of what looked like severe pathology to the researchers were put to constructive use by the subjects. . . . [64]

Even if accurate predictions were possible, a fundamental problem would remain. What set of values is a judge to use to determine what is in the child's best interests? Should the judge be concerned with happiness? Or should he or she worry about the child's spiritual goodness or economic productivity? Are stability and security for a child more desirable than intellectual stimulation [65]? Should the best interests of the child be viewed from a short-term or a long-term perspective? The conditions that make a person happy at age ten or fifteen may have adverse consequences at age thirty.

The neglect statutes themselves are of little help in providing guidance about the values that should inform the decision. And, our pluralistic society lacks consensus about child-rearing strategies and values. By necessity, a judge is forced to rely upon personal values to determine a child's best interests.

## The Problem of Fairness

What is wrong, one may ask, with reliance on individual values and judgments? For one thing, it offends a most basic precept of law. As John Rawls wrote: the rule of law "implies the precept that similar cases be treated similarly" [66]. This aspiration is not always met, but any legal test that requires impossible predictions and reliance on the decision-makers' own values invites injustice.

As long as the best interests standard or some equally broad standard is used, it seems inevitable that petitions will be filed and neglect cases will be decided without any clear articulation or consistent application of the behavioral or moral premises on which the decision is based. This conclusion is supported by a simulation study which analyzed the factors influencing a judge's decision whether to provide a child with services within the child's own home or to remove the child [67]. Three judges, each with at least five years experience, were independently given the actual files for 94 children from 50 families. Each judge was asked to decide whether the child should be removed or services should be provided. The three agreed in less than one-half of the cases (45 out of 94). Even more significantly, when the judges were asked to indicate the factors influencing their decisions, the study concluded, "Even in cases in which they agreed on the decision, the judges did not identify the same factors as determinants, each seeming to operate to some extent within his own unique value system" [68].

A judge's reliance on personal values is especially risky when class differences confound the problem. The foster care system is frequently accused of being class biased, one "in which middle-class professionals provide and control a service used mostly by poor people, with upper-lower and lower-middle class foster parents serving as intermediaries" [69]. The fact that most foster children come from poor families does not, of course, prove that there is an inherent class bias in the system. There are other plausible explanations for the high proportion of poor children. The condition of poverty may lead to family breakdown and a greater likelihood that children are endangered in times of crisis. Alternatively, since poor families are more subject to scrutiny by social workers who administer welfare programs, their faults, even if no more common, may be more conspicuous. Finally, since poor families have access to few resources in the event of family crisis, their children may be forced into the foster care system because other forms of substitute care, such as babysitters, relatives, and day care centers, are not available [70].

Although these other explanations are plausible, the fact remains that the best interests standard allows the judge to import his personal values into the process, and leaves considerable scope for class bias. An examination of available reported cases dramatically illustrates how a judge's attitude toward child rearing, sexual mores, religion, or cleanliness can affect the result of court proceedings. These cases, while not typical, clearly reveal the risks of "individualized" decisions under vague judicial standards. There are a number of reported cases, for example, where a judge has decided parental behavior was immoral and, without any systematic inquiry into how the parental conduct damaged or was likely to harm the children, the judge then determined the children to be neglected and removed them from their home [71]. A New York judge declared five small children neglected, and ordered custody to be transferred to the father on the ground that the mother "frequently entertained male companions in the apartment . . . and, on at least one occasion, one of them spent the night with the (mother) and, in fact, slept with her, to the knowledge of the children." The court openly acknowledged:

> The statutory definition of neglect, therefore, being in general terms, has resulted in a dearth of cases reported; and the tendency has been to leave it to the judge in a particular case to make his own decision as to whether or not there is neglect, based upon the particular and unique set of facts in the case at bar. It therefore has developed upon the courts to establish the moral standards to be followed by persons to whom is entrusted the care and custody of children. And never has there been a greater need for the courts to maintain a high level of moral conduct than exists today. This court intends to give more than lip service to the principle that the fabric of our society is composed of the family unit and when the family unit is damaged, the fabric of society suffers. Our courts will continue to insist upon a high level of moral conduct on the

> part of custodians of children, and will never succumb to the "Hollywood" type of morality so popular today, which seems to condone and encourage the dropping of our moral guard. We have not yet reached the point where, when parents who have tired of each other's company, may be free to seek other companionship with complete disregard of the moral examples they are setting for their children. This is the crux of the case at bar. [72]

In deciding whether to remove a child from parental custody, various other judges have thought it relevant that a mother had extramarital sexual relations [73], was a lesbian [74], or had several illegitimate children [75]. Religion, like sex, has also triggered strong responses from judges. Religious fanaticism and unconventional beliefs of parents [76] have been considered relevant factors in neglect proceedings.

Finally, there are cases where a child is removed from his parental home because the court determines the *physical conditions* in the home are unsuitable for the child. In a recent California case, an appellate court affirmed a juvenile court decision removing children from a dirty home. The parents claimed there was no evidence showing that the children had been harmed, but the appeals court maintained that the state "was not required, as appellants assert, to prove that the conditions of the above cause 'sickness and disease of mind or body' in order to establish 'neglect' . . . the welfare of the child is of paramount concern, and a purpose of the juvenile court law is to secure for each minor such care and guidance as will serve the spiritual, emotional, mental, and physical welfare of the minor and the best interests of the state" [77]. Some "dirty homes" may seriously endanger a child's growth and well-being, but most may merely offend middle-class sensibilities. One suspects courts may sometimes be enforcing middle-class norms of cleanliness where both economic and cultural circumstances make it both unfair and inappropriate [78].

During the past ten years there have been several appellate court decisions [79] rejecting extreme attempts by trial court judges to use neglect laws "to impose middle-class mores upon families and to punish a parent's undesirable conduct unless that conduct can be shown to result in damage to the child" [80]. For two reasons, however, these cases do not significantly limit the discretion of the judge who hears the case. First, the appellate decisions suggesting that specific factors are not appropriate for consideration also emphasize the continuing need for individualized determinations and wide latitude for trial judges [81]. Second, juvenile court judges can often disguise a decision based on an "improper" factor by vague recitation of general language. The real reasons may be very different than the stated ones.

David Matza thought individual treatment in juvenile court dispositions was a "mystification" and his observations have relevance to the best interests standard:

> To the extent that it prevails, its function is to obscure the process of decision and disposition rather than enlighten it. The principle of individualized justice results in a frame of relevance that is so large, so all-inclusive, that any relation between the criteria of judgment and the disposition remains obscure. [82]

## The Risks of Foster Care Placement

The best interests test also makes it too easy for a judge to ignore the possible detrimental effects of removing a child from parental custody. The dangers of leaving a child at home often seem compelling, and because the judge is often unaware of or unable to evaluate the psychological risks of foster care, an individualized determination under a best interests standard may be biased in favor of removal. An assessment of the risks involved in separating children from their parents requires explicit knowledge of the foster care system. What happens to foster children? Are they happy while in foster care? What harm, both short-term and long-term, can result from being put into this system? How many children "fail" in foster homes?

Since predictions of how an individual child will fare in foster care have not proved reliable [83], there is no reason to believe a judge can accurately assess the risks of placement. For the social scientist, analysis of the differential effects of foster placement on a child's development raises severe methodological problems; these include defining a control group, establishing a standard of "successful development," and isolating the factors responsible for any noticeable effects. No studies prove either that foster care benefits or harms children. The most famous longitudinal study, published in 1924, traces what happened to 910 former foster children who had spent one year or more in a foster home. The research question was, "Has the subject shown himself capable (or incapable) of managing himself and his affairs with ordinary prudence" [84]? The results of the study showed 615 subjects (67.5 percent) as "capable," 182 subjects (20.0 percent) as "incapable," and 113 subjects (12.5 percent) as of "unknown capability." Needless to say, criteria for success were defined in only the most vague and arbitrary terms. Moreover, one cannot judge whether these results were good or bad without a control group, and definition of such a group presents overwhelming problems. More recent studies have not been able to overcome the methodological difficulties nor provide definitive answers about the long-range effects of foster care [85].

Empirical studies *do* exist, however, to illustrate the conditions of children while in foster care. These suggest there is "rather persuasive, if still incomplete, evidence that throughout the United States children in foster care are experiencing high rates of psychiatric disturbance" [86]. Maas and Engler, for example, in their study, found that "forty to fifty percent or more of the children in foster care in every one of our nine communities showed symptoms of maladjustment" [87]. Other studies concur with this finding [88].

The factors responsible for the emotional problems observed in foster care are difficult to isolate. For years, the effects of "separation trauma" were studied [89], with the argument that the "act of placement in itself creates what is known as a separation trauma" and therefore may be harmful [90]. Many psychologists would agree.

> Any child who is compelled for whatever reason to leave his own home and family and to live in foster placement lives through an experience pregnant with pain and terror for him and potentially damaging to his personality and normal growth. It is abnormal in our society for a child to be separated for any continuing length of time from his own parents and no one knows this so well as the child himself. For him placement is a shocking and bewildering calamity, the reasons for which he usually does not understand. [91]

Later, some psychologists modified this position arguing that children who remained in their own homes with neglectful or indifferent mothers experienced greater psychological harm than children in foster homes [92]. However, when researchers observed the effects of separation on older children, concern was again expressed about the risks of removing a child for placement in foster care [93]. Although the debate is far from over, it is generally assumed that separation carries substantial risks for the child, risks that are related to the age of the child at the time of separation. Concern has been expressed particularly about children separated between six months and three years of age, at about six years of age and at puberty [94].

Another way the foster care system itself may cause psychological harm involves the anomalous position of a child within a foster home. "Family life can be complex indeed for the foster child" [95]. The child often experiences conflict over which set of parents, natural or foster, to trust and rely on when in trouble. Moreover, the child may observe power struggles among the natural and foster parents, the social workers, and the judge, each of whom has a reason to be concerned about the child's care and future. A foster home is supposed to provide, insofar as possible, a normal family environment. But agencies often become concerned if the foster parents grow too attached to a child. In one case, the highest state court in New York approved the transfer of a child from a foster home to an unknown alternative because the foster parents "had become too emotionally involved with the child" [96]. The court upheld an agency determination "that the child's best interests necessitated her placement in another environment where she would not be torn between her loyalty to her mother and her boarding parents" [97]. Although the effects of ambiguous relationships are impossible to measure, there is a good theoretical argument and some suggestive evidence that a child's basic security and ability to form other relationships are shaken when he or she is torn by conflicting expectations and loyalties [98]. Lack of a solid identity, which most children acquire largely in their relationship with their parents, perhaps causes the most harm [99]. "Without an adequate conception of who he is, where he is, and why he is there, it is difficult to see how the foster child could develop well in a situation that is as complex and problematic as placement" [100].

A third psychologically detrimental factor in foster care is the instability of the system itself. As noted earlier, children are often moved from home to home [101], and there is rapid turnover of social workers [102] and judges [103] involved in the case. Studies strongly indicate that personality problems are more frequent among children who have been moved often [104]; Maas and Engler, for example, concluded that "instability in relationships fosters personality disturbances" [105]. On the other hand, the frequency of moves may depend on the child's adjustment before he or she even enters foster care: a "disturbed child who enters foster care is more likely to experience more numerous replacements, and his symptoms increase accordingly" [106]. Whatever the reason, both former foster children and experienced social workers agree that moving a child from foster home to foster home is a painful and at times damaging experience [107].

## Present Legal Standards Fail to Make Removal a Last Resort

It would seem that foster care entails substantial risks of psychological harm. This does not imply that a legal standard should be adopted to make it impossible to take children from their parents and place them in foster care. But it does suggest a child's life may not be improved by removal unless the dangers of remaining at home are immediate and substantial and there are no means of protecting the child within the home.

Placing a child away from home is often referred to as a "last resort," but in fact most communities offer few preventive or protective services for children within the home while a family is helped through a crisis. Day care or baby sitting services, along with parental counseling, might make removal unnecessary in a wide variety of circumstances; such services typically are unavailable. A national survey conducted by the American Humane Association in 1967 concluded that "*no state* and *no community* has developed a child protective service program adequate in size to meet the service needs of all *reported* cases of child neglect, abuse, and exploitation" [108]. Even when such services are available, neglect statutes and the best interests standard do not require that before ordering removal a court conduct an inquiry into whether the child can be protected if left in parental custody [109]. Anecdotal evidence strongly suggests that children are often placed in foster care without a careful analysis of whether less drastic forms of intervention might be preferable. Thus, for instance, children have been placed in foster care because their parents' home is filthy even though a homemaker's services might have remedied the situation and done so at far less cost to the state [110]. Also, an undernourished child may be taken from the home without any prior effort to educate the parents about nutritional needs [111]. Even in child abuse cases, where removal from the home is very likely, many experts believe that the child can often be left safely at home if the parents receive appropriate treatment and support [112].

Removal would seem appropriate only when there are no means to protect the child within the home. Given the size and quality of present institutional arrangements for children who are removed, and given the widely shared view that parents, not the state, should ordinarily be responsible for child rearing, any legal standard should incorporate a substantial presumption favoring a parent who has expressly indicated that he or she wishes to retain custody. Because of the importance of the parent-child relationship and because of the risks of removal, I believe the state should not be allowed to remove children unless less drastic means of intervention cannot protect the child.

## Is Judicial Application of the Best Interests Standard the Issue?

My analysis has been couched largely in terms of how *judges* behave in the *dispositional* phase of neglect proceedings. Despite problems with the best interests standard, it might be thought that the statutory standards determining when a juvenile court should assume *jurisdiction* are sufficiently stringent to exclude all but the most extreme cases from the dispositional phase of any juvenile court proceeding. But the jurisdictional phase of the court's proceeding provides no such safeguard. As already noted, some courts now appear to use the best interests standard for determining jurisdiction [113]. As indicated earlier, the statutory standards for jurisdiction are extremely vague and broad, and require findings of parental unfitness or neglect [114]. These standards provide no more guidance to a court than does best interests and do little to limit judicial discretion. Indeed, the jurisdictional provisions have been subject to a steady barrage of criticism in the legal literature for the last two decades [115].

Finally, and I think this is the nub of the problem, the jurisdictional decision is the same whether a court is going to supervise the child within the home or remove the child. Consequently, to assume jurisdiction need not in itself be seen as a particularly important decision. My own strong impression based on interviews and courtroom observation is that the judge and social worker consider the dispositional decision of whether to remove the child from the home as the key issue and that courts are not at all reluctant to assume jurisdiction. The fact that the juvenile courts assume jurisdiction in a very high percentage of cases suggests the same conclusion [116].

It might be argued that social workers, probation officers, psychologists, and psychiatrists involved in the foster care system actually are the ones who decide when children should be removed, and that standards governing the judicial process therefore are of secondary importance. It may be true that judges rely on the advice of these other professionals. But deciding the direction of the causal link is no easy matter, since social workers are known to sometimes shape their recommendations according to what they think a particular judge will want to decide. In all events, the same problems that plague a judge plague these professionals too: lack of information, lack of predictive models, and the need to rely on individual values.

## THE AGENDA FOR LAW REFORM

Is there something better than the "best interests of the child" standard? Can an adequate legal standard be developed, given our limited knowledge of human behavior, our pluralistic value system, and the realities of present foster care arrangements? Any standard devised will necessarily involve values—values that can be questioned and attacked. But it is essential that the new standard expose for analysis what is now hidden behind the "best interests" shield. I believe any new standard must be premised on three basic principles, implicit in much of the previous discussion.

> 1. Removal should be only when the child cannot be protected within the home.
>
> 2. To the extent possible, the decision to require foster care placement should be based on legal standards that can be applied in a consistent and even-handed way.

3. The state should make every effort to provide children who must be removed with as much continuity and stability as possible.

## Two Unlikely Solutions

Against the backdrop of these principles, it is useful to analyze why two plausible methods of legal reform hold no great promise. These are, first, stricter enforcement of criminal child neglect statutes and, second, additional procedural safeguards in neglect proceedings. Every state now has criminal child neglect, abuse, or cruelty statutes. Better articulation or enforcement of these standards of minimum parental conduct, and greater use of criminal sanctions, will not improve the foster care system and will do little or nothing to correct the causes of child neglect, and does not serve two goals of criminal law, deterrence and rehabilitation. Insofar as poverty and emotional problems are at the root of many child neglect cases, increased reliance on the criminal sanction would probably be counter-productive [117], and would have little deterrent effect. "A command impossible to fulfill does not alter the incentives of the person subject to it" [118]. A jail sentence provides no rehabilitation for the parent and at the same time forces a separation betrween the parent and child. Retribution against the parent is achieved, but at what cost to the child?

There also have been frequent proposals in dependency and neglect cases for procedural reform [119]. Presently, neglect proceedings are highly informal. Few parents, and far fewer children, are represented by counsel; typically hearsay evidence of all sorts is admissible. The trial court often decides neglect cases without insisting on specific findings to reveal the basis for its determinations. Appellate review, infrequently sought, usually results in a rubber stamp affirmation of the trial court's decisions, particularly with regard to dispositional determinations. This procedural picture is not a happy one. Convincing arguments can be advanced that due process requires something more [120]. I believe that certain procedural reforms might have beneficial effects. If lawyers were introduced into the process, for instance, they might play a significant role in finding witnesses, presenting evidence, and suggesting alternative dispositions not considered by the state's social workers. If judges in turn were required to make factual findings, the involvement of lawyers in the process might make judges more self-conscious about how their values affect their decisions. Also, procedural reforms would impose higher transaction costs on an agency seeking to remove a child, perhaps reducing the number of petitions filed or limiting them to the most egregious cases.

But procedural reform alone cannot correct the fundamental fault in the system: the court's wide discretion [121]. Imagine a procedural reform guaranteeing parent and child separate legal representation in all neglect cases. How would the child's advocate determine what to advocate under a best interests standard? Ordinarily, a lawyer can look to the client for direction, and if the child is fourteen years old or even seven years old, the child is an appropriate source for information, even guidance. But a majority of children involved in neglect proceedings are younger. A lawyer with a very young client is placed in a position not dissimilar to that of the judge. He must make his own set of predictions and use his own set of values to ascertain what is in the child's best interests, and then advocate that position. The judge might agree with the lawyer's recommendation, but why should we assume the lawyer's recommendation is any more appropriate than the judge's would be? In all events, if the judge reaches some other conclusion, the chances of reversing this decision in an appellate court are slight. If the best interests standard is applied, even with additional procedural safeguards at the hearing, appellate courts will continue to give wide latitude to the trial court's individualized decision.

## The Direction of Legal Change

First priority for legal reform must involve changing the underlying legal standard for removal. Although I will not attempt here to formulate a definitive legal standard, the direction of change is clear; judicial discretion to remove children should be more limited, and if possible the standard should be made more objective. One example of such a standard would be the following:

> A state may remove a child from parental custody without parental consent only if the state first proves: a) there is an immediate and substantial danger to the child's health; and b) there are no reasonable means by which the state can protect the child's health without removing the child from parental custody.

Before removing the child, I would further require the court to specify in writing the basis for the conclusion that the child was immediately and substantially in danger, with an explanation of which less drastic means of intervention had been contemplated, and why these were inadequate for the child's protection. Unlike the best interests test, the proposed standard is very explicit in its value premises; children are to be left at home except when there is real danger to them. It would take courts away from evaluating parental morality or sexual conduct, except in those rare cases when the child's health is endangered by it. The test would also focus judicial inquiry on whether the child could be protected within the home. A dirty-home case would no longer justify removal, because the state could usually protect the child by sending in a homemaker or housekeeper. Similarly, a child who was malnourished because a mother did not know anything about nutritional needs could be protected either by having a social worker teach the mother about nutrition, or by having someone sent into the home to prepare the child's meals.

Within the context of these new standards, additional procedural safeguards, such as separate counsel for the parents and the child, are desirable. When removal is sought, the attorney for the state would have the burden of demonstrating why the child's health is endangered and why the child cannot be protected within the home. Counsel for the parents would attempt to show why the child is not in danger, and would propose alternative methods that might allow the family to remain intact. Counsel for the child might sometimes side with the parents, other times advocate alternative services, or other times urge removal. The child's lawyer would be responsible for evaluating the case after consulting with the child and making an independent investigation.

In addition, requiring the trial judge to make findings on these issues could make appellate review of the initial determination more meaningful. Although appellate courts would not often second guess a judge's conclusions about a witness's credibility, appellate review could serve an important role in defining how much danger was sufficient to justify intervention, and how far the state would have to go in providing alternatives. Indeed, standards of general applicability could evolve by a process not unlike that of common law.

The trial judge's role under the proposed standard would still not be easy. Judges would face the problem of predicting when the risks to the child were so great that the stricter standard for removal would be met. The terms "immediate" and "substantial" are not self-defining and would require interpretation. Nevertheless, the proposed standard is much more restrictive than existing standards. The justification for a more restrictive standard was best put by Ernst Freund, who observed: "in the absence of scientific certainty it must be borne in mind that the farther back from the point of imminent danger the law draws the safety line of police regulation, so much the greater is the possibility that legislative interference is unwarranted" [122].

The term "health" poses particularly difficult policy issues. When there is an immediate and substantial danger to a child's *physical* health and the child cannot be protected at home, it is reasonable to predict that his or her lot will be improved by placement in foster care. Foster care does a reasonable job of protecting a child's physical health. But there is, of course, good reason to be concerned about a child's emotional health as well. Regarding the mental health of the child, it strikes me as extraordinarily difficult to predict when a child is emotionally endangered. Moreover, there is no evidence whatsoever that foster care is psychologically therapeutic. I am therefore very concerned that individualized determinations concerning emotional health could, on balance, do more harm than good by introducing a highly speculative element into the process. On balance I think "health" should be limited to "physical health," although this is a very difficult issue and requires more thought.

Another policy problem associated with the new standard relates to the question of how far a state must go in order to demonstrate that alternatives to removal will not work. The economic questions posed here are not trivial. For example, what if the means of protecting the child in the home are extraordinarily expensive? In a dirty-home case, what if a child could be protected only if a full-time maid were available in the house? The word "reasonable" allows the court to take into account the costs of alternatives, and to consider the economic question in the context of a specific case. Two general observations should be made, however. Because the costs of foster care are substantial, always several thousand dollars per year [123], any method of protecting the child within the home which costs less than foster care would certainly be reasonable. I do not think it would be reasonable for a state to allow the level of resources available for home-based services to vary substantially among local jurisdictions merely because their capacity to raise revenue differs.

One clear goal of the new standard is to require states to devote more resources to the protection of children within the home. It is important that certain types of services such as homemakers, housekeepers, and public health nurses be available. But one unintended consequence of the proposed standard might be that the state would neither provide services to protect children within their homes, nor remove them when they are in danger. If this were the state's response the situation might well end up worse than it is today. Children who need protection would be left in danger. Fortunately, I think this response is unlikely, both because of public concern about children and because of the vested political interest of the existing social welfare bureaucracy.

## Standard for Stability

A principal objective of law reform should be to establish a legal process ensuring a greater degree of stability for the child. For children who must be removed, there should be a statutory requirement fixing the maximum length of time they can remain in "temporary" foster care. The most direct way of doing this would be to require the judge at the end of a *fixed* period (perhaps twelve or eighteen months after placement) to choose between returning the child to the parents and placing the child either in an adoptive home or some other stable long-term environment. To allow this, I would change existing laws to provide for final termination of parental rights at the end of the required period if the child could not be safely returned to the home, and if the state had made reasonable efforts to rehabilitate the parents while the child was living away from the home.

At the time of removal, I would require the state to outline to the court the services it would make available to the parents. A court hearing might be required every three months during the interim period to ensure that the social welfare agency reported on its efforts and results. I would also put the burden on the state at these interim hearings to show that the child could not be safely returned to the home [124]. If the child could not safely be returned home at the end of the statutory period, adoption would be the favored alternative. Some foster children would be difficult to place for adoption because of age, health, or behavior. Subsidized adoption would be an appropriate way to expand adoption possibilities. Short of adoption, certain other alternatives exist which are rarely employed today. Several years ago it was suggested, for instance, that social welfare agencies should encourage the grant of legal guardianship to foster parents who had a long-term interest in a child [125]. Guardians do not have a legal duty to support a child from their own funds, but unlike foster parents they do have the legal right to custody of the child and do have powers much like normal parents with regard to the everyday guidance and control over the child's life. Guardianship thus would promote a degree of continuity often lacking in foster care.

I am not prepared to state categorically what the fixed time unit should be when the court must make a permanent decision. Although no recent national data are available, Maas and Engler found that most children who are in foster care for more than eighteen months never return home. This suggests the necessity of research for the development of such criteria. It might be possible to develop different time limits for different kinds of cases. But in all events, the fixed time limit should be established at the time of removal on the basis of criteria that could be consistently and fairly applied. For example, a shorter period might be appropriate for very young children [126]. Future research might show that rehabilitative prognosis of the family in certain identifiable types of cases is sufficiently poor to allow a quick decision. The great advantage of a fixed time period rather than an open-ended one is that it eventually requires courts and social welfare agencies to make permanent plans. In the past, periodic review procedures have not been sufficient to break bureaucratic inertia. Instead, routine extensions have been the rule.

Any fixed time period is necessarily arbitrary; a slightly longer or shorter period might be better for a particular case, and inevitably some parents' rights will be finally terminated even though with more time they might have been able to pull themselves and their families together. Nevertheless, I think this method is more desirable on balance than a system based on individualized determinations giving a judge the discretion to leave children in the limbo of foster care, granting extension after extension even though it is highly improbable that the child will return home.

The proposed standard also does much more than the present law to require the state to work with the natural parents in the home situation after removal. By working with parents, social welfare agencies could acquire information to assess what should be done for the child at the end of the statutory period. This raises difficult questions of confidentiality; if the state has access to information from the parents' therapy, for example, this may in itself inhibit the therapy. On the other hand, the state has a very substantial interest in making permanent plans for the child with the best information possible.

## How Reform Can Occur

Litigation has been used to challenge existing neglect statutes, on the ground that they are unconstitutionally vague [127] and on the ground that the state has ordered removal without first assessing whether the child could be protected within the home [128]. To my knowledge no court has upheld either kind of claim. But the legal arguments available for such challenges are substantial, and a victory would move the operation of the system in the right direction. Alternatively, a state court might interpret existing neglect statutes to allow removal only under the circumstances described in the new standard. Although litigation is a possible avenue for improvement, reforms along the lines outlined here can be best achieved through new legislation. The American Bar Association has spurred legislative reform recently by establishing a Juvenile Justice Standards Project. This project will make a comprehensive reassessment of laws relating to minors, reexamining among other things all the legal standards concerning dependent and neglected children [127].

## Conclusions

The standards proposed in this article are intended to limit the wide discretion presently given to the professionals involved in the foster care system. There are costs associated with limiting this discretion. Some children who would substantially benefit from placement in foster care might be excluded from the system under the new standard. Similarly, there would undoubtedly be parents whose rights would be terminated under the proposed standard who might, given more time, have been able to work things out. The underlying issue, however, is whether we would have a fairer system, and one that on balance was more helpful to children.

Although this article has been directed primarily at the problems of children who are coercively removed from their parents, the analysis has broader implications, particularly for children who are "voluntarily" placed in state-sponsored foster care with the consent of the natural parents. Usually there is no court supervision of these children, even though from the *child's* perspective, placement is no less coercive simply because the state and parents agree. While state provision of foster care for children whose parents seek it may often be desirable, it must be remembered many children voluntarily placed remain in the limbo of foster care for years. In San Francisco, for example, the average stay for these children appears to be slightly *longer* on average than for court-ordered placements [130]. Moreover, social workers have suggested in interviews that many parents who voluntarily place their children are ambivalent about wanting to raise them, but also feel guilty about waiving parental responsibility. Consequently, they often are unwilling either to keep their children at home or to allow a stable alternative to develop. Their children, like ping pong balls, are paddled back and forth between parents and the social welfare system.

In voluntary placements, consideration should be given to imposing standards similar to those suggested for court-ordered placement. Before a child is voluntarily placed, the state might offer, but not compel, alternative services to enable the parent to keep the child at home. If placement were nevertheless desired by the parent, the parent might be told that the child can remain in such care for no more than a fixed period of time. At the end of that period, if the parent were unwilling or unable to have the child return home, the state would make another permanent arrangement for the child. While not without problems requiring further analysis, such a standard might have two benefits. First, some parents might decide to keep their children at home in the first place rather than placing them unnecessarily in the foster care system. Second, both parents and the social welfare bureaucracy would be required to make a permanent decision after a reasonable period of time.

The new standard also might have implications for dispositions in juvenile court cases where jurisdiction rests not on neglect, but on the wrongful behavior of the minor—i.e., in delinquency and "pre-delinquency" cases. In a delinquency case, for example, the critical question is often what the juvenile court judge does in the dispositional hearing. Although jurisdiction turns on the issue of whether the state has proved beyond a reasonable doubt that the minor has committed an act which for an adult would be a crime, the judge's analysis in that hearing very often focuses on neglect-type considerations: the quality of the child's home life, his relationship with his parents, etc. Many of the criticisms I have leveled against the use of an individualized "best interests" standard in the dispositional phase of neglect proceedings can be made with regard to dispositions in delinquency cases [131].

Finally, the questions examined in this article are closely related to those involved in a number of other areas of the law where officials are given the power to make coercive individualized determinations even though they lack information, theoretical tools to make predictions, proven methods of therapy, and a consensus with regard to values. The use of the best interests standard poses issues analogous to those raised by discretionary sentencing in the criminal law, where the therapeutic ideal has been used to justify giving judges, probation officers, and parole boards enormous discretion [132]. Indeterminate sentences are justified on the grounds that experts should shape the length of a prison term to the time required to bring about rehabilitation, a period which may be short or extend over many years. Similar problems are raised by the involuntary "civil" commitment of those thought to be mentally ill. In all these areas, I think it would be useful to analyze closely whether additional procedural safeguards alone can ever be enough, and whether less individualized standards might not be the more important legal reform. "Ignorance, of itself, is disgraceful only so far as it is avoidable. But when, in our eagerness to find 'better ways' of handling old problems, we rush to measures affecting human liberty and human personality on the assumption that we have knowledge which, in fact, we do not possess, then the problem of ignorance takes on a more sinister hue" [133].

In closing it is wise to acknowledge that changing the legal standard for removing children is by no means the only strategy for bringing about needed reforms in the foster care system. It is arguable, in fact, that political efforts for reform should be devoted not so much toward changing the law as toward improving the foster care system by securing additional resources and devising "better ways" of providing useful services. Certainly facilities should be improved; more public support also would be useful. Dramatic improvements in the operation of the foster care system or new information about its present effects might influence my conclusions. But in analyzing the present foster care system, I am impressed by the relevance of an observation made in another context by Francis Allen:

> We shall be told that progress is obstructed by the lack of public interest and support and by the absence of adequate funds. That these factors are real and their consequences devastating few

would care to deny. Yet, these familiar scapegoats do not provide the most fundamental explanations. We should not overlook the fact that, in many areas, our basic difficulties still lie in our ignorance of human behavior and its infinite complexities. [134]

## NOTES AND REFERENCES

1. Language in several Supreme Court opinions can be read to suggest that these are constitutional underpinnings for the primacy of the parental role. See, e.g., *Pierce v. Society of Sisters*, 268 U.S. 510, 534–35 (1925) where the court struck down an Oregon statute that required parents to send their children to public schools, stating that the statute "unreasonably interferes with the liberty of parents and guardians to direct the upbringing and education of children under their control." See also *Meyer v. Nebraska*, 262 U.S. 390 (1923). Compare *Prince v. Massachusetts*, 321 U.S. 158 (1944) where the court affirmed the child labor law conviction of an aunt who had a nine-year-old niece in her custody sell Jehovah's Witness literature at night on the street in her presence. The Court emphasized that "the state has a wide range of power for limiting parental freedom and authority in things affecting the child's welfare; and that this includes, to some extent, matters of conscience and religious conviction," *id.* at 167.
2. HEW estimates that on March 31, 1970, there were 326,700 children under eighteen in foster care, approximately 284,500 of whom were under the complete or partial auspices of a public welfare agency. Of the 284,500, 243,600 were in foster family homes; 3,600 were in group homes; and 37,300 were in child welfare institutions. An additional 42,200 children were in foster care under the auspices of voluntary child welfare agencies. See U.S. Dept. of Health, Education and Welfare, *Children Served by Public Welfare Agencies and Voluntary Child Welfare Agencies and Institutions March 1970*, Publication No. [SRS] 72-03258, March 10, 1972, Table 6.
3. U.S. Bureau of the Census, Census of Population: *1970 General Social and Economic Characteristics, United States Summary*, PC(1)-C1, (Washington, D.C.: U.S. Government Printing Office, 1972), Table 85, pp. 1–380.
4. California State Social Welfare Board, *Report on Foster Care, Children Waiting* (Sacramento, Calif.: Department of Social Welfare, 1972), p. 7.
5. See Shirley Jenkins and Mignon Sauber, *Paths to Child Placement, Family Situations Prior to Foster Care* (New York: Community Council of Greater New York, 1966), p. 74.
6. See e.g., *Escobedo v. Illinois*, 378 U.S. 478 (1964).
7. *Johnson v. Zerbst*, 304 U.S. 458 (1938).
8. See 42 U.S.C. §608(a).

9. See Robert Bremner, ed. *Children and Youth in America* (Cambridge, Mass.: Harvard University Press, 1970), I, pp. 64–70.
10. Bremner, p. 68.
11. Story, 2 *Equity Jurisprudence* Sec. 1341 (1857) (footnotes omitted from quote). For a discussion of the history of child neglect laws, see Mason P. Thomas, "Child Abuse and Neglect, Part I: Historical Overview, Legal Matrix, and Social Perspectives," *North Carolina Law Review*, 50 (1972), p. 293.
12. A recent collection of the citations to these provisions can be found in Sanford N. Katz, *When Parents Fail, The Law's Response to Family Breakdown* (Boston: Beacon Press, 1971), pp. 83–85.
13. See, e.g., Colo. Rev. Stat. Ann. Sec. 22-1-1 (1963).
14. See, e.g., Mass. Ann. Laws ch. 119, Sec. 24 (1965).
15. See, e.g., Cal. Welfare and Institutions Code Sec. 600 (d) (West 1972).
16. See, e.g., Ohio Rev. Code Ann. Sec. 2151.03(c) (1969).
17. See, e.g., Minn. Stat. Ann. 260.015 (b) (d) (1969).
18. For a historical description of how neglected children were cared for, see generally, Homer Folks, *The Care of Destitute, Neglected, and Delinquent Children* (New York: Macmillan, 1902). Various documents can be found in Robert Bremner, ed., *Children and Youth in America*, Vols. I, II(A) and II(B) (Cambridge, Mass.: Harvard University Press, 1970).
19. The child is sometimes taken into custody by the state at the time of this initial report—before any court hearing. The laws of many states authorize "emergency" removal from parental custody without prior court authorization by police, and sometimes social workers and doctors. In California, for example, a policeman with "reasonable cause for believing" the child is neglected or abused can take a child into custody without prior judicial authorization (Cal. Welfare & Institutions Code Sec. 625). The child must be released to the parents within forty-eight hours, however, unless a petition is filed to institute a juvenile court proceeding (Cal. Welfare & Institutions Code Sec. 631). Moreover, even if a petition is filed, the statute requires the court to hold a detention hearing within twenty-four hours to determine whether the child should remain in state custody during the pendency of the judicial proceedings (see Cal. Welfare & Institutions Code Sec. 632), which can often take several weeks. Because there are situations in which swift removal is of crucial importance to a child's safety, the power to remove for short periods of time without prior court approval seems plainly desirable. The important questions relating to what the standard for emergency removals should be and how prompt judicial review of such interim actions can be insured are beyond the scope of this paper.
20. Thomas Gill, "The Legal Nature of Neglect," *National Probation and Parole Association Journal*, 6 (1960), p. 14.
21. Letter dated September 25, 1973, from Los Angeles County Department of Public Social Services. Calculations based on this same source suggest that in

1972, the 3,518 juvenile court petitions filed by the Los Angeles Department of Public Social Services were disposed of as follows: Total Petitions 3,518; Dismissed by Department of Public Social Services before final court determination 1,480; Transfer to other jurisdictions 75; Decided by Juvenile Court 1,963, dismissed by Court 307; Jurisdiction Assumed by Court 1,656, supervised within home 628; Removal Ordered 1,028, placed with relatives 149, placed in foster care 879.

22. Unpublished yearly statistical compilation for the San Francisco Juvenile Court Annual Report for 1972. These data show that in 1972, there were hearings in cases involving 544 children; the court transferred 22 to other counties and dismissed 119 more without assuming jurisdiction. Of the 402 children for whom the court took jurisdiction, 141 were supervised within their own home, 59 were ordered placed with relatives, and 203 were placed in foster care.

23. See N.Y. Joint Legislative Committee on Court Reorganization: Report No. 2—The Family Court Act, McKinney's Session Laws of New York 3428, 3443 (1962).

24. "The Relationship Between Promises and Performance in State Intervention in Family Life," *Columbia Journal of Law and Social Problems*, 9 (1972) p. 30, citing Note, "An Appraisal of New York's Statutory Response to the Problem of Child Abuse," *Columbia Journal of Law and Social Problems*, 7 (1971), p. 72.

25. See, N.Y. Jt. Legislative Committee on Court Reorganization; p. 3442. (In neglect proceedings, fifty percent are children under age six, ninety percent under twelve.)

26. See, e.g., Shirley Jenkins and Elaine Norman, *Filial Deprivation and Foster Care* (New York: Columbia University Press, 1972), pp. 2, 25–30; Martin Rein, Thomas E. Nutt, and Heather Weiss, "Foster Care; Myth and Reality," in Alvin Schorr (ed.). *Children and Decent People* (New York: Basic Books, forthcoming). For a careful analysis of how the judicial system treats custody decisions for the poor, see Herma Hill Kay and Irving Phillips, "Poverty and the Law of Child Custody," *California Law Review*, 54 (1966), p. 717. See also Jacobus ten Broek, "California's Dual System of Family Law: Its Origin, Development, and Present Status," *Stanford Law Review*, 16 (1964), p. 257 (Part I); p. 900 (Part II); *Standard Law Review*, 17 (1965), p. 614 (Part III).

27. See e.g., Jenkins and Norman, *Filial Deprivation*, p. 35, indicating that only eleven percent of the foster children in their sample of 533 foster children in New York City were living with both parents at the time of placement.

28. Jenkins & Sauber, *Paths to Child Placement*, p. 80.

29. See Jenkins & Norman, *Filial Deprivation*, p. 55.

30. See Michael H. Phillips, Ann W. Shyne, Edmund A. Sherman, and Barbara L. Haring, *Factors Associated with Placement Decisions in Child Welfare* (New York: Child Welfare League of America, 1971); Bernice Boehm, "An

Assessment of Family Adequacy in Protective Cases," *Child Welfare*, 41 (January 1962), pp. 10–16; Eugene Shinn, "Is Placement Necessary? An Experimental Study of Agreement Among Caseworkers in Making Foster Care Decisions," Diss., Columbia University School of Social Work, 1968.

31. In California, for example, for the period from January 1, 1967, through August 30, 1973, there are a total of fourteen reported appellate opinions for neglect cases—not one by the California Supreme Court. At the present time there are about 15,000 children in foster care for whom a court ordered removal. Most of these were first placed during that period. It seems reasonable to assume that at least as many children both entered and exited foster care during that period as were initially placed before 1967.

32. This conclusion, based on observations of juvenile court and interviews with social workers and probation officers is consistent with the findings of Phillips, *Factors Associated with Placement*, pp.72–79, 88, based on a simulation study of the behavior of three juvenile court judges.

33. For 1968, David Gil estimated that a total of 10,931 reports of child abuse were made under state reporting laws. *Violence Against Children, Physical Child Abuse in the United States* (Cambridge, Mass.: Harvard University Press, 1970), p. 92. At that time every state had a law requiring that child abuse be reported. For that same year HEW estimated that Juvenile Courts in the United States handled approximately 141,000 dependency and neglect cases. See United States Children's Bureau, *Juvenile Court Statistics 1968* (Statistical Series No. 95, 1970), p. 15. Although many cases of child abuse go unreported, it is reasonable to assume that most abuse cases that go to court are reported. Moreover, some reported cases of abuse do not result in juvenile court petitions. Therefore, one could reasonably estimate for that year that less than nine percent of the dependency and neglect petitions handled by juvenile courts involved child abuse. There has apparently been an increase in reported abuse cases since 1968, however, while the number of neglect cases handled by courts declined to 130,900 for 1971. See *Juvenile Court Statistics 1971*. Moreover, abuse cases are perhaps more likely to lead to removal than other cases. Based on preliminary work here in California, I would estimate that probably fifteen to twenty percent, and certainly no more than a quarter of the cases where removal is ordered involved intentional physical abuse by a parent.

34. See Alfred Kadushin, "Child Welfare: Adoption and Foster Care," in *Encyclopedia of Social Work*, ed. R. Morris, 16th ed. (New York: National Association of Social Workers, 1971). Vol. 1, p. 104.

35. See *Children Served by Public Welfare Agencies*, at Table 6. Part of the reason for the preference for foster family care over institutional care is cost. In California, as of June, 1973, for example, the average monthly payment for residential care per child in a foster family home was $124.96; the average monthly payment for children in the institutions was $487.87, California State Department of Social Welfare, *Aid to Families with Dependent Children*—

*Boarding Homes and Institutions Case Load Movement and Expenditure Report* (Department of Social Welfare, Sacramento, June, 1973).

36. In California the monthly rates per foster child paid to foster families are set by the county and vary widely among counties—from $72 to $160 in 1972. California State Department of Social Welfare, Aid to Families with Dependent Children. Differences in the cost of living do not justify these differentials, and one suspects that—as is true for school spending—the differences are in part related to the local wealth. Compare *Serrano v. Priest*, 5 Cal. 3d 584,487 P.2d 1241, (1971). The financing of foster care is extremely complex, with funds coming from both state and federal government. The federal government, as part of the Social Security Act, reimburses states for a portion of cost of foster care for children meeting financial eligibility. See 42 U.S.C. Sec. 608(a). For a complete description of the complexities of the financing of foster care in California, see Childhood and Government Project, Earl Warren Legal Institute, University of California, Berkeley, "The Finance of Foster Care," (Staff Working Paper), 1973.
37. See, e.g., Martin Wolins, *Selecting Foster Parents* (New York: Columbia University Press, 1963), p. 201; Alfred Kadushin, *Child Welfare Services* (New York: Macmillan, 1967), p. 371.
38. Joseph Goldstein and Jay Katz, *The Family and the Law, Problems in Decision in the Family Law Process* (New York: Free Press, 1965), pp. 1021–22.
39. Kadushin, *Child Welfare Services*, p. 411.
40. Henry S. Maas and Richard E. Engler, Jr., *Children in Need of Parents* (New York: Columbia University Press, 1959), p. 356.
41. David Fanshel, "The Exit of Children from Foster Care: An Interim Research Report," *Child Welfare*, 50 (February 1971), pp. 65–81.
42. Kermit Wiltse and Eileen Gambrill, "Decision-Making Processes in Foster Care," unpublished paper, School of Social Welfare, University of California, Berkeley, Calif., 1973.
43. See Ralph W. Crary, "Neglect, Red Tape and Adoption," *National Probation and Parole Association Journal*, 6 (1960), p. 34.
44. Maas and Engler, *Children in Need*, pp. 390–91.
45. Maas and Engler, p. 383.
46. Wiltse and Gambrill.
47. Mass and Engler, p. 379.
48. Helen Jeter, *Children, Problems and Services in Child Welfare Programs* (Washington, D.C.: U.S. Government Printing Office, 1963), p. 87.
49. Jeter, p. 5; fifty-eight percent had more than one placement; Wiltse and Gambrill state that the foster children in their sample typically had two placements.

50. Jeter, p. 87. This same study anticipated only twelve percent would return home. See also Mary Lewis, "Foster-Family Care: Has It Fulfilled Its Promise?" *The Annals*, 355 (1964), pp. 31, 36.
51. See Crary, p. 39.
52. Maas and Engler, p. 390. "In community after community it is clear from the data in the study that unless children move out of care within the first year to year and a half of their stay in care, the likelihood of their ever moving out sharply decreases."
53. *Finlay v. Finlay*, 240 N.Y. 429, 433–34, 148 N.E. 624,626 (1925).
54. Zuchman & Fox, "The Ferment in Divorce Legislation," *Journal of Family Law* 12 (1972), p. 515; 571–576.
55. See e.g., In Re Rocher, 187 N.W.2d 730, 732 (Iowa, 1971): "Neither the trial court nor this one has—or claims—omniscience. It is never a pleasant task to separate parent and child. We can only take the record as we find it and reach a conclusion which appears to be for the best interest of the children. Both the statute and our previous decisions demand that we do so." *In re East*, 32 Ohio Misc. 65, 288 N.E.2d 343 (C.P. Juv. Div. Highland County 1972); *In re Kindis*, 162 Conn. 239, 294 A.2d 316 (1972); *In re Johnson*, 210 Kan. 828, 504 P.2d 217 (1972); *In re One Minor Child*, 254 A.2d 443 (Del. Sup. Ct. 1969); *In re* B.G. & V.G., 32 C.A. *3d 365,108 Cal. Rptr. 121 (1973); Hammond v. Department of Public Assistance*, 142 W.Va. 208, 95 S.E. 2d 345 (1956).
56. See *In Re Cager*, 251 Md. 473, 479, 248 A.2d 384, 388 (Md. Ct. App. 1968): "It is clear that the ultimate consideration in finding neglect which will serve as a basis for removing a child from its mother's custody is the best interest of the child."; *Todd v. Superior Court*, 68 Wash. 2d 587, 414 P.2d 605 (1966); *State v. Pogue*, 282 S.W. 2d 582 (Springfield Mo. Ct. App. 1955).
57. David Matza, *Delinquency and Drift* (New York: John Wiley & Sons, 1964), pp. 114–15.
58. The best interests test has been criticized in the divorce context. For a thorough review of the behavioral science research as it relates to the effects of divorce custody determinations, and an excellent argument for specific statutory presumptions for divorce custody disputes, see Phoebe C. Ellsworth and Robert J. Levy, "Legislative Reform of Child Custody Adjudication," *Law & Society Review*, 4 (1969), p. 167.
59. Anna Freud, "Child Observation and Prediction of Development—A Memorial Lecture in Honor of Ernst Kris," *The Psychoanalytic Study of the Child*, (New York: International University Press, 1958), XIII, pp. 92, 97–98. After this article was submitted for publication, I discovered two fascinating essays, one by Anna Freud entitled, "The Child is a Person in His Own Right" and one by Joseph Goldstein, "The Least Detrimental Alternative to the Problem for the Law of Child Placement." Both are found in *The Psychoanalytic Study of the Child* for 1972 (New York: Quadrangle Books 1973), and are parts of a

soon-to-be-published book co-authored by Freud, Goldstein, and Albert Solnit entitled *Beyond the Best Interests of the Child*. Goldstein's essay, which takes the form of a judicial opinion, suggests that courts should seek out the "least detrimental available alternative" rather than ask what is in a child's best interests in custody cases. Goldstein's analysis is consistent with my own in that it emphasizes the importance of stability and consistency in parent-child relationships; it criticizes the best interests standard for misleading judges into thinking "they have more power for 'good' than for 'bad' " in what they decide; and it suggests that courts should focus on available alternatives. Although I wonder whether in terms of information, predictions and values Goldstein's alternative standard (if applied to removing children from parental custody for initial placement in foster care) might not be subject to many of the same criticisms as the best interests standard, I do not wish to base my judgment on the two essays alone for they are obviously part of a more elaborate analysis presented in the forthcoming book. In my expansion of this article that will be published this coming May in the *California Law Review*, I hope to analyze in some detail the Freud, Goldstein, Solnit book, which should soon be available.

60. Sibylle Escalona, *The Roots of Individuality: Normal Patterns of Development in Infancy* (Chicago: Aldine, 1968), p. 13.
61. H.R. Schaffer, *The Growth of Sociability* (Baltimore: Penguin, 1971), p. 16.
62. Arlene Skolnick, *The Intimate Environment, Exploring Marriage and the Family* (Boston: Little Brown, 1973), p. 372.
63. Joan W. Macfarlane, "Perspectives on Personality Consistency and Change from the Guidance Study," *Vita Humana*, 7 (1964), pp. 115–126.
64. Skolnick, pp. 378–79.
65. See *Painter v. Bannister*, 258 Iowa 1390, 140 N.W. 2d 152 (1966).
66. John Rawls, A *Theory of Justice* (Cambridge, Mass.: Harvard University Press, 1971), pp. 237.
67. Phillips *et al.*, pp. 69–84.
68. Phillips *et al.*, p. 84.
69. Rein *et al.* See also Katz, *When Parents Fail*, p. 91.
70. See Rein, *et al.*
71. See generally, Michael F. Sullivan, "Child Neglect: The Environmental Aspects," *Ohio State Law Journal*, 29 (1968), p. 85.
72. In re Anonymous, 37 Misc. 2d 411, 238 N.Y.S. 2d 422, 423 (Fam. Ct. Rensselaer County, 1962).
73. See *In re Booth*, 253 Minn 395, 91 N.W. 2d 921 (1958).
74. *In re Tammy F.*, Cal. Dist. Ct. App., 1st Dist. Div. 2, No. 32643 (1973).
75. *In re Three Minors*, 50 Wash. 2d 653, 314 P.2d 423 (1957), See *In re Fish*, 288 Minn. 512, 179 N.W. 2d 175 (1970).

76. See *In Re Watson*, 95 N.Y.S. 2d 798 (Dom. Rel. Ct. 1950): three children were declared neglected because their mother was "incapable by reason of her emotional status, her mental condition and her allegedly deep religious feeling amounting to fanaticism to properly care, provide and look after the children."; *Hunter v. Powers*, 206 Misc. 784, 135 N.Y.S. 2d 371 (Dom. Rel. Ct. 1954): mother, an ardent Jehovah Witness, who left the child alone while she attended Bible discussion, compelled the child to distribute religious literature on the streets during parts of the day and night; *In Re Black*, 3 Utah 2d 315, 283 P.2d 887 (1955): children removed from their parents' home because their parents believed in and practiced plural marriage which they thought to be the law of God.

77. In the Matter of Deborah Gibson, decided June 29, 1973, Cal.Court of Appeal, 2nd App. Dist., Div. 1 (2d Civil No. 40391). See *In Re Q*, 32 Cal. App. 3d 288, 107 Cal. Rptr. 646 (1973).

78. See Monrad G. Paulsen, "Juvenile Courts, Family Courts, and the Poor Man," *California Law Review* 54 (1966) p. 694.

79. See, e.g., *In Re Raya*, 255 Cal. App. 2d 260, 63 Cal. Rptr. 252 (1967): reversing neglect determination premised only on the fact that the parents were living unmarried, with new partners, because they were unable to afford divorce; *State v. Greer*, 311 S.W.2d 49, 52 (Ct. App. Mo.) (1958): reversing a juvenile court decision to remove a baby girl who was "concededly adequately housed, fed, clothed and attended, personally and medically" simply on the ground that mother had on occasion visited taverns, had been arrested for reckless driving, and had a child out of wedlock.

80. Katz, *When Parents Fail*, p. 69.

81. See *In re A.J.*, 274 Cal. App. 2d 199, 78 Cal. Rptr, 880 (1969).

82. David Matza, *Delinquency & Drift*, p. 115.

83. Compare Roy Parker, *Decision in Child Care* (London: Allen & Unwin, 1966) with Harry Napier, "Success and Failure in Foster Care," *British Journal of Social Work*, 2 (Summer, 1972), pp. 187–204.

84. Sophie Theis, *How Foster Children Turn Out* (New York: State Charitable Aid Association, 1924), p. 19.

85. Joan McCord, William McCord, and Emily Thurber, "The Effects of Foster-Home Placement in the Prevention of Adult Antisocial Behavior," *Social Service Review* 34, (1960), pp. 415–420. This study matched a group of nineteen potentially delinquent boys living at home with nineteen boys placed as a last resort in foster care. Contrary to their hypothesis, the results showed that "a significantly higher proportion of those who had been placed in foster homes had criminal records in adulthood. See also Elizabeth Meier, "Current Circumstances of Former Foster Children," *Child Welfare* 44 (1965), pp. 196–206. A group of eighty-two persons who had been in foster care five years or more were interviewed and their "adjustment" was evaluated. A higher

than normal incidence of marital breakdown and a higher proportion of illegitimate births were found. On the other hand, one-half owned or were buying their own homes, few needed social services, and nearly all were self-supporting. See also Elizabeth Meier, "Adults Who Were Foster Children," *Children*, 13 (1966), pp. 16–22; Anne Roe, "The Adult Adjustment of Children of Alcoholic Parents Raised in Foster Homes," *Quarterly Journal of Studies on Alcohol*, 5 (1944), pp. 378–393. Since 1964, a research group at Columbia University has been engaged in longitudinal research relating to foster care. The volume on what happens to the children in the long-run has not yet been published.

86. Leon Eisenberg, "The Sins of the Fathers: Urban Decay and Social Pathology," *American Journal of Orthopsychiatry*, 32 (1962), p. 14.

87. Henry Maas, "Highlight of the Foster Care Project: Introduction," *Child Welfare* 38 (July 1959), p. 5.

88. Gordon Trasler, *In Place of Parents: A Study of Foster Care* (London: Routledge & Kegan Paul, 1960); Eugene Weinstein, *The Self-Image of the Foster Child* (New York: Russell Sage Foundation, 1960); Jessie Parfit, ed., *The Community's Children: Long-term Substitute Care: A Guide for the Intelligent Layman* (New York: Humanities Press, 1967).

89. Esther Glickman, "Treatment of the Child and Family after Placement," *Social Service Review*, 28 (September 1954), p. 279. See also John Bowlby, *Maternal Care and Mental Health*, Monograph No. 2 (Geneva: World Health Organization, 1952). Ner Littner, *Some Traumatic Effects of Separation and Placement* (New York: Child Welfare League of America, 1956).

90. Glickman, p. 279.

91. Leontine Young, "Placement from the Child's Viewpoint," *Social Casework*, 31 (1950), p. 250.

92. See, e.g., *Deprivation of Maternal Care; A Reassessment of Its Effects* (Geneva: World Health Organization, 1962); Lawrence Casler, *Maternal Deprivation: A Critical Review of the Literature*, Monograph No. 26 (Chicago: University of Chicago Press for the Society for Research in Child Development, 1961); Anna Freud and Dorothy Burlingham, *Infants Without Families; The Case for and Against Residential Nurseries* (New York: International University Press, 1944). Much of the early "separation" literature was addressed to the question of institutionalizing children—especially infants. The maternal deprivation literature began focusing on the need for a continuous relationship with the child-caring person—whether at home, in an institution, or in a foster home.

93. Martin Wolins and Irving Piliavin, *Institution or Foster Family: A Century of Debate* (New York: Child Welfare League of America, 1964). Rosemary Dinnage and M.L. Kellmer Pringle, *Foster Home Care, Facts and Fallacies: A Review of Research in the United States, Western Europe, Israel and Great Britain between 1848 and 1966* (London: Longmans, Green, 1967).

94. See Bowlby, Freud, and Napier.

95. Weinstein, p. 47.

96. In *re Jewish Child Care Ass'n*, 5 N.Y. 2d 222, 226, 156 N.E. 2d 700, 702 (1959).

97. Id. For some intriguing materials on the *Jewish Child Care Association* case see Goldstein and Katz, pp. 1027–34.

98. See Weinstein, pp. 47–57, 66–70.

99. J. Bowlby, *Forty-four Juvenile Thieves: Their Characters and Home-life* (London: Bailliere, Tindall & Cov, 1946). Bowlby concludes that children separated from their parents often develop "affection-less characters," incapable of forming lasting attachments and of adhering to society's rules. Elsewhere Bowlby states "The impairment of the capacity for successful parenthood is perhaps the most damaging of all the effects of deprivation," in *Maternal Care and Mental Health*, p. 327.

100. Weinstein, *Self-Image*, p. 66.

101. See footnote 49, and Lewis, p. 37.

102. See Lela Costin, *Child Welfare: Policies and Practice* (New York: McGraw-Hill, 1972); Alfred Kadushin, *Child Welfare Services*, p. 476.

103. In many states, such as California, judges are typically rotated through the juvenile court on a yearly basis.

104. Maas and Engler, p. 389. See Elizabeth Meier, "Adults Who Were Foster Children," *Children*, 13 (1966), pp. 16–22.

105. Maas and Engler, p. 422.

106. Wiltse and Gambrill.

107. See Young, p. 251. "One child in the process of replacement expressed his bitterness well, 'The social workers are the bat and I'm just the ball they sock from one place to another.' "

108. American Humane Association, *Child Protective Services, A National Survey* (Denver, Colo.: American Humane Association, 1967), p. 20. See Monrad G. Paulsen, "Juvenile Courts, Family Courts, and the Poor Man," *California Law Review*, 54 (1966), p. 694.

109. Minnesota is an exception for its statute provides that a child may be removed from the parents "only when his welfare or safety and protection of the public cannot be adequately safeguarded without removal." Minn. Stat. Ann. Sec. 260.011.

110. See Children's Aid Society of New York, "Nine-to-Twenty-four Hour Homemaker Service Project," *Child Welfare*, Part 1, 41 (March 1962), p. 99, and Part II, 41 (April 1962), p. 103; Sue Minton, "Homemaker Classes: An Alternative to Foster Care," *Child Welfare*, 52 (March 1973), pp. 188–91.

111. See *In Re Q*, 32 Cal. App. 3d 288, 107 Cal. Rptr. 646 (1973).

112. See Ray Helfer and C. Henry Kempe, *Helping the Battered Child and His Family* (Phildelphia: Lippincott, 1972).

113. See footnote 56.

114. See pp. 601, 604–605 above.

115. See, e.g., Sullivan.

116. I think the jurisdiction/disposition division of the judicial process in neglect cases is not a useful one. Substantive standards should be established for each type of coercive intervention, with more intrusive forms of intervention. In other words, there might be one standard for a court to be able to compel protective services; a different standard for a court to allow a child to be removed from his home during the pendency of the case; and yet another standard (such as that suggested in the last section of this article) for the court to remove the child for indefinite period.

117. See Monrad G. Paulsen, "The Law and Abused Children," in *The Battered Child*, ed. Ray Helfer and C. Henry Kempe (Chicago: University of Chicago Press, 1968).

118. Richard Posner, *An Economic Analysis of the Law* (Boston: Little, Brown, 1973).

119. Since *In Re Gault*, 387 U.S. 1 (1967), held that some safeguards available in criminal trials had to be applied in juvenile court delinquency proceedings, there have been numerous articles that have advocated more stringent requirements in dependency proceedings as well. An especially thoughtful analysis of the procedural requirements appropriate in child protective cases is Robert A. Burt, "Forcing Protection on Children and their Parents: The Impact of *Wyman v. James*," *Michigan Law Review*, 69 (1971), p. 1259. Other articles on the subject include Thomas T. Becker, "Due Process and Child Protective Proceedings: State Intervention in Family Relations on Behalf of Neglected Children," *Cumberland-Sanford Law Review*, 2 (1971), p. 247; Dianne M. Faber, "Dependent-Neglect Proceedings: A Case for Procedural Due Process," *Duquesne Law Review*, 9 (1971), p. 651; Joseph J. Mogilner, "Admissibility of Evidence in Juvenile Court: A Double Standard or No Standard," *Journal of the State Bar Association of Colorado*, 46 (1971), p. 310; Note, "Child Neglect: Due Process for the Parent," *Colorado Law Review*, 70 (1970), p. 465; Note, "Representation in Child-Neglect Cases: Are Parents Neglected?" *Columbia Journal of Law and Social Problems*, 4 (1968), p. 230.

120. Two cases have held recently that due process requires state assigned counsel for parents when the state is seeking permanently to remove their children. See *Nebraska v. Caha*, decided June 8, 1973 (Neb. Sup. Ct.); *Danforth v. Maine Dept. of Health*, decided April 17, 1973 (Me. Sup. Ct.).

121. Lon Fuller develops a distinction between "person-oriented" and "act-oriented" legal rules which usefully explains why procedural reform is not likely to

eliminate discretion if the legal standard is the best interests of a child "which by its nature cannot be rule-bound." Lon L. Fuller, "Interaction Between Law and Its Social Context," *Sociology of Law*, Summer 1971, University of California, Berkeley (bound class materials), Item 3.

122. Ernst Freund, *Standards of American Legislation* (Chicago: University of Chicago Press, 1917), p. 83.

123. See David Fanshel and Eugene B. Shinn, *Dollars and Sense in the Foster Care of Children: A Look at Cost Factors* (New York: Child Welfare League of America, 1972).

124. Despite these procedural safeguards, an occasional case might arise where the state failed to make reasonable efforts to rehabilitate the parents. Termination of parental rights after the fixed time period might nevertheless be appropriate for the child's sake. Alternatively, because of the unfairness to the parent, perhaps the judge should be allowed to do everything short of termination to provide a stable environment for the child, give the parents a damage action against the state for the failure to provide past services, and compel the provision of such services for an additional period of time.

125. Hasseltine B. Taylor, "Guardianship or 'Permanent Placement' of Children," *California Law Review*, 54 (1966), p. 741.

126. Professor Michael Wald of Stanford University Law School suggested to me the possibility of a shorter time limit for younger children.

127. See, e.g., Minor Children of F.B. v. Caruthers, 323 S.W. 2d 397 (Mo. Ct. App. St. Louis 1959); *In re Black* 3 Utah 2d 315, 283 P.2d 887 (1955); *In re Cager*, 251 Md. 473, 248 A.2d 384 (Md. Ct. App. 1968).

128. See, *In re Jeannie Q.*, 32 Cal. App. 3d 288, 107 Cal. Rptr. 646.

129. Through conversations with Professors Michael Wald and Robert Burt of the University of Michigan, the Reporter's for the relevant portion of the ABA Project, after I was well into writing this paper, I know that they were independently giving consideration to standards that would narrow the grounds that should justify removal and that would establish time limits for foster placement after removal.

130. I am grateful to Professor Kermit Wiltse, School of Social Welfare, University of California, Berkeley, for this finding.

131. See Matza; Edwin M. Schur, *Radical Non-Intervention: Rethinking the Delinquency Problem* (Englewood Cliffs, N.J.: Prentice-Hall, 1973).

132. See American Friends Service Committee, *Struggle for Justice, A Report on Crime and Punishment in America* (New York: Hill and Wang, 1971).

133. Francis A. Allen, *The Borderland of Criminal Justice* (Chicago: University of Chicago Press, 1964), p. 13.

134. Allen, p. 12.

# Part VI
# Importance of Parents for the Placed Child

# Part VI

## Importance of Parents for the Placed Child

Children who are placed away from their parents from earliest infancy, regardless of the reason, experience loss related to the separation. This loss, the severing of the parent-child tie, has a differential impact, depending on the child and the circumstances. The tie between parent and child is an invisible cord that provides a child with a biological, emotional, and symbolic sense of connectedness to his environment, and affects his basic identity and sense of self. As Germain eloquently states:

> The child who must be placed in substitute care at any age, and regardless of the reason, is torn from the biological and symbolic context of his identity. No matter how nurturing the substitute care, the child's ongoing task will always be to reweave the jagged tear in the fabric of his identity, to make himself whole again.[1]

Recognition of the significance of the parent for the child's sense of identity is a large part of the motivation in the movement for "open adoption" and "unsealed records." As discussed earlier in this book, other cultures have given more weight to this bond than has ours. Perhaps our culture could not afford to recognize such attachments, given the exigencies of industrialization and urbanization, which create mobility and uproot individuals.

The three articles included here attest, from different viewpoints, to the importance of the parents to the child. In Chapter 14, Colón emphasizes the

[1]Germain, Carel, Editor, *Social Work Practice: People and Environments*. New York: Columbia University Press, 1979: 175–176.

primacy of the child's experience of biological familial continuity in establishing his sense of self and personal significance. His argument is all the more convincing because he is a former foster child who, when older, went in search of his own parents. Exploring the broad scope of parent-child separation in foster care and adoption, Colón singles out concepts that are "common denominators" in child placement. These include: continuity of care; visitation rights; relinquishment; and the conflicts inherent in the various configurations of triangles consisting of the parents, the child, and either the foster parents or the child welfare worker. Colón stresses a balance between the child's connection to his or her family and a strong degree of consistent, secure, continuous care for the child.

Littner, long a proponent of attention to the tie between parents and child, describes in Chapter 15 the significance of this bond from a psychoanalytic perspective. He reiterates that unless the child is allowed to come to terms with the internalized image of the parents, preferably through contact with them, his or her sense of identity is impaired. Contact with the parents may also help the child deal more effectively with repressed separation feelings, which, if not directly expressed, often become displaced onto other adults in the environment, such as the foster parents. Such repressed feelings tie up a great deal of energy and interfere with the child's ability to function properly. Littner feels that the poorer the child's relationship to the foster parents, the more imperative it is that the child see his or her parents. Although Littner's article is addressed primarily to foster parents, it is useful for anyone interested in child placement issues.

As reported in Chapter 16, Fanshel found in his longitudinal study of 624 children in foster care in New York City that visiting with parents was indeed the "key to discharge." Children who were discharged from care were visited children; those who remained in care were unvisited. Fanshel's study also discovered that visiting varied by ethnicity: Jewish children were visited most; black children least; white and Puerto Rican children fared relatively well. Other factors also affected the rate of visitation. Older children were usually visited more. Frequency of visitation was higher for children who were placed because of the mother's mental illness or the child's behavior. Children who were abandoned had a low level of visitation. Of particular significance for practitioners is that high frequency of caseworker-parent contact was linked to a higher level of visitation. Fanshel's findings corroborate the ongoing importance of the parents for the child in placement.

## SUGGESTIONS FOR FURTHER READING

Bryce, Marvin E. and Ehlert, Roger C., "144 Foster Children," *Child Welfare*, 50: 9 (November 1971): 499–503.

Colón, Fernando, "In Search of One's Past: An Identity Trip," *Family Process*, 12: 4 (December 1973): 429–438.

Fraiberg, Selma, "A Therapeutic Approach to Reactive Ego Disturbances in Children in Placement," *American Journal of Orthopsychiatry*, 32: 1 (January 1962): 18–31.

Hallowitz, David, "The Separation Problem in the Child Care Institution," *Journal of Social Casework* (now *Social Casework*), 29: 4 (April 1948): 144–148.

Jenkins, Shirley, "The Tie That Bonds," in Maluccio, Anthony N. and Sinanoglu, Paula A., Editors, *The Challenge of Partnership: Working with Parents of Children in Foster Care*. New York: Child Welfare League of America, 1981.

Jolowicz, Almeda R., "A Foster Child Needs His Own Parents," *The Child*, 12: 2 (August 1947): 18–21. (Reprinted elsewhere in this volume.)

Jolowicz, Almeda R., "The Hidden Parents," in Sourcebook of Teaching Materials on the Welfare of Children. New York: Council on Social Work Education, 1969: 105–110.

Littner, Ner, "The Child's Need to Repeat His Past: Some Implications for Placement," *Social Service Review*, 34: 2 (June 1960): 128–148.

Ludlow, Bonnie and Epstein, Norman, "Groups for Foster Children," *Social Work*, 17: 5 (September 1972): 96–99.

MacIntyre, J. McEwan, "Adolescence, Identity, and Foster Family Care," *Children*, 17: 6 (November–December 1970): 213–217.

Mahoney, Kathryn and Mahoney, Michael J. "Psychoanalytic Guidelines for Child Placement," *Social Work*, 19: 6 (November 1974): 688–696.

Moss, Sidney Z., "How Children Feel About Being Placed Away from Home," *Children*, 13: 4 (July–August 1966): 153–157.

# 14

# Family Ties and Child Placement

FERNANDO COLÓN

In a real sense, this paper can be thought of as a sequel to my identity paper [6], in which I describe my experience as a foster child and my successful reestablishment of contact with my biological-extended families. At the end of that paper I raised a number of questions about the need and the right of the individual to "know" his biological and familial roots. This paper is an attempt to begin to answer those questions and, I hope, deepen our understanding of the complex and rich relations between a person and his biological families, both immediate and extended.

The central premise of this paper is that the child's experience of biological-familial continuity and connection is a basic and fundamental ingredient of his sense of self, his sense of personal significance, and his sense of identity. It is my contention that consistent consideration given to this premise would result in better child placement practice and procedure. Painful ruptures that particular life circumstances cause for some children and their biological parents and extended families can be offset. The critical issue is the maintenance of the child's and the biological families' mutual emotional bondedness so that the child grows up, at the very least, emotionally connected to his biological families and, if possible, with tangible

---

Reprinted from *Family Process*, Vol. 17, No. 3 (September 1978), pp. 289–312. By permission of the author and Family Process, Inc.

connections as well. Both child and parents can retain a reciprocal sense of themselves and a sense of their roles in a still larger family system.

The goal of this paper is to examine the effects of current child placement practices on the child's ties to his biological families and, in some cases, foster families. Although the relation between family ties and the placement of children has received attention in the past and there is an extensive literature on the topic summarized by Kadushin [10], this issue has not been addressed systematically across a variety of child placement settings such as care of children of divorced parents, foster care, adoptive care, and the placement of children in crossracial and crosscultural settings. This paper will explore the way child placement policy and practice might function if the reality of both the child's ties to his biological family and their ties to him were deliberately considered in planning for her or his placement.

For the purposes of this paper the family system is defined as all members of the child's family both living and dead who are biologically related to one another. As well as all members of the step-family, foster family, or adoptive family, included are all members of the nuclear family and extended family on both sides.

Murray Bowen [3, 4] was one of the first family theorists to understand and to describe the interconnectedness among the various parts of the nuclear and extended family systems. Ivan B. Nagy and Geraldine Spark [2] have richly enlarged our view of the way family ties function in their book, appropriately entitled, *Invisible Loyalties: Reciprocity in Intergenerational Family Therapy* [2]. Salvatore Minuchin et al. [19, 20, 21], in their work with ghetto families, have focused their attention upon the continuously impacting ecological system composed of the larger social-economical-political contexts such as neighborhood, school, church, courts, and welfare agencies that daily affect the life of the family. They are concerned also with familial intergenerational contextual factors.

It is becoming increasingly clear that when a child is cut off from his biological family system there is for the child, the parents, and the families involved a deep mutual sense of personal loss. Weiss [27] and Roman [23] speak of this loss with regard to the children and parents of divorced families. Colón [6] and McAdams [17] speak of this loss for children and parents who experience foster-child placement. Benet [1] and Trisiliotis [24] address this loss as it applies to children and parents who experience adoptive placement. Haley's book, *Roots*, [8] does not focus directly upon the crossracial and crosscultural placement of children, but the story still speaks powerfully to such arrangements. The uprooting of African blacks for the slave market and the crossracial and crosscultural adoption of Korean and Vietnamese children inevitably involve profound loss of racial, ethnic, and cultural ties in addition to familial cut-offs.

These considerations suggest that the hypothesis that persons who experience unresolved emotional cut-offs from significant others are persons at higher risk emotionally and psychologically than those who have resolved such cut-offs. The psychological response on the part of the person who has lost contact with a "familial-other" because of permanent cut-offs in family ties is strikingly similar to the reaction one sees in persons who are bereaved by the death of a loved one. When my ten foster brothers left our foster home at different times, there was no opportunity for further contact with them. I experienced their leaving and the permanent cut-offs from them as a series of depressions. I was forced to work my way through a series of mourning reactions [6]. The empirical evidence for this hypothesis is not as yet well established, but the work of Weiss [27], Wallerstein and Kelly [25, 26], and Hetherington et al. [9] with divorced families and the work of Trisiliotis [24] with adopted persons clearly support such a hypothesis.

Implicit in the principle of continuity with biological-familial roots is an assumption that deep, enduring, reciprocal loyalty commitments throughout the course of life are better for the child, the individual, the family, and the larger community. As one observes contemporary American culture, one is impressed by the degree to which powerful societal forces operate toward the loosening and the breaking down of family ties. There is a decline of tradition as essential. There is a disregard of moral and social restraints on all levels of behavior. There is an increasing preoccupation with self and self-realization at the expense of the family or the community. There is an endemic mobility to American life that contributes to a deep inner sense of rootlessness and emptiness whereby we pursue success at the expense of personal and familial relationships. The divorce rate is truly alarming. People seem to be less willing to make deep long-term and enduring commitments.

Given such societal forces it is no wonder that child placement practices are not conscious of the need for a child and his family to retain mutual ties but tend rather to accentuate further society's acceleration toward fragmentation. When one moves from the placement of children of divorced parents, to foster care, to adoptions, to crossracial and crosscultural adoptions, to artificial insemination, and finally to the latest development, i.e., embryo transplants, what one sees is a progressively increased degree of being cut off from one's biological rootedness. This is not to say that all child placement workers deliberately set out to pull children further and further away from their roots. Indeed, many workers are acutely aware of these societal pressures and consciously act to resist them. Rather, it is to say that some child care workers do place children without adequate attention to the principle of family continuity largely because societal forces do not seem to value the maintenance of family ties.

This paper makes a plea for the primacy of the child's and the adult's *birthright* to have access to the biological rootedness of their existence. The birthright can be given in a variety of ways. This paper will explore the birthright issue as it plays itself out in our concern for . . . foster children and adopted children. The sympathetic reader will like what he reads. The unsympathetic reader will be critical because he substantially disagrees and because the applications of the idea of family continuity in this paper will be fragmentary and incomplete. Nevertheless, I hope whether or not you are sympathetic, you will join me in our common struggle to understand this emotionally loaded but compelling human issue. . . .

## FOSTER-CHILD PLACEMENT

When a child is placed in foster care, he is unavoidably wrenched from his biological family. No matter how benign the foster family, both the child and his biological parents react to and profoundly experience the rupture of their mutual family ties. Foster care of children, by definition, is meant to provide *temporary* care for the child when his biological family is unable to care for him adequately. One of the best single-volume sources that addresses this complex issue sensitively and comprehensively is Kline and Forbush-Overstreet's book, *Foster Care of Children—Nurture and Treatment* [11].

When an agency receives a family's request to place their child in foster care, the agency's initial response should focus on placing the child with some other member of the child's extended family. All too often agencies fail to look beyond the nuclear family, when in fact there may be cousins, aunts, uncles, or grandparents ready and willing to care for the child. Placement in the extended family would keep the child in the context of his biological family system and enable both child and parents to maintain their mutual ties. The following cases illustrate such a placement.

> When Mario was 3 years old, his father was killed, and his mother had a nervous breakdown. He was placed in the custody of his maternal grandparents. He grew up in violent surroundings both within and outside of his home. At age 14, when the home became intolerably violent, he was placed in a half-way house because of acting-out behavior. After one year he was returned to his grandparents' home. He also lived occasionally with his mother who had remarried by then and was raising a large family. For a while he was involved with the street life of violence and drugs, but, seeing that this was leading nowhere, he enlisted in

the army. After his discharge, he visited a friend in college who encouraged him to apply for an opportunity award; he did, was accepted, and went on to college.

When Mario sought therapy he was in an academic crisis, felt socially isolated, and was cut off from ongoing contact with his family. He had developed a pattern of letting all of his studies go until the day before the final exam. Then he would cram and expect himself to do better than anyone else. The pattern worked through his junior year but failed during his senior year. Once he realized that he did this to pump up his self-esteem, he saw that it was self-destructive and was able to change.

When we started therapy, Mario was estranged from his family. He felt he was the black sheep and that they had no interest in him. Since Christmas vacation was approaching, I encouraged him to be in touch with his family and to plan to visit them. He was able to do this and established meaningful contact with them for the balance of his senior year. He experienced a great sense of welcome and support from his family and no longer felt he was fighting the world all by himself. This support undergirded his academic effort, and he excelled. His senior year culminated in his being accepted by a prestigious law school. As therapy ended, he was aware that he still had a lot of unresolved rage that he believed he experienced because of his minority status. He realized that at some point in the future he might need to resume therapy in order to resolve those feelings.

Often we automatically go along with a family's request to put the child in foster care without fully examining why the family wants to extrude the child. The desire suggests that the child may be a symptom of trouble in the family, and if the symptom is removed, the family may move much slower toward addressing the family problem. By resisting the impulse to remove the child, the agency may be able to help the family directly and may not have to resort to foster placement at all.

One foster-care agency used to place twenty to thirty children each year in foster care. After shifting to a family perspective that made them scrutinize the reasons for foster placement, they offered family therapy instead and were able to reduce the number of placements to three to five a year [12].

This practice in no way negates the need to place children in foster care who truly need it. However, if foster care must be used, a major effort should be made to enable the child and biological families to retain mutual ties. This would involve the selection of foster parents who would support the child's continuing interest in and contact with his natural family, who would cooperate rather than compete with the natural parents for the attention of the child. The ideal foster parents would view themselves as additional parenting figures, *not* as replacement parents and would try to attenuate the foster child's inevitable loyalty conflict. B. Kranser, who is both a mother and foster mother, speaks pointedly to this issue:

> Most significant . . . is the fact that our foster children's primary loyalties lie with their family of origin, and try as we did, we could not remake that reality. [13]

Agencies should especially seek out foster parents who not only enjoy mutually satisfying marital relations but who also maintain "active" and mutually satisfying relations with their own families of origin. These will be the kind of foster parents who can cooperate with the child's biological family rather than seek to replace them. If the foster parents have distant relations or chronic conflict with their own families, they might be prone to overinvest in the foster child and seek to meet needs they were not able to satisfy in relations with their own families.

It is not at all uncommon for the child's ties to his biological family to be fragmented, ruptured, or even severed after he is placed in foster care. However, there are ways to heal such ruptures in familial continuity through periodic visits; yearly family reunions; and giving the child access to family scrapbooks, family photo albums, and family geneologies. Because in the past it was assumed that the child's continued contact with his biological family would cause loyalty conflicts and interfere with adjustment to his new foster home, the above suggestions are contrary to traditional practice. But if the child can maintain ties with both biological and foster family systems, his loyalty can be encouraged in both directions, thus reducing the possibility that the foster parents or the biological parents will be treated as scapegoats.

During its routine visits, the foster care agency can take a leadership role in enabling this process to occur. The practice, carried out consistently and sensitively, could keep the foster family from developing distorted fantasies about the biological family and vice versa. It would be enormously comforting to the foster child, reassuring him that he had not been abruptly cut off from his family as if suddenly they had all died. He would have a clearer sense of the distinction between the foster parents and biological parents and what the limits of those relations could be.

This practice would change the whole nature of the foster child's experience because it would provide stability, continuity, predictability, and a subsequent sense of security. It would enable her or him to develop strong realistic ties to *both* sets of parents and to resolve loyalty conflicts. The reality of the circumstances that necessitated the placement could be more readily assimilated. Thus the child would not be left bereaved but would still have access to rich options of identity and connection. Ideally, the child would be returned to his natural family and, because of the continued contact between both families, the return would be considerably less problematic. If the child is not returned to his natural family, however, the periodic visits should continue until he achieves majority; they will continue to enhance his sense of self and to counteract any feeling of being "different" because of having had no contact with the biological family. (Although my father's visits to me when I was a foster child were aperiodic, they were extremely valuable. I "knew" who my father was, and by knowing him I came to know myself. This enabled me to have a clearer and stronger sense of myself. It is also worth noting that my foster mother had the wisdom to encourage me to take Spanish in high school even though she spoke German. I recall being at college and writing to my father in Spanish and my foster mother in German. Visits from my maternal great-uncle and first cousin and a paternal aunt and cousin when I was between 7 and 8 later turned out to be of rich significance to me as I succeeded, finally, in reconnecting with my extended families [6].)

People often criticize proposals for ongoing visits between the foster family and the biological family by asking what happens if the child's father or mother is psychotic, if the father or mother is in prison, or if the biological family has no interest in the child. What then? The human tendency in such cases is to shield the child from the pain of such unfortunate reality. And yet whenever there is such an extreme disruption in the continuity of a parent-child relationship, there is a profound sense of loss on both sides. A child cut off from his parent—even if the parent is imprisoned or hospitalized—could react to that loss with rebellious, delinquent, or depressed behavior. The parent who is cut off from his child could react to that loss with hostility or apathy to the child or active rejection. Again it would seem to be extremely important to maintain or reinstitute the ties that were broken. Parents in psychiatric hospitals and in prisons can be visited. Both parent and child can benefit from such visits. They can work out a relationship based on reality, not fantasy, and clarify any misapprehension of the child that she or he is to blame for his parents' condition. Understandably, this would be a painful process. However, it is hard to imagine that it would not be emotionally corrective to both parent and child or child-now-adult if ample time were devoted to the effort. The following case illustrates these issues:

> Miss R., a 22-year-old graduate student, was the oldest of three sisters. Her mother had abdicated her maternal role to Miss R., who was often left with the care of her younger sibs. Miss R.'s

mother would become violent when drunk, was diagnosed as schizophrenic, and was hospitalized on several occasions, once by Miss R. herself. Finally, because of her mother's violence, Miss R., from the age of 14 to 17, was placed in a half-way house for delinquent teen-age girls. She had always done well academically and was able to get scholarship support for college.

When Miss R. was 5 years old her father killed a man and had been in prison most of the years since that event. Before his imprisonment she had been his favorite child. They corresponded occasionally from the time she was 5 until she was 20, when their correspondence ceased. She had seen her father a few times during her childhood when he was on parole, but he was jailed again after being involved in an armed robbery.

Miss R.'s relationships to men were conflictual and unsatisfying. At the time of therapy, she had not seen her father for over five years. Her contact with her mother was minimal and limited to occasional visits. When she sought therapy, she was depressed, anxious, over-extended, and socially isolated. She had poured her energies into four years of academic work and was emotionally and physically exhausted. In the process she had become more and more distant from her ghetto roots.

After establishing trust, we focused upon her lack of contact with her past, which understandably she was eager to forget. She began making every-other-weekend visits to her mother, her sisters, her old friends, her parish priest, nuns, and her old church choir. She was warmly received by these people, and she found that by reconnecting to them, her depression disappeared and she felt renewed energy to pursue her degree.

Then she was encouraged to visit her father in prison. As we prepared for this visit, she acknowledged that she still felt like a 5-year-old emotionally in relation to him. The visit was very significant for her. She was able to meet with him for three hours, and they spent the time reviewing their histories for each other and getting reacquainted as adults. She discovered that he had kept a scrapbook of all her accomplishments and activities throughout her high school and college years. It was made up of clippings and reports sent to him and told to him by friends and relatives.

This was a pivotal experience for Miss R. She felt an additional source of emotional support. As therapy terminated because of her graduation, we began to explore her still unresolved tie to her mother. Time did not permit us to complete this task. Nor did her visit with her father magically resolve her problems with men. Nevertheless, she ended therapy having made significant gains.

Although caseworkers often do make genuine attempts to keep a child within the biological family, the pressure on the caseworker to place a child in foster care can be tremendous, as illustrated by this case:

> A caseworker was working with a single parent who had been reported to protective services for abusing her 7-year-old son, Dan. The whereabouts of the boy's father was unknown. Dan was extremely difficult for his mother to handle and was also stealing in school. The caseworker had instituted a behavior modification program with mother, son, and school. Dan stopped stealing, his mother stopped abusing him, and she responded to the care and support of the worker.
>
> When the caseworker brought up the issue of termination, the whole situation collapsed. The mother began to beat Dan, and Dan started to act out again. The mother returned to the caseworker and demanded that her child be placed in foster care and that he not be returned to her until he was good. The caseworker felt exhausted by this turn of events and wanted to resolve it by placing the child in foster care because of her concern about Dan and because after a year of treatment she felt the mother was intractable.
>
> The caseworker recounted her last session with the mother and Dan when the issue of his placement was addressed in a very heated emotional interview. The climax occurred when the child indicated his willingness to go to foster care and the mother, for the first time, showed some tearful emotion, which she quickly covered up. Assessment of the mother's history revealed that her own mother was ill from cancer from the time of the daughter's birth until her maternal grandmother died when the child was 6 years old. At that point the care of her alcoholic father fell upon the child's shoulders.
>
> It became apparent that the event of termination triggered strong unresolved feelings in the mother about her own losses. It also did not appear to be accidental that the mother was having problems with her 7-year-old son at about the parallel age she was at the time of her own mother's death. Thus, the session signaled not the end of therapy but a new beginning.

> As the case unfolded, the caseworker felt the support of her supervisor for her feelings of frustration. As she began to comprehend more fully what was happening within the mother, she began to believe that it could be of value to continue to see the mother and Dan. She decided not to place Dan in foster care but to continue to work with both of them to help them resolve their relationship as well as to help the mother resolve her ties to her own mother.

This turnabout did not come easily because powerful emotional forces were operating on both the mother and caseworker to place the child. But by taking a position of holding off on placement as long as possible, the worker was able to reassess the situation and to see more fully what was occurring, thereby envisioning ways that she could continue to work in an effective way with the mother and her son.

Fortunately, this worker had the support of a supervisor who did not rush in and agree that placement of the child was the appropriate solution. Many workers do not have that support. Indeed, they often feel great pressure to cool the situation down. Thus, many of the ideas in this paper that suggest to workers that family ties should be maintained confront workers with seemingly insoluble problems. Not only families, supervisors, and agency directors, but schools and courts often are on the side of placement of children without continuity of family ties.

Although finding alternatives to foster care is not easy, it can and is being done. Minuchin [21] makes use of an ecological approach to address this issue. The ecological approach seeks to find natural systems of support that are available to the family. Such natural sources of support can include not only the extended family but the neighborhood, the school, the church, etc. By moving into the home and the community, the worker can frequently discover sources of support that can help sustain families rather than make interventions that shatter them.

The Lower East Side Family Union of New York City is an agency that was created in March 1974 to prevent the breakup of families. The Family Union coordinates and monitors the efforts of agencies such as the school, the court, the Public Health Department, and the Welfare Department by working out family service contracts by which the agencies agree to provide specific services and the families agree to cooperate. The Family Union puts a great deal of effort into building and reestablishing the informal neighborhood social networks that can also provide self-help. In 1976 the Family Union worked with 390 families, 141 of which were seen as high-risk families because they had problems that were similar to other families whose kids were being placed in foster care. As of the date of Bush's [5] article, in only ten of the 390 families was it necessary to place children in foster care. These placements were temporary and lasted only a few months; the average foster placement by traditional agencies is five years. Placing children in foster care is expensive. Preventive family counseling is significantly cheaper, the savings in emotional costs to the family immeasurable.

Although the last case had a positive outcome at that point, it would be naive to assume that thereafter all will go well for the caseworker and the family. Many families have extremely limited resources both economically and emotionally. There is still a tremendous need for good foster homes—in fact the demand far exceeds the supply.

I would like to suggest that we deliberately set out to develop *long-term* foster care homes for such children. Long-term foster care would be more permanent than temporary foster care but less permanent than adoptive care. It could be used in those situations in which limited economic, social, and emotional resources make it unlikely that the child's biological family would be able to take him back in the foreseeable future. The foster family in long-term foster care would have custody rights that would assure to the child the continuity of care so critical in developing his sense of basic security. Guardianship rights and visitation rights for the biological family would ensure familial continuity. Since it is conceivable that the biological family could develop the necessary resources to be able to care for the child in the future, custody rights for the child should remain revocable. However, if they are revoked, the long-term foster family should have visitation rights to assure continuity for them and their foster child with whom they now share mutually significant ties.

A glimpse into how such an arrangement could work is offered by McAdams [17] whose six children were placed in foster care. After several years they were returned to her when she was able to care for them. Her experience strongly illustrates the need for the biological and the foster family to be able to work together in their mutual concern for the child.

Long-term foster care defined in this way might make it possible to find more foster homes. It is very difficult to find families that are willing to make short-term commitments to foster children. Even though the placement may last only a few months, significant attachments develop so that separations are inevitably painful. If the foster family had the assurance that they would be able to foster the child on a long-term basis, it is likely they would find it easier to make the kind of emotional commitment so necessary for the child's well-being.

Madison and Schapiro [16] propose still another category of foster placement that they call *permanent* foster care. This would apply to those cases in which the children are surrendered by their biological families and become legal wards of the state with guardianship vested in the agency. They believe this is a viable option for children unlikely to be adopted and whose continued contact with their biological families is thought to be destructive. Thus, in this category the biological parents' ties to the child are completely severed.

I am quite opposed to such a practice because, again, by severing the ties the long-term cost to the child may well outweigh the short-term gains. Again, I believe that the biological family should be able to retain visitation rights to their children at times that would be constructive. Visitation rights could still be retained *even though* the guardianship of the child rests with the agency. The guardianship with the agency secures the long-term continuity of care for the child while the visitation rights of the biological parents and child maintain the biological family ties.

## ADOPTIVE CHILD PLACEMENT

The adoption of children is a time-honored practice that has the effect of ensuring adequate parenting for children who might otherwise be sadly neglected. There is no question about the value of adoption in this regard. However, it is my working assumption that all children should have not only adequate parenting but also access to information about, and perhaps eventual contact with, their biological families. For most of us, knowledge of and parenting by our biological family occur simultaneously in an organic, unifying way. For the adopted child whose ties are legally severed from his biological family, there is a profound separation of his biological sense of himself and his experience of being parented by his adoptive family.

Indeed, when the final adoption decree is awarded to the adoptive family, it is the court's and society's intention that the adopted child's ties to his biological family be permanently severed. "The effect of the final decree is to establish a parent-child relationship between the petitioner and the adopted child and to terminate all relationships between the child and the biological parents. When the final adoption order is granted, the child legally assumes the surname of his adoptive parents. A new birth certificate may be issued in his new name and the record of the adoptive proceedings is sealed" [10: 560].

However well intentioned the above process, there is a growing awareness of a dilemma resulting from the practice of attempting to *erase* the actual roots of a child's biological existence. Lifton, in the foreword of Benet's *The Politics of Adoption*, says:

> The adoption experience cannot be free of dislocated human arrangements. For the most part our society handles the

> dislocation by offering a substitute family, but at a price. That price is the suppression of the adoptee's "life story"—the psychological and practical excision of his or her personal history and biological connectedness. What has been excised is replaced by fantasy—the adoptee's, the adoptive parents', and society's. The fantasy . . . begins with the falsification of the birth certificate and extends indefinitely around most of the adoptee's life processes.[15:1]

The unique feature of the adopted children's experience is that in a deep sense they do not really know who they are. This feeling can and does persist even though the adoptive child's early years in the adoptive family may have been quite positive. The desire to know one's biological origins and parentage results from a deeply felt psychological and emotional need, a need for roots, for existential continuity, and for a sense of completeness. To know who one's biological parents are or were, to know where one's skin color, facial features, body build, temperament, and talents come from is a powerful human desire that drives a person as he seeks to achieve a sense of wholeness about herself or himself. However, says Lifton:

> The main message to the adoptee . . . is that he must suppress his urgent impulse to know. The power of that impulse, whether overt or suppressed, is underestimated. It is commonplace for adoptees, from childhood through adulthood, to search faces on the street for signs that some anonymous person may be his mother, or his father, sister or brother. But to actively seek concrete information, whether through organized search procedures or even persistent questions to adoptive parents, is apt to be equated (by adoptee and adoptive parents) with disloyalty and ingratitude. Every family has secrets, but the adoptee is unique in the extent to which his quest for the most fundamental details of his existence is a direct source of guilt. He has no choice but to adopt a pervasive sense of separateness and half-life [15: 2–3].

Trisiliotis [24] has done research on 70 adoptees who chose to uncover their biological and historical heritage. He was interested in the motivations for their search, their needs, and how they used the information they received. His book has much useful information. He divided his group of 70 into two groups: one wanted to meet the natural parents, the other wanted to secure family background information. He concludes:

> . . . the majority of adoptees searching into their genealogical background and especially most, but not all, of those trying to find

> their birth parents were unhappy and lonely people and a considerable number had had psychiatric help. [24: 160]

One could mistakenly conclude from his finding that those adoptees who seek to know their birth parents are disturbed in some way. Although it is likely to be true that the adoptee is upset on some level about his lack of full knowledge about himself, I suspect that underneath that disturbance lies a healthy drive to know himself fully and completely in a biological, existential, and historical sense. Powerful statements regarding these issues may be found in Rod McKuen's [18], Ann Fisher's [7], and Betty Jean Lifton's [14] accounts of their search for ties to their biological families.

When the adoptees succeed in identifying and locating their biological parent(s), there is a fairly typical sequence of events. Again, Lifton says it well:

> The sequence usually includes a desperate, intense search; exhilaration and deep satisfaction at finding one's natural mother (or father); and then a profound letdown, a sense of disillusionment and sometimes depression, as one painfully surrenders the fantasies of a lifetime and absorbs the realization that the found parent is an ordinary human being, sometimes a troubled one, and that neither party knows quite well what to do with this relationship. The long-range sense, however, is that the search and reunion have been profoundly valuable and necessary, the source of the adoptee's newly experienced sense of being grounded in reality, no longer a phantom or a replacement but a renewed human being who has re-entered the world on a different plane. What these emotions suggest is that everyday feelings of connection and self-definition depend upon being able to locate oneself in the larger human continuity. [15: 5].

This need to know, however, is not a one-sided issue for the adoptee. There is growing evidence indicating that the adoptee's biological parents have a reciprocal need to know their relinquished children:

> Many natural mothers (according to recent psychiatric studies) when "found" by the children they long ago gave up, experience emotions described as "relief" at learning that the child has made his or her way reasonably into adulthood, and above all, diminution of guilt. Feelings vary and no situation is free of ambivalence. But increasing numbers of natural mothers are themselves embarking on a "search," and it turns out that many, over the years, experience symptoms similar to those of their children—studying faces, newspaper pictures and stories,

> marriage announcements, and yes, obituaries, looking for signs of the lost connection. What is at stake for each in the reunion is not the sudden formation of a new or ideal mother-child relationship but rather the re-establishment of connection, the filling in of a vital biological and historical story, the emergence of the self from a half-life to something approaching full existence. [15: 5–6]

Unfortunately, the biological father, or so called putative father, has been all but neglected in the past in adoption proceedings. However, this is changing, and it is noteworthy that the biological father also has strong feelings about what is to become of his child when he is given a chance to explore his reactions to the adoptive event. Contrary to popular belief, the relationship of most parents who have out-of-wedlock children and give them up for adoption are not short-term, casual relationships. Kadushin [10] reports that in two recent studies, not only was the mother available for interviews to plan for the child's adoption but 70 to 80 percent of the fathers were available as well.

Benet [1] notes that prior to two 1972 United States Supreme Court decisions (Stanley vs. Illinois and Rothstein vs. Lutheran Social Service of Wisconsin), the out-of-wedlock mother could, by herself, give consent to the adoption of the child. The child in this sense was fatherless. Benet suggests that because of these decisions the U.S. Department of Health, Education and Welfare warns that the putative father has custody rights to the child that must be considered at the point of the decision to relinquish the child for adoption. He must be given the opportunity to show that he is capable of being the child's custodian and must be personally served in any litigation that could affect his rights. It is hoped that these events will increase the putative father's involvement in the adoption process of *his* child.

Given the above considerations, how might we redefine our adoption procedures to meet the child's needs for secure, permanent parenting, on the one hand, and his right to know the roots of his existence, on the other hand? This is an extremely complex question, and I would be foolhardy indeed to suggest that what follows is anything more than an initial proposal. Nevertheless, I believe we need to begin to develop a better answer to this important question.

The rationale for *severing* all ties of the child to his biological family is to protect the privacy of the biological parent, to ensure the security of the adoptive child's relation to his adoptive parents, and to enable the adoption agency to carry out its task of placing the child in adoption. New thinking in this area must focus upon the issue of "severing all ties" and seek ways to either retain those ties or to enable the adoptee to reactivate them at a later date if he so chooses.

There are two major categories of adoption: *early adoption*, in which the aim is to place the child as quickly as possible in a permanent home *before* the child develops any conscious memories of his biological family, and *late adoption*, in which older children are placed in adoptive homes *after* they have acquired conscious, or preconscious, memories and experiences of their biological families.

## Early Adoption

For the early adoptee, significant steps toward addressing the biological family ties could be taken by adoption agencies, biological parents, and adoptive parents *at the point of application* for such services. The biological parents could be told that the child, as it moves through childhood, adolescence, and young adulthood, will probably want to know something about her or his origins. The child may indeed choose to seek a reconnection with them at a later date in order to obtain an even more complete sense of self. Both biological and adoptive parents will need help in being able to accept the fact that it is the child's existential *birthright* to know who he is.

The biological parents must recognize that they have a major responsibility to take steps to ensure that their child will be able to know who he is. To this end, they can leave on file at the agency a complete social and medical history that includes names, ages, and addresses of themselves and family relatives. The adoptive family should be given all of this information at the point of adoption, except specific identifying data of the biological parents and family. Then, as the child grows, he can be given this information so that at the outset he has *factual* information about himself.

Trisiliotis' [23] work suggests that this can be done in response to the child's questions, and at an early age, well before adolescence. If the birthright data were handled in this manner, the child could, at his own pace, assimilate the knowledge into his sense of self. When the early adoptee reaches majority, he should be given the option of learning the specific identifying data about himself and of seeking a reconnection with his biological family.

The adoptive parents must be helped to understand that their adoptive child's interest in his biological family in no way negates the importance and significance of his relationship with them. Their mutual tie to each other *cannot* be erased. The biological family, at the point of application for adoptive services, and at the point the child might seek a reconnection, needs to be assured that the reconnection in no way puts upon them the demand that they resume the parental role with their child, now young adult. Indeed, the adoption process resulted from their earlier decision to relinquish that parental role. Reality would not permit them to assume a role that is no longer appropriate, since the adopted young adult is now at majority. This is a lesson we all learn whether we have natural, foster, or adoptive children.

Ideally, the adopted child should be encouraged to relate to the biological family to the extent that he and the biological family desire to relate, while retaining his ties to his adoptive family. Adoption care agencies would have to play a major, post-adoption role in enabling families to negotiate such a relationship. This mode of handling the early adoptive placement of the child has obvious merit. It enables the child to be reared by a family able to care for him. It does not tamper with the realities of the child's actual roots of existence. It enables the child to activate his ties to the biological family at a time in his life when he is more capable of doing so. It does not force him to make a choice but helps him to have, if he so chooses, a meaningful tie and relationship with both his adoptive and his biological families. But, above all, it gives him a readily available way of completing sense of self, if and when he is ready to do it, without going through the trauma that our current system of handling adoptions forces upon the person who seeks to know (i.e., hiring lawyers, detectives, going to court, etc.)

In the absence of such a procedure, all three sides of the adoption triangle are not prepared for later reunions nor provided support during the reunion event itself. Painful encounters can and do occur. When the adopted person sets out on his search alone, he may succeed in reconnecting to his biological family only to discover that they want nothing to do with him and indeed actively reject him. Or they react the other way and seek to totally and hungrily absorb him into their life. The adoptee in such a predicament can be helped to work out a connection with the biological family based on reality. If the biological parent rejects him, he can be encouraged to persist in his need for reconnection by contacting other members of his biological family; it is highly unlikely that *all* members of the biological family will actively reject a family member who "returns." In time, if the adoptee establishes ties to members of the extended family, he may succeed in effecting a connection with the rejecting biological parent himself. The adoptee can also defuse an overinvestment in himself by his biological mother or father by establishing ties with other members of his biological family.

For the adoptee who decides to find out who he or she is, the move itself toward the reunion will have the effect of reactivating many old and long-buried questions such as: What are my biological parents like? Which one do I look like? Why did they really give me up for adoption? Will they react acceptingly or reject me if I succeed in locating them? How would or could we relate to each other now?

If the adoptee succeeds in reconnecting with his biological mother or father or other family member, the event can be upsetting and traumatic, as well as exhilarating. It can be confusing and anxiety-provoking to find a biological parent who is less than the fantasied ideal, especially if the parent turns out to be psychotic, imprisoned, alcoholic, or physically ill. The clash of fantasy and reality can be painful and lead to an even greater state of confusion for the adoptee. Thus, the adoptee who succeeds in his search for connection to his biological family will need a strong, supportive relationship with a mature friend or professional counselor to help resolve such issues. Sometimes the "strong other" is the adoptee's adoptive parents. However, the fundamental fact at this point is that now with the reality available, the issue *is* resolvable.

Sometimes an adoptee who has had an unhappy adoptive childhood experience hopes to undo this circumstance by finding his biological parents in the hope that they will love and accept him unequivocally and thereby give him what he feels he didn't get from his adoptive family. Even if the biological family responds positively to the reunion, they cannot, in reality, "redo" the adoptee's childhood. Nevertheless, the reunion can be an occasion for working through realistic relations with both adoptive parents and biological family.

Some adoptees will choose *not* to know anything about their biological roots. Or they may be interested in whatever information is available but have no interest in seeking a reunion with their biological family. I think it is important to honor these choices as well. The primary concern is that all adoptees at least be given the opportunity to make a decision themselves as to whether or not they wish to pursue the issue. The recent phenomenon of hundreds of adoptees joining together in adoptees' associations to seek "open records" is poignant evidence that most adoptees still do *not* have that choice.

The usual passages of life often reactivate the adoptees' feelings about their human connectedness. The onset of adolescence, marriage, having one's own child, the death of a loved one, or a divorce can all have the effect of raising again the biological-tie issue for the adoptee. In the following case, an early adoptee, who was adopted at four months and whose adoptive parents had died, began her "search" after her marriage ended in divorce:

> Mrs. J., a 41-year-old divorcee and mother of four children, entered therapy because she was having difficulty in her relations with men. The divorce reactivated her feelings about her human connectedness; her unresolved conflicts about her deceased, adoptive parents; and her fantasies about her biological parents. She felt a strong need to find her biological parents. She succeeded in locating and reconnecting with her mother within a year. This was a profoundly significant event for her because she was able to fill in gaps about herself, thus feeling more complete and secure. She did not look to her biological mother to be a

parent but to be a person who enabled her to make a reconnection with her biological heritage and existence. Circumstances did not permit us to work through her concerns about her relations with men, to whom she tended to cling in an urgent, needy way that inevitably alienated them. However, I suspect that in the future these relations might take on less of an all-or-nothing quality because the reconnection to her biological extended family attenuated her urgent need for emotional connectedness. Had it been possible to work longer, I would have encouraged her to seek out other members of her biological family, especially the men. Thus she could have been enabled to address and resolve the issue of her relations with a number of significant men—her adoptive father, her ex-husband, the men in her biological family, and the current men in her life.

## Late Adoption

Because of the scarcity of infants available for adoption—owing to the expanding use of contraception and abortion as well as to the fact that increasing numbers of young mothers are keeping their babies—the phenomenon of adopting older children has become more widespread. The situation for the late-adoptee child, who has conscious or preconscious memories of his biological or foster family or both, is decidedly different from that of the early adoptee. How best to handle this issue has not been clear. I am leery, however, of any practice that attempts to make the child forget his tie to his biological family or foster family. Indeed, the older the late-adoptee child, the bigger the eraser would have to be and the larger the piece of reality the child would have to erase. This approach cannot be constructive because reality cannot be erased.

The better course would be to work out ways in which the child could maintain his ties to the previous families *and* be adopted as well. This practice already exists and works well in those cases in which the adoption experience and the previous family connections are handled sensitively. It calls for adoptive families to cooperate with the previous families to maintain the child's family connections via visitation. "Adoption-with-connection" would appear to be a good choice for the older child whose biological family is unable to provide continuous care and is unlikely to be able to do so for the remainder of the child's childhood. It is a step further in the relinquishment process for the biological family than is expected when the child is placed on long-term foster care.

If "adoption-with-family-connection" were instituted, it would make sense for these children to retain their own surnames so that this important part of their actual identity would not be denied. In order to recognize the crucial contribution of the adoptive parents as well as their needs and responsibilities, the last name of the child could be a hypenated combination of his *own* last name and that of his adoptive father. It seems to me realistic to give *both* names *equal* weight and significance because that most aptly fits the actual reality situation.

These suggestions would enable the late-adoptee to fashion a whole sense of himself from ties to *both* his adoptive family and his previous families.

Sometimes the older child articulates the dilemma of being adopted and taken away from the biological family.

> For example, a 9-year-old girl in the process of becoming adopted, said to her caseworker, "But I don't know how to say good-bye to my parents."
>
> A 13-year-old adolescent girl, who initially refused to be placed in adoptive care when her elderly maternal grandmother was no longer able to care for her, feared that she would lose her very significant familial tie to her grandmother. Subsequent discussion involving the child, the grandmother, the worker, and the adoptive family clarified the issue. It was agreed that after adoption the child would be able to visit her grandmother. The girl then accepted the adoption.

The implementation of this approach is not easy because the emotional voltage surrounding these issues is so high. Each case is unique and has to be handled with great sensitivity and care.

> Maggie was 5 years old when she placed in foster care because her mother was too emotionally incapacitated to provide adequate maternal care. During the first year of the placement, with the goal of returning her to her biological home, the agency actively supported Maggie's ties to both her biological mother and the foster family by arranging for visits on neutral ground.
>
> However, the visits proved to be extremely upsetting to Maggie. Although she asked that they be stopped, the visits were continued for another year. Eventually the agency did end the visits, which had continued to upset the child. The foster family then tried to adopt Maggie but her biological mother successfully appealed to the court to stop their action. Another year went by, and she was placed in another home for adoption. Again the biological mother appealed as yet another year went by, but this time the adoption was upheld.

During the final court proceedings, two psychiatrists stated opposing views: the child *should* have the reality of seeing her biological mother; the child should *not* be subjected to that painful reality and should be allowed, as much as possible, to grow up as a carefree child. The biological mother's lawyer believed that she should be allowed visitation rights but acknowledged that he was not sure it would be healthy for the child. He thought the biological mother was not ready to take the child back at that time and that she might never be ready. The judge awarded custody to the adoptive agency, which placed Maggie, now 9 years old, in adoptive care after four years of foster care.

Currently, the adoptive agency doesn't want Maggie to have any further contact with her biological mother because Maggie has been adopted. Maggie's biological mother doesn't feel that way and has already visited the adoption agency in an attempt to see Maggie again. The agency stood firm and said no. I do not know if the agency plans for the child to have contact with the foster family, who after four years had become significant others to Maggie. Maggie's father has dropped out of sight. He is reported to be schizophrenic.

Maggie's adjustment to her adoptive placement has been good. Although she still doesn't want to see her biological mother, she does write to her, thus maintaining some tie. Her adoptive family believes that the visits with the biological mother had been too devastating—they tore Maggie in two and left her very depressed. Her adoptive parents are firmly convinced that what Maggie needs now is no direct contact with her biological mother and ample opportunity to be a child free of such dilemmas.

The adoptive mother, Mrs. D., feels very sorry for Maggie's biological mother because she gave Maggie a lot when she was with her as an infant and toddler. The adoptive mother hopes that at some distant point in the future, Maggie and her biological mother will have direct contact.

Mrs. D also has knowledge of how to reach Maggie's biological father's extended family. Mrs. D. believes that Maggie should have this connection too, but again at a later date when Maggie is mature enough to handle it with their support.

This case clearly suggests the inadvisability of insisting upon visits with the biological family without taking into account the psychological needs of all the parties involved. The critical measure in the situation is an assessment of how destructive visits were for the child and the biological mother and an assessment of the adoptive family's capacity to provide secure continuity of care. Only when all three corners of the adoptive triangle are considered can a specific plan be designed. In this case it seems that the child's tie to her biological mother needs to be necessarily quite thin for the present and the immediate future. Later the connect can be thickened via visitation when the child and the biological mother are able to handle such visits in a mutually beneficial way. However, the visits cannot be constructive until Maggie knows that her adoptive home is secure and permanent to the extent that visits with her biological mother will not overwhelm her with the devastating fear that she will lose her adoptive home if she sees her biological mother.

In the following exceedingly difficult case, the issue is raised again of severing or maintaining the late adoptee's ties to the biological family.

> Angie, a 2½-year-old girl, witnessed her father brutally beating her mother before he succeeded in killing her. He had also sexually abused Angie. Since the traumatic event of her mother's death, Angie was placed in temporary foster care. Her father was convicted of his wife's murder and imprisoned.
>
> Although Angie was doing well in her foster care, she was still a very traumatized little girl. The goal of the social agency was to place her in permanent adoptive care and to sever all ties with the biological family. However, a paternal aunt and her family initiated court action to block the adoption, claiming their natural right to the child as blood relatives.
>
> The agency's psychologist believed that the placement of Angie in her father's sister's home would be the worst place for the child to be. To do so would force her to live with the fact that her father murdered her mother or that her father was in prison wrongfully convicted of murdering her mother. He felt that it would be impossible for her paternal aunt to prevent Angie from being reminded of her father and the traumatic events. He also felt that living with the aunt, Angie would very likely have subsequent contact with her father directly or indirectly. Another psychologist agreed that Angie deserved a new start at her age, and the agency concurred in recommending a permanent adoption without connection to the biological family.

As difficult as this case is, it is unfortunately not that uncommon. It confronts everyone involved with a series of agonizing human decisions. It is easy to identify with the social agency in their concerns about the child. But would placing the child in permanent adoptive care and severing all ties to the biological family actually resolve the issue? I think not. It will bury the issue, which is appropriate for now, but it will not resolve the issue for the child if the cut-off is permanently maintained. The child would lose her ties not only to her father and paternal extended family but to her maternal extended family as well. Such a loss would be considerable.

A possible solution to the complex problem of Angie's placement would be to place her in a late-adoptive-care setting with a planned, later reconnection with her biological family. This would be consistent with the fact that at her age she would be highly likely to retain conscious or preconscious memories of her mother and father and other extended family members. For the balance of her childhood she could be nurtured in the adoptive home. During this period her ties to her biological family would be dormant. After her psychological and emotional roots were solidly secured in her adoptive home, her ties to her biological family could be reactivated through visitation at an age when she could handle such meetings with adequate support. The tie to her biological father necessarily needs to be quite thin until she reaches a level of maturity to be able to deal with the painful reality that was a part of her life. At that time, perhaps after majority, she may need professional help to resolve her tie to her father. This would be a difficult task for her but one that would lead to important psychological and emotional gains. Again, I believe that the impulse to cut Angie off totally and permanently from her biological father and her biological extended families in an effort to protect her goes too far. Whether or not one chooses to move in the particular ways suggested above would depend necessarily upon a full assessment of Angie's biological extended family. My point is simply that, even in cases like this, I would not advocate the complete severance of all family ties.

## Crosscultural Adoption

The issues regarding crosscultural adoptions are extremely complex. Often the lack of a means of support for these children in their own cultural setting dictates that they be transplanted to an alien culture in order to save their lives. But when, for example, children from Vietnam are adopted into American families, important familial, racial, linguistic, and cultural ties are severed simultaneously. The full impact of the disruption is often obscured when the children are young and in the process of adapting themselves to the new family, culture, and ethnic group, but when they reach adolescence, those severed ties resurface as each child asks the (by now almost impossible to answer) question, "Who am I?"

As they seek to answer this question, they will be faced with an array of very likely unanswerable questions, since the cut-off is probably permanent. We have to be available to these children and be committed to providing them with long-range follow-up. Without that commitment many of them will be unable to fully resolve and mourn their original familial losses. Very likely they will have difficulty handling their subsequent marriage and parenthood because of the feelings of abandonment and loss they will still carry.

This issue is movingly illustrated in the case of a young woman who was crossculturally adopted from Asia into an American family. This woman went through the poignant and painful process of resolving her early feelings of being attached to and abandoned by her biological family. As a mother, this resolution enabled her to begin feeding her own infant adequately and to reverse a pattern of abandonment so strong that she had been leaving her child to die slowly of malnutrition. Not all severed familial ties lead to such devastating outcomes, but that they do occur is evidence that the issue of rootedness is not to be taken lightly.

## CONCLUSION

This paper has explored a design for child placement practice that would deliberately consider the reality of both the child's ties to his biological family and their ties to him. Four factors emerged repeatedly that bear on these child placement issues: continuity of care, visitation rights, the various configurations of parent-child triangles, and relinquishment.

The paper suggests a range of *continuity-of-care options* that can be thought of as a series of placement possibilities running along a continuum of familial connection with a strong, consistent degree of secure, continuous care for the child. On the continuum would be joint custody of children, short-term foster care, long-term foster care, adoptive care with familial connection, and finally adoptive care without familial connection.

*Visitation rights*, which ensure continuity of ties with the biological family, are inextricably interwoven with the factor of continuity of care. The meaning of the visit with the biological family must be clearly spelled out to the child so that he will not be overwhelmed by the fear and threat of losing his secure home base; the visits should not have the effect of making him feel that his placement situation is jeopardized in any way. Although there are many exceptions, generally the frequency of the visits can be seen to fall along a continuum. In the divorced family the child's visits may be quite frequent; for foster children and adoptive children, they may be progressively less frequent. But the visits, even if limited, have enormous value to all parties involved in maintaining a sense of wholeness about themselves. The issue of visitation is a salient one not only for biological parents but for biological grandparents as well. Some grandparents whose son has been divorced are beginning to press for visitation rights to their grandchildren [22] (maternal grandparents typically have greater contact).

Nevertheless, one can still ask, "Are there no exceptions to the principle of visitation for the child and his biological family?" The answer is, yes, of course. Visits at the wrong time will be more destructive than constructive. Necessarily, the thread of connection to one's biological family may need at times to be very thin, indeed—dormant perhaps, but never broken. Later when conditions are favorable, the dormant ties can be reactivated through photo albums, letters, phone calls, and eventually visits. There will, of course, always remain the option for anyone, at majority, to decide whether he or she wishes to maintain biological family ties or any other family ties.

The third factor operating inevitably in all child placement situations is the various *child-parent triangles*. . . . In the foster-care setting, it will be a triangle consisting of the child, the biological family, and the foster family. In the adoptive-care option it will be the child, the biological family, and the adoptive family. Bowen's work with family system triangles, Nagy's work with family loyalties, and Minuchin's work with current familial-contextual arrangements all have obvious applicability here. The aim would be to have the agency or the worker involved help the child and the families to resolve the harmful loyalty conflicts that such triangles set up. This would call for continuous contact of the child with *both* sides of the triangle but only at times that such contact could be constructive.

In general, the thinner the biological familial connection, the longer the resolution process is likely to take. Significant ties to both biological families and foster and adoptive families need not be seen as different from children's ties to *both* biological families in the standard family pattern.

This paper suggests that we can develop degrees of *relinquishment* defined by the particular child placement option that is used. Again, as one moves from foster care to adoptive care without familial connection, a greater degree of relinquishment is appropriate. In crosscultural adoptions, although family ties are typically severed, efforts can be made to maintain racial, ethnic, and cultural ties.

Although this paper has focused upon the question of familial connectedness, when a child moves in the direction of such family continuity, the issue is raised of separation and individuation from the biological and placement-care families in order to achieve a sufficient whole sense of self. It is clear that it will be necessary to help children establish ties that are life-giving and life-supporting but not overly suffocating nor overly distant. Indeed, we all need to strike a realistic balance between togetherness and separateness, with freedom to move from one to the other.

Finally, I am acutely aware that the caseworker, the mental health professional, or the parent who wishes to implement some of the ideas suggested in this paper will inevitably be confronted with seemingly insoluble dilemmas. If the parent or worker attempts to help the child maintain biological family ties, he is not unlikely to encounter strong resistance from the other parent, his field supervisor, the child's family, the court, the school, or all of these. Nevertheless, the more we confront and think about these problems, the more we will find ways to solve them. To move in this direction will require a shift in orientation that will not come easily. I have no doubt that many persons and professionals will strongly disagree with the ideas presented in this paper. This would trouble me only if the disagreements do not lead to better solutions that enhance our ability to place children in ways that enrich them. Much more work needs to be done in this area in terms of exploration, practice, and definitive research. I hope readers will assist in this venture by active criticism and suggestions. In this way, we all stand to gain a more profound understanding of the processes by which human beings can become *whole* persons.

## REFERENCES

1. Benet, M. K., *The Politics of Adoption*, New York: The Free Press, 1976.
2. Boszormeniyi-Nagy, I., and Spark, G. *Invisible Loyalties: Reciprocity in International Family Therapy*, New York: Harper and Row, 1973.
3. Bowen, M., "The Use of Family Therapy in Clinical Practice," *Comp. Psychiat.* 7: 345–374, 1966.
4. Bowen, M., "Toward the Differentiation of Self in One's Family of Origin," in F. D. Andres and J. Lorio (Eds.). *Georgetown Family Symposia: A Collection of Selected Papers*, vol. I, Family Section, Department of Psychiatry, Georgetown University Medical Center, Washington, D.C., 1971–72, 1974.
5. Bush, S., "A Family Program That Really Works," *Psychol. Today*; 1977, 10, no. 12: 48–50.
6. Colón, F. "In Search of One's Past: An Identity Trip," *Fam. Proc.* 12: 429–438, 1973.
7. Fisher, F., *The Search for Anna Fisher*, Greenwich, Connecticut, Fawcett Publications, 1974.
8. Haley, A., *Roots*, Garden City, New York, Doubleday, 1976.
9. Hetherington, E. M.; Cox, M.; and Cox, R., "Divorced Fathers," *Fam. Coord.* 25: 417–427, 1976.

10. Kadushin, A., *Child Welfare Services* (2nd ed.). New York, MacMillan Publishing Co., 1974, Chapters 9, 10, 11.
11. Kline, D., and Forbush-Overstreet, H., *Foster Care of Children, Nurture and Treatment*, New York, Columbia University Press, 1972.
12. Kramer, C., "Foster Care Tomorrow," Paper read at 4th Statewide Conference of the Child Care Association of Illinois, Chicago, Illinois, March 26, 1968.
13. Krasner, B., "The Issue of Conflicting Loyalties in Foster Care Relationships," Paper read at the Foster Parents Recognition Dinner, Reading, Pennsylvania, June 1, 1975.
14. Lifton, B. J., *Twice Born*, New York, McGraw-Hill, 1975.
15. Lifton, R. J. Foreword to *The Politics of Adoption*, by M. K. Benet, New York, The Free Press, 1976.
16. Madison, B., and Schapiro, M., "Permanent and Long-Term Foster Family Care as a Planned Service," *Child Welfare*, 49: pp. 131–136, 1970.
17. McAdams, P. J., "The Parent in the Shadows," *Child Welfare* 51: 51–55, 1972.
18. McKuen, R., *Finding My Father: One Man's Search for Identity*, New York, Coward Publishing, 1976.
19. Minuchin, S.; Montalvo, B.; Guerney, B.; Rosman, B.; and Shumer, F., *Families of the Slums*, New York, Basic Books, 1967.
20. Minuchin, S., *Families and Family Therapy*, Cambridge, Massachusetts, Harvard University Press, 1974.
21. Minuchin, S., "The Plight of the Poverty Stricken Family in the United States," *Child Welfare* 49: 124–130, 1970.
22. New York Times News Service, "Grandparents Robbed of Their Role by Divorce," *The State Journal Register*, Springfield, Illinois, December 28, 1977, p. 14.
23. Roman, M., "The Disposable Parent," Paper read at the Association of Family Conciliation Courts, Minneapolis, Minnesota, May 11–14, 1977.
24. Trisiliotis, J., *In Search of Origins—The Experiences of Adopted People*, London, Boston, Routledge and Kegan Paul, 1973.
25. Wallerstein, J., and Kelly, J., "The Effects of Parental Divorce: The Adolescent Experience," in E. J. Anthony and C. Koupernik, (Eds.). *The Child in His Family*, vol. 3, New York, John Wiley and Sons, 1974.
26. Wallerstein, J., and Kelly, J., "The Effects of Parental Divorce: Experiences of the Pre-School Child," *J. Am. Acad. Child Psychiat.* 14: 600–616, 1975.
27. Weiss, R., *Marital Separation*, New York, Basic Books, 1975.

# 15

# The Importance of the Natural Parents to the Child in Placement

NER LITTNER

As many foster parents see it, the child's natural parents are a necessary evil. To be a foster parent is not easy. It requires being much more than just a parent to the child. Actually the foster parent has to juggle three tasks simultaneously. The first task is to be the best possible parent to the child. The second task is to cooperate as best he can with the placement agency and its social workers. And the third task is, very often, to do all this while maintaining a working relationship with the child's natural parents. It is understandable that some foster parents wish they could be relieved of this third task.

## WHY ARE SOME NATURAL PARENTS DISTURBING?

There are at least five reasons why foster parents may resent the natural parents:

1. Realistically, the natural parents may be difficult people to get along with and their presence may make the work of the foster parents harder. Some natural parents have severe emotional problems. They may be uncooperative, unpredictable and inconsistent. They may show up at inconvenient times, or

Reprinted from *Child Welfare*, Vol. LIV, No. 3 (March 1975): 175–181.

early or late or sometimes not at all. They may return the child to the foster parents' home at the wrong time. They may be argumentative, critical or drunk. They may unrealistically promise the child anything. They may be sabotaging of the foster parents' best efforts. They may treat the foster parents like hired help. They may show up with a different boyfriend or girlfriend each time.

2. In addition to these realistic problems with the natural parents, their visits with the child may result in a temporary worsening of the child's behavior and functioning. The child may become quite tense prior to the visit and extremely upset and unhappy and difficult to handle after the visit.

3. The child may worsen the situation by attempting to play the foster parents and the natural parents against each other. He does so, of course, as one way of trying to deal with his own inner emotional problems. But even though the foster parents may understand this theoretically, it still may be quite difficult for them when the child quotes selected comments made by the natural parents that seem critical of the foster parents or when the child unrealistically magnifies what the natural parents are like while simultaneously minimizing the care received from the foster parents.

4. A fourth reason for foster parents having difficulties with the natural parents may occur when the foster parents are clearly aware of how the child has been emotionally damaged by the natural parents. It is difficult for foster parents to be friendly with the natural parents under such circumstances, particularly if the damaging behavior continues, making it harder for the child to respond to the foster parents' care.

5. Finally, because foster parents are normal human beings they may have personal problems of their own. They may feel inadequate and unsure of their own role as parents. They may feel frustrated over their difficulties in helping a difficult child. They may feel guilty over how angry they get when the child behaves badly. All of these feelings may contribute to their feeling excessively competitive with the natural parents and needing to depreciate them in order to feel better about their own handling of the child.

These are five reasons—there undoubtedly are many others—why foster parents may resent the child's natural parents, may see them as a natural enemy, or even wish to exclude them competely from the child's life.

## WHY ARE NATURAL PARENTS IMPORTANT?

Yet, despite these problems, the foster parent is also aware of how important the natural parents are to the child.

There are many reasons why placement agencies go to a great deal of trouble to keep some contact between the natural parents and the child, even when, as a result of this contact, the child becomes upset and the foster parents feel that their work is made harder.

1. When the child has had living experiences with his natural parents, he identifies with many of their personality traits. He carries images of his natural parents within his own mind. They become, in effect, a part of the child. This occurs even when the child has no conscious memories of his natural parents, e.g., when he is placed away from his parents before the age of 6 years. Because of these identifications and images, any criticism of the natural parents—even when it is completely justified—is usually experienced by the child as a criticism of and attack upon the child.

2. If a child has emotional problems, he may develop highly unrealistic pictures of his natural parents in his own mind. He may overidealize them and their treatment of him, or he may exaggerate their problems and how badly they handled him. These unrealistic pictures in the child's mind serve to reassure the child about himself. They help the child deal with his own lack of confidence in himself, his own poor self-image, his anxieties, guilts and shame. No amount of logical discussions with the child can alter these unrealistic pictures. Only when the child gains self-confidence and feels better about himself is he able to see his natural parents as they really were and are.

3. A third reason for the natural parents' importance to the child is because he may miss them deeply. (I am discussing, of course, only those natural parents who actually had living experiences with the child. Those natural parents who never looked after the child prior to the placement are parents in name only.) No matter how troubled or difficult they may be, to the child—who is dependent upon them for life or death—they may be his entire security. They are all he has ever known. For better or worse, they are his roots to the past, his support and his foundation. When he is separated from them, he feels that he has lost a part of himself.

4. Finally, the placed child never really understands why his natural parents have left him. No matter what the realistic reason for the placement, the placed child develops a series of irrational explanations that he buries deeply in his mind. These unconscious feelings about his separation from his natural parents usually include such frequently illogical thoughts as the following: He was placed because he was bad and the placement is punishment; his natural parents have rejected and abandoned him and he will never see them again; his natural parents have died; etc., etc. The placed child's unconscious explanations of his separation from his parents are always enormously exaggerated, irrationally fearful and completely illogical. For these reasons, and despite the problems posed by our attempts to keep the natural parents in the picture, there are many advantages to the placed child of having continuing contact with his natural parents.

## THE PLACED CHILD GAINS FROM CONTACTS WITH HIS NATURAL PARENTS

These advantages[1] include the following:

1. As I have mentioned, the process of separation from his parents evokes in the placed child a variety of painful feelings, many of them highly exaggerated and illogical. Some of these separation feelings can be discharged by the child by his talking about them at the time of placement. In effect, he can get some of his feelings about leaving his parents off his chest. When he is able to do so, these separation feelings will bother him less. However, many of his feelings about separation are so painful that the child is unable to face them and so ventilate them. Instead he buries these feelings in his mind and represses them.

These repressed separation feelings pose a continuing danger to the child. The effort at keeping them buried ties up a lot of the child's energy and thus interferes with his ability to function properly. In addition, the repressed feelings may manifest themselves indirectly through such symptoms as behavior problems or difficulties in getting along with people. Finally, the repressed separation feelings may be displaced onto mother and father substitutes and so interfere with the child's ability to relate to them.

In other words, the child may have problems with his foster parents because his repressed feelings about his natural parents may color the spectacles with which he views his foster parents.

Placed children frequently are upset after a visit with their natural parents. This upset behavior may be due in part to the natural parents' tense or traumatic handling of the child. But usually most of the child's upset behavior after the visit is due to the fact that the act of seeing his natural parents again triggers the child's repressed separation feelings about the parents.

This is why it is so important for the visits to take place. It's not that we want the child to be upset, but rather because we want to help the child get as much of his repressed feelings off his chest as possible, so that these buried feelings will stop bothering him. The short-term disadvantage of the child being upset by the visit is outweighed by the long-term benefit.

The more emotionally disturbed the child, i.e., the more problems he has prior to placement, the greater will be his difficulty in ventilating his

[1]It is important to maintain a diagnostic attitude toward a placed child's questions about his natural parents or wish to see them. Sometimes—and this is particularly true when the child had no living experiences with them—his questions have really nothing to do with his natural parents. Instead they may reflect an inner concern about himself, as in adolescence, or worries about his relationship with his foster parents.

separation feelings. Therefore, the child with few problems when placed will be able to discharge most of his separation feelings—if the placement is carried out properly. The sick child, on the other hand, will repress most of his separation feelings.

In other words, the sicker the child is emotionally the more important it is that he have regular visits with his natural parents. Another way of saying this is as follows: The child who is able to establish an excellent relationship with his foster parents has the least need to have visits with his natural parents. The child who has the most difficulty in getting along with his foster parents has the greatest need for continuing contacts with his natural parents. A child must have roots somewhere. Until he can establish roots in present relationships, we need to protect his roots to the past no matter how deformed they may be. Without roots, the child will die of emotional starvation.

2. This brings us, then, to the second benefit of continuing contacts between the placed child and his natural parents. On a long-term basis, it helps the child relate better to his foster parents. As the child, through his contacts with his natural parents, is able to discharge or come to peace with some of these buried separation feelings he will not need to displace them onto the foster parents. Instead he will be better able to view the foster parents as they really are and so develop with them a more appropriate, realistic relationship.

3. The continuing contacts with his natural parents have a third dividend. They give the placed child continuing opportunities to see them also realistically. As I have mentioned, the placed child develops a series of highly irrational feelings and fears concerning the natural parents. If the child has no further contacts with them after placement, these irrational images will merely blossom, unimpeded by the truth of reality. The contacts are needed to keep demonstrating to the child what his natural parents are really like. Because of the child's own inner problems, he may still need to cling to various irrational notions about his natural parents even though they keep visiting him. But without the visits it will be much more difficult for him to reach the point where he can view them rationally.

4. The child is not the only one who has unrealistic fantasies about the natural parents. The foster parents may also visualize them in a completely illogical manner. These unreal fantasies of the foster parents develop in part from the child's attempts to paint an unreal picture of his natural parents, and in part from unresolved problems of the foster parents concerning their own parents. These unreal fantasies can be kept under control by regular contacts between the foster and natural parents.

5. Another advantage of the visits is that they help calm some of the child's irrational separation fears. For example, one can tell a placed child

repeatedly that his natural parents are still alive even though they do not visit him; he probably won't believe what he is told. But if he is able to see them, this particular fear is more easily dealt with. Similarly, the child can correct his belief that his parents placed him because he was totally unimportant to them. No matter how rejecting the natural parents may be when they visit the child, their behavior will never be as frightening to the child as are his exaggerated fantasies about them—fantasies that will blossom unchecked if he never sees them.

6. A sixth benefit may occur when the natural parents are able to treat the child decently during the visits. Every parent wants to be a good parent. He isn't able to be when he has problems and the problems get in the way of his parenting abilities. The social worker who works with the natural parents has the opportunity to help them be better parents to the placed child by the help that he is able to give the natural parents and by the way the visits are structured. It is possible, even with the very disturbed natural parents, to help them bring out their best attitudes when with the child, and also help them to subdue their more upsetting ones. When this is possible, everyone benefits. The natural parents feel better about themselves. The placed child receives corrective living experiences from his natural parents, which help him function better with, and feel less distrust toward, the foster parents.

7. A seventh benefit from the child's continuing contact with his natural parents has to do with the fact that many placed children come from homes where they were exposed to and traumatized by constant fighting between the adults. A placed child who comes from such a background can greatly benefit from experiencing a living situation where the foster parents not only get along with each other (with the usual average problems) but also get along with the natural parents. The child who was brought up by quarreling parents frequently tries unconsciously to stir up quarrels between the foster parents or between the foster and natural parents. If the child's efforts to provoke such quarrels are unsuccessful, he will mature much more quickly and learn instead more appropriate ways of relating to people.

8. Finally, an eighth benefit from such visits occurs in those situations when the natural parents are able to reestablish their family. It is rather difficult for a child to fit into a family where he has become a stranger. It is much easier when the child has been able to maintain some form of an ongoing relationship with the other members of his family.

## CONCLUSION

It is understandable that some foster parents would regard natural parents as their natural enemies. The presence of the natural parents in the placement picture frequently complicates and renders difficult the foster parents' attempts to help the child and to cooperate with the placement agency.

It is frequently difficult to realize that behind the mask and facade of the provocative, neglecting or difficult actions of the natural parents is a completely different face. Most natural parents feel a sense of deep failure as parents and as human beings. They feel inadequate, guilty and ashamed. They feel totally helpless to deal with either the child or the placement situation. Their neglect, their anger, their criticism, their unrealistic competitiveness—all are defensive maneuvers. Unfortunately, their defensiveness only serves to perpetuate their own problems, problems that originated in their own traumatic childhood experiences at the hands of *their* parents.

When the foster parent feels hit on the head by the defensive actions of the natural parents, it is hard for him mentally to step back and sympathize with their problems. While he is being hurt by the behavior of the natural parents, it is difficult for the foster parent to remember that one cannot love unless one was first loved. Many disturbing natural parents received little love as children. It is hard for them to give to their own children unless they are first given to, either by the social worker or by the foster parents themselves.

To the degree that the foster parent can be understanding of the natural parent, and particularly of the crucial significance of the natural parents to the placed child—to that degree will the foster parent make his own job more interesting, more rewarding and more fulfilling.

# 16

# Parental Visiting of Children in Foster Care: Key to Discharge?

DAVID FANSHEL

The longitudinal study of foster children at the Columbia University School of Social Work focused upon 624 children who entered foster care in 1966 and were followed for a five-year period. The age of the children at the time of their entry spanned a range from infancy to twelve years. They had never been placed before, and each subject experienced a minimum of ninety days in care. At the time data collection ended, in 1972, 36 percent of the children were still in care. Fifty-six percent of the children had been discharged, 5 percent placed in adoptive homes, and 3 percent transferred to mental institutions or training schools for delinquent children.

I here provide data about parental visitation of the children while they were in placement and explore the ramifications of visiting patterns for the discharge of the subjects over the five years of longitudinal investigation. The research team has previously reported on selected findings from the investigation of the children dealing with such topics as discharge patterns, the cost of care, and the special problem of children whose mothers were

---

Reprinted from *Social Service Review*, Vol. 49, No. 4 (December 1975), pp. 493–514, by permission of The University of Chicago Press. 

identified as drug abusers [1]. Reports have also been issued on parallel studies of the families and the agencies serving the children [2]. From the beginning of the study, parental visiting was viewed as highly important for the welfare of the children. Prior experience in working with foster children had sensitized me to this. I had witnessed the dismay and acute pain caused children by the failure of their parents to visit. Anyone who has observed this phenomenon quickly becomes appreciative of the emotional turmoil that can be experienced by the unvisited youngster [3]. I also was aware that several studies had indicated that the visitation of parents had beneficial effects with respect to the emotional adjustment of foster children [4].

The matter of parental visitation has received only spotty attention in the professional literature, which may reflect a lack of appreciation of its critical importance in shaping the course of a child's career in foster care. Here and there, however, one finds important references in the research literature. In the well-known study of foster care reported by Maas and Engler, there is a commentary by Joseph H. Reid, executive director of the Child Welfare League of America, indicating the massive failure of parents to visit their children in the nine communities included in the study: "We can only conclude that there are roughly 168,000 children today who are in danger of staying in foster care throughout their childhood years. And although in a third of their cases at least one parent did visit the child, in approximately half the parents visited infrequently or not at all" [5].

More recently there have been similar findings about the low level of parental visiting in two statewide studies. An investigation in Massachusetts reported the following finding: "Related to the issue of parental interests, the social workers were asked about the frequency of parent contact with the child. The statistics remained consistent on this point. It was found that less than 30 percent of the children had seen one of their parents in a given three-month period. Approximately 38 percent had seen their parent(s) sometime within the last six months. The remaining children have no substantial parental contact" [6].

In a study of foster children in Arizona, less than 30 percent of the children interviewed reported receiving visits from their parents and only 14 percent reported visiting their parents in their own homes [7].

## THE VISITING SCALE

My data on visiting are derived from a series of four sequential telephone interviews carried out over the course of the five years of investigation [8]. The first round of interviews (time 1, 1966–67) took place when most of the 616 children covered had been in placement between six and nine months

[9]. The second round (time 2, 1967–68) covered 496 children at a time when most had been in placement between eighteen and twenty-three months. The third round (time 3, 1969–70) covered 389 children, most of whom had been in care between thirty-five and forty-eight months. The fourth round (time 4, 1971) covered 275 children, most of whom had spent the entire five-year span of the study in care. The declining number of subjects in each round of interviewing reflects the discharge of children from care; social workers were no longer available for reports when the cases were closed. Parental visiting was, of course, not a relevant matter for discharged children.

The social workers who had primary responsibility for work with the children and their families were queried about the nature of the contact between the parents and their children. The questions covered such details as the frequency with which fathers and mothers visited, restrictions imposed by the agency upon visiting, conditions preventing the parents from availing themselves of the opportunity to visit, and whether the child visited his parent(s) at home.

In the presentation here I focus upon frequency of parental visiting, and for this purpose, a "visiting scale" was created reflecting the following categories of visitation:

*No visiting:* Neither parent had visited in the time period covered by each round of interviewing.

*Minimum visiting:* A parent had visited rarely or occasionally in the period covered; many had visited only once or twice.

*Frequent irregular visiting:* A parent had visited fairly often, but visiting was irregular and not up to the maximum permitted.

*Maximum permitted visiting:* A parent had visited regularly and took full advantage of all opportunities to do so.

*Child visits home*. The predominant form of contact was the child visiting in his own home [10].

It should be noted that the visiting scale was created on the basis of each child being classified according to an optimal criterion. The parent whose visiting was most frequent became the source of codification. Thus, if a mother of a child was reported as having engaged in "minimum visiting" and the father as having visited on the basis of "maximum permitted visiting," the visiting pattern was categorized according to the father's behavior [11].

## PARENT VISITING OVER FIVE YEARS OF STUDY

Table 1 displays the pattern of parent visiting over the five years of longitudinal investigation. The data show a dramatic decline in visitation

**TABLE 1**

**Frequency of Parental Visiting over Five Years of Longitudinal Investigation***

| Visiting Behavior | Series | | | | | | | |
|---|---|---|---|---|---|---|---|---|
| | Time 1 | | Time 2 | | Time 3 | | Time 4 | |
| | N | % | N | % | N | % | N | % |
| No visiting | 112 | 18.2 | 146 | 31.3 | 136 | 36.0 | 153 | 56.9 |
| Minimum visiting | 125 | 20.3 | 49 | 10.5 | 58 | 15.3 | 20 | 7.4 |
| Frequent irregular visiting | 75 | 12.2 | 90 | 19.4 | 45 | 11.9 | 16 | 5.9 |
| Maximum permitted visiting | 304 | 49.3 | 150 | 32.3 | 96 | 25.4 | 58 | 21.6 |
| Child visits home† | ... | .... | 30 | 6.5 | 43 | 11.4 | 22 | 8.2 |
| Total | 616 | 100.0 | 465 | 100.0 | 378 | 100.0 | 269 | 100.0 |

*Each data-gathering occasion represents a round of telephone interviewing of agency caseworkers.

†At time 1, this category was included within "maximum permitted visiting."

from time 1 to time 4. As children are discharged from care over time, the residual populations of children show an increasing proportion of those who are unvisited. Whereas 18 percent of the children in care at time 1 were not visited at all, this is true of 31 percent at time 2, 36 percent at time 3, and 57 percent at time 4. When the cases where there was *no visiting* are consolidated with those where there was *minimal visiting*, it is apparent that about two-thirds of the children remaining in care five years after their entry had essentially lost contact with their parents. This is a striking and dismaying finding but not very different from those of the studies previously cited.

The data provided here tend to be in accord with a 1979 survey of the New York City foster-care system undertaken to determine the number of children who should be considered for adoptive planning. The investigators found that nearly one-third of all children in foster homes and institutions had had no communication with either parent for six months or longer [12]. Since this reflected a cross-sectional analysis of all children in care including recent arrivals who were more apt to be visited—in contrast to the data reported here for children in care for five years—the findings can be seen as quite compatible.

I will not take the occasion at this point to dwell upon the significance of the social data provided. This issue will be explored analytically in the material that follows. I am aware, however, that revealing that large numbers of foster children are unvisited must awaken considerable consternation among those charged with program planning and legislative responsibility in this area of service.

## ETHNICITY AS A FACTOR IN VISITING

An analysis of parental visiting according to the ethnic background of the children was undertaken in order to determine whether the children were differentially handicapped with respect to having ongoing contact with their parents. The children were grouped within the following categories: white Catholic and Protestant, Jewish, black Catholic, black Protestant, and Puerto Rican. White Catholic and white Protestant children were grouped together because there were relatively few of the latter in our sample and because the two groups appeared relatively undifferentiated for almost all our measures of child adjustment. The black children were separated into two groups on the basis of religion because there were a fairly substantial number of black Catholic children and they tended to be cared for by a different network of agencies than were the Protestant children.

Table 2 displays the visiting patterns of the parents according to the ethnicity-religious breakdowns cited. Parental visiting was characterized as high if the parent(s) engaged in frequent irregular visiting or the maximum visiting permitted by the agency, or if the child visited home. It was characterized as low if the parent(s) engaged in minimum visiting or did not visit at all. At time 1, reflecting the situation in the early phase of our study, all groups showed a significant proportion of children whose parents engaged in a high degree of visiting. However, quite distinct intergroup differences are readily apparent. The Jewish children, coming most often from intact family units, tended to receive the most frequent visitation; more than nine out of ten were visited at a high level. The white Protestant and Catholic children fared well, with about two-thirds being frequently visited, as did the Puerto Rican children, with 70 percent being visited the maximum amount permitted or on a frequent but irregular basis.

The black children, both Catholic and Protestant, experienced the least amount of parental visiting. About half of both groups were either unvisited or visited minimally compared with a third of the white Catholic and Protestant children and 30 percent of the Puerto Rican children. Less than 7 percent of the Jewish children were visited minimally.

For the children remaining in care at time 2, we observed that the visiting of the Jewish and Puerto Rican children was high, comparable to that reported at time 1. The white Catholic and Protestant children showed a small decline in the group of highly visited children, while the black Protestant children showed a decline of about 10 percent. Only 39 percent of the latter received a high level of visiting. The black Catholic children were visited at about the same level as time 1.

At time 4, an erosion can be observed in the proportion of visited subjects still left in care. Only 22 percent of the black Protestant children, 35 percent

TABLE 2

**Frequency of Parental Visiting for Four Time Occasions by Ethnicity-Religion**

| Visiting Behavior | White Catholic and Protestant | Jewish | Black Catholic | Black Protestant | Puerto Rican |
|---|---|---|---|---|---|
| Time 1 (*N*=616): | | | | | |
| High visiting (%) | 66.7 | 93.5 | 47.1 | 48.9 | 70.2 |
| Low visiting (%) | 33.3 | 6.5 | 52.9 | 51.1 | 29.8 |
| N cases | 126 | 31 | 68 | 190 | 201 |
| | $x^2$=64.117, df=16, P<.001 | | | | |
| Time 2 (*N*=465): | | | | | |
| High visiting (%) | 59.8 | 92.6 | 48.1 | 38.6 | 72.7 |
| Low visiting (%) | 40.2 | 7.4 | 51.9 | 61.4 | 27.3 |
| N cases | 87 | 27 | 52 | 145 | 154 |
| | $x^2$=82.758, df=16, *P*<.001 | | | | |
| Time 3 (*N*=378): | | | | | |
| High visiting (%) | 48.6 | 100.0 | 40.9 | 35.9 | 54.9 |
| Low visiting (%) | 51.4 | ..... | 59.1 | 64.1 | 45.1 |
| N cases | 72 | 21 | 44 | 117 | 124 |
| | $x^2$=51.176, df=16, *P*<.001 | | | | |
| Time 4 (*N*=269): | | | | | |
| High visiting (%) | 34.8 | 70.0 | 50.0 | 22.2 | 39.6 |
| Low visiting (%) | 65.2 | 30.0 | 50.0 | 77.8 | 60.4 |
| N cases | 46 | 10 | 36 | 86 | 91 |
| | $x^2$=49.045, df=16, *P*<.001 | | | | |

Note. — In this and subsequent tables, "high visiting" includes children who received frequent irregular visiting or maximum permitted visiting or who visited their own homes. "Low visiting" includes children whose parents engaged in minimum visiting or did not visit at all. Chi squares are calculated on the basis of 5×5 contingency tables reflecting full visiting scale instead of the collapsed version presented here.

of the white Catholic and Protestant children, and 40 percent of the Puerto Rican children were receiving frequent visiting. Fifty percent of the black Catholic children were receiving high levels of visiting, as were 70 percent of the few (ten) Jewish children remaining in care. The special disadvantage of the black Protestant children is noteworthy.

## REASONS FOR PLACEMENT

The major reasons for the placement of the children as displayed in table 3 provide some clues about the different patterns of parental visitation. Children who entered care because of their own behavioral and/or emotional disorders received a high level of visiting in all four time periods. They tended to come from intact families whose economic circumstances were relatively superior. Surprisingly, children who came into care because of the mental illness of a parent were among those who were relatively advantaged with respect to parental visiting. By the end of the study, only one out of three children in the neglect or abuse category and only one in five of those who had been abandoned by a parent was visited.

As might be expected, unmarried mothers who were unwilling to assume care of their newborn babies were among those who tended to engage in a low level of visiting. By the end of the study, when their children were about five years old, only one of ten such mothers engaged in frequent visiting of their children.

## PARENTAL VISITING AND DISCHARGE FROM CARE

In approaching the task of analyzing the relationship between parental visiting and the discharge of children from foster care, I was prepared to find a significant association between these phenomena. It seemed reasonable to expect that parents who maintained steady contact with their children would be more likely to arrange to take them home than would those who hardly visited or who completely dropped out of the picture. The latter were apt to include the most disabled among the parents as well as the most socially deprived. One would also anticipate that those not motivated to visit—or prevented from doing so by circumstances beyond their control—would feel under less pressure from their children to take them home than would parents who had regular face-to-face contact with their offspring. I should point out, however, that while I anticipated a fairly strong association between parental visiting and child discharge, I was not sure how visiting behavior interacted with other variables, nor was I well informed about the influence of visiting in the later years of the child's placement experience as opposed to the first year after entry into care. I wanted to know more about the relationship between visiting and discharge from a longitudinal perspective.

In table 4 cross-tabulations between the reported visiting of parents and the discharge of children are provided. For simplicity of presentation I have dichotomized the status of the children as discharged or still in care after five

TABLE 3

Frequency of Parental Visiting for Four Time Occasions by Reason for Placement

| Visiting Behavior | Mental Illness of Child-Care Person | Neglect or Abuse of Child | Behavior of Child | Physical Illness of Child-Care Person | Abandonment or Desertion by Parent | Parent Unwilling to Continue Care | Family Problems | Parent Unwilling to Assume Care | Death of Parent |
|---|---|---|---|---|---|---|---|---|---|
| Time 1 ($N$=616): | | | | | | | | | |
| High visiting (%) | 77.2 | 55.0 | 84.9 | 57.4 | 43.3 | 68.2 | 40.4 | 49.0 | 35.7 |
| Low visiting (%) | 22.8 | 45.0 | 15.1 | 42.6 | 56.7 | 31.8 | 59.6 | 51.0 | 64.3 |
| N cases | 136 | 91 | 73 | 68 | 67 | 63 | 57 | 47 | 14 |
| | $x^2$=102.792, df=24, $P$<.001 | | | | | | | | |
| Time 2 ($N$=465): | | | | | | | | | |
| High visiting (%) | 70.0 | 46.5 | 86.5 | 54.3 | 50.9 | 42.0 | 45.5 | 40.0 | 72.7 |
| Low visiting (%) | 30.0 | 53.5 | 13.5 | 45.7 | 49.1 | 58.0 | 54.5 | 60.0 | 27.3 |
| N cases | 100 | 71 | 67 | 35 | 57 | 50 | 44 | 30 | 11 |
| | $x^2$=100.288, df=32, $P$<.001 | | | | | | | | |

**TABLE 3** *(Continued)*

| | | | | | | | | | |
|---|---|---|---|---|---|---|---|---|---|
| Time 3 (N=378): | | | | | | | | | |
| High visiting (%) | 56.0 | 41.8 | 81.2 | 42.0 | 47.0 | 37.1 | 38.4 | 29.2 | 27.3 |
| Low visiting (%) | 44.0 | 58.2 | 18.8 | 58.0 | 53.0 | 62.9 | 61.6 | 70.8 | 72.7 |
| N cases | 84 | 55 | 48 | 31 | 51 | 35 | 39 | 24 | 11 |
| | $x^2$=79.285, df=32, $P$<.001 | | | | | | | | |
| Time 4 (N=269): | | | | | | | | | |
| High visiting (%) | 48.3 | 33.4 | 63.0 | 37.9 | 18.9 | 33.3 | 32.1 | 10.0 | 12.5 |
| Low visiting (%) | 51.7 | 66.6 | 32.0 | 62.1 | 81.1 | 66.7 | 67.9 | 90.0 | 87.5 |
| N cases | 56 | 42 | 25 | 29 | 37 | 24 | 28 | 20 | 8 |
| | $x^2$=88.360, df=32, $P$<.001 | | | | | | | | |

Note. — Chi squares calculated on basis of five categories of visiting instead of collapsed high-low version presented here.

TABLE 4

**Discharge of Children from Foster Care According to Frequency of Parental Visiting for Four Time Occasions**

| Discharge Status | No Visiting | Minimum Visiting | Frequent Irregular Visiting | Maximum Permitted Visiting | Child Visits Home |
|---|---|---|---|---|---|
| Time 1 (N=577): | | | | | |
| Discharged (%) | 34.0 | 46.2 | 68.9 | 73.4 | ....* |
| Still in care after 5 years (%) | 66.0 | 53.8 | 31.1 | 26.6 | ..... |
| N cases | 97 | 117 | 74 | 289 | ..... |
| | $x^2$=60.799, df=3, $P$<.001 | | | | |
| Time 2 (N=422): | | | | | |
| Discharged (%) | 31.7 | 24.4 | 44.7 | 64.0 | 76.7 |
| Still in care after 5 years (%) | 68.3 | 75.6 | 55.3 | 36.0 | 23.3 |
| N cases | 123 | 45 | 85 | 139 | 30 |
| | $x^2$=47.630, df=4, $P$<.001 | | | | |
| Time 3 (N=349): | | | | | |
| Discharged (%) | 17.3 | 27.3 | 35.7 | 48.3 | 78.0 |
| Sill in care after 5 years (%) | 82.7 | 72.7 | 64.3 | 51.7 | 22.0 |
| N cases | 122 | 55 | 42 | 89 | 41 |
| | $x^2$=57.756, df=4, $P$<.001 | | | | |
| Time 4 (N=245): | | | | | |
| Discharged (%) | 7.9 | ..... | 7.1 | 29.6 | 28.6 |
| Still in care after 5 years (%) | 92.1 | 100.0 | 92.9 | 70.4 | 71.4 |
| N cases | 139 | 17 | 14 | 54 | 21 |
| | $x^2$=22.411, df=4, $P$<.001 | | | | |

Note. — Table excludes 29 children who left care because they were adopted, 16 who were transferred to state mental institutions, and two who were transferred to state training schools for delinquent children.

*At time 1, this category was included within "maximum permitted visiting."

years rather than indicate the year in which the child exited from care (e.g., first year, second year). Note also that twenty-nine cases of adopted children have been excluded from this analysis, since their exit from the foster-care system is a phenomenon not related to parental visiting. I have also excluded sixteen cases where the children left foster care through transfer to state mental institutions and two cases involving transfer to state training schools for delinquent children. While the discharge of children is generally construed as a positive outcome, such orientation is not appropriate for these latter cases.

Table 4 shows that there is a strong association between the frequency of parental visiting and the discharge of children from foster care. The first year's visiting data illustrate that a considerably higher proportion of subjects was eventually discharged whose parents visited the maximum permitted by the agency or who visited frequently but irregularly than those not visited at all or visited minimally. Sixty-six percent of the children whose parents engaged in no visiting at time 1 were still in foster care five years after their entry. This was true of 54 percent of those whose parents visited on a minimum basis. By contrast, 31 percent of the children whose parents visited on a frequent but irregular basis and 27 percent of those whose parents visited on all occasions permitted by the agency were still in care at the end of five years. The strength of the relationship between visiting and discharge is impressive and demonstrates the centrality of visiting as a key element in the return of foster children to their own homes.

Inspection of the data in table 4 shows that the visiting behavior of parents is significantly associated with discharge status on the three subsequent data-gathering occasions. Even at time 4, when the children were in care over four years, highly visited children left the system in significantly greater proportions than did children whose parents did not visit or visited minimally. For all four data-gathering occasions high parental visiting appears to be a good omen with respect to discharge. At the same time, it is important to observe that the association between visiting and discharge becomes attenuated over time, so that high visiting at time 1 is more closely linked to discharge than at time 4. Thus 73 percent of the children whose parents engaged in maximum visiting as assessed at time 1 succeeded in returning home. This was true for 64 percent at time 2, 48 percent at time 3, and only 30 percent at time 4. When children whose parents did not visit at all are considered, 34 percent were discharged with respect to the time 1 visiting pattern, 32 percent for time 2, 17 percent for time 3, and only 8 percent for time 4.

I believe that the saliency of visiting as a predictive variable in the discharge of children from foster care has been demonstrated. The association is indeed striking. The reader should also bear in mind that, while the fact of no parental visiting or minimal visiting bodes ill for the discharge of children, the absolute number of nonvisiting parents kept increasing in our sample even as the study population in care diminished over the five years of the study. Thus an object of concern is not only that nonvisiting parents at time 1 do poorly in retrieving their children from foster care but also that their ranks are increased over time by parents who have slipped into a nonvisiting pattern.

## PATTERNS OF VISITING OVER FIVE YEARS AND DISCHARGE

Since there were four data-gathering occasions when information on parental visiting could be obtained over the five years of the longitudinal study, a variety of visiting patterns could logically emerge. Some parents could

**TABLE 5**

**Pattern of Parental Visiting over Five-Year Period Related to Discharge of Children**
(N=577)

| Selected Patterns of Visiting | *N* Children | *N* Discharged |
|---|---|---|
| Uniformly high visiting patterns: | | |
| Hi$_1$ ——$_2$ ——$_3$ ——$_4$ | 107 | 107 |
| Hi$_1$ ——$_2$ Hi$_3$ ——$_4$ | 2 | 2 |
| Hi$_1$ Hi$_2$ ——$_3$ ——$_4$ | 45 | 45 |
| Hi$_1$ Hi$_2$ Hi$_3$ ——$_4$ | 49 | 47 |
| Hi$_1$ Hi$_2$ Hi$_3$ Hi$_4$ | 43 | 11 |
| Total | 246 | 212 |
| Uniformly low visiting patterns: | | |
| Lo$_1$ ——$_2$ ——$_3$ ——$_4$ | 37 | 37 |
| Lo$_1$ ——$_2$ ——$_3$ Lo$_4$ | 3 | 0 |
| Lo$_1$ Lo$_2$ ——$_3$ ——$_4$ | 8 | 8 |
| Lo$_1$ Lo$_2$ Lo$_3$ ——$_4$ | 9 | 5 |
| Lo$_1$ Lo$_2$ Lo$_3$ Lo$_4$ | 71 | 2 |
| Total | 128 | 52 |
| Mixed pattern: low to high visiting pattern: | | |
| Lo$_1$ Lo$_2$ Lo$_3$ Hi$_4$ | 5 | 1 |
| Lo$_1$ Lo$_2$ Hi$_3$ ——$_4$ | 6 | 5 |
| Lo$_1$ Lo$_2$ Hi$_3$ Hi$_4$ | 7 | 0 |
| Lo$_1$ Hi$_2$ ——$_3$ ——$_4$ | 12 | 12 |
| Lo$_1$ Hi$_2$ Lo$_3$ Hi$_4$ | 2 | 0 |
| Lo$_1$ Hi$_2$ Hi$_3$ ——$_4$ | 10 | 9 |
| Lo$_1$ Hi$_2$ Hi$_3$ Hi$_4$ | 6 | 4 |
| Hi$_1$ ——$_2$ Lo$_3$ Hi$_4$ | 1 | 0 |
| Hi$_1$ Lo$_2$ Lo$_3$ Hi$_4$ | 8 | 3 |
| Hi$_1$ Lo$_2$ Hi$_3$ ——$_4$ | 6 | 4 |
| Hi$_2$ Lo$_2$ Hi$_3$ Hi$_4$ | 4 | 3 |
| Hi$_1$ Hi$_2$ Lo$_3$ Hi$_4$ | 13 | 1 |
| Total | 80 | 42 |

**TABLE 5** *(Continued)*

| Selected Patterns of Visiting | N Children | N Discharged |
|---|---|---|
| Mixed pattern: high to low visiting pattern: | | |
| Lo$_1$ Lo$_2$ Hi$_3$ Lo$_4$ | 9 | 0 |
| Lo$_1$ Hi$_2$ Lo$_3$ ———$_4$ | 5 | 2 |
| Lo$_1$ Hi$_2$ Lo$_3$ Lo$_4$ | 15 | 2 |
| Lo$_1$ Hi$_2$ Hi$_3$ Lo$_4$ | 9 | 0 |
| Hi$_1$ ———$_2$ Lo$_3$ ———$_4$ | 2 | 2 |
| Hi$_1$ ———$_2$ Lo$_3$ Lo$_4$ | 1 | 0 |
| Hi$_1$ ———$_2$ Hi$_3$ Lo$_4$ | 2 | 2 |
| Hi$_1$ Lo$_2$ ———$_3$ ———$_4$ | 15 | 14 |
| Hi$_1$ Lo$_2$ Lo$_3$ ———$_4$ | 5 | 5 |
| Hi$_1$ Lo$_2$ Lo$_3$ Lo$_4$ | 12 | 0 |
| Hi$_1$ Lo$_2$ Hi$_3$ Lo$_4$ | 3 | 0 |
| Hi$_1$ Hi$_2$ ———$_3$ Lo$_4$ | 1 | 1 |
| Hi$_1$ Hi$_2$ Lo$_3$ ———$_4$ | 14 | 12 |
| Hi$_1$ Hi$_2$ Lo$_3$ Lo$_4$ | 14 | 1 |
| Hi$_1$ Hi$_2$ Hi$_3$ Lo$_4$ | 16 | 3 |
| Total | 123 | 44 |

| | N | % | % Discharged |
|---|---|---|---|
| Summary: | | | |
| Uniformly high | 246 | 42.6 | 86.2 |
| Mixed: low to high | 80 | 13.9 | 52.5 |
| Mixed: high to low | 123 | 21.3 | 35.8 |
| Uniformly low | 128 | 22.2 | 40.6 |
| Total | 577 | 100.0 | ..... |

maintain a uniformly high level of visitation over time, while others could uniformly engage in no visiting. For many parents, it was expected that changes in visiting patterns would reflect the ebb and flow of events in their lives—departure from mental hospitals, movement to new housing, and new responsibilities with the birth of a baby.

In table 5, the various patterns of parental visiting are displayed. The first procedure was to dichotomize the visiting scale information as previously cited into a low category (including children whose parents did not visit at all or visited only on a minimum basis) and a high category (including children whose parents visited frequently but irregularly, engaged in maximum permitted visitation, or took the child home to visit).

Inspection of table 5 shows that 246 children (43 percent) were the recipients of uniformly high levels of visiting. They had never been exposed to being in foster care without the active presence of their parents. The table demonstrates a very high proportion of discharges for these children. An exception is the pattern identified as $Hi_1$ $Hi_2$ $Hi_3$ $Hi_4$. These are children who remained in foster care despite consistently high visiting by a parent. These were mainly situations involving totally disabled mothers; the fathers could not take care of their children but nevertheless sustained contact with them. These also involved a few situations where the child came into care because of behavioral disturbance and was still in care five years later.

About 22 percent of the children were exposed to uniformly low patterns of visitation. The seventy-one children whose parents showed this pattern on all four time occasions ($Lo_1$ $Lo_2$ $Lo_3$ $Lo_4$) tended to remain in care; only 3 percent were discharged. On the other hand, it should be observed that thirty-seven children returned home during the first year after entry whose parents were reported to have engaged in low visiting during that period. These tended to reflect cases in which the mother was not able to visit because she was hospitalized or otherwise disabled. As soon as she recovered, she resumed care of her children.

About 35 percent of the children were exposed to parental visiting which included high visiting during one period and low visiting during another. The table presents data divided into two mixed patterns: (1) those cases in which the last visiting pattern was high, representing 14 percent of the study population, and (2) those cases in which the last reported visiting pattern was low, representing 21 percent of the cases. Where parental visiting moved into a high direction, the discharge rate was fairly good; about 53 percent of the children affected by this pattern were discharged within five years after entering care. This was true of only 36 percent of the children whose parental visiting pattern alternated between high and low visiting and where the last reported level of visiting was low.

## VISITING FREQUENCY AND DISCHARGE BY RACE/ETHNICITY

Having established that the visiting patterns of parents are strongly associated with discharge and highly differentiated by race, I proceeded to a somewhat more elaborate three-variable analysis to test whether the correlation between visiting and discharge holds within racial and ethnic groups. For simplicity of presentation I have consolidated the ethnicity variable into three categories (white, black, and Puerto Rican) and the visiting variables into the dichotomy employed earlier (low and high visiting). The results of this analysis are set forth in table 6.

A close examination of the data shows that, with a few exceptions, parental visiting is linked to discharge from foster care and that this holds

TABLE 6

Discharge of Children from Foster Care by Frequency of Parental Visiting for Four Time Occasions Controlling for Ethnicity

| Discharge Status | White | | Black | | Puerto Rican | |
|---|---|---|---|---|---|---|
| | Low Visiting | High Visiting | Low Visiting | High Visiting | Low Visiting | High Visiting |
| Time 1 (N=577): | | | | | | |
| Discharged (%) | 44.5 | 85.5 | 37.0 | 69.2 | 45.8 | 65.4 |
| Still in care after 5 years (%) | 55.5 | 15.0 | 63.0 | 30.8 | 54.2 | 34.6 |
| N cases | 36 | 107 | 119 | 120 | 59 | 136 |
| | $x^2$=23.574, df=1, $P$<.001 | | $x^2$=24.865, df=1, $P$<.001 | | $x^2$=6.612, df=1, $P$<.01 | |
| Time 2 (N=422): | | | | | | |
| Discharged (%) | 48.5 | 72.6 | 21.5 | 58.1 | 35.9 | 50.4 |
| Still in care after 5 years (%) | 51.5 | 27.4 | 78.5 | 41.9 | 64.1 | 49.6 |
| N cases | 31 | 73 | 98 | 74 | 39 | 107 |
| | $x^2$=5.633, df=1, $P$<.05 | | $x^2$=24.279, df=1, $P$<.001 | | $x^2$=2.438, df=1, N.S. | |
| Time 3 (N = 349) | | | | | | |
| Discharged (%) | 34.5 | 72.0 | 14.3 | 44.7 | 22.2 | 44.0 |
| Still in care after 5 years (%) | 65.5 | 28.0 | 85.7 | 55.3 | 77.8 | 56.0 |
| N cases | 32 | 50 | 91 | 56 | 54 | 66 |
| | $x^2$=11.291, df=1, $P$<.001 | | $x^2$=16.667, df=1, $P$<.001 | | $x^2$=6.227, df=1, $P$<.05 | |
| Time 4 (N=245): | | | | | | |
| Discharged (%) | 18.5 | 42.1 | 5.1 | 20.0 | 3.9 | 22.9 |
| Still in care after 5 years (%) | 81.5 | 57.9 | 94.9 | 80.0 | 96.1 | 77.1 |
| N cases | 27 | 19 | 78 | 35 | 51 | 35 |
| | $x^2$=3.060, df=1, N.S. | | $x^2$=6.081, df=1, $P$<.05 | | $x^2$=7.242, df=1, $P$<.01 | |

across ethnic groups and is persistent over time. Thus it appears that there is a beneficial payoff in superior discharge rates for the black and Puerto Rican subjects visited frequently as well as for those who are white.

The findings should be interpreted further to indicate that, while there is an apparent advantage within each ethnic group for highly visited children, white children experience higher discharge than the minority subjects when compared within the high and the low visiting categories. Factors other than visiting are obviously operating to depress the discharge rates of the black and Puerto Rican children. Note particularly the rapidity of the decline in discharge of the black children who received low visiting: only 14 percent were discharged at time 3 and 5 percent at time 4. For the low-visited Puerto Rican children, 22 percent were discharged at time 3 and 4 percent at time 4. By contrast, 35 percent of the low-visited white children were discharged at time 3 and 19 percent at time 4.

## FURTHER UNDERSTANDING OF VISITING BEHAVIOR

Thus far, the role of two independent variables has been examined in seeking to determine the sources of variation in parental visiting behavior: ethnicity and reason for placement. In an effort to develop further understanding of the visiting phenomenon through employment of a larger group of explanatory variables, multiple regression procedures were used rather than contingency tables. This procedure is capable of providing an assessment of the predictive utility of a fairly large number of variables. This approach was chosen because the limited sample size prohibited extending the contingency analysis much further than already carried out.

In the search for predictive correlates of parental visiting, a number of variables were examined in terms of their correlations with the dependent and other independent variables. Some were discarded because they showed little potential for enhanced understanding of the visiting phenomenon. Among others, these included the sex of the child, wedlock status of the mother at the time of his birth, and court versus public welfare agency as the source of placement. The following independent variables were selected for the multiple regression analysis:

*Child's age at placement:* I theorized that older children, having experienced longer contact with their parent(s), would have more solid ties with them than would infants.

*Number of children in family:* I theorized that having multiple children would provide greater pull on the parent to offspring than would the case of a single child.

*Ethnicity:* This was a dummy variable coded in binary form (coded 1 if the observation fell into the category, 0 if it did not) [13].

*Reason for placement:* As demonstrated earlier, categories such as unwillingness to assume care of an infant, neglect and abuse, and abandonment were associated with low levels of parental visiting while child behavior as a reason for placement showed a positive correlation. Through dummy-variable coding, seven reasons were created for placement variables.

*Evaluation of mother:* This is a five-item index covering the agency caseworker's assessment of the mother in five areas: (*a*) adequacy of maternal functioning; (*b*) degree of disturbance; (*c*) outlook for working with her; (*d*) prediction of whether she would drop out; and (*e*) quality of the caseworker's attitude toward the mother as rated by the agency study staff. This information was collected on the same four data-gathering occasions during which visiting behavior was recorded.

*Log total contact rate of caseworker with parent:* This variable is a seven-item index measuring the average monthly case contacts by the agency's caseworker. Information about contacts with the child, child-caring persons, parents, collaterals, and other agencies is included. The contacts include in-person interviews, home visits, and extended telephone calls. A logarithmic form of the index was developed to pick up some of the nonlinearity of the scores. Contact scores were created to reflect each of the four time phases.

In table 7, the zero-order correlations between the variables just cited and the visiting behavior of the parents at times 1–4 are provided. While there are fairly numerous instances where the correlations are statistically significant, none is higher than .36. The correlations must thus be seen as relatively modest.

For all four time phases, older children tended to be visited more frequently. The correlations are statistically significant for each time phase. The finding tends to support the view that older children, having had more extended contact with their parents, enjoy a greater claim on their loyalty and attentiveness than do younger children, such as newborns, whose mothers decided not to assume care of them early after birth.

The variable specifying the number of children in the family tends to show trivial and insignificant correlations with parent visiting, except for time 2, when there was greater visiting by parents of larger family units ($r$ = .10). On the whole, this variable is not impressive in its ability to contribute to the prediction of visiting behavior.

As previously displayed in the contingency tables, ethnicity is one of the stronger predictors of parental visiting, at least through time 3. Black children tended to be significantly undervisited for times 1, 2, and 3 while Puerto

TABLE 7

Correlations of Selected Background and Other Variables with Visiting Behavior of Parents (Times 1–4)[a]

| | Time 1 (N=577) | Time 2 (N=422) | Time 3 (N=349) | Time 4 (N=245) |
|---|---|---|---|---|
| Child's age at placement | .16*** | .32*** | .27*** | .21*** |
| No. of children in family | .00 | .10* | .04 | .07 |
| Ethnicity: black vs. others | −.22*** | −.29*** | −.19*** | −.10 |
| Ethnicity: Puerto Rican vs. others | .10* | .20*** | .08 | .07 |
| Reason for placement:[b] | | | | |
| Child behavior vs. others | .15*** | .25*** | .25*** | .21** |
| Unwilling to assume care vs. others | −.02 | −.09 | −.10 | −.12 |
| Abandonment vs. others | −.12** | −.04 | .01 | −.15* |
| Neglect or abuse vs. others | −.05 | −.11* | −.07 | −.03 |
| Mental illness of parent vs. others | .17*** | .14** | .05 | .14* |
| Physical illness of parent vs. others | −.04 | −.03 | −.04 | .02 |
| Unwilling to continue care vs. others | .04 | −.10* | −.06 | −.06 |
| Evaluation of mother (times 1–4)[c] | .21*** | .35*** | .30*** | .36*** |
| Log total casework contact rate times (1–4)[c] | .22** | .26*** | .35*** | .08 |

*$P<.05$.
**$P<.01$.
***$P<.001$.

[a]The visiting behavior variable is a dichotomy: low (coded as 0) and high (coded as 1).
[b]Ethnicity and reason for placement variables, dummy variable coded (each category is coded as 1 and "others" as 0).
[c]Variables come from the same time phase as the visiting behavior variable with which it is correlated.

Rican children received somewhat higher levels of visiting. As previously shown in the contingency tables, white children, particularly Jewish youngsters, fared better than minority children in being the recipients of frequent visiting from their parents.

The reason for placement variables coded in dummy-variable form show a number of categories which are significantly correlated with parental visiting. This information reflects the findings reported in table 3. Children coming into care because of their own behavior difficulties tended to be visited at a higher level when contrasted with others for all four time phases. Children who came into care because of the mental illness of their parents also were visited on a significantly greater basis for times 1, 2, and 4. Children who were abandoned tended to be visited significantly less than the other children at times 1 and 4, and children who were admitted into care because of neglect or abuse were significantly less visited at time 2.

Children of mothers who received more positive evaluations by the caseworkers, as reflected in the five-item index, showed significantly more visitation over each of the four time phases. The correlations for each data-gathering occasion are significant beyond the .001 level. The fairly strong correlations are not surprising; one would expect that parents perceived as functioning on higher levels would visit their children more steadily. It would also seem logical that caseworkers' assessments would be influenced by knowledge of parents' visiting patterns.

The index measuring the amount of investment of caseworker effort in a case showed significant association with parental visiting for times 1–3, but little association for time 4. The fact that frequency of casework contact is associated with frequency of parental visitation does not necessarily suggest a causal relationship between the two phenomena. It is quite possible that an underlying dimension of accessibility of the parent accounts for the correlations found. This will be examined in the material that follows.

## MULTIPLE REGRESSION ANALYSIS OF VISITING BEHAVIOR

Table 8 shows the standardized regression coefficients ($\beta$ weights) and unique variance contributions which relate parental visiting, the dependent variable, to the independent variables just cited. The multiple regressions were carried out for each of the four time phases in which visiting behavior information was secured through agency study research interviews.

Among the statistically significant variables in the time 1 analysis are mental illness of the mother and child behavior as reasons for placement. Both were linked to enhanced visiting of the parent. The influence of these

TABLE 8

Standardized Regression Coefficients (β Weights) and Unique Variance Contributions of Selected Variables in the Analysis of Parental Visiting (Times 1–4)

| Independent Variable[a] | Time 1 Visiting β Weight[b] | Time 1 Visiting Unique Variance | Time 2 Visiting β Weight | Time 2 Visiting Unique Variance | Time 3 Visiting β Weight | Time 3 Visiting Unique Variance | Time 4 Visiting β Weight | Time 4 Visiting Unique Variance |
|---|---|---|---|---|---|---|---|---|
| 1 | .04 | 0.10 | .17 | 1.70** | *.13* | 1.10* | *.09* | *0.50* |
| 2 | .01 | 0.00 | .05 | 0.20 | .00 | 0.00 | .05 | 0.20 |
| 3 | *.16* | *1.40*** | *−.14* | *1.10* | −.10 | 0.60 | −.08 | 0.30 |
| 4 | −.02 | 0.00 | .09 | 0.40 | −.03 | 0.10 | −.01 | 0.00 |
| 5 | *.21* | 2.20*** | .10 | 0.40 | .13 | 0.70 | .12 | 0.80 |
| 6 | .08 | 0.40 | .01 | 0.00 | .01 | 0.00 | −.06 | 0.20 |
| 7 | .06 | 0.20 | −.02 | 0.00 | .07 | 0.30 | −.05 | 0.20 |
| 8 | .13 | 0.90 | −.03 | 0.10 | .02 | 0.00 | −.01 | 0.00 |
| 9 | *.27* | 3.00*** | .07 | 0.20 | .03 | 0.00 | .08 | 0.30 |
| 10 | .05 | 0.20 | −.04 | 0.10 | −.03 | 0.10 | −.03 | 0.00 |
| 11 | .13 | 1.00* | −.11 | 0.70 | −.01 | 0.00 | −.04 | 0.10 |
| 12 | *.15* | 2.00*** | .24 | 5.10*** | .28 | 7.40*** | *.31* | 8.50*** |
| 13 | *.15* | 2.10*** | *.11* | 0.90* | .23 | 4.40*** | −.04 | 0.10 |
| Multiple $R$ | .41 | | .53 | | .50 | | .44 | |
| Multiple $R^2$ | .17 | | .28 | | .25 | | .19 | |
| N cases | 577 | | 422 | | 349 | | 245 | |

*$P<.05$.
**$P<.01$.
***$P<.001$.

[a]Variable numbers represent the following: 1=age of child; 2=N children in family; 3=ethnicity: black; 4=ethnicity: Puerto Rican; 5–11: reasons for placement (5=child behavior, 6=unwilling to assume care, 7=abandonment, 8=neglect or abuse, 9=mental illness of parent, 10=physical illness of parent, 11=unwilling to continue care); 12=evaluation of mother (times 1–4); 13=log total caseworker contact rate (times 1–4).

[b]Italicized standardized regression coefficients are at least twice as large as their standard errors.

variables was greatly diminished, however, in accounting for visiting behavior at times 2–4. Ethnicity is also a significant factor in time 1 parent visiting, with black children tending to be visited less in comparison with both white and Puerto Rican children. A similar tendency is noted in the time 2 analysis, but ethnicity loses cogency as a regressor variable at times 3 and 4; this may be due to the discharge of visited children over time, leaving those behind in a greater state of parity so that ethnicity is less salient as a predictor.

Evaluation of the mother and the logarithm of total contacts made by the caseworker (with child, parents, collaterals, etc.) show quite substantial $\beta$ weights; this is sustained through times 2 and 3. At time 4, the evaluation of the mother is still very salient but casework activity is diminished in importance in accounting for variability in visiting.

When the effects of other relevant variables are removed, the age of the child at placement does not loom large at time 1 although some predictive variance is contributed; the variable does, however, show greater usefulness as a predictor for the analyses of times 2–4.

When the multiple regression analyses for times 2–4 are examined, the lack of cogency of reason for placement as a set of explanatory variables is apparent. On the other hand, evaluation of the mother, extent of casework investment, and age of the child at placement appear fairly potent as explanatory variables. The number of children in a family makes a modest predictive contribution at time 2 and time 4, with children in larger family units receiving greater visitation.

The coefficient of determination ($R^2$) ranges between .17 and .28 for the four analyses. This reflects a relatively modest amount of variance accounted for and makes clear that other sources of explanation of visiting by parents should be examined in future research.

## IMPLICATIONS OF FINDINGS

One must be impressed with the fact that the proportion of parents who visit their children declines rapidly as one proceeds from the time 1 to the time 4 data. At the end of five years, 57 percent of the children still in care were not being visited. Behind this figure may well exist acute feelings of pain for the children involved. The findings that discharge rates are quite closely linked to the frequency of parental visitation underscores the need to assign high priority to monitoring this phenomenon.

It is my view that it ought to be mandatory for all agencies to keep a log on the visitation of parents to their children in foster care. This information should be readily available as part of the computerized management information systems currently being developed in this area of service. The requirement that this information be available should be formalized into state law, and agency practices in this regard should be carefully monitored by the state departments of social service as part of their licensing function. Like the frequent monitoring of body temperature information for assessing the health of patients in hospitals, the visitation of children should be carefully scrutinized as the best indicator we have concerning the long-term fate of children in care. Consider the fact that 66 percent of the children who received no visits during the first year of care were still in care five years later.

The reader should be aware that only a modest amount of the variance in parental visiting was accounted for by the variables utilized in these analyses. Further work remains to be done in illuminating the factors that deter parents from maintaining contact with their children. The extent to which agencies encourage visiting demands attention as well as other "systems" variables [14].

Failure of parents to visit their children cannot long be tolerated unless the parent is physically or mentally incapacitated. The question of termination of parental rights naturally arises when a parent drops out of a child's life. Agencies should be held accountable for efforts made to involve the parent in more responsible visitation. The finding that frequency of casework contact, independent of the valuation of the mother, is associated with greater frequency of visiting is a good omen.

Further research to replicate and extend the findings reported here should be encouraged.

## NOTES AND REFERENCES

The ideas expressed in this paper are being developed further for a book by David Fanshel and Eugene B. Shinn entitled *Children in Foster Care*, to be published by Columbia University Press. The study has been supported by grant SRS-89-P80050/2 (formerly PR600R) from the Child Welfare Research and Demonstration Grants Program, Community Services Administration, Social and Rehabilitation Service, U.S. Department of Health, Education, and Welfare. The author wishes to thank John Grundy for help in computing and programming.

1. See David Fanshel, "The Exit of Children from Foster Care: An Interim Research Report," *Child Welfare* 50 (February 1971): 65–81; David Fanshel and Eugene B. Shinn, *Dollars and Sense in the Foster Care of Children: A Look at Cost Factors* (New York: Child Welfare League of America, 1972); and David Fanshel, "Parental Failure and Consequences for Children: The Drug-abusing Mother Whose Children Are in Foster Care," *American Journal of Public Health* 65 (June 1975): 604–12.

2. For a parallel study of the families of the children, see Shirley Jenkins and Elaine Norman, *Filial Deprivation and Foster Care* (New York: Columbia University Press, 1972) and *Beyond Placement: Mothers View Foster Care* (New York:

Columbia University Press, 1975). For a parallel study of the agencies serving the children, see Deborah Shapiro, *Agencies and Foster Children* (New York: Columbia University Press, 1976).

3. We assume that for most children in foster care, contact with their own parents is to be desired. There are, of course, cases where parents are so disturbed or destructive in relationship to their children that contact may not be in the latters' interest. In this study, 2–4 percent of the parents were restricted from visiting by agencies over the course of the four research interviews encompassing five years of investigation.

4. See Eugene A. Weinstein, *The Self-Image of the Foster Child* (New York: Russell Sage Foundation, 1960), pp. 68–69; and M. L. Kelmer Pringle and L. Clifford, "Conditions Associated with Emotional Maladjustment among Children in Care," *Education Review* 14, no. 2 (February 1962): 112–23.

5. Henry S. Maas and Richard E. Engler, Jr., *Children in Need of Parents* (New York: Columbia University Press, 1959), p. 380.

6. Alan R. Gruber, *Foster Home Care in Massachusetts* (Boston: Governor's Commission on Adoption and Foster Care, Commonwealth of Massachusetts, 1973), p. 18.

7. Edmund V. Mech, *Public Welfare Services for Children and Youth in Arizona* (Tucson, Ariz.: Joint Interim Committee on Health and Welfare, 29th Legislature, State of Arizona, 1970), p. 72.

8. The interviews were carried out as part of the parallel study of the agencies serving the children under the direction of Dr. Deborah Shapiro.

9. It was not possible to obtain interviews covering situations related to eight of the 624 children in the sample.

10. This category was not coded separately in the time 1 interview; such children were included under "maximum permitted visiting."

11. It should be pointed out that the data presented here differ somewhat from the findings reported by Shapiro (n. 2 above). She reports the mothers' visiting behavior, whereas the data presented here reflect the optimal visiting of either parent.

12. Gwen Bellisfield, Miriam Allen, and Virginia Hyde, "Census of Children Who May Need Adoptive Planning," mimeographed (New York: City Department of Social Services, 1971), p. 2.

13. As pointed out by Cohen, creating dummy variables from nominal scales requires no more than $g - 1$ independent variables to represent $g$ of a G nominal scale. Thus it is not necessary to create a dummy variable for the white group after black and Puerto Rican children have been accounted for. See Jacob Cohen, "Multiple Regression as a General Data-analytic System," *Psychological Bulletin* 70, no. 6 (1968): 428.

14. In interviews with the parents of the children during the last year of the study, it was found that complaints of lack of encouragement of visitation were quite numerous (see Jenkins and Norman, *Beyond Placement*).

# Part VII
# Impact of Placement on Parents

# Part VII

## Impact of Placement on Parents

Loss of a child through placement is often traumatic for parents. Since the child has most commonly been the focus of child welfare practice, the effects of the placement experience on the parent have been given relatively little attention. Keith-Lucas focused on this apparent oversight in the mid-1960s. He criticized the zeal of the child-centered worker who, by claiming a superior love of children, might misquote Jesus: "Unto the least of these," he proposed, does not refer to children, but rather to the less considered and often least attractive—the parents.[1]

Most parents whose children enter foster care are identified as having many problems: they are poor, mentally or physically disabled, jobless, single, abusing, neglecting, and/or under high stress. Also, the child whom they relinquish may have behavior difficulties. S/he may be mentally retarded, autistic, or manifest behavior problems the parents are unable to handle. If these parents are "multiproblem," they already no doubt have poor self-images and probably regard themselves as failures in living. The fact that their child is removed is yet another testimony to their feelings of low self-worth, failure, and guilt.

The articles in this section reflect perspectives on the removal of a child. McAdams is a parent whose children were removed. Mandelbaum considers the effects of separation on parents from a psychoanalytic perspective. Jenkins reports on a research project that led to the concept of "filial deprivation."

In Chapter 17, McAdams poignantly describes her ambivalent feelings about having her six children placed in foster care. On the one hand, she identifies the positive aspect of her experience: in a time of family crisis and emotional turmoil her children were provided with a stable home

[1]Keith-Lucas, Alan, "Child Welfare Services Today," in Bremner, Robert H., Editor, *Children and Youth in America—A Documentary History*. Vol. III. Cambridge, Mass.: Harvard University Press, 1974: 666–677.

environment in which they were able to develop. On the other hand, she points out that the fact that one's children are in foster care and one must visit them in a foster home is a reminder that one is a failure as a parent. The order, calm, and often materially superior environment of the foster home make the parent feel that the children would be better off left there. Visiting is often painful for the parent and her reluctance to visit often indicates that she cares too much, rather than that she is indifferent. McAdams firmly believes that social workers should strongly advocate visiting "on the part of the reluctant parent."

In Chapter 18, Mandelbaum argues that the issue of separation is the most significant of all the problems involving work with parents and children and that an understanding of the impact of separation on the parent is essential in helping both parent and child. Mandelbaum believes that what he describes as "the long satiation experience of nurturing and security" is a prerequisite to the parents' being able to let go of a child and vice versa. He points out that most children going into residential care have been deprived of this experience.

Mandelbaum discusses the fact that parents often react to the decision for placement by agreeing, and then running away from the child. Running away seems preferable to them than facing thoughts about losing the child and about their inadequacy as parents. They may feel that their anger has damaged the child beyond repair and that they have been of no value whatsoever to the child. Moreover, many parents feel that separation means that they are irretrievably lost. They often experience this loss as a vacuum, feeling that they no longer have any momentum in their lives and no reason for existence. Mandelbaum sees this reaction as an egocentric one, a massive defense, and a stalemate in which no forward action is possible. He believes that the worker must indicate to the parents that "placement is not the end, but the beginning." He concludes that the contribution of the social worker is to teach the parents that "separation is . . . not an act of death, but of life and growth."

As reported in Chapter 19, Jenkins interviewed 297 mothers and 137 fathers of 624 children in foster care in New York City, focusing on the feelings of these parents at the time of placement. She found that parents felt loss, anger, and guilt—a phenomenon that Jenkins labels "filial deprivation." On the basis of this extensive research, Jenkins contends that unless these feelings are recognized and dealt with by the parents and those helping them, they are displaced onto the child when s/he returns home. The child then has two problems to deal with: the trauma s/he has experienced upon being separated from his/her parents and the turmoil caused by the unresolved feelings of the parents. It becomes the task of the social worker to be sensitive to the parents' feelings in order that they may be worked through.

## SUGGESTIONS FOR FURTHER READING

Adler, Jack, "Separation—A Crucial Issue in Foster Care," *Journal of Jewish Communal Service*, 46:4 (Summer 1970): 305–313.

Flynn, Laurie, "A Parent's Perspective," *Public Welfare*, 37:3 (Summer 1979): 28–33.

Freud, Clarice, "Meaning of Separation to Parents and Children as Seen in Child Placement," *Public Welfare*, 13:1 (January 1955): 13–17 and 25.

Hersh, Alexander, "Changes in Family Functioning Following Placement of a Retarded Child," *Social Work*, 15:4 (October 1970): 93–102.

Jenkins, Shirley, "Filial Deprivation in Parents of Children in Foster Care," *Children*, 14:1 (January–February 1967): 8–12.

Jenkins, Shirley and Norman, Elaine, *Beyond Placement: Mothers View Foster Care*. New York: Columbia University Press, 1975.

Olshansky, Simon, "Chronic Sorrow: A Response to Having a Mentally Defective Child," *Social Casework* 43:4 (April 1962): 190–193.

Pannor, Reuben; Baran, Annette; and Sorosky, Arthur D., "Birth Parents Who Relinquished Babies for Adoption Revisited," *Family Process*, 17:3 (September 1978): 329–337.

# 17

# The Parent in the Shadows

PHYLLIS T. McADAMS

What is it like to have your children placed in foster care? How does it feel to find yourself in the role of a visitor in your own child's home?

These are a few of the questions I've been asked by groups of foster parents and social workers during the past few years. I've tried to answer them honestly and objectively, but it is pretty hard to be objective about something as painfully personal as losing custody of your children and having them placed in foster homes. Probably any parent who has gone through this experience sees it differently.

I became mentally ill during the early 1960s. My depressive state gradually became so severe that I could no longer maintain the home or care for my family and myself properly. I was committed to a state hospital and my children were declared dependents of the court. The six children were first placed in Snedigar Cottage and subsequently placed by pairs in three foster homes.

I remained in the hospital about a year, and upon my release continued intensive outpatient therapy. It was several years before I was able to assume full responsibility for the care of all six children.

I maintained close contact with both the social worker and the children during this period in which the children were being gradually returned to their own home. Sometimes in my attempt to maintain contact with all my children I felt like I was running an obstacle course, and if it hadn't been for a

---

Reprinted from *Child Welfare*, Vol. LI, No. 1 (January 1972): 51–55.

couple of workers who just refused to let me give up I think I would have thrown in the towel on a number of occasions.

## THE ADVANTAGES

As a natural parent I have very ambivalent feelings toward the foster care program in general. I tend to concentrate on the negative aspects of foster care and sort of push the positive points in the background. Perhaps I should list some of the advantages, as far as my children's situation was concerned, and then go on to the criticisms.

The first and most obvious advantage in the case of my kids was that foster care answered an immediate need for a stable home environment and parental supervision at a time of crisis and emotional turmoil.

The four oldest children were boys aged 8 through 12. Several of the foster fathers were hikers and campers, and this made it possible for the boys to take part in activities of this sort at a time in their life when they were of great importance. This opportunity probably would not have been available to them in our fatherless urban home.

All the children were instilled with certain habits of routine and order, something that I had not stressed enough in the home.

Their study habits improved, and this had a direct influence on their performance in school during the past several years that they have been back in their own home. The oldest boy, at 19, finished his first year of college on the honor roll. The second boy, at 18, was offered two excellent academic scholarships—one at UC Berkeley, and the other, which he accepted, at a very highly rated private university. The other four children give every indication of doing at least as well. Sure, these kids were very bright, but it was only through the efforts of some very perceptive and persistent foster parents and social workers that they continued to work up to their potential in school at a time when it would have been easy to goof off, with the very good excuse that they were being shifted around from place to place and school to school.

## SOME PROBLEMS

I just wish that my impression of foster care were limited to the preceding, but although some of the negative aspects cannot be eliminated, there are quite a few problems which I feel would not have to exist at all, if there were just more of an attempt at communication and understanding between workers, parents, and foster parents.

The fact that you are visiting your child in a foster home is a reminder you are, at least for the time being, a failure as a parent. You are very sensitive, especially during the first visits. Sometimes a foster parent, in a well-meaning effort to let you know that your child is doing well in a foster home, will make comments on how well the child is eating, how neat he keeps himself and his room, how happy he is, etc. To me, this type of remark was just an implied criticism of the care I had given my child, and was a verbal slap in the face.

It would have been easier to talk to my children if I had been kept up to date on what they had been doing. I understand that frequent phone calls can be very disruptive, but perhaps if a foster parent could just have dropped a brief note on a postcard once a week, it would have made communication between my child and me less strained.

It is surprising how many legitimate excuses you can come up with to avoid visiting your children in foster homes. Sometimes a failure to visit frequently on the part of the natural parent is not an indication that they don't care, but that they care too much.

You see your child in a home situation where everything is apparently orderly and calm, and quite often materially superior to anything you are going to be able to offer them, and you wonder why the hell you are bothering to rock the boat . . . maybe it would be better to leave your child there, it would be a lot less upsetting for everyone involved if you would just drop out of the picture. Quite often this is true. As the parent you would like to avoid the pain the visit causes you. The child, though he loves you, probably isn't too thrilled over the prospect of the emotional upheaval of the visit. The foster parent, who has to cope with the behavioral problems that a visit might bring up in the child, is just as content not to have the routine of the home shaken up. Yes, sometimes staying away is the easiest thing for everyone, but when your whole life has been torn up and you are somehow trying to reassemble the pieces, I don't see how things could be easy.

I blame the social workers for not pushing visiting on the part of a reluctant parent. If there is a natural parent in the picture, there is always a chance, even in long-term placements, that that parent is going to regain custody of the child. A parent who is out of contact and then, after a year or two, is in a position to have the child returned, is going to have a very rough time trying to establish a workable relationship with that child. It is very important that the social worker make every effort to gain the confidence of natural parents and if necessary force them to take an interest in their child, even when they are away from home.

The foster parent who gives you orders and instructions in the presence of your child is another problem. You are told that you should have the child back in the foster home at 5 o'clock, and admonished not to be late, or you are told to be sure little Tommy doesn't go outside without his sweater, as he has just recovered from a cold. These instructions may be necessary, but your kid, no matter how young, is already aware of the fact that you have little authority at this time, and this only increases the child's concern as to how responsible you are. If it is necessary to give the natural parent instructions about taking the child away from the foster home on an outing, it would be better to do so out of the child's presence.

No matter how courteous a foster parent is, the natural parents still have the feeling that they have very little to say in the decisions made for their child. There is no reason why the natural parents can't be consulted on some of the decisions regarding the child, even if they are only small ones, such as the color of a soon-to-be-purchased coat, or the advisability of getting a haircut. Being asked your opinion on matters concerning your child is a step toward the time when you will be making decisions yourself again, and will help restore your confidence in your ability to do so. I think it is the responsibility of both the social worker and the child's foster parent to involve the natural parent even if she doesn't show too much interest in being involved.

## PARENT COMPETITION

I think it is possible for foster parents and natural parents to have mutual respect for each other, but the very nature of their relationship makes it impossible to avoid elements of jealousy and competition. In the case of my children, finding themselves in the position of having foster parents whom they loved and admired and yet having to cope with me trying to strengthen their love for me and regain their trust was almost too much. As far as they were concerned they couldn't have two sets of parents, and the only solution was to reject one and keep the other. Often it was just simply not wanting to give up the sure thing, a stable foster home, for the uncertainty of when I would be able to reestablish a home for them. This problem took a lot of effort at all levels, before they accepted the fact that love for one set of parents did not imply disloyalty to the other.

I know quite often children return from visits with the natural parents with all sorts of plans and promises given them during the visit. It is very difficult to deny a child any hope when the immediate situation seems to be pretty bleak. My kids were able to extract tentative promises of when we would all be reunited, because my pride was killing me and I didn't have the heart to say that I had no home, no money, and no definite time when I would have sufficient emotional and financial resources for getting these things.

I believe one of the most damaging things a foster parent may do to a child, quite often without conscious intent, is to undermine the child's opinion of the natural parent. It must be very difficult for a foster parent to refrain from passing moral judgement on a natural parent whose offenses have been particularly unpleasant or even criminal, but that person is still the child's parent and the more the foster parent knocks him, the more the child is obligated to defend him.

A foster parent should always keep in mind that the child who has come to him from a deprived atmosphere may very likely be returned to an environment that will be materially inferior to the one he can offer the child. This is a condition which he can help the child to accept gracefully and even with pride. A foster parent can be very helpful by letting the child know that it is a fact that certain people live differently, but that home condition has no real bearing on the child's worth as a person.

If it is the habit of the foster family to attend church regularly, but it is unlikely that this will be possible when the child returns to the natural home, the foster parent should not make the child feel that this is the only way to live. Encouraging the child to participate in community activities, and belong to organizations such as the Boys Clubs, where they can continue when they return home, is another way a foster parent can help the youngster make the transition from one environment to another.

A couple of my kids ran into a situation in which foster parents in a misguided effort to show my children how much they cared for them told them that they enjoyed and cared for the children so much that they would keep them even if they were not being paid for their care. My children, instead of being flattered and pleased, were resentful. They did not like to feel that they were receiving charity from either the county or the foster parents. I think a simple explanation about the purposes of taxes would be helpful to all foster children. When they understand that everyone pays taxes as sort of insurance toward the day when they may be in need, and that the child himself will someday be a taxpayer for this same purpose for someone else, it may be the start of teaching the child that he too will have a responsibility to assist other people. If the child's parents contribute to his care while he is in a foster home, he should know this too.

Although I have a number of criticisms of foster care, I never allowed my children to involve me in a discussion of personalities while they were living in a particular home. As long as they have to live in the home, I think they must learn as much as possible to resolve their own differences with the persons they are living with in the foster home. If these conflicts of personality become too marked, then I think the child should feel close enough to the social worker to be able to discuss the problem.

My children were returned to me gradually, one or two at a time. During this period I relied very much on the social worker. I had little or no faith in my ability to manage a home and family. My children were skeptical as to how much they could depend on me. I found myself having to prove myself over and over again. I couldn't blame them, for I was their mother and, for whatever reason, I had allowed them to be separated and go through the foster home routine. Learning to live together was a big task, but we managed it, and it has been well worth the effort required of everyone to make it work.

# 18

# Parent-Child Separation: Its Significance To Parents

ARTHUR MANDELBAUM

Understanding the anxieties that parents suffer in separating from a child is essential if parents and child are to be helped. This paper is particularly concerned with the significance of separation to parents in the residential treatment of children. Of all problems the social worker encounters in casework with parents and children, none is more significant than separation. But is it not true that separation is central to all life experiences?

Albert Camus stated, "Separation is characteristic of the human condition. It is often the rule of the world . . . It is in the essence of things that all who love should be separated" [1]. Of course, Camus was speaking of the separation that inevitably accompanies all growth and development and is therefore impossible to resist: birth, infancy, childhood, adolescence, adulthood, old age, and death. Throughout each stage of this growth and development, from birth to death, there is a gradual giving-up of the old for the new in an orderly sequence within which there may be great variation but where the pattern follows a major form. Separation through growth and development is a process whereby parents and child learn to differentiate themselves from each other and to part gradually, a process made possible by the satisfactions experienced by each individual in the family which bring a

---

sense of growth, achievement, and contentment. The transition from one developmental period to the next during the early years is smoothed by the ever consistent, ever present parents, who create a sense of outer continuity, predictability, and harmony which becomes transformed in the child into a sense of inner security. Erikson has described this as essential for giving the child an identity and a sense of inner goodness and basic trust [2].

The mother, who gives early essential nurturing experience to the child, is assisted by biological, social, and cultural factors. After the child is separated from her body, holding him close and feeling his softness and warmth comfort her for the loss of sensations and unity that she experienced prior to his birth. The encompassing love of her husband and his consistent support and attention mean that the child is loved as well, because now, although the biological unity is gone, she and the child are, in the emotional sense, still one. The culture approves of her caring for the child and sanctions her motherhood as the major priority. If she is always present for the child, alert and responsive to his needs, and if he is somewhere within the circle of whatever major interests occupy her, then he will absorb into himself an image of his mother that will become deeply etched into his personality. He will then go on to relate himself to his father and others who enter his life. Wherever he goes, he will carry an image of his parents that will remain unshaken; because he knows he belongs to them, he does not have to be physically bolted to them. Such a child will be able to separate. Psychoanalyst Christine Olden has stated, "It could be that you renounce complete possession of the baby more easily if these first months were a satisfactory experience, if you are satiated and feel free to go on to different joys with your child [3].

This long satiation experience of nurturing and dependency between mother and child is characteristic of the human species, in contrast to the pattern in lower animal life. With the latter, instincts transmitted from one generation to the other enable the mother to force a separation from her young after a relatively short period of time; then, instinctively, the young know how to survive and care for themselves. But the human infant, who is so long dependent on his parents, develops slowly and painstakingly, acquiring in the process a permanent capacity to learn from experience, which is a more creative and flexible way of existence.

> Without a protected childhood in which there is time to play, mankind would probably never have arisen above an animal existence. Perhaps in the future, the playing of children will be recognized as more important than technical developments, wars and revolutions. . . . it was precisely the protection of children from the struggle to survive which favored learning and new developments. [4]

Some fear of separation is universal to children and their parents. When the young child enters kindergarten or when the young adult goes away to college, parents experience vague apprehensions and anxieties. In a study of a group of normal parents whose children were to begin school for the first time, the parents expressed concern that the streets were busy with traffic, the child would be bullied by older children, he would come home with ugly words expressing dangerous aggressive and sexual thoughts, he might even eulogize the teacher as attractive, competent, and omniscient. Many mothers expressed a sense of loneliness after the first few days of school, and both parents shared some concern that now there would be a real test as to whether they had done a good job of rearing their children during those first five years when they were all theirs [5]. Harry Golden, with great sensitivity and insight, expresses the dilemma of parents upon separation.

> I believe the most stirring moment in this experience of a parent comes on the day he leaves the child in school for the first time. This can be so sharp an experience that, where there are two or three children, this ritual has to be alternated between parents. I remember leaving one of mine there all starched up with a look of bewilderment on his face such as I never want to witness again. I held his little hand and got him registered. As we walked through the yard and corridors of the school he never took his eyes off me and never said a word: Then came the moment to put him in a line and—leave him.
>
> I tried to be nonchalant as I walked away but I quickly hid behind a pillar; he had never taken his eyes off me. He just looked and looked, but I could see that he filled up, but, since I am bigger, I filled up more. What an ordeal! Yet I know that the final decision could not be delayed for long. There was no law that forced me to keep watching him. I turned my back and started out slowly and then I practically ran out the door. You have to make a break [6].

## THE DISTURBED CHILD

The child who is considered a suitable candidate for residential treatment is not likely to have had the long satiation experience of nurturing and security essential to the development of identity and basic trust. His world had been chaotic, inconsistent, uncertain. His family has suffered breakdown because of events happening to his parents: separation, divorce, death, physical or emotional illness, or imprisonment. He himself may contribute to family breakdown through physical or emotional illness, severe retardation, acts of delinquency, or a combination of some or many of these factors which in their interaction are so intense and malevolent that the family can no longer tolerate or endure their impact.

One outstanding characteristic of a disturbed child is that he cannot relate to his parents without demanding infantile, primitive gratifications. He explodes with rage and aggression when these needs are frustrated. His world is filled with glaring hatred, disorganized behavior, wildly fluctuating ego states, bizarre symptoms, and distorted realities. This child cannot bear separation except to withdraw into the loneliness of himself where the dangers of abandonment are less likely and where he does not have to depend on the whim and uncertainty of adults and their world of terror. Because of the illness within him and in the parent-child relationship, he requires residential treatment.

The purpose of residential treatment is to arrange life sensibly for those children whose lives have not been sensible, to bring order to lives which have not had order, to give an experience within a new framework of security where the events of each day and the child's reaction to them are examined for meanings which gradually will appear consistent and logical to him. George Santayana said that those who cannot remember the past are condemned to repeat it [7]. In residential treatment the child repeats his past—it is the only behavior he knows. But he repeats it to have it examined by himself and others in a heightened, ordered way so that he can take up once again the torn threads of his interrupted and halted development and, from the fragment left of his life, revitalize himself into a whole human being.

> The essence of the residential process is that as each child projects his inner world against the macrocosm of the residence, by and large the staff will find from each other and within each other, the strength to resist stepping into the role of the feared parents, and give the child the nurturing and protection he needs to restore his faith in himself. [8]

It is this knowledge and conviction about the purpose and value of residential treatment that the social worker brings into his process with the parents.

## FACING THE NEED FOR RESIDENTIAL TREATMENT

As the parents face the formidable question of the child's need for residential treatment, their great fear of separation brings a feeling of isolation and loneliness. Their impulse to act, to agree quickly to place the child, to make this profound decision impulsively, is slowed and eased in casework. Indeed, it is characteristic of resistance to placement that the parents wish to bypass an understanding of the child's difficulties and the problems that exist in their relationship with him as unfolded by the study. To understand the child and their problems with him is to understand themselves, and there is a wish to avoid this pain. But there is also a wish to avoid understanding the fearful recommendation of placement—to run quickly from the child and leave him behind. The decision to run away seems less intolerable than facing thoughts about losing him, and later the parents must undo their act by returning to claim the child.

The study process, which every family is required to go through prior to any admission, aims not at a decision for residential treatment but rather at a beginning understanding of the nature of the total problem. Once the parents understand this as the first goal, the first essential, they will not feel urged or pushed, and a major part of their anxiety will be relieved with their realization that their child will not be placed until he is understood and until they share in that understanding. It is only from such a process that the importance of the need for this kind of total inpatient care begins to crystallize. When the study process deeply involves the parents and when their rights for making any decision are held foremost, treatment once embarked upon is less likely to suffer disruption. Since residential treatment is a contractual arrangement involving considerable time and expense, there must be as much assurance as possible prior to placement that both the parents and the treatment center will abide by the treatment. The important questions are consistently examined: "Can the child live with you at home?" "Can you live with him?" "If not, can you find the strength in yourself to permit the child, for an indefinite period of time, to live without you?" "But can you also see it as more than a matter of living—that it is a matter of growth, too?"

If these questions are not carefully deliberated, there will be treatment disruption at the first sign of stress. When this occurs it constitutes additional trauma for the parents, the child, the staff of the treatment center, and the children already in residence (who suffer when one of them comes and goes unexpectedly and abruptly and then begin to doubt the power and wisdom of the setting to give them protection from disruption and the logic and predictability their lives require).

The study process is not accomplished by one or two hours of work. To think that it could be is to depreciate the many-faceted aspects of the parents' thoughts and emotions and the depths of their concerns; it is also to overevaluate casework, expecting a persuasive power and magic from it which can then only bring disillusionment and a futile search for new and magical treatment methods. The process begins from the moment the parents make contact with the setting. It continues through the evaluation and study of the child, in which both parents must be deeply involved. It lasts until the parents have given enough consideration to their conflicting feelings and have arrived at sufficient understanding to risk separation.

## BEFORE AND AFTER PLACEMENT

What are the feelings of parents who face the prospect of residential treatment for their child? During the study and later, during the admission procedure, a universal reaction is that the child's need of residential treatment reveals their inadequacy as parents. They have been found deficient in qualities of goodness. Their past and present anger has been evil and destructive to the child; their power to hurt him is unlimited. This anger has assumed such power, they believe, that it has damaged the child beyond repair and he will never recover. There is also anger at the recommendations (but perhaps relief, too) and a secret hope that the treatment center will fail, for if it succeeds, and the child succeeds, it will mean they have solved things in the past in the wrong way. These are forbidden thoughts that arouse guilt and the fear that if discerned further disapprobation will be brought on themselves and they will be rejected as worthless. On the other hand, if the treatment center should fail, it will mean that their own failure is less, for the child is beyond anyone's power to help.

Many parents consider residential treatment as meaning they have been of no value to their child whatsoever. The good things they have done for him, the warm, tender moments, are swept away by the totality of their bitter thoughts. They no longer have a useful function; their parental rights are entirely severed. They feel that the treatment center will now do all the work and this confirms their helplessness, their inadequacy, and their feelings of being unwanted. They feel that even if the child is given the opportunity to grow, to get well, he may fail, and perhaps it would be better not to risk this failure after a series of so many—why gamble and risk finding out that there is no hope whatsoever? And because some parents tend to undervalue themselves, they depreciate the child and his potential strength or undervalue the child and thus themselves.

Separation from the child means that he is irretrievably lost. "Out of sight, out of mind" was the expression used by one parent. The disorganized parent, whose internal personality organization is fluid and fragmented, fears that he will lose the image of his child (the inner picture-making mechanism is broken), and this is equivalent to death. Because he feels his inner self is so chaotic, he fears that the child has similar problems of disorganization and that during the child's absence from his parents he will lose his image of them, which is the equivalent of their death. They will die and he will die.

During the interim period (after the study of the family and before admission), the social worker continues to explore with the parents the meanings of their fears, doubts, and expectations. They learn to look forward to residential treatment with hope that this, at last, is the long-hoped-for solution. They see it as having value for the relief it will give from the intolerable demands the child makes on them, and perhaps the demands they make on the child. They partially recognize that some of the chains that bind them to the child are forged with anger and guilt. These feelings are so strong that the act of giving the child into someone else's care is felt to be an act of aggression on their part. They see this reflected in the anger and doubts of the child about leaving home and their fear that as he grows big and powerful he will retaliate and destroy them. But this is because they see the child as having failed to renounce the pleasures of his instinctual life and feel that they have failed to help him move in this direction.

As the parents continue to exchange thoughts with the social worker during this period, it becomes clear to them that they have one direct way to assist the child to begin the education of his instinctual life: by separating from him. This step calls for their work and sacrifice, the renunciation of whatever unhappy gratifications they have from the primitive aspects of the child's behavior. This renunciation is the decision for placement. Through carefully planned admission procedures in which grief reactions and depression are expressed, the social worker continues to help them understand and master their feelings. Once these are mastered, the parents are rewarded by the gradual recognition that they have accomplished something good for their child, because it brought him growth and growth to themselves as well.

After placement the parents fear that the great force, the great energy they have put into the struggle, will now be gone and that the vacuum created in their lives because of the child's absence will cause them to lose their momentum, their reason for struggle, their reason for existence. One mother said that her son was like a great wind against which she could lean and remain upright and strong; now, with him gone, she would collapse. Another mother wrote her son shortly after admission:

> Hello, Honey,
>
> Well, we have had it around here. Workmen all over the place. And now the roof is falling in. Then the painters again. Then the gardener. If you lose me, just check the local nut houses—that's where I'll be!
>
> I missed you yesterday . . . there is no news here . . . worth listening to that is. I forgot to tell you my bathroom window is

> disintegrating and both balconies are gone. I tell you, Allan, I'm getting tireder and tireder. If there is no such word as "tireder" you can take your choice and you can have it. I love you.

The parents are also afraid that they who are "bad" parents will be replaced by "good" parents. This fear is sometimes reinforced by the residential staff.

> And it will be found that categorizations of good and bad, loving and rejecting, eager to help and uncooperative, which are used subtly to dichotomize treatment staff and parents are current in some measure in all settings where children are treated. . . . Some of the many seemingly insuperable difficulties which frequently beset the relationship between the real parents and the residential center can be linked to these feelings. Generally children who have endured a particularly unhappy life experience, or whose conditions call forth immediate pity, are more likely to evoke these fantasies and feelings in total staff with extraordinary swiftness and intensity. [9]

When rescue fantasies from the "bad" parents do occur among staff, these are accompanied by feelings of righteous indignation and passion, with the result that diagnostic and treatment goals are blurred. The parents, alert to negative attitudes, can only react with a deeper pessimism about themselves. They fear the residential staff will alienate the child from them with these hostile feelings. And attitudes of contempt for the parents are sensed by the child as an estimate of him, for he feels himself a part of his mother and father. The parents may soon develop counterrescue fantasies and wish to remove the child from this "bad, critical place," especially as the child in correspondence and during visits describes his anger toward staff, his loneliness, his wish to be withdrawn. The strength of the parents to resist the temptation to return to the former unhealthy relationship with the child is sorely tested. If these elements in the separation are carefully predicted in advance, if the parents are prepared for these actions by the child, and if the meanings of the actions are correctly interpreted, they are then able to sustain the treatment.

Some parents communicate their distress after the child is admitted by excessive letter writing and a constant stream of gifts and clothing. These mean to the child, "Do not forget me," or "I am sorry that I have sent you away, please forgive me," or "I do not wish you to forget that I am the major person in your life, you need me, I need you and I do not want you to relate yourself to others; please stay young for it is the way I love you best."

These expressions may also indicate to the child that he remains the only source of gratification for his parents, the only reason for their existence, and that they have no other avenues available to them for satisfactions and a fruitful life. Thus, loyalty struggles become inextricably confused in the process of separation. If the child is to get well, he must have his parents' permission and be sure of their conviction that it is all right for him to love others, to have regard for himself, and, finally, to regard his parents with esteem, dignity, and without fear that they will withdraw from this healthy, mature expression of his need and love for them.

## WORKING WITH STAFF AND PARENTS

It is one of the essential responsibilities of the social worker to convey to all staff his knowledge and feeling about the parents, giving a whole picture of them as they really are—vital, human, and tormented. Social workers may become angry when a child's spirit is mutilated, but if they go to the other extreme and turn this anger against the parents they fail to see the mutilation of the parents' spirits, and the negative effects on their own spirits as well. When the social worker succeeds in identifying himself sufficiently with the suffering of the parents and can catch a glimpse of the extent of their terror, he is better able to provide staff with a framework of understanding. Staff will thus know better what the child carries within himself of his parents, what his life has been before he came, and what he is likely to do and repeat; they will know what the parents have within themselves that corresponds to what is in the child and, then, how these forces continue to interact even though there is physical separation.

> Mrs. B recalled that as a youngster she had been like the patient, whining and clinging to her mother, frightened of separation. When Mrs. B left her son with us, she was depressed, and at home she felt confused, disorganized, helpless and without strength to do much. In the residence, a child care worker who had noticed Mrs. B's son meandering aimlessly and morosely about reported: "Instinctively I put my hand on Ben's shoulder. He spun around and embraced me tightly. I sat down and still holding on he sat on my lap. He squeezed me for a moment and I commented on his wish to be small. He said, 'I'd like to be smaller than the youngest child here. I'd like to be one year old. No! I'd rather be no months old and be small enough to crawl back in my mother's stomach.'
>
> "At this point he moved off my lap and sitting next to me continued, 'I'd like to be smaller than a dot.' I said, 'Maybe you'd like to start all over again.'

"Ben said, 'Yes I would so I could be in my mother's stomach and she would eat and eat and I'd get bigger and she'd get fatter and fatter; so fat, two by four, can't get through the bathroom door. And she'd try and try and she'd break down the wall of Southard School and get into the bathroom and then I could start all over and I wouldn't have to come to Southard School.'"

During the first months of residential treatment, the social worker listens to what the parents say, write, or telephone to him, translating back to them the essence of their concerns. Hannah Arendt has written, "True understanding does not tire of interminable dialogue and 'vicious circles,' because it trusts that imagination will eventually catch at least a glimpse of the frightening light of truth" [10]. And if the social worker translates this light of truth with kindness, warmth, clarity, and intelligence, it will become clear that there are no absolutes. Placement is an intervention which at first may seem all injury, all loss. As the child struggles to be without his parents and solve his problems and as they struggle to live without him, antagonism and despair seem paramount. This is often revealed through correspondence.

Dear Dr. W,

Would it be possible for me to visit. It's hard not hearing from Don himself. I get the feeling that I have to see him before something snaps. Who says the world is round? Don is way out in Kansas and that may be beyond the edge of the disc, where things drop off.

One if by land and two if by sea!

Dear Mousie,

Those hamsters are as smart as they can be. I guess it gripes them that we are just a little bit smarter. They have discovered that if they work real hard they can squeeze out of their cage. I had them out in the patio yesterday . . . All of a sudden, one of the little monsters escaped . . . Finally Daddy looked behind the wall, and there the little thing was trembling and looking all around. I guess he was kind of scared, being out in the big world all alone. Served him right . . . because now I won't let them out of the house again.

Dear Cindy,

It has been a tough day. I believe that I am getting old for somehow I tire more easily . . . What is more those things which used to act as incentives no longer do so . . . I am dog tired. It just seems as though things just pile up. Believe me Cindy, it is a tough life and no one knows it better than you do.

The feeling that all is lost is an extremely egocentric one. The parents attach to their feelings an absolute value that obscures everything but their own dilemma. This position is a massive defense and as long as it exists there is a stalemate in which no forward action is conceived as possible. When the worker indicates that placement is not the end, but the beginning, that their involvement is not only desired, but necessary, the parents are relieved; but anger comes from the opposite extreme position—that placement in and of itself does not absolve the parents of struggle, of the need to understand the child and themselves and to come together with him when there is a strategic need to do so. Slowly, parents are able to re-enter the struggle, but now from the designed, protected position of carefully timed contacts in which there is no overloading of such severe emotional intensity that the parents and child are injured. It is as if once powerful magnets come together with such force that separation meant a ripping-apart rather than a coming-together and leaving when the life situation demanded it.

> Dear Mr. M:
>
> Nice to see you and talk with you again. I did have a good visit with Harry. Feel much better about him. At times he displays a good deal of hostility toward me. If he has that much then it is better that he can display it, although it is a little difficult to take at times. He is mighty precious to us, and we are so glad that you people took him. He would not have had a chance otherwise. Usually when I return, I am depressed for several days, sometimes for weeks. Now it is different. I get over things much more quickly. Each time I have more strength to walk. This was the best yet. I believe that slowly I am emerging from the woods.

Absence from the child is more than a matter of suspended animation, a continuation of old routines; it is a matter of healing and growth, too. For absence, sustained by the relationship with the social worker, has a healing power. When the parents are encouraged to assure the child that as he grows stronger they do not get weaker, and that he is not expected to return home in order to take care of them, they will examine this need and expectation from their child and trace its irrational sources. For some parents, the closeness to the child has served to ward off their fears of facing other relationships in which their own inadequacies might be uncovered; a fear of facing life situations whose demands would be too harsh, too perfectionistic. Placement gives the parents the needed opportunity and freedom to seek a reunion with each other, to test carefully available strengths, to relate to others, to enter new activities and pursuits. To their surprise, the collapse they expected to undergo does not occur. Much of the resistance of professional people to separation of the child from his family for the purpose of residential treatment is based on the fear that the family will disintegrate. The current crisis in the family brings so much to the fore that is regressive that underlying strengths of parents to sustain themselves are covered over and underestimated.

When the parents reveal their feelings that it is *they* who have been abandoned, these feelings are gently highlighted by the worker. The perception of the parents is then widened to permit them to assure the child that he has not been abandoned and that he has their permission to feel less lonely for them. Much of the unconscious protest of the parents about the child's growth seems based on the fear that should he achieve levels of maturity they have not been able to gain he will then be beyond their control and his power will be used destructively. Thus, sexual strivings are feared lest they go awry, and aggression and learning are feared because they might be turned into delinquent activities—all this corresponding to what is tenuous and poorly integrated in the personality of the parents. But it is possible to master these fears as the parents observe the child mastering them in his new environment. And as they understand some of the barriers overcome by the child, to some extent they overcome their own.

What further gives the child freedom to move on is the confidence that his parents have other gratifications in their lives which occupy them. He is not the center of their universe and they are not totally stricken at his loss. The knowledge that he can crush his parents because he is everything in their lives is too awesome a power for any child. Once he is relieved of this power a tremendous burden is lifted from his shoulders and he is no longer an omnivorous monster but a small child who wants care from powerful but safe adults. Further, the child must have his parents' optimism that a new world is offered him and that they are not jealous or resentful of it. "After all there is freedom in not being loved too deeply, in not being thought of too often. Possessive love makes most of the complication and nearly all of the unhappiness in the world" [11].

## LIFE—NOT DEATH

The interpretation in casework of these feelings in the parents does not deal with their unconscious. True, these are deep feelings, but they are sharply apparent as the parents react. They are expressed directly or through metaphor, analogy, displacements, and projections, but very close to the surface of awareness. As the worker urges the parents to think with him, crosslacing back and forth what the child does and its consequences to them, and what they do and its consequences to the child, the worker couches his language, thoughts, and feelings in terms of what is logical and consistent with societal expectations. And if these societal expectations are logical and consistent, they are consonant with principles of healthy growth and development. Through such a process, strength and positive feelings gain ascendancy. And as the parents lose their exclusive self-preoccupation and turn outward toward the child and toward work and friends as other sources of gratification, they do not fear loneliness. Separation is then not an act of death, but of life and growth. This is the contribution of the social worker in helping heal the parents. His efforts coincide and intertwine with those of other disciplines invested in residential treatment, where united energy in a collective enterprise frees the human gifts in parents and their children.

## REFERENCES

1. Philip Thody, *Albert Camus* (London: Hamish Hamilton, 1957), p. 28.
2. Erik Erikson, *Childhood and Society* (New York: W. W. Norton & Co., 1950), p. 219.
3. "Notes on the Development of Empathy," *Psychoanalytic Study of the Child*, Vol. 13 (New York: International Universities Press, 1958), p. 515.
4. Henno Martin, *The Sheltering Desert* (New York: Thomas Nelson & Sons, 1958), p. 140.
5. Donald C. Klein and Ann Ross, "Kindergarten Entry: A Study of Role Transition," *Orthopsychiatry and the School*, Morris Krugman, ed. (New York: American Orthopsychiatric Association, 1958).
6. Harry Golden, *Only in America* (Cleveland: World Publishing Company, 1958), p. 49.
7. Clifton Fadiman, *The Lifetime Reading Plan* (Cleveland: World Publishing Co., 1960), p. 14.
8. Rudolf Ekstein, Judith Wallerstein, and Arthur Mandelbaum, "Countertransference in the Residential Treatment of Children," *Psychoanalytic Study of the Child*, Vol. 14 (New York: International Universities Press, 1959), p. 186.
9. *Ibid.*, p. 189.
10. Hannah Arendt, "Understanding and Politics," *Partisan Review*, Vol. 20 (July-August 1953), p. 392.
11. Ellen Glasgow, *The Sheltered Life* (Garden City, L. I.: Doubleday, 1932), p. 252.

# 19

# Separation Experiences of Parents Whose Children Are in Foster Care

SHIRLEY JENKINS

When a child enters foster care, the child care worker is concerned not only with making an optimal placement, but with ameliorating the separation trauma and deprivation the youngster is assumed to have experienced. Although "irreversibility of damage" is no longer accepted without question, there are substantial research findings offering evidence of maternal deprivation in placement experiences.

When parents place a child in foster care, the reciprocal aspect of the transaction—the filial deprivation—is not a primary concern of the child care worker. In the research literature, meager attention has been given to what happens to parents when children enter placement. The study reported on here sought to fill this gap in understanding the total placement experience, by investigating feelings of several hundred mothers and fathers when their children entered foster care. The data were derived from intensive field interviews with 297 natural mothers and 137 natural fathers of New York City foster children. This research was part of the longitudinal study of 624 children in care conducted under the Child Welfare Research Program at the Columbia University School of Social Work [1].

Feelings were only one aspect of the family study. Other areas studied included reason for placement, family composition, attitudes on childrearing,

---

Reprinted from *Child Welfare*, Vol. XLVIII, No. 6 (June 1969): 334–340.

social orientation of parents, male and female role preferences and performances, family pathology, and socioeconomic status. This report is focused on separation feelings, relating them where appropriate to demographic and other characteristics of mothers and fathers.

Exploratory interviews with parents other than those in the study sample whose children were in care, supported the hypothesis that parental feelings on placement did not follow a single dimension; they were mixed, seemingly contradictory but actually organized in patterns related to reason for placement and to other variables. Spontaneous responses in the pilot study to the question, "How did you feel the day your child was placed?" produced a "sad-mad-glad" trilogy, with 12 main feeling areas emerging as most frequently expressed. These became the basis for a checklist of 12 feelings for inclusion in the research interviews.

Field interviews for the family study were conducted in the homes of the mothers and fathers by trained social workers on the research staff. The average interview extended for about 2 hours, and began with an exploration of the reason for placement and of the placement experience. Respondents were then asked to express spontaneously their feelings about the child's going into care, and to react to the 12 feelings noted on the checklist. They were asked in turn whether or not each feeling had been experienced. The feelings studied were: sadness, anger, bitterness, relief, thankfulness, worry, nervousness, guilt, paralysis, shame, emptiness, and numbness.

## PARENTS' FEELINGS AT PLACEMENT OF CHILDREN

For both parents, who were interviewed separately, sadness was the feeling reported most frequently, being expressed by 87 percent of mothers and 90 percent of fathers. Also high in frequency among the feelings noted were worry, expressed by 76 percent of mothers and 68 percent of fathers, and nervousness, reported by 68 percent of mothers and 56 percent of fathers. From 40 to 60 percent of both mothers and fathers reported feelings of emptiness, anger, bitterness, thankfulness, and relief. From 30 to 39 percent of mothers and father reported guilt and shame, guilt being higher for mothers and shame higher for fathers. Relatively small numbers of either parent, from 10 to 20 percent, reported numbness or the feeling of being paralyzed.

It was not possible to interview all fathers of the children, primarily because many fathers, or their whereabouts, were unknown. In 88 cases, however, both parents of the sample child were interviewed, and these cases present an excellent base for comparison of parental feelings. The feeling responses of mothers and fathers corresponded closely, with statistically

TABLE 1

**Percent of Parents Reporting Feelings Experienced on Day of Placement and Commonality of Feelings**

| Feeling | Mothers N=297 | Fathers N=137 | Parent Pairs* N=88 Mothers | Parent Pairs* N=88 Fathers | Commonality† |
|---|---|---|---|---|---|
| Sad | 87% | 90% | 83% | 91% | 88% |
| Worried | 76 | 68 | 75 | 69 | 76 |
| Nervous | 68 | 56 | 54 | 54 | 60 |
| Empty | 60 | 42 | 54 | 44 | 53 |
| Angry | 45 | 50 | 44 | 56 | 59 |
| Bitter | 43 | 43 | 40 | 45 | 51 |
| Thankful | 42 | 57 | 48 | 54 | 51 |
| Relieved | 40 | 42 | 47 | 44 | 50 |
| Guilty | 39 | 30 | 37 | 32 | 52 |
| Ashamed | 36 | 39 | 26 | 40 | 38 |
| Numb | 19 | 14 | 15 | 16 | 15 |
| Paralyzed | 16 | 11 | 15 | 14 | 24 |

*Refers to families where both the natural mother and father were independently interviewed. This subsample is part of the larger N reported here.

†Refers to mother and father feelings held in common — all mother and father feelings.

significant differences noted only in the category of shame, expressed by more fathers than mothers. At the time of placement, the mothers and fathers lived together in 47 cases, and apart in 42. Mothers and fathers differed in feelings expressed, but whether the parents lived apart or together was not a significant factor. Proximity in household arrangements was apparently not crucial in determining parental feelings or the extent to which mothers and fathers agreed or disagreed.

## FEELINGS AND DEMOGRAPHIC VARIABLES

Data on the expressions of feelings were then related to other family characteristics. One complexity in making such an analysis is that interrelationships are frequently found among the following factors: ethnic group, religion, jurisdiction of case, and socioeconomic status. None of these can be identified as the primary factor related to expression of feelings, but significant differences were noted for some of these variables and parental reactions when children enter care.

## Differences Among Ethnic and Religious Groups and by Referral Source

Of all mothers in the study, 27 percent were white, 42 percent Negro, and 31 percent Puerto Rican. No significant differences relevant to ethnic groups were noted for feelings of sadness, emptiness, anger, or guilt. Thankfulness, however, was expressed by significantly more white and Puerto Rican mothers than by Negro mothers, and worry by significantly more Negro and Puerto Rican mothers and by fewer white mothers. Shame and nervousness were expressed by significantly more whites and by fewer Negroes and Puerto Ricans. The feeling of paralysis tended to be expressed to a significantly greater degree by the Puerto Rican group. Within one ethnic group, the Negro mothers, a difference emerged on the basis of religion. With 30 Negro Catholic and 93 Negro Protestant mothers, it was found that a significantly higher percentage of Catholic mothers expressed anger than did Protestant mothers.

In the total study sample, about 19 percent of families had children who entered placement under the supervision of the Family Court; the other 81 percent entered under the Bureau of Child Welfare of the Department of Social Services. Mothers whose children entered under the aegis of the Family Court were significantly angrier and more nervous, whereas mothers who were clients of the Bureau of Child Welfare tended to express significantly more relief and more thankfulness about the placement. The extent to which guilt was expressed was of particular interest. The court cases included situations in which severe abuse and neglect of children had occurred. This was not reflected in feelings of guilt by abusive parents, however, and there were no significant differences between court and Bureau of Child Welfare cases in this regard.

## Feelings and Socioeconomic Status

The study sample of families comprised a generally low-income group, and included 45 percent of families for whom public assistance was the main source of support at the time of placement. Forty-three percent of families were supported primarily by earnings, but the median family income for this salaried group was under $100 a week. The study was concerned with examining, even within this low income range, any differences between families relatively better off and those with the most disadvantaged circumstances.

The usual scales for measuring socioeconomic status were not applicable for this sample, because of the large numbers of cases involving one-parent households, where there had never been any paid employment, and where income was fixed by welfare standards. Therefore, the study staff developed a scale of five criteria particularly relevant to an impoverished group. The first was support, which included source of support, amount of income, and, for families on public assistance, duration of dependency. The second criterion was the highest educational attainment of any related adult in the household. The third criterion was extent of dilapidated or deteriorated housing conditions, and the other two were based on neighborhood data on comparative median family income and juvenile delinquency rates. Combined weighted scores for each family on all five criteria became the measure of socioeconomic circumstances. Within the range for the total group, the study sample was divided into high, middle, and low subsamples, based on socioeconomic level. It should be noted that for this population the high group's typical family had an earned income of $75 a week or more, and included an adult who was a high school graduate. A typical family low on the scale included long-term public assistance recipients who lived in dangerous housing conditions, in one of the lowest-income and highest-delinquency neighborhoods in New York, and for whom an adult with eighth-grade education represented the highest level of schooling.

When feelings on entry of children into care were related to socioeconomic circumstances, there were four feeling dimensions with significant differences. Mothers in relatively high socioeconomic circumstances were significantly more thankful and more relieved upon placement. Mothers in low socioeconomic circumstances were more nervous and more worried on the day their children entered foster care.

## Reason for and Necessity of Placement

Feelings were particularly relevant to reason for placement. Eleven percent of children, for example, were placed because of physical illness of the mother. In these cases, thankfulness on the part of the mother was significantly higher, and guilt and anger significantly lower, than when other reasons for placement were involved. A total of 17 percent of children were placed because of child behavior and difficulties in adjustment. In these cases guilt and relief were both significantly higher on the part of the mother, and anger and bitterness significantly lower, than for the overall group. Significantly more anger was expressed by mothers when children entered care because of severe parental neglect and abuse (14 percent) or for reasons of family dysfunction including conflict, fighting, alcoholism, drugs, and incompetence (10 percent), than when other reasons were involved.

An important factor in the feelings expressed was the mother's perception of how necessary she felt placement to be. In the field interview, mothers were asked to react on a four-point scale to the question, "How necessary was it that your child enter placement?" There were 37 percent who said it was "absolutely necessary," 21 percent said "very," 18 percent said "somewhat," and 24 percent said "not at all." The more necessary the mothers viewed placement, the more thankful and relieved they were on the day the child entered care. They also expressed significantly fewer feelings of emptiness or worry. On the other hand, mothers who said placement was not at all necessary tended to be significantly angrier, more ashamed, and more bitter.

## FEELING REFERENTS

In addition to asking parents whether they had experienced each of the 12 feelings, the interviewer inquired further on every positive response, asking what the feeling was about. For example, if a mother said, "I feel sad," she was asked, "About what?" The respondent then described what she felt sad about. This response was called the "feeling referent." When these spontaneous feeling referents were reviewed by the research staff, they fell into seven main categories. The first category was one of respondents expressing feelings about themselves—the self-referent; the second was of feelings related to the separation from the child; and the third was of feelings referred to the child himself. A fourth referent category related to feelings about child care, a fifth to feelings about the agency, and a sixth involved interpersonal feelings, referring to relatives or friends. The seventh referent category was one of feelings referred to society in general, or what might be termed "generalized other."

It was possible for any of these seven referents to apply to any of the 12 feelings. If a mother said, "I'm angry at myself," this would be noted as self-referent. If she said, "I am angry at being away from my child," that was listed as a separation referent. If she said, "I am angry at Johnny for the way he behaved," that was put down as a child referent. The other categories covered anger at the way the child was taken care of; anger at the agency as such; anger at her former husband or her mother-in-law, an interpersonal referent, or anger "at everything and everybody," which was listed as "generalized other."

When feeling referents were analyzed, it was apparent that some feelings tended to be directed toward specific referents, whereas others could be referred to a variety of sources. Guilt, for example, was referred to self by 84 percent of the mothers and 94 percent of the fathers who reported having feelings of guilt. Shame was another feeling that was highly focused, and tended to be self-referred. Sadness was referred to the separation experience by 69 percent of mothers and 62 percent of fathers who were sad. The feeling of anger was primarily interpersonal. It was usually expressed as anger against an individual—either a relative, friend, or neighbor—whom the respondent blamed for the child having gone into care. Often this individual was the absent husband or wife. The same pattern of interpersonal referents was noted for the feeling of bitterness. The feelings of relief and thankfulness tended to be expressed in relation to the agency care of the child. The feelings related to a variety of referents included those that can be described as generalized anxiety. Nervousness, for example, was distributed among many referents, including separation, child, agency, and generalized other. Worry was similarly diversely ascribed.

Considering referents without regard to particular feelings, the data show that 28 percent of all feelings expressed by these parents were referred to the separation experience, 20 percent to self, and 17 percent to agency care. Child referents and interpersonal referents each make up 11 percent of the total. Seven percent of feelings were referred to generalized other, and 6 percent to the agency as an institution. This distribution gives some insight regarding the channels into which feelings flow, and the direction of emotional reactions expressed at the time of separation. The separation experience itself was the main focus, but next to this the parent's major attention was directed to herself or himself. Attention to the child as an independent actor in the placement experience was not primary. The parents did not express concern with the operation of foster care as a system, or with other larger social problems. This was shown by the low incidence of referents as "generalized other" and to the agency as an institution.

Further analysis of feelings and referents was undertaken through the statistical intercorrelation of the variables, which were then factor-analyzed. The purpose was to show combinations of variables that tended to be related, in order to discover common dimensions. The following six factors were identified for mothers: interpersonal hostility; separation anxiety with sadness; self-denigration; agency hostility; concerned gratitude; and self-involvement. For fathers there were three factors: separation anxiety with numbness; personal shame with relief about care; and personal guilt with interpersonal hostility.

A further examination of the relationship between feelings and other aspects of the family study, such as attitudes toward agencies, toward society, and toward childrearing patterns, identified some relationships that were statistically significant [2]. There was a significant relationship, for example, between those parents who expressed feelings of anger on placement, and those who regarded agencies as usurpers of parental rights. There was also a significant relationship between the feeling of anger and expressions of alienation from society. Shame tended to be associated with a more trusting orientation toward agencies. Nervousness in relation to placement was significantly related to strong evidence of authoritarian childrearing attitudes. Both shame and nervousness, however, were also significantly related to low socioeconomic status. Fathers who tended to be thankful at the time of placement also tended to regard the agency as a surrogate taking over parental rights.

## RELATIONSHIP OF FEELINGS TO LENGTH OF TIME IN CARE

One goal of the research was to see whether data on feelings at the time of placement were relevant to predictions of length of stay in foster care. So far, data on discharges occuring up to 1 year following placement have been analyzed. Approximately one-third of the children in the study were discharged. Since children entered the study sample only after 3 months in placement, discharge data were noted for the following categories: children who went home in from 3 months to 6 months after entering care; children who went home in from 6 months to 1 year after placement; and children who were still in care 1 year after entry. This analysis showed that parental expression of anger, bitterness, and worry were significantly associated with those cases in which children were discharged from care prior to 1 year.

At present, the study staff is returning to the field to reinterview parents of children in care, and see how they have fared over the last year. For families whose children remain in care, perceptions of the foster care system will be explored, including the role of the natural mother or father in relation to the perceived role of the child care worker. In cases where children have returned home, the resolution of the original problem necessitating care will be reviewed, and information on family functioning will be obtained. In all cases, feeling data will be gathered on either continued separation of parents and childen, or on filial reunion. Length of time in care will be reviewed for relevance to possible diminished level of parental feeling, and further detachment.

The importance of giving serious attention to the needs of mothers and fathers when children enter care goes beyond the perception of them as individuals in need of help. Unless expressed needs and feelings have been worked out so that the parent can understand the placement experience, it is likely that the trauma suffered by the child upon separation from the mother or father will only be reinforced upon return home by the unresolved problems suffered by the parent upon separation from the child.

## NOTES

1. The research was supported by a grant from the Children's Bureau, U. S. Department of Health, Education, and Welfare. The sample included children from birth through age 12 who entered care in New York City in 1966, and remained in care at least 90 days.
2. Statistical significance was determined by application of the chi-square test (P = .05 or less).

# Part VIII
# Perspectives on Programs and Methods

# Part VIII

## Perspectives on Programs and Methods

The common thread in this selection of articles on programs and methods of working with parents is emphasis on active participation of parents in the child's placement and in permanent planning for their child. A variety of newer as well as long-established approaches to work with parents are represented. The readings may also stimulate other, more creative solutions to the challenge of working with parents. Finally, in addition to suggesting possible interventions, the authors offer a "way of seeing" parents as a constructive force and a partner with others involved in decision making about children in foster care.

Perception of the client clearly influences the nature of the intervention. If parents are given recognition as being important to the child, programs that include them will evolve. It is also true that the choice of intervention depends largely on the services available. Until recently, parents were ignored; consequently, there existed few programs that fully involved them. With the emerging focus on the significance of parents, new programs and methods have been developed that emphasize their participation.

The first three chapters in this section underline the urgency of preventing extended foster care. The authors agree that the primary goal should be reunion of the child with the parent. If reunion is not possible, they believe that relinquishment for adoption within a limited period of time should be the preferred alternative.

Writing about the well-known Oregon Project in Chapter 20, Pike notes that while staff members help parents to decide whether their goal is reunion or relinquishment, the project is based on the philosophy that foster care placements could be prevented through comprehensive support services to families. Pike reiterates that the early identification of problems and intensive work with families (such as crisis intervention, counseling services, and day care) could make even necessary placements short ones. As the Oregon Project has demonstrated in recent years, through consistent work with parents permanent plans can be made for most children who enter the foster care system.

As described in Chapter 21, Chestang and Heymann have developed an approach to working with parents that has as its main tenet: "Only two roads to permanence exist for the child: rehabilitating his natural parents or family, or helping them to free him for adoption." This conviction comes from over ten years of experimentation with various methods of reducing the length of foster care. Like Pike, these authors stress the need to work with parents to achieve permanency for children. They assert that "Ineffective handling of the natural parents' resistance and indecisiveness is most often the factor that perpetuates extended foster care." Chestang and Heymann provide concrete practice guidelines and case examples for the worker who must help parents make and follow through on a decision to keep or relinquish their child.

Responding to the lack of systematic case planning in the foster care system, Stein, Gambrill, and Wiltse, in Chapter 22, describe the use of contracts with parents in the Alameda Project. The project had as its goal the creation of an intensive relationship between parent and child that would help "rebuild the parent's sense of parenthood and sense of authority to make the decision about his or her children." The authors consider three decisions acceptable: return of the child to the parent; relinquishment of the child for adoption; or placement of the child in long-term foster care with either an agreement with the parent or a guardianship arrangement. Contracts, which are used as a means of encouraging parental participation in planning and early decision making, serve these purposes: recognizing parental participation as an integral part of the planning process; identifying the exact changes required of the parents if their child is to be returned; establishing a time frame in which these changes must occur; and strengthening parental commitment to change by requiring them to sign a contract. The authors are convinced that the contracts provide a viable and successful instrument for practice with parents. Their chapter outlines the specifics of setting up contracts and includes a sample one.

The next three chapters in this section present varied programs set in group homes, foster homes, and residential treatment centers that actively involve parents in the helping process. These programs use the concept of "part-time parenting," which focuses on rebuilding the strengths in the family. They recognize that although the stress of parenting may be overwhelming, removal of the child in the traditional sense may not be the answer.

In Chapter 23, Simmons, Gumpert, and Rothman describe a small group home called a "family residential center" in Brooklyn, New York. The program stresses helping parents through group approaches, providing services to families as entities rather than to children as isolated individuals, and making social work services available to all in the child's environment—parents, siblings, and kin. Although the children of six families were housed in the group home, parents and other significant family members were encouraged to participate in the care of their children. Every effort was made to avoid displacement of feelings about a parent onto a foster parent and replacement of a parent by a parent surrogate. The parents were regarded as "partners." Simmons, Gumpert, and Rothman conclude by questioning whether separation of the biological family from the foster parents or from the direct caretakers of the child can be justified, except in the case of relinquishment for adoption.

Loewe and Hanrahan, also using a "part-time parenting" concept, describe in Chapter 24 a five-day foster care program in Cleveland that was created in the wake of failure of traditional foster care. Five-day foster care is geared toward assisting parents who are unable to carry full parental responsibility. Five days a week, children live with, and are cared for by, foster parents. Weekends, holidays, and vacations are spent with their own parents. Goals of the program are to reduce separation trauma for parents and children, and to maintain the child's relationship and identification with the biological family. The program strives to reunite child and parents within less than a year. Foster parents are regarded as assistant rather than as substitute parents. Social workers, parents, and foster parents are viewed as a team. Placement is considered a means of solving a family problem, not as a punishment for parents. Intrinsic to the philosophy of this program, which has been quite successful in reuniting children and parents, are the concept of "sharing parental burdens rather than assuming them" and the worker's task of assisting parents to learn to fill their parental role on a full-time basis.

In Chapter 25, Oxley reports on a followup study of a small residential treatment center for boys in San Francisco. The center stressed active participation by the parents in the form of weekly counseling sessions. In addition, parents were assigned various child-care roles and the boys went home for weekends and one month during the summer. In the followup research, responses to the treatment were elicited from the boys, who were, on an average, four years postdischarge, as well as from members of their families. The study showed that mandatory involvement can be effective: parents showed strong interest in becoming partners with child-care staff and achieved changes in their functioning and in their parenting skills that were maintained at the point of followup. These findings are all the more impressive since these parents were for the most part involuntary clients. As Oxley concludes, the study suggests that shifting priorities in use of clinical time from child to parent might increase benefits without increased cost.

Closely akin to the goal of helping parents grow so that they may more easily assume parental roles is the concept of role modeling. In Chapter 26, Davies and Bland describe a program in Hartford, Connecticut, that utilizes foster parents as role models. The basic assumption of the program is that many parents are inexperienced in parenting and are unclear as to what is expected of them as parents. In addition, many of the children are emotionally disturbed and have special needs. The goal is reunion of child and parents as soon as is realistically possible. Within this context, foster parents serve as "teachers of parenting behavior." Davies and Bland's approach reflects the movement toward greater involvement of foster parents as members of the child placement team and as resources in behalf of biological families.

Other programs making similar use of resources in the environment look to older or more experienced persons to model parental behavior for parents in situations involving child abuse or emotional disturbance.[1] Some of these programs are also designed to meet the multiple, concrete needs of families. As an example, in Chapter 27 Spinelli and Barton discuss the experience of the Southern Home for Children in Philadelphia. As the Home has expanded its interventive modalities in response to the changing needs of its population, it took on the task of confronting social and environmental factors such as poverty, poor housing, and unemployment through intensive "Home Management Services." Home Management Specialists are individuals who have overcome many of the difficulties facing their clients and who help parents deal with concrete issues and locate needed services. As a result, some children are able to remain at home; some are returned home sooner than would otherwise have been expected; and re-placement of children is frequently averted. Family environments are strengthened and the emotional and financial costs of residential treatment are forestalled or reduced.

In Chapter 28, Murphy presents an educational approach to helping parents from her experiences with courses for parents of children in foster care offered by the San Francisco Department of Social Services in conjunction with a community college. These grew out of classes for foster parents, who felt that parents might also profit from similar learning experiences. The success of this program suggests that workers should give greater attention to

[1]Cf. Arch, Shirley D., "Older Adults as Home Visitors Modeling Parenting for Troubled Families," *Child Welfare*, 57: 9 (November 1978): 601–605.

the potential use of educationally oriented approaches in work with parents. At the same time, there should be further use of self-help groups such as Parents Anonymous that also mobilize people's own resources.

Most of the programs presented in this section explicitly or implicitly take heed of the ecological model. They recognize the parents as a significant factor in the ecosystem of the child. The means by which different programs choose to involve the parents vary. Some focus on removing barriers in the family's environment and enriching it through the introduction of resources such as foster parents or home aides. Some use contracts, while others stress teaching methods. Emphasis is placed on the parents' need for concrete support services as well as opportunities to practice and enhance their parental capacities. As illustrated by the programs described in this section, both child and parents can be helped even more effectively if they are regarded as part of an ecological system, interrelated and interdependent.

## SUGGESTIONS FOR FURTHER READING


Arch, Shirley D., "Older Adults as Home Visitors Modeling Parenting for Troubled Families," *Child Welfare*, 57: 9 (November 1978): 601–605.

Edinger, Hanni B., "Reuniting Children and Parents Through Casework and Group Work," *Children*, 17: 5 (September–October 1970): 183–187.

Emlen, Arthur et al., *Overcoming Barriers to Planning for Children in Foster Care*, Washington, D.C.: U.S. Department of Health, Education and Welfare, Children's Bureau, 1978. DHEW Publication No. (OHDS) 78-30138.

Gitelson, Paul, "A Model Program to Avoid the Institutionalization of Children," *Journal of Sociology and Social Welfare*, 6: 6 (November 1979): 805–813.

Hammond, John W., "Child Care Workers as Helpers to Parents," *Child Care Quarterly*, 2: 4 (Winter 1973): 282–284.

Holmes, Sally, "Parents Anonymous: A Treatment Method for Child Abuse," *Social Work*, 23: 3 (May 1978): 245–247.

Horejsi, Charles R.; Bertsche, Anne V.; and Clark, Frank W., *Social Work Practice with Parents of Children in Foster Care—A Handbook*. Springfield, Ill.: Charles C Thomas, 1981.

Hoxworth, D. and Alsup, Theresa, "Group Work with Parents in a Day-Care Center," *Hospital and Community Psychiatry*, 19: 8 (August 1968): 256–258.

Jones, Mary Ann, "Reducing Foster Care Through Services to Families," *Children Today*, 5: 6 (November–December 1976): 6–10.

Keith-Lucas, Alan and Sanford, Clifford W., *Group Child Care as a Family Service*, Chapel Hill, N.C.: University of North Carolina Press, 1977.

Krona, David A., "Parents as Treatment Partners in Residential Care," *Child Welfare*, 59: 2 (February 1980): 91–96.

Magnus, Ralph A., "Teaching Parents to Parent: Parent Involvement in Residential Treatment Programs," *Children Today*, 3: 1 (January–February 1974): 25–27.

Maluccio, Anthony N. and Sinanoglu, Paula A., editors, *The Challenge of Partnership: Working with Parents of Children in Foster Care*, New York: Child Welfare League of America, 1981.

Maybanks, Sheila and Bryce, Marvin, editors, *Home-Based Services for Children and Families*, Springfield, Ill.: Charles C Thomas, 1979: 260–71.

Stein, Theodore J.; Gambrill, Eileen D.; and Wiltse, Kermit T., *Children in Foster Homes—Achieving Continuity of Care*, New York: Praeger Publications, 1978.

Ten Broeck, Elsa, "The Extended Family Center: A Home Away from Home for Abused Children and Their Parents," *Children Today*, 3: 2 (March–April 1974): 2–6.

# 20

# Permanent Planning for Foster Children: The Oregon Project

VICTOR PIKE

When April was 18 months old, her young, unwed mother suffered a psychotic episode and, in an effort to "spare the child from degradations of the devil," stabbed April and held her under a hot shower. April survived and, after a long hospitalization, was placed in foster family care. The mother was committed for a year to a state hospital. After her release, the child welfare agency caseworker helped her to receive a variety of community services, including psychiatric treatment, job training, health services, financial aid and public housing.

When the caseworker cautiously initiated visits between the child and mother, April cried and clung to the worker. Later, she learned to run and hide whenever the mother visited the foster home. Gradually, however, the child began to accept the visits, although she never responded warmly to her mother.

After the mother had received a year of treatment, the worker began to consider the possibility of returning April to her—but problems persisted. April began to have nightmares every night, and her foster mother would rock

Reprinted from *Children Today*, Vol. 5, No. 6 (November–December 1976), pp. 22–25 and 41. By permission of the author and the journal.

her until her screaming stopped and April fell asleep. As the situation appeared to approach an impasse, the mother experienced another psychotic episode and was hospitalized for three months.

By the time of her mother's release, April was three years old and had been in foster family care more than half of her life. April began visiting her mother again, and her nightmares continued.

After consulting with hospital psychiatrists and private psychologists, the worker arranged psychiatric examinations for the mother and April. All involved professionals concurred that while the mother would be capable of some degree of self-support, she would never be intact enough to care for April even minimally.

Agency and community efforts to rehabilitate the mother were well documented. A petition to terminate parental rights was filed, expert witnesses testified and the court terminated the legal rights of April's mother. At age 4½, April was free for adoption.

The foster parents, who wanted to adopt April, explained the court decision to her. Although there was little visible reaction from April, there were no nightmares that night—nor on succeeding nights. In fact, April, who was adopted by her foster parents, has never had another nightmare.

April's case was one of 509 which the Children's Services Division of the Oregon State Department of Human Resources had selected for special attention as part of a 3-year demonstration project funded in 1973 by the Children's Bureau, OCD. The project—Freeing Children for Permanent Placement—emphasized aggressive planning and casework techniques to achieve permanent homes for children like April who were adrift in long-term foster care.

## THE OREGON PROJECT

One of three possibilities can usually be considered when making permanent plans for a child in foster care: returning the child to his biological parents; freeing him for adoption through the termination of parental rights; or contracting for a formal long-term foster care arrangement. Since proceedings to terminate parental rights were foreign to many circuit courts, we decided to focus our efforts on working toward this goal. In Oregon, existing appellate court decisions had reversed about 40 percent of the cases appealed, and line staff members knew little about properly preparing cases for court. In addition, we felt that termination of parental rights was a "heavy" matter with which state attorneys and judges were reluctant to deal.

After funds for the project were received in November 1973, 2,300 children in foster care were screened according to three criteria. These were that the child must have been in foster care for one year or more; that the child was unlikely, in the referring worker's judgment, to return home; and that the child was considered to be adoptable. More than 500 children were accepted for the project, fewer than those meeting the criteria but the maximum number possible under the protected caseload arrangement. Caseloads were limited to 25 children per worker (as opposed to the usual caseload in Oregon of 50 to 60 children per caseworker). Fifteen of the state's 36 counties participated in the demonstration project.

We believed that children involved in termination of parental rights proceedings should have separate counsel. Consequently, the Children's Services Division negotiated a contract with the Metropolitan Public Defender's office in Portland for the services of a full-time attorney, David Slader, and supporting staff, to represent the children in this project. It was recognized that the counsel had to be an independent legal agent, representing neither the project nor the Children's Services Division.

To meet the grant requirement that the project be evaluated by a third party, a contract was arranged with the Regional Research Institute for Human Services of the Portland State University School of Social Work. The Institute, directed by Arthur Emlen, provided the structure and direction for screening activities and collection and analysis of data.

The goals and casework tactics for each case were defined, and the project began with concentrated efforts to locate absent parents and to assess the available parents' capacities to provide care for their children. Despite the screening criteria bias toward identifying cases suitable for termination of parental rights proceedings, project staff members were convinced that the primary goal of permanent planning should be the reuniting of biological families. Thus, an exhaustive effort was made to accomplish this goal before steps were taken to resolve cases through termination of parental rights. These efforts resulted unexpectedly in a surprising number of children being returned home—26 percent have now been reunited with their biological families.

One of the children returned home was Chris, a 9-year-old boy who had been in a foster family home since age two, when he was sexually abused by his father. The father had been convicted and sent to prison.

Chris' mother, who was Japanese, had married the father when he was stationed in Japan and Chris had been born shortly after their return to the United States. Further investigation and a visit to the mother's home revealed that she had divorced Chris' father after his conviction and was now remarried, had a child and seemed content. Reports from the prison indicated that the father was seriously disturbed and was not anticipating parole in the near future.

Chris had been meeting with his mother about three times a year, when she initiated a request to the agency. Although she had been described in the case record as "apathetic," the project caseworker discovered that she really had not understood the juvenile court proceedings through which Chris had been placed in foster care, due to her poor grasp of the English language. She had accepted the decision, believing that planning by the "State" was not to be questioned or thwarted.

Chris was apparently happy, living in a stable foster home in which he received loving care and was treated as a member of the family. However, as the caseworker began to know Chris better, she learned that he was puzzled by the separation from his mother and nurtured a desire, although rarely expressed, to be a member of his own family. The worker's initial steps to increase Chris' involvement with his mother, stepfather and 3-year-old half brother were met with pointed resistance by the foster parents, who were understandably reluctant to relinquish him.

A psychological examination of Chris indicated that, despite his positive foster care experience, emotional ties to his own mother were strong. After seven years in foster care, Chris was returned to his mother's home. The foster parents accepted the decision and now fulfill the role of "aunt" and "uncle" to him. Even though Chris' behavior had usually been good, the former foster parents were the first to recognize a new, relaxed freedom in him and Chris' school grades improved noticeably.

In Chris' situation, placement in foster care was counterindicated from the beginning, since the perpetrator of the problem had been removed from the home. A prompt evaluation-treatment effort would have indicated that Chris belonged at home—and seven years of separation and $14,700 in foster care expenditures could have been avoided.

## BARRIERS TO PERMANENT PLANNING

What obstacles may hinder permanent planning for children in foster care? Many factors operate to maintain the foster care status quo. These may include, for example, overburdened caseworkers; lack of case management procedures or case review mechanisms; lack of commitment on the part of the agency and workers to change the characteristics of foster care practice; the absence of statutory authority or a poor statute upon which to seek termination of parental rights decisions; and lack of skills in preparing cases for court. We found the techniques and casework tactics described here to be effective in overcoming many of these barriers.

The first step to permanent planning might be termed prevention—reducing unnecessary placements by helping parents function at a minimum level of adequacy. Crisis intervention and counseling services, homemakers, day care—all alternatives must be tried to help keep the family intact.

However, if these efforts fail and a child must be placed in foster care, planning for his or her return home should begin immediately with a thorough assessment of the parents' capacity to provide care. Are the problems which necessitated the child's placement chronic or situational, profound or superficial? Are they remediable—and how?

When a child is first removed from home, parents' emotions are running high. They haven't yet settled into apathy and complacency, and the family dysfunction is usually identifiable. This is the time to engage parents in treatment and to draw up a written agreement between the caseworker and parents, stating the goal of the treatment program—the return of the child within a specified period of time—and spelling out the steps both parents are expected to take to accomplish the goal [1].

Visits between biological parents and child should begin instantly. Only if parents are destructive in their contacts with the child should visits be restricted. Although a loving relationship between foster child and foster parents should certainly be promoted, the persistent presence of the child's biological parents can help to control the overpossessiveness that might develop on the part of foster parents and which might interfere with the child's subsequent return home.

All casework activity should be carefully documented. Interviews with families should be followed up promptly with a letter reiterating the salient points discussed. This reinforces the worker's contact with the parent and provides the agency with a record of the worker's attempts to help reunite the family. An accurate and running chronology of all activities should be included, and the record kept free of hearsay, rambling opinion or value judgments.

Although the treatment program should be reasonably structured, the caseworker cannot be expected to "hold the parent's hand" throughout the process. If parents are not cooperating, they should be advised—not threatened—that continued unacceptable performance will jeopardize their parental rights.

In deciding whether to return a child home or to work toward termination of parental rights, attention must be directed objectively toward the dangers that may exist for the child if he or she were to return home. Would there be danger of physical abuse? If not, the possibility of physical neglect must be considered. Perhaps the child would be left unattended, without adequate nutrition and medical care. Poor housing or a parent's lack of housekeeping skills might pose a distinct threat to his or her physical health or safety. Can these problems be rectified? Would the child be subject to emotional neglect?

Both legal statutes and the casework process direct how cases are structured for resolution so that permanent plans for children can be realized. In general, the situations of parents whose children are in foster care fall into four categories or cases: *condition cases,* in which parents have a professionally diagnosed incapacity that precludes their fulfilling a parental role; *conduct cases,* in which parents do not display a significant, clinically diagnosable condition but either cannot or refuse to respond acceptably as parents; *abandonment cases,* in which parents, through statement or action, evidence a determination never to resume the care of their children; and *desertion,* when a parent is simply absent for a specified period (in Oregon law, one year).

## CONDITION CASES

If parents suffer from a chronic condition such as mental or emotional illness, serious mental retardation, alcoholism, drug addiction, etc., they may never be able to fulfill their parental roles and the child may never be able to return home. Any condition that precludes the child receiving a minimum degree of emotional nurturing should be documented by psychiatric or psychological examination which addresses both diagnosis and prognosis. If in the evaluator's professional opinion the condition is seriously detrimental to the child and is not remediable, a termination case should be brought to court. The evaluator will necessarily be someone who can be established in court as an expert witness.

Parents who present clear-cut, clinically diagnosed conditions that cannot improve should not be coerced into an involved treatment program.

## CONDUCT CASES

Typical conduct cases involve families with some history of psychiatric and/or marital problems, drinking problems, transiency, chronic and severe financial difficulties, minor law violations, serious housing and housekeeping inadequacies, incidences of abuse or neglect of children, etc. The presence of any one of these symptoms would not support a petition to terminate parental rights, but the collective impact of several will reduce the parents' ability to perform at a level of minimum functioning. These families have a right to a comprehensive, community-oriented treatment program in which the agency matches client problems with appropriate treatment resources—and coordinates the process. Through such efforts many families can be rehabilitated and a surprising number of children returned home.

If, however, the caseworker, supervisor and representatives of community agencies involved in the case agree that efforts have failed to motivate or rehabilitate the parent within a specified period of time, a petition to terminate parental rights should be prepared. Consensus decision making is imperative at this point to minimize the chance for bias or error.

Again, accurate documentation of all efforts through the use of case records and correspondence can provide the information needed to establish allegations. A comprehensive and chronologically organized case record is indispensable for workers testifying in court.

When termination of parent-child relationships is indicated, parents should be offered the option of voluntarily releasing their children before a petition is prepared. Proposing the subject of voluntary release is often difficult, even for experienced caseworkers and the worker's inclination usually is to discuss it at "the opportune time"—when the parent himself brings up the subject. However, since this rarely occurs, caseworkers should initiate discussion of voluntary release as a part of the agency's service options. A surprising number of parents are not aware of this possibility. Although parents may initially reject the idea, it often becomes more acceptable once their defensiveness is overcome and they realize that they may again have to face the task of childrearing—or the unpleasant experience of a termination of rights hearing.

## DESERTION AND ABANDONMENT CASES

Termination of parental rights based on abandonment or desertion requires that a reasonable search be made for missing parents. If it is established that parents know where their children are and have chosen to remain absent, perhaps they should have the right to be spared a vigorous search. However, if desertion could possibly be considered involuntary, the search must be exhaustive.

The past known addresses of parents and relatives, registration lists of the motor vehicles departments of any state in which they were known to have lived, records of utility companies and unions—all must be carefully searched. Knowledge of parents' personal characteristics may produce leads as to their whereabouts. If there is a history of mental illness, for example, admissions to mental hospitals in areas where they had lived should be checked. If they have a pattern of criminal activity, police department "rap sheets" for arrests should be investigated and a further search conducted to determine whether convictions had followed those arrests. Many of these time-consuming chores should be turned over to agency employees other than the already overburdened caseworker.

A search for missing parents should be launched as soon as the child comes into care, rather than mounting a crash effort after the statutory time has passed.

## BRINGING CASES TO COURT

When any termination of parental rights case is presented in court, the district attorney and judges will be more inclined to act if the social agency has (1) searched for absent parents as soon as possible after the child was placed and documented the absence; (2) secured psychiatric or psychological evaluations in condition cases; and (3) tenaciously pursued a treatment plan in conduct cases and carefully recorded the rehabilitation effort if the parent has failed to respond. In addition, the worker should assemble a list of witnesses, indicating which facts each witness can testify to. The worker should also have a thorough knowledge of the applicable statutes, be familiar with the relevant case law and the principles of due process, and have some expertise in being a good witness.

Some psychiatrists and psychologists will be reluctant to leave the security of their offices to face cross-examination on the witness stand by aggressive defense attorneys who will probably try to badger, discredit and sometimes disparage them. In condition cases, a professional evaluator's testimony is the primary means through which to resolve the litigation. The worker should feel free to appeal to the social conscience of the evaluator, explaining that the child's chance for a permanent plan is dependent upon his willingness to testify. However, in those cases where the parent or his attorney resists a psychological or psychiatric examination, and the parent's behavior is bizarre and has been so demonstrated in the community, lay witnesses can testify to their direct observations of such behavior and a doctor can diagnose, in court, from a hypothetical standpoint.

The effectiveness in accomplishing needed litigation in our project has been enhanced immeasurably by our arrangement with the public defender's office to provide legal counsel for the children. When the state is the moving party against the parent, the child's status in the litigation is somewhat nebulous, despite the fact that the child is in a position to suffer the greatest impact from the court's decision. An attorney retained for a specific client assumes a different posture than one who represents "the interests of the State." Also, in the event of a judicial decision that is adverse to the child's interest, the child's attorney is in a more politically desirable position to appeal than is the district attorney.

We have found that this arrangement also has the benefit of providing children with legal counsel who are more experienced and sensitive to the child's predicament than are most attorneys appointed randomly from the bar list.

## OUTCOME OF THE PROJECT

As of October 31, 1976, 26 percent of the 509 children in the project had been returned home to their parents and 36 percent had been freed for adoption and placed in adoptive homes—19 percent with their former foster parents and 17 percent with new families. Three percent of the children are living with relatives.

Seven percent of the children will continue in formalized, long-term foster care. For these children who may never return home and who are not adoptable, the drawing up of placement contracts by the agency is encouraged to offer them maximum security and stability of care. In arranging contracts for long-term foster care, the concerns of all parties involved must be considered: the foster children, the biological parents, the foster parents and the agency.

Nine percent of the total number of project cases have not been satisfactorily resolved, but 19 percent are in process and most of these children will be adopted.

During the third year of the project, now ending, we focused on the resolution of cases remaining in litigation, the analysis of research data, the establishment of a statewide staff training effort to implement the demonstration project throughout the state child welfare system, and the production of various written materials, including a compendium of Oregon case law and a resource manual to assist caseworkers in permanent planning [2].

The project has recently received funding from OCD for a fourth year to continue following the children's placements, to ascertain the continuity and success of the plans made for them.

## DISSEMINATION

In response to the growing awareness of the phenomenon of drift in foster care, the Children's Bureau, OCD, is planning to disseminate nationally, over a 4-year period, the concepts and procedures relative to definite decision making and action for foster children. In the first year a number of states will be selected to receive incentive monies to replicate all or parts of the Oregon project or to initiate other approaches that will reduce unnecessary long-term foster care. The Regional Research Institute, which will work in cooperation with others who participated in the Oregon project, has recently been awarded a contract from OCD to provide technical assistance to that effort, to disseminate the results of the Oregon project and to further develop other useful materials.

The participants in the Oregon project are convinced that significant numbers of children now in limbo in foster care can enjoy the benefits of legally secure futures. It takes a concentrated effort and reasonable workloads to screen cases and provide appropriate treatment resources, and tenacious resolve to bring appropriate cases for judicial determination. The results, however, are valuable in terms of both improved planning for children and in increased staff knowledge and skills.

## NOTES

1. For a discussion of the use of contracts with natural parents as a tool for encouraging parental participation in planning and early decision making, see "Foster Care: The Use of Contracts" by Theodore J. Stein, Eileen D. Gambrill and Kermit T. Wiltse, *Public Welfare*, Fall 1974, reprinted in *Foster Care*, a collection of articles available from the Children's Bureau, OCD, P.O. Box 1182, Washington, D.C. 20013.
2. A summary of the project entitled *Barriers to Planning for Children in Foster Care: A Summary*, is available from Regional Research Institute, Portland State University, Harder House, P.O. Box 751, Portland, Oreg. 97207.

# 21

# Reducing the Length of Foster Care

LEON W. CHESTANG
AND IRMGARD HEYMANN

What has been long known from experience and practice has now been established through empirical research: the child who remains in foster care for more than eighteen months is likely to remain there indefinitely [1]. If he is older or black or for other reasons "hard to place," the obstacles to making permanent living arrangements for him are increased. These facts, together with the growing realization that foster care is not the best plan for children, provided the impetus for developing the techniques described in this article.

These approaches are the result of experience gained from over ten years of experimenting with various methods of reducing the length of foster care. Underlying them is a philosophy whose main points can be summarized as follows:

1. Every child has a right to a permanent home.
2. Foster care is a temporary arrangement, not a solution.
3. Extended foster care, with its vicissitudes, is damaging to children.
4. Only two roads to permanence exist for the child: rehabilitating his natural parents or family or helping them to free him for adoption.

---

5. Inactivity on the part of the caseworker and/or the child's parents perpetuates the state of extended foster care.
6. Adoption is a realistic alternative for the older child. [2]

In fact, permanent living arrangements, including adoptions, can be made for far more children than at present. To accomplish this, it is crucial to develop approaches to the child's natural parents because ineffective handling of the natural parents' resistance and indecisiveness is most often the factor that perpetuates extended foster care. This discussion, therefore, is focused on work with the child's natural parents. The objective is to reach a decision to effect the child's return to them or to free him so he can have the opportunity to live in an adoptive family.

The aim of the casework approach with natural parents is to achieve a permanent home for the child, with rehabilitation of the natural family or adoption as the options. The parent and the social worker are free to elect the option best suited to the parent's capacity. In working with parents, the worker would make these points:

*Focus on the demands of parenting.* "The law and society require that parents meet the basic physical and emotional needs of children. We will help you assess your ability to fulfill these responsibilities and the reality of your plan to resume care of your children."

*Use of time.* "We want you to have every opportunity to resume your role as a parent. How much time do you think you will need to accomplish your plan? If you are unable to achieve your goals within the time you have set, we will examine together whether this is because you are unable to achieve them, you need more time, or some unidentified problem is impeding progress [3]. Perhaps some alternate plan such as adoption should be considered."

*Recognizing the parent as a person with needs.* "You, like everyone else, are a person with needs that must be satisfied. However, each person has different capacities and abilities. Let us evaluate yours. It may be that you are capable of being a good parent to all or only some of your children or you may require all your energy to meet your own needs. We will accept whatever your capacities are and we will not blame you if you cannot meet your child's needs."

*Interposing adoption as a leverage.* "Your child is entitled to a stable, permanent family. During your child's placement, you have failed to maintain contact with him. If this limited parenting is hard for you, total parental responsibility will be even harder. Perhaps, we should consider adoption as an alternative so that your child may have the opportunity to have a new family of his own."

*Allowing the parent to abandon the child.* "The parent who abandons his child abdicates his role as parent. A three-month period of no contact with your child is viewed as abandonment by the laws of this state. We will use this law if necessary."

*Use of the extended family.* If members of the extended family are available and competent, they may be called on to support a parent in his decision to free the child for adoption, thereby relieving the parent of the fear that he will be rejected because of his decision.

## STRESSING ADOPTION

At intake the worker stresses that foster care is a poor, only temporary solution and explores the parents' interest in placing the child for adoption. Although most parents state they would not consider giving up the child for adoption, the question is raised routinely in each situation, thereby emphasizing the alternatives available to the parent—effecting the child's return home or placing him for adoption. Thus prolonged and often futile efforts at rehabilitation can be avoided. Instead, the options are increased and parents are pushed toward a resolution of the problem.

Can a parent be rehabilitated? Will giving up the child for adoption best meet the needs of both the parent and child? These questions involve complex diagnostic issues, including an assessment of the parents' personality and strengths, the true parent-child relationship, and the parents' capacity for problem-solving. Such an assessment requires much time and can delay decision-making by both parents and the caseworker. Hence talking about adoption as a viable alternative from the beginning can promote rehabilitation, save years in foster placement, and make it easier for the parent to reach a decision. In this process, the parents are told that prolonged foster care is harmful both to them and to the child and that the worker will help them find another solution as soon as possible.

Discussing adoption in a nonthreatening manner and at the same time maintaining a meaningful relationship with the parent are keys to the ongoing process that begins at intake and continues until a decision is reached. Some of the topics discussed include the family history, with particular attention to events that have contributed to family breakdown; the parents' ability to deal with stress; and alternate resources for placement. Throughout, the worker's general focus is on the demands of parenting, which allows the client to examine what is expected of him as a parent and whether he is able to fulfill these demands and at the same time meet his own needs.

The process of evaluating the parent's own needs usually requires examining past events. But many of the inadequate parents with whom the authors deal have not developed the ability to analyze and learn from the past. Thus, in order to reach these parents, the worker concentrates on such present events as visits with the child. He sees the parents shortly after the visit so that feelings and events are not forgotten or denied and a realistic assessment can be made of what is happening between them and the child.

In evaluating parent-child visits, the following questions are raised:

1. How frequent are the visits?
2. Is the parent on time and does he stay for the allotted time?
3. Does the parent spend time alone with the child or take him to visit friends and relatives, thus diluting the relationship and minimizing the demands of parenting?
4. Can the parent relate to the child's needs and feelings, or is he able to think only of his own immediate needs?
5. Is the parent angry at the child for having positive feelings toward the foster family?

All these questions yield rich material that may spur the parent to find more quickly a resolution to the problem of taking the child home or putting him up for adoption.

Parents' plans are often vague and unrealistic. Frequently the parents complain about their difficulties in making plans. Thus it is essential to help the parents learn to make decisions. To encourage the parents, the worker generally gives his approval to any plan the parents suggest that is at all realistic, and he helps them explore alternatives. Because many of the parents have made poor decisions in the past, it is particularly important to help them feel they can make good decisions.

## MRS. JONES

The Jones case is a prime example of a parent's ability to take decisive steps when supported by a worker who suggests specific alternatives.

> Mrs. Jones, an attractive 24-year-old woman, contacted the agency for help in placing her 1½ year-old daughter. She had just separated from her husband, eighteen years her senior, whom she had married for convenience two months before the birth of her

> first daughter. Her husband had convinced her he was sterile and therefore not the father of the child so that she surrendered that child for adoption. When she became pregnant with her second child, Jane, she realized her husband was not sterile and that he had a pattern of pathological lying.
>
> Mrs. Jones's family life had been severely unstable. Her father was an alcoholic, two siblings were mentally ill, her mother was controlling, and as a child she had had severe problems in school.
>
> Her faulty perception of reality was apparent from the beginning. In spite of a high intelligence, she reasoned poorly and dissociated affects from events. Because she viewed herself as a helpless victim of fate, she felt that the only answer to her future security was to find a rich husband. The worker did not oppose this solution but demanded that she set a time limit for accomplishing it. In the interview they discussed ways of finding a rich husband, and in addition the worker brought up the alternative of placing Jane for adoption. Although this angered Mrs. Jones, the worker persisted, and Mrs. Jones became increasingly more realistic.
>
> After six months Mrs. Jones moved to a better neighborhood, hoping to attract eligible men, but she did not do so. She then began to inquire about local child care agencies and nursery schools. After a year she took the child home to the two-room apartment she had previously considered unsuitable. She stated that the worker's suggestion of placing the child for adoption had given her the impetus to make alternative plans.

Even when parents choose to surrender their child for adoption, they do so with ambivalence. Some parents can only act through inaction. For example, although parents are advised at intake that three months of no contact with the child constitutes legal abandonment and they can be taken to court to surrender their child for adoption, they remain inactive. Unable to muster enough strength to go to court to sign a surrender, they prefer to discontinue all contact with the child so that the agency will then take positive steps toward placing the child for adoption.

Other parents will appear in court when they receive a summons, but in most instances this represents a feeble attempt to make themselves feel they are not giving up the child. These parents usually disappear before the final court hearing, as occurred in the following case.

## MRS. CLARKE

When Mrs. Clarke abandoned the family, Mr. Clarke asked the court's help in planning for their sons, aged 5 and 6. By the time the court referred the case to the agency, Mrs. Clarke had returned home. In the first joint interview, neither parent showed affect, although Mr. Clarke admitted he too had abandoned the family several times and Mrs. Clarke appeared to be a person who acted on impulse.

Mrs. Clarke proudly admitted she engaged in prostitution whenever her husband left her. Raised by indulgent grandparents, she did not go to live with her mother, also a prostitute, until she was an adolescent.

The children had been referred to agencies three years earlier for fire-setting and running away. They were clearly responding to their home environment. When they were placed in a foster home, they expressed fear that they would be forced to return to the Clarkes.

Mrs. Clarke continued her pattern of running away and reappearing, but did not visit the boys or even inquire about them. It was not long before Mr. Clarke agreed that adoption was best for the children. Finally Mrs. Clarke was charged with abandonment (in keeping with the statutory definition of no contact for three months) and requested a jury trial. During the delay caused by the Christmas holidays, she made an appointment to visit her children, which she did not keep. She disappeared when the trial date was announced, and no one knew her whereabouts, not even her lawyer.

Surrendering a child has important implications for the parent's self-respect. A close member of his own family can be of tremendous help in preserving the parent's self-esteem and resolving his ambivalence. The knowledge that his own family approves of his act and is saying in effect that he is a good person to undertake this crucial step can be most supportive.

Many of the families have more than one child in foster care, but decisions about each child must be handled individually. Frequently, the parents prefer one child whom they want to keep and reject a child whom they want to be rid of. The rejected child usually has been invested with badness and is the one around whom the family breakdown has occurred. Because it is better to be a good parent to one child than a bad parent to two, the worker encourages the family to place the rejected child for adoption, as in the following example.

## MRS. MURPHY

Mrs. Murphy, aged 22, had been exploited and abused by her southern white share-cropping family. At age 16, deserted by the man by whom she had become pregnant, she married on the rebound. Chris, the first child, born of what she thought was a love relationship, was always her favorite. Mrs. Murphy bitterly resented Jean, the first child by her husband, and when Jean was 4 years old, she locked her out of the house in freezing weather.

The third child, Tom, was 1 year old when Mr. Murphy deserted the family. A week later Mrs. Murphy asked the police for child care when she entered the hospital to give birth to her fourth child, Lee. With Mr. Murphy gone, she realized she could not care for the children because she had to support herself. She requested ongoing foster placement for three of the children and took Chris, now aged 6, home.

In casework, Mrs. Murphy explored her feelings about herself and the children. She realized she was treating Jean as harshly as she had been treated as a child. Because she did not think she could change her feelings toward Jean, she accepted the idea of placing Jean for adoption—an alternative the worker had suggested from the beginning.

As she took stock of herself further, Mrs. Murphy decided that, as a factory worker with limited earnings, she could only care for two children. Therefore, she decided also to give up Lee, who was still an infant.

## CONCLUSION

Far too many children unnecessarily remain in foster care for extended periods of time. That this situation persists in the face of mounting evidence both from practice and research that for most children foster care is a stop-gap measure filled with pitfalls, is due, in large measure, to our failure to devise techniques to help parents act decisively. Agencies and caseworkers, clinging to traditional and value-laden notions about the sanctity of parenthood or caught up in their own ambivalence, are equally at fault.

If we are to give life to our belief in the right of every child to a permanent home, then we must reexamine our practice in the field of foster care. Such an examination must include questioning our present posture of permitting parents to flounder in indecision. Instead, we must move to help them follow through on their decisions, whether to effect the child's return home or to release him for adoption. Such indecision posing as objectivity and self-determination is damaging to both parents and children. The authors' experience in placing older children with severe problems attests to the validity of the changes in technique and philosophy discussed in this article.

The crucial questions then are not whether natural parents can be rehabilitated or which children are adoptable, but whether we can be creative in working with natural parents and inventive in finding adoptive homes for the hundreds of children whose physical, emotional, and social circumstances have caused them to be denied their birthright.

## NOTES AND REFERENCES

1. Henry R. Maas and Richard E. Engler, *Children in Need of Parents* (New York: Columbia University Press, 1959), p. 421.
2. For an approach to preparing foster children for adoption, *see* Laura Epstein and Irmgard Heymann, "Some Decisive Processes in Adoption Planning for Older Children," *Child Welfare*, 1 (January 1967), pp. 5–9.
3. This process combines Glasser's concept of responsibility with the use of time as a limit. For a fuller discussion of the concept, *see* William Glasser, *Reality Therapy* (New York: Harper & Row, 1965), p. 27.

# 22

# Foster Care: The Use of Contracts

THEODORE J. STEIN, EILEEN D. GAMBRILL, AND KERMIT T. WILTSE

The literature in foster care has faulted the service delivery system in two basic aspects: children enter out-of-home care too readily and they remain unnecessarily long [1]. A lack of systematic case planning has been identified as one deficit in service delivery [2]. In order to assess the possible impact of alternative case management methods, a joint project between the Children's Home Society of Oakland, California, and the Alameda County Foster Care Department was undertaken as of April 1974 (The Alameda Project). The aim of this project was "to introduce an intensive relationship which will help to rebuild the parents' sense of parenthood and sense of authority to make the decision about his or her children" [3]. Three types of decisions are possible, namely (1) the children are returned to their natural parents; (2) parental rights are terminated, ordinarily followed by placement for adoption; (3) long-term care is decided upon, usually followed by either a guardianship arrangement or a long-term foster care agreement.

The project employs three full-time M.S.W. social workers who offer intensive casework services to the natural parents of children in foster care [4], while county child welfare workers focus their efforts on the children in their foster homes. By comparing the efforts of these workers with those of a control

---

Reprinted with the permission of the American Public Welfare Association from *Public Welfare*, Vol. 32, No. 4 (Fall 1974), pp. 20–25.

group, we hope to observe whether or not such intensive services can facilitate movement of the children in the foster-care system.

The purpose of this article is to discuss the use of contracts with natural parents as a tool for encouraging parental participation in planning for their children and early decision making.

*The problem.* National estimates of the number of children in foster home care vary, ranging between 285,000 and 326,000 [5]. In the state of California alone, there are approximately 28,000 children living under state supervision, either in family or group homes, or institutions [6]. In considering the future of these children, the available evidence suggests that the majority of them will "grow to maturity" in out-of-home care. As Gruber (1973) reports from his study of foster care in the state of Massachusetts:

> Forty-nine percent entered foster care for a specified length of time, while 31.4 percent had specific discharge dates, that in fact, 83 percent never returned to their biological parents, even for a trial visit. [7]

A critical concern raised by these data lies in recognizing that such long-term care is rarely a planned outcome. Rather, as Gambrill and Wiltse (1974) note, many children "drift" into this situation [8]. The consequences of such drift are serious indeed, as evidenced by frequent changes in foster homes; absence of adults who are responsible for major decisions regarding the children; changing yearly expectations as to whether or not a child will be returned to biological parents; and the amount of social service manpower that is devoted to resolving these issues. Therefore, identification of criteria which would allow for the earliest possible determination of the probabilities of either returning a child, or of making alternative plans, is of crucial concern to foster-care workers. While most of the critical variables that are involved in decision making have yet to be identified, one consideration that seems crucial in this area is that of "time." Researchers are in agreement that the optimal period for a return to occur is within the first year of a child's career in the foster-care system, and the probabilities decrease markedly beyond that point [9]. As Maas and Engler (1959) state:

> Once a child is in care beyond one-and-one-half years, his chances of being adopted or returned to his biological family greatly decrease. [110]

Therefore, it seems reasonable to suggest that the thrust of a worker's efforts to reunite a family must take place during this first year. Frequently, however, this does not occur for several reasons: (1) parents do not make themselves available for treatment; (2) large caseloads frequently preclude intense involvement even when the parents are available, and (3) such ancillary resources as homemaker services which might be employed to facilitate such a return are not always available.

The purpose of having written contracts between caseworkers and natural parents are fourfold: (1) the parents are recognized as integral participants in the process geared to restore their children; (2) the exact changes required of them are described so that they can identify what will have to be different if their children are to be restored; (3) a time limit is established within which the changes must be accomplished; and (4) signing of the contract hopefully strengthens parental commitment to participate in the change effort [11].

*The concept of contracts.* While contracts are referred to in the social work literature, the concept suffers from a lack of shared definition [12]. Opinions vary, for example, as to whether they should be made explicitly with clients, or are an implied aspect of treatment. Further, with the exception of the writings of Gambrill, Thomas, and Carter (1971), Stuart (1971, 1972), and Gruber (1973), reference is to oral, as opposed to written, agreements [13]. Nowhere in the social work literature are examples of contracts presented.

Some authors in the socio-behavioral literature have provided specific examples of written contracts [14], while others have discussed their use in treatment settings [15]. However, with the exception of Tighe and Elliot (1968), and Mann (1973) reference is made to an agreement between clients, not between the caseworker or therapist and the client [16].

In our work in the project, contracts have been defined as written documents specifying particular agreements between the project and the county worker, and a client. There are two parts to a contract, the first of which contains the following statements:

1. The client's objective (e.g., restoration of a child on a permanent basis or for a specified time period, such as a trial visit);
2. The goals for a treatment program focusing specifically on the identified problems to be remedied prior to the return of a child or upon goals to be accomplished during a trial visit;
3. The agreement of both the project and the county workers to support the parent's objectives (number 1) by making the appropriate recommendation to the juvenile court provided that problems are remedied;
4. A statement of the potential consequences of nonparticipation by the parent (e.g., that the objectives cannot be recommended to the court) and that alternative planning for the child's future will have to be considered;

5. The time limits within which the treatment goals are to be accomplished.

The second part of the contract focuses upon the specific treatment methods to be employed and includes:

1. The steps to be engaged in to achieve the goals that are outlined as point number 2 above;
2. The tasks of the client and others in the client's environment who may be involved in treatment;
3. The environmental resources that will be brought to bear in addressing the problem; and
4. The role of the caseworker in achieving the specified goals.

*The project contracts.* The contract presented in figure 1 focuses upon the long-range objective of returning a child to his natural parents and is illustrative of items 1 through 5 noted above. Figure 2 contains an example of a short-term contract designed to cover the period of a trial visit. These contracts differ from each other in that the former focuses upon changes that must occur prior to achieving the parents' objective, while the latter contract is concerned with behavioral expectations of the parent while her children are at home for the trial visit.

*Selection of contract objectives.* The clients' expressed wishes for the future of their children (e.g., restoration) are the basis for formulating contracts [17]. To understand the process of selecting treatment goals, it is useful to differentiate between major and secondary goals.

*Major goals.* The source for selection of goals in long-term contracts (figure 1) is either the original allegations that lead to court removal of a child, or the presenting problems of the parents in a voluntary placement agreement. Both of the cases in the illustrative contracts are court dependency cases, with alcohol abuse specified as the allegation in case 1 and neglect resulting in malnourishment of the children in case 2.

By focusing upon the reasons for the original removal of a child, the common uncertainty on the part of the worker as to what has to be changed in order to bring about restoration becomes less of a problem [18].

*Secondary goals.* A systematic assessment is conducted in each case to identify any conditions and/or behaviors, in addition to those originally identified, that require change prior to the return of a child. This assessment focuses upon such areas as housing, finances, parent-child interaction and parent-parent interaction. The thrust of this effort is to identify only those problems that, if left unaltered, would hypothetically result in a child's being returned to foster-care placement. An example of such a secondary goal can be seen in point 5 of the contract presented in figure 1. In this situation, the parents' housing situation had deteriorated following the removal of their child, and new accommodations were seen as necessary before the child could be returned.

In establishing secondary goals, we are particularly concerned that we do not set standards for parents that go beyond reasonable expectations of children's safety and well-being. Too frequently, restoration becomes "mired"

---

**FIGURE 1**

Sample Contract

This contract is entered into between ______, Social Worker for the Alameda Project of Children's Home Society, ______, Child Welfare Worker for the Welfare Department of the Alameda County Human Resources Agency, and ______, parents of ______, at present a dependent child of the Alameda County Juvenile Court.

In keeping with the wish of both parents to have their son returned to their home on a permanent basis, both ______ and ______ agree to recommend such a return on a trial basis to the Alameda County Juvenile Court contingent upon the compliance of the parents to engage in a program to modify the following behaviors which all parties agree are currently problematic and, further, which all parties agree require modification prior to such a return. It is understood by the parents that failure to comply with such a program will result in a statement to the Alameda County Juvenile Court that, in the opinion of both social workers, such a return is not feasible at the present time and that alternate plans for the care of the child, such as guardianship or adoption, should be explored.

The general goals of the modification program are as follows:

1. Elimination of drinking behavior by both parents;
2. Participation by both parents in the program sponsored by the Alcohol Abuse Program;
3. Visit their child, ______, in the foster home, according to the prescribed schedule;
4. Increase the amount of time ______ engages in employment;
5. Obtain suitable housing;
6. Demonstration by both parents of adequate parenting skills.

The specific plan for each particular problem area, as well as the roles of the parents and of the social workers are attached. The first stage of this contract relates to problem areas (1), (2), and (3). Development of plans for the remaining problem areas is contingent upon the parents' successful completion of the first stage of the contract.

This contract will be in effect for a period of six (6) months. The first stage of the contract will be for a period of two (2) months, August 8, 1974 to October 8, 1974.

| Parents: | Social Workers: |
|---|---|
| ______________________ | ______________________ |
| Mother | Children's Home Society |
| ______________________ | ______________________ |
| Father | Alameda County Human Resources Agency |
| ______________________ | |
| Date | |

Note: This contract sample focuses on long-term goals which must be achieved prior to restoration.

---

in attempts to elevate parenting to a level far beyond that minimally necessary to secure a child's well-being [19].

Only those problems that are identified as major and/or secondary goals are focused upon during intervention. Should new problems arise, new contracts are negotiated.

*Unclear goals.* It has been our experience that most parents, when asked about long-term planning for their children, are quite clear in the wish to have their children returned to their care. However, cases do arise in which such clarity is not present. The only difference in contracts in these situations is that the wording of the first goal indicated that "decision making" for the future of the children is a primary focus for the parents.

Our hypotheses in these cases is that by reducing parental stress through alteration of identified problems, and by encouraging open dialogue on the options that are open for the child's future, parents will be enabled to reach decisions.

*Treatment programs.* The specific programs that are designed to alleviate parental problems vary considerably, and include the use of "hard" services (e.g., housing and financial assistance), as well as direct casework counseling.

In developing programs, particularly in the area of drug, alcohol, and child abuse, the worker's plans are guided by two considerations. First, the court will frequently mandate parental participation in an already existing community program. In such situations, the contract will clarify the frequency with which a parent is to present himself for treatment to these programs, and it is understood by the parent that the information that is

**FIGURE 2**
Sample Contract

This contract is entered into between ______, Social Worker for the Alameda Project of Children's Home Society, ______, Child Welfare Worker for the Welfare Department of the Alameda County Human Resources Agency, and ______, parent of ______, at present children of the Alameda County Juvenile Court.

In keeping with the wish of ______ to have her children returned to her home on a one-week trial visit, from July 26 to August 2, 1974, both ______ and ______ agree to recommend such a trial visit to the Alameda County Court.

The purpose of the contract is to specify certain behaviors ______ is to engage in for the period of the return. The specific plan, as well as the roles of the parent and of the social workers are attached.

| Parent: | Social Workers: |
| --- | --- |
| ________________ | ________________ |
| Mother | Children's Home Society |
| ________________ | ________________ |
| Date | Alameda County Human Resources Agency |

Note: This contract focuses on specific desired behaviors during a planned visit.

supplied relative to progress in these programs will contribute to the final recommendation to the courts.

In the absence of court directives, the workers rely on the empirical literature (particularly focusing on a behavioral approach) for selecting treatment methods for specific problems.

*Time limits.* There are two general guides used in the selection of time limits: (1) suggestions from the empirical literature as to recommended times for altering specific problems; and (2) the number of identified problems and the temporal sequence in which change must occur.

These points must be considered together in establishing time limits. For example, in the case covered by the contract in figure 1, the drinking problem is somewhat complicated by the fact that both clients drink and reinforce each other in this behavior, plus the fact that the clients live in an environment heavily populated by bars and others who also drink, further occasioning and reinforcing this behavior. As such, the six month time limit is seen as necessary. To illustrate the importance of considering both points 1 and 2, we can cite a project case where drinking was also the identified problem. In this situation, however, variables maintaining the drinking behavior were far less inclusive, and thus reduction of drinking and recommended return of the child were accomplished in three months.

The necessity of considering temporal sequence is also illustrated by the case represented in figure 1. The problems of increasing the father's employment, and subsequently having the finances to acquire new housing, required the prior reduction in the drinking behavior.

*Consequences of parental behavior.* As presently constituted, the foster-care system frequently reinforces a parent for "operationally abandoning" a child [20]. Parents are not infrequently allowed to establish their own rules for maintaining contact with their children, as well as for participating in social service programs. As suggested above, this contributes to the current status of many children as unplanned, long-term foster care cases. Therefore, informing parents of the potential consequences of different courses of action is seen as an integral aspect of written contracts.

Such a statement of consequences can be seen in the second paragraph of the contract presented in figure 1. The specific wording here is quite important; the phrase "will recommend to the juvenile court" recognizes the fact that, at the present time, the court is not a participant in the signing of these contracts. While it is our hope to enlist court involvement, until this comes about we cannot guarantee that the recommendations made by the caseworkers will be acted upon by the courts.

Contracts, currently employed in the project, are signed with the parents of children who have already been accepted into foster care. An important issue to be considered is their use at intake in order to explicate parental responsibility to the county or state that is offering substitute parenting, and to the children in care.

In conclusion to his Massachusetts study, Gruber recommends the signing of such contracts at intake, and suggests that they include the following statements of parental responsibility:

1. Continued financial support of the child;
2. Continued visiting with the child while in care;
3. Participation in school and medical issues involving the child;
4. Participation in treatment programs to remedy identified problems. [21]

Signing a contract at this first stage of foster placement serves several purposes. First, it has an "educational" function [22]. Some parents may not understand the ramifications of placing a child, and supplied with this information, may reconsider their decision to do so. Next, the issue of establishing parental goals (e.g., as to whether or not they wish to have their child returned) is simplified insofar as parents understand that foster-home care is a short-term situation. In addition, a parental lack of interest in participating in future planning for their children would become apparent in the early stages of the children's career in foster care, hence facilitating alternative planning.

## SUMMARY CONCLUSIONS

In the above pages we have discussed the use of written contracts between caseworkers and the biological parents of children in foster-home care.

It has been suggested that contracts provide a focus for casework services by explicating long-range objectives for children; the identified problems that require remedy to achieve these objectives; the treatment methods to be employed in resolving the identified problems; the alternative outcomes of parental participation; and finally, the time limits within which the above are to be accomplished.

By directing the workers' attention to each of these areas in the early stages of a child's career in foster-home placement, it has further been suggested that the process of early decision making for the child's future would be facilitated.

## NOTES AND REFERENCES

1. See, for example, Henry S. Maas and Richard E. Engler, *Children in Need of Parents* (New York: Columbia University Press, 1959); David Fanshel, "The Exit of Children from Foster Care: An Interim Research Report," *Child Welfare* 50, no. 5 (February 1971): 65–81; Alan R. Gruber, *Foster Home Care in Massachusetts: A Study of Foster Children and Their Biological and Foster Parents* (Boston: Governor's Commission on Adoption and Foster Care, 1973).
2. Eileen D. Gambrill and Kermit T. Wiltse, "Foster Care: Plans and Actualities," *Public Welfare* 32, no. 2 (Spring 1974): 12–21.
3. Page one of Attachment A to the contract formally executed January 24, 1974, between the Alameda County Board of Supervisors and the Children's Home Society of California.
4. The maximum caseload of project workers is 20 families, unlike their colleagues in the county who are responsible for a caseload of 49 children, frequently equalling 25–35 families. As such, the project workers are able to visit with clients

at least once a week, and frequently two or three times a week. The services offered vary considerably; specific information describing these will be the subject of future articles.

5. Robert H. Mnookin, "Foster Care: In Whose Best Interest?" *Harvard Educational Review* 43, no. 4 (November 1973): 599–638.
6. Jessica Pers et al., "Somebody Else's Children: A Report on the Foster Care System in California" (unpublished paper from the Childhood and Government Project, School of Law, University of California at Berkeley, 1974).
7. Gruber, *Foster Home Care in Massachusetts*, p. 17.
8. Gambrill and Wiltse, "Plans and Actualities," p. 12.
9. See, for example, Maas and Engler, *Children in Need*, and Fanshel, "The Exit of Children."
10. Maas and Engler, *Children in Need*, p. 351.
11. E. Burstein, "Interpersonal Strategies as Determinants of Behavioral Interdependence," in *Experimental Social Psychology*, edited by Judson Mills (New York: Macmillan Co., 1969), pp. 390–396.
12. A.N. Maluccio and W.D. Marlow, "The Case for the Contract," *Social Work* 19, no. 1 (January 1974): 28–37.
13. Eileen D. Gambrill, Edwin J. Thomas, and Robert D. Carter, "Procedure for Sociobehavioral Practice in Open Settings," *Social Work* 16, no. 1 (January 1971):51–62; Richard B. Stuart, "Behavioral Contracting Within the Families of Delinquents," *Journal of Behavioral Therapy and Experimental Psychiatry* 2 (1971): 1–11, and "Behavioral Contracting with Delinquents: A Cautionary Note," *Journal of Behavior Therapy and Experimental Psychiatry* 3 (1972): 161–169; and Gruber, *Foster Home Care In Massachusetts*.
14. See, for example, Gerald R. Patterson, *Families: Applications of Social Learning to Family Life* (Champaign, Ill.: Research Press, 1971); and Roland Sharp and Ralph Wetzel, *Behavior Modification in the Natural Environment* (New York: Academic Press, 1969).
15. See, for example, Robert M. Browning and Donald O. Stover, *Behavior Modification in Child Treatment* (New York: Aldine-Atherton Press, 1971); Lloyd Homme, "Human Motivation and the Environment," in *The Learning Environment: Relationship to Behavior Modification and Implications for Special Education*, edited by N. Haring and R. Whelan (Lawrence, Kan.: University of Kansas Press, 1966); Lloyd Homme et al., *How to Use Contingency Contracting in the Classroom* (Champaign, Ill.: Research Press, 1970); T.J. Tighe and R. Elliot, "A Technique for Controlling Behavior in Natural Life Settings," *Journal of Applied Behavior Analysis* 1 (1968): 263–266; and R.A. Mann, "Contingency Contracting: Design Requirements of a Technique for Demonstrating Control of Adult Behaviors in Natural Settings" (paper presented in 1973 in Miami, Florida, at the Seventh Annual Meeting of the Association for Advancement of Behavior Therapy, New York).

16. Tighe and Elliot, "A Technique for Controlling Behavior"; and Mann, "Contingency Contracting."

17. At the conclusion of the discussion of goal selection, we shall consider contracts in situations where the client is not sure of his immediate goals for a child.

18. Gambrill and Wiltse, "Plans and Actualities," p. 15.

19. At present, too little is known about what constitutes a good or productive environment for a child, and while gross problems that might result in danger to a child are not too difficult to identify, the majority of cases fall outside such boundaries. We are at present struggling to identify minimum levels of parental performance in each area of child care in order to guide intervention precisely to those areas of deficiency and away from those areas where the minimum is met.

20. Gruber, *Foster Home Care in Massachusetts*, p. 3.

21. Ibid., p. 83.

22. Theodore J. Stein, "A Content Analysis of Social Caseworker and Client Interaction in Foster Care," (D.S.W. diss., School of Social Welfare, University of California at Berkeley, 1974), p. 285.

# 23

# Natural Parents as Partner in Child Care Placement

GLADYS SIMMONS,
JOANNE GUMPERT,
AND BEULAH ROTHMAN

How to involve the natural parents of children in foster care has been an issue much discussed in social work in recent years. Earlier beliefs that the child must be "rescued" from an unrehabilitated family have been replaced by more optimistic views. There is a growing recognition that physical separation does not put an end to the emotional and psychological ties that bind a family together, even the most disorganized one. The much-noted irrepressible longing of the child in placement for his natural family and the undiminished guilt and episodic incursions by natural parents into the life-space of the child in placement suggest the probability of psychological continuity of the family's coexisting with disruption and physical separation. This conception has stimulated the development of time-limited care, and it also provided the hypothetical cornerstone for the project described in this article.

The fact that many children now return more frequently to their own families after placement or, more precisely, cyclically move between their own homes and placement intensifies the need to determine the nature and extent of involvement of the natural parent in the child care situation.

---

Reprinted by permission of Family Service Association of America, publisher, from *Social Casework*, Vol. 54, No. 4 (April 1973), pp. 224–232.

Changes in agency programs and policies do not always keep step with changes in professional conceptions or values. Although committed to serving the total natural family, most child care agencies continue to emphasize the relationship of the child and the foster family after the placement of the child has been effected, to the detriment of rebuilding the strengths of the natural family. Such ritualistic practices as rigidly scheduled visitation of natural parents with their children, usually confined to the antiseptic environment of the agency office, and containment of contact between the natural and the foster parents are some of the ways by which professional goals for rehabilitation of the natural family are diverted, if not made impossible to achieve. It appears that the stability of the foster placement plan is too often tied to controlled involvement of the natural parent, thus tending to diminish meaningful communication between the natural parent and the child in placement. This fact clearly suggests that increased involvement of the natural parent in child care may be more dependent on the structure and organization of services than on the attitudes of professional practitioners. Professional commitments have little opportunity for implementation without sufficient support of agency structures.

## MODEL OF SERVICE DELIVERY

In the summer of 1968, Brookwood Child Care instituted a program devised as a possible alternative to the placing of children in foster homes and as an opportunity to explore the full range of untapped potential towards sustaining and modifying interfamilial relationships. The program was based on the flexible use of a physical nucleus called a "family residential center." It consisted of two connected apartments in a housing project, that could accommodate eight boys and girls between the ages of six and twelve. Although similar in many ways to the conventional group home in which a small number of children live together under the supervision of houseparents or other adults, the agency's version incorporated several innovative concepts. Parents of children assigned to the center were given almost unlimited visiting privileges and—to the extent of their ability to do so—were encouraged to share with the agency the responsibility for the care of their children.[1]

[1]Annual Report, Brookwood Child Care, 1972, p. 3.

The idea of part-time parenting was conceived as a viable possibility, to be nurtured and supported through a new child care structure.

Because the residence was a group setting, it was expected that small group phenomena would occur that would markedly affect the behavior of the children in residence. Previous experiences in agencies working with natural parents also indicated that group approaches are more successfully sustained and utilized by them. Group treatment methods, therefore, were to be the methods of choice initially both with the children and the natural parents. Individual treatment methods were to be added in combination with, and in support of, group methods as identifiable needs naturally flowed from the group life of the children in residence and from the regular meetings of the parent group.

It was anticipated that the parents would develop various degrees of involvement in the center through attendance at parent group meetings and through participation in various center activities. Identification of parents with the group of parents and with the center was viewed as the initial goal, preceding expectations of parental motivation or ability to assume partial care for their own individual children. In order to avoid increased anxiety or threat to the parents, care was taken not to expect too much of the parents early in the placement plan. In the process of identifying with the center, families would develop ties with one another which could serve to extend the resources and strengths of any particular family. To provide service to families as entities, rather than to children as isolates, all siblings and other significant family members within the network of the child's natural environment were to be provided with social work services by the staff of the Family Residential Center.

It was expected that the result of the above assumptions would be a stream of interactions within the center and among parents, child, staff, and family at home. These interactions comprised the substantive base for the multiple services that were eventually to emerge during the three years of experimental operation of the center.

## SELECTION AND INTAKE PROCEDURES

Six families with children between the ages of six and eleven years who required long-term placement were selected for the project in the order of their referral from the Bureau of Child Welfare and the Family Court. These families did not differ greatly from families with children in traditional foster care. In three families there was court-adjudicated neglect. All of the families, however, were beset with problems often associated with need for placement. Most had insufficient income, were inadequately housed, and were suffering from severe social and interpersonal deprivations. In many instances, siblings were already in placement with Brookwood or other agencies. Some older siblings remained with the natural parents. Most of the children accepted in the residence had previously been placed in temporary shelters for periods of six months to one and one-half years.

The intake procedures of the Family Residential Center reflected its innovative approach, beginning with the direct request that the parent play a significant role at every step in the intake process and in the initial placement of the child. For example, intake interviews included joint meetings between the staff, the child, and the parent in an effort to break through the myth that "they are taking the child away." A preplacement luncheon was held at the center for the mothers and their children, and informality and spontaneity were encouraged. On the actual day of placement, each mother brought her child to the center.

Immediately following placement, parents were invited to participate in the medical examination required by the agency, to assist staff in making decisions on the purchasing of toys and other supplies for the center, and to contribute their suggestions and services in decorating the rooms of the children. Parents were invited to visit their children at their convenience, and both children and parents were encouraged to remain in telephone communication with each other.

## STAFFING

The staff consisted of two basic groups: child care staff and professional staff. Every effort was made to engage child care staff members who could provide warmth and acceptance without overinvolvement with the children at the expense of displacing or competing with the parents. The child care staff were responsible on a twenty-four-hour basis for the daily care of the children. Unlike child care workers in traditional group homes, child care staff in the center were expected to relate to natural parents and siblings and to carry a helping role to facilitate communication and interaction between the parents and their children. Within this context, child care staff were often called upon to perform such extraordinary functions as sobering up a parent who spontaneously appeared at the residence, accompanying a natural parent to the school, visiting children at camp, and participating in special activities involving natural parents and their families. Thus, child care workers had to be prepared for emergency situations not only in regard to the children in placement but with natural parents and siblings as well. They had the difficult task of maintaining their authority in the daily care of the children, yet relinquishing control if and when a parent wished to assume greater responsibility.

The complex nature of staff and client interaction called for continuous monitoring of communications at all levels. A team structure was used by professional staff to deal with regular as well as crisis needs. The professional team was the unit for establishing basic diagnostic understanding and for managing the treatment process. The responsibilities of the professional staff can be characterized within the following major areas: work with groups within the center, work with individual children and individual parents, and work with families within their own homes.

Because the entire residence was viewed by the professional staff as a system consisting of four subgroups in constant interaction with each other—the children, the natural families, the child care staff, and the professional staff—subgroup linkages were identified and reinforced by the professional staff. A consistent theme under discussion at team meetings was examination of strains within or between subgroups and the means by which these could be dispelled or used constructively. Professional staff, therefore, in addition to their specific assignments with individuals or groups, viewed their role as mediating between the subgroups and strengthening cohesive ties within the total residence.

## SERVICES TO CHILDREN

Continuity in the relationship between the child and his natural parent was regarded as a significant factor in the maturation and development of the child. Services to children were directed to strengthening this bond and avoiding any displacement of the parent by a parent surrogate in the daily life of the child. Parenting tasks were distributed among a variety of adults including the child care workers, the professional staff, and the tutorial and part-time recreation workers. It was expected that the children would develop natural affinity or differential affectional ties with various child-caring persons, but institutional structures did not impose a single child care staff member as a substitute for the parent. It was hoped that within such a system children in placement in the residence center would feel more intact, less exploited, and better able to develop their own identities. This assumption, with its concomitant practices, created some problems initially.

The first problem was that the children in the residence could not accept the extended family and its visible differences from other families in the community. They did not wish to be identified as children living under special circumstances in a residential program. Secondly, the children who were being supported in their yearning and their desires for maintaining their ties with their natural families had to simultaneously deal with the fact that their parents could not be relied on for stability of relationship. Parents, acting out their own problems and pathology, would often fantasize expectations that could not be fulfilled. These problems had to be dealt with at all levels in the residence program and were the subject of discussion in group meetings and in individual conferences with the children, their parents, and the child care staff. The behavior of the children when they felt particularly frustrated or disappointed with their parents was displaced on all others in the residence and had to be understood in that framework.

Throughout the three years of this program, treatment methods were directed toward providing the children with some understanding of their parents, some ability to cope more realistically with their frustration and anger at their parents, and the development of more appropriate behavior to help sustain themselves and their parents. An underlying belief in this project was that children were not only the victims of their parents but that they had some power and some strengths which could be brought to bear in helping their parents. Parents and children were viewed as partners in an interdependent system with the behavior of one affecting the other.

Wherever possible, individual problems and experiences were shared by the group, and treatment was offered on a collective basis. A boys' group, a girls' group, and a total residence government group were the major vehicles in carrying out treatment, but these groups were augmented by individual treatment, recreation, tutorial service, and summer camping. In many respects, the residence was similar to other experimental small group homes in that it utilized all modalities of service.

However, it did differ in two major aspects. First, the children were purposefully exposed to the role of their parents in decision-making processes that directly affected their lives. The children observed and frequently participated with their parents and staff in problem-solving meetings and discussions. Second, the children collectively planned for and carried out activities with their parents and in turn were participants in activities planned and executed collectively by the parent group.

## SERVICES TO NATURAL FAMILIES

During the beginning phase of the project, the parents could be described as fearful, suspicious, and impulsive. They appeared at meetings poorly groomed, at times in clothing bordering on the bizarre. They appeared to be immersed in a sea of ongoing crises with which they were unable to cope and from which they attempted to flee. They displayed severe pathology, both physical and psychological.

The mothers internalized society's view of themselves as "unfit." In turn, they viewed the agency as bureaucratic and doubted the staff's desire to be helpful to them. Most of the parents attended the early meetings of the group in conformity with the initial contract established by the agency. But after the beginning phase, the group attendance was sporadic and corresponded to the mothers' sense of relief that their children were being cared for at the residence. This feeling was particularly reflective of their life-style, involving an inability to sustain continuous involvement when unrelated to immediate crises.

Reaching-out methods employed by the staff emphasized daily problems occurring in the center that needed parent cooperation for resolution. It was in connection with planning the family Christmas party at the residence that the parents finally crystallized for themselves the deeper significance of their group and their participation in the center.

Ensuing development in the group was largely self-propelled by the members and related to broader policies in the center, as well as personal problems of the families. During this phase, several services were instituted upon the recommendation of the parents and in response to their needs. These services included a parent loan fund and a group treasury for allocation of carfare for parents' meetings. Members developed and expressed more intimacy toward and with each other and appeared more trustful of the worker. During this phase, a systematic plan for children's visits to their homes on weekends was worked out by the parent group.

By the beginning of the second year, the parents' group became an active vehicle for change within the center and a therapeutic channel for helping families to meet their own internal needs. Concomitant with the emerging strength of the group was the increased pressure felt by all staff to respond to the organized demands on the part of the parents. Structures were developed to capitalize on these positive changes so that gains could be made more visible to the parents and the children.

The following discussion of the specific areas of parent involvement presents in greater detail the growth in part-time parenting that unfolded over the three years.

## PURCHASE OF CLOTHING

The idea of the parents' assuming responsibility for spending the agency clothing replacement allowance for the purchase of their children's clothing was born out of the concern that was expressed toward the end of the first project year. One mother had indicated dissatisfaction with her daughter's lack of clothing. She was suspicious that some of her daughter's clothing allowance was being withheld by the child care staff. Other parents questioned whether favoritism was influencing the child care staff in purchase of clothing. In exploring these concerns, as well as the amount and disbursement of clothing money budgeted by the agency, it was concluded that if each mother purchased her own child's clothing, many of these problems would be eliminated. The mothers would be more satisfied that their children were adequately clothed according to their own taste. The mothers had indicated also that the children might take better care of their clothing if purchased by them instead of the child care staff.

Displacement of the child care staff in this area provoked open competition which had earlier been camouflaged and quiescent. Child care staff tended to be either overbearing in their suggestions for clothing purchases which the mothers resented or withheld suggestions, leaving the parents unable to know what their children actually needed. Child care staff were also uncomfortable in insisting on receipts from the mothers. A different method for determining clothing needs prior to purchase was instituted at the next three-month clothing check and was acceptable to parents and child care staff.

In the course of taking responsibility for clothing purchases, parents educated each other in better consumer practices. They explored resources that sold good quality clothing at low prices. They established an exchange of outgrown clothing between families and initiated a review of agency practices regarding increased budgets for special clothing needs.

The actual transfer of monies to parents (previously handled only by agency personnel) signified to the parents a social and institutional recognition of their competence as functioning adults. Moreover, many of these mothers who had a history of using their children as tools for manipulating more money for their own needs reversed this pattern. Most of the mothers added money to the children's clothing allowances from their own meager resources at a personal cost to themselves. If good parenting were to be measured by the degree of economic sacrifice that parents make for their children, these parents would have met the criteria.

## INVOLVEMENT IN DECISION-MAKING

The initial thrust for the involvement of the parents in decision-making developed from anger expressed by the parents about treatment of them and their children by the child care staff and the professional staff. In particular, a newly employed child care staff member became involved in arguments with the children in which the mothers were spoken of derogatorily. Two mothers, particularly infuriated by the attitude of the child care staff member, introduced the subject at a meeting. The discussion led to a request for a meeting between the child care staff, the professional staff, and the mothers. At this meeting, the mothers verbalized their complaints and confronted the staff. The right of the parents to demand change was acknowledged by the staff, who in turn made known the problems they were having with the children and requested assistance from the parents. Decisions on specific behavioral problems were made and implemented on a joint basis.

Subsequent monthly joint meetings were planned to develop a set of working rules for the Family Residential Center and to share complaints about the residence or difficulties and achievements of the children. The parents considered these meetings important, and in the second year of the project they limited their own meetings to once a month in order to make time for the joint meetings. A set of regulations providing more direction to the children was compiled by the joint group as were decisions about how to handle infractions. Interestingly, the regulations covered situations that normally create conflict in a family and over which a parent exercises considerable control: for example, time to come in from outdoor play, bath time, homework time, the use of television and the phonograph, privacy of telephone use between parent and child, assignment of household chores, and care of room and clothing.

Another outgrowth of these meetings was a family conference of parent, child, child care staff, and social workers regarding an individual child. As a result of these conferences, the sphere of involvement of individual parents was extended. Parents participated in making school visits with the social worker. They were regularly given their children's report cards to sign and to keep at the end of the year. In general, interest in their children's learning became another means of engaging parents and their children.

The question of which camp the children should attend in the second year was discussed at great length by the parents, children, and staff. Some children and a few parents had raised questions about returning to the former summer camp where the children had been part of a small minority of black campers. It is to be noted that although some of the families did not feel the factor of race to be extremely important to them they were willing to accede to the needs of those who felt differently. When the children and parents were convinced that the services of a second camp would be equally as good and that there would be no personal loss, the decision was made that the children would attend the integrated camp in the second summer.

The gains noted by the staff were that this critical decision was carried almost exclusively by the families on the basis of considerable exploration, undiffused by irrational or panic reactions, and that ample time and thought went into the decision. In this process too, the staff, the parents, and the children faced more fully the issue of black identity and its meaning in the lives of maturing youngsters. The emergence of black identity as a significant and positive factor in the residence and in the families approximated the changes taking place in black communities, thus further reducing within the residence the isolation from the community so often associated with residential care.

## PROJECTS OF THE PARENTS' GROUP

The parents continued to plan and carry out projects for themselves and their children. These projects included a trip to a state park over the Labor Day weekend, an annual Christmas party for the families of the residents, a family Easter trip, and a family camp weekend just prior to the camp season. Parents took on more responsibility as a group in arranging these activities and increasingly involved their entire families rather than just the children in residence. These events were viewed as successful by the parents and gave them a sense of accomplishment in providing an enjoyable experience for their children. These events have become a tradition in the residence.

The big event of the second year was the family camping weekend. In the previous year when parents had viewed the pictures of their children at camp, they had commented on their desire for such an experience and the deprivation they felt in never having had such an opportunity. In preparation for the second summer of camp, the social worker suggested the possibility of a family camping weekend. This idea was enthusiastically discussed and explored by the parents. In preparing for the family camping weekend, the parent group assumed responsibility for purchasing and preparing the food for their families and staff, a group of about forty people. They divided the money according to the size of the families, and each mother shopped and cooked for her own family and three extra staff members. When the mothers were first confronted with the tasks of carrying full responsibility for the food preparation, they suggested that the child care staff take over, but they were held to their responsibility. This task was an achievement, since all food had to be prepared in advance and transported to the camp.

At the camp, sleeping and eating arrangements were family-centered. Mothers were expected to assume responsibility for their own children with the assistance of the staff when necessary. The spaciousness and freedom that a camp setting affords were particularly gratifying to the families. Conflicts were at a minimum, even in the use of the kitchen, swimming, and boating facilities. The children were cooperative in accepting limits at the waterfront and in taking responsibility for equipment. A major stride was made in identification of all families with the residence as an extended family facility.

## IMPROVED FUNCTIONING OF PARENTS

Because these parents have severe pathology, crises have continued to erupt in their lives. They have learned, however, to cope with some of these crises by selectively turning to the residence for help. Although regression can be seen from time to time, a general and overall forward movement was observed by the staff. One mother managed to sustain herself in employment for the last year and a half of the project. Another mother faced her problem of alcoholism and committed herself for a six-week stay in an Alcoholics Rehabilitation Unit; she remained sober through the last year. A notable change was also observed in her relationship with her children. Another mother with a long history and pattern of denial of her problems has more realistically accepted them, offering more support and nurturance to her thirteen children. She requested and used family therapy and has taken on a more active parenting role both at home and in the center. As part of this change, this mother has successfully managed to assist her oldest son in maintaining himself out of a mental hospital for an entire year, the longest this man has ever been able to live in the community in the past six years.

The major change for all these parents over the three years seems to be in the recognition that they are indeed an important influence in the life of their children. They are willing to risk assuming increased responsibility for the parenting role. The classical anger of natural parents toward the foster care agency diminished appreciably as the project progressed. It is interesting to note that this sense of trust and positive feeling appear to be extended only toward the staff of the Family Residential Center. Parents with other children placed in foster homes retained the usual hostility toward foster parents and toward the foster care agency.

One rather dramatic service was the use of the residence by an entire family during a holiday period when most of the other children returned to their natural homes. In a sense, the residence was utilized by a family almost as a vacation facility. It provided a physically more attractive setting than their own home and an escape from its constricted and dismal atmosphere. The use of the residence by a single family reflected identification with the residence and increasing comfort and confidence on the part of the child care staff in leaving the residence in the care of a family. Also significant is that all of the families using the residence for this purpose left it in good condition.

In addition, utilization of the residence as a temporary shelter for both natural parents and siblings at times of crisis differentiated the residence from other small group homes. Provisions for such contingencies had been made in advance by the purchase of two folding beds. Although innovative, this service did not seem particularly unusual to the staff since they had so fully integrated the more comprehensive goals of total family rehabilitation into their practice at the center.

## RESEARCH FINDINGS

Independent evaluative research was conducted during the three years of this experimental project.[2] Hypotheses tested related to two lines of inquiry: the effectiveness of the Family Residential Center in facilitating contact between children and their natural parents and the effects of such increased contact upon the behaviors and attitudes of the children and their natural parents.

More explicitly, it had been anticipated that the Family Residential Center would promote greater involvement and participation by the parents in the daily lives of their children. Not only would this involvement increase beyond what normally occurs in traditional child care, but the involvement itself would be qualitatively more positive in terms of the growth needs of children and the satisfactions derived by adults from functioning more successfully as parents and people.

It was expected that the children would show improvement in their general functioning, including their relationships with parents, siblings, other adults, and with peers in the residence and in the community. Predominantly hostile, aggressive social behaviors were expected to change to more collaborative and cooperative behaviors. It was expected that the children would improve in their school functioning and increase their learning skills. It was hoped that learning disabilities so often observed in children after placement could be reversed or prevented.

Because a healthier self-image is generally associated with greater success in interpersonal relationships, it was expected that both the children and the parents would demonstrate such growth through changes in physical appearance and self-care, in their increased ability to face new situations, and in increased confidence in themselves to undertake responsibilities and make decisions. Thus, it was anticipated that the children and the parents would exhibit more rational approaches to problem-solving. As a result of the egalitarian and participatory milieu promoted in the center, it was assumed that the attitudes of children and parents toward the center as an institution, and toward the staff, would become more favorable. The eventual return of a child to his natural home and family was not necessarily envisioned as a desirable outcome. Whether a child returned home permanently was not at issue in this project. More important was the increased ability of the parent and the child to maintain family identification and feelings of closeness during placement. It was expected that the child's visits to his home would increase at a frequency greater than is usually found in traditional foster care

[2]See Daniel Rosenblatt and Florence Rosenstock, *The Evaluation Study*, Brookwood Child Care, 1972.

and that he would develop a more realistic perception of his own and his parents' needs and capacities.

The experimental research design compared the experimental group, consisting of the nine children placed in the Family Residential Center, with two control groups. Control Group I consisted of thirteen children entering a Brookwood foster care home during the same intake period. Control Group II consisted of ten children already placed in a Brookwood foster care home who remained in the same placement throughout the experimental period.

Children were randomly selected, as far as possible, for the experimental group and for Control Group I. Factors held constant for all three groups, however, were age, sex, family composition and size, and reason for placement. It was subsequently found through testing that the groups were virtually equivalent in terms of their I.Q. scores.

Research findings indicated that the family center was substantially more effective in fostering child-natural parent contact. Children and natural parents saw each other more frequently and had a greater volume of telephone contact, and parents had a wider range of involvement in aspects of child care than did those in the control groups. Children in the experimental group were also more closely identified with the natural parent and felt stronger ties to their natural family.

Research findings also indicated substantial gains made by natural parents through involvement in the Family Residential Center. It was indicated that the quality of an individual natural parent's relationship with his child's foster parents would in part determine his access to information about his child, but it was also determined that the communication structure developed in the family center permitted all parents access to information despite any variation in interpersonal warmth between parent and child care staff. The residence program not only made children more available to parents, but also enabled a quality of contact that was more acceptable to parents. The majority of experimental group parents indicated that the presence of child care staff did not affect their comfort in visiting their children in the residence. Thus, it seems likely that the residence structure was successful in helping natural parents to remain secure in their roles, whether or not they regarded child care staff as competitive figures.

In use of individual contacts with the social worker, natural parents expressed more concern about aspects of their children's development. This change was related to the fact that they had a much higher level of information about their children and were closer to the issues involved in the child's development.

Research findings about the children's functioning indicated that those in the Family Residential Center showed some improvement in academic performance but were less compliant and conforming in their behavior at school and in the residence. They developed relatively strong self-concepts, had stronger ties to their natural families, and were able to establish effective peer relationships.

In retrospect, staff's expectations of marked change in the children's behavior and school functioning were probably unrealistic in view of the short time span of the research project. The findings in relation to changes in the children are open to interpretation, and it is impossible to draw firm conclusions from them. The small sample of children involved in the project further limits generalizations to be derived from the findings.

The most dramatic results of the Family Residential Center project were the increased parent-child contact and the effects on natural parents. These conclusions leave little room for debate on the positive value of parent involvement. The effect of continued involvement on the improved functioning of the parents as individuals, with their children at home and those in placement, reinforces this point. The fact that it is possible for parents with severe problems to increase, sustain, and improve upon their parenting role with children in placement is validated by the research findings.

A question raised by this project is whether separation of the natural family from the foster family or from the direct caretakers of the child in placement can any longer be justified, except, of course, where freeing the child for adoption is indicated. Unless the natural parents are directly involved with their children's caretakers and in their children's daily lives, there seems little likelihood for growth of the natural parents. Moreover, active or potential competition between the natural parents and direct caretakers does not appear to produce excessive negative results in the children, a result traditionally feared by most professionals in child care practice.

Further exploration is indicated toward developing new services that support continuous interaction between natural parents, parent surrogates, and children in placement. Such explorations should continue to examine the relationships between parent involvement and group process and focus on the family as a total unit.

# 24

# Five-Day Foster Care

BESSIE LOEWE
AND THOMAS E. HANRAHAN

Five-day foster care, started by Children's Services, Cleveland, in November 1970, grew out of two major movements that converged in the late 1960s.

A changing social climate created new challenges for the child welfare agency and demanded new priorities. Illegitimate births increased but the number of children surrendered for adoption fell sharply. Divorce rates rose, leaving more single-parent families. Economic need brought more working mothers into the labor force. Court decisions, reflecting changed values, granted child custody to more fathers than before. Increasingly, requests for help reflected the need for child care services that would supplement the efforts of parents.

At the same time, expanding research on traditional foster care programs led professionals to question both the soundness and the results of the programs and practices.

In 1959, after a 2-year study of children in foster care in nine communities, Maas wrote:

> It is a delusion to consider foster care primarily a means for providing children with temporary substitute homes, while parental conditions which have led to and maintained the separation of parent and child are being remedied. For once

Reprinted from *Child Welfare*, Vol. LIV, No. 1 (January 1975): 7–18.

> children have been in foster care 3 months, it gives promise of being long term for most of them. Moreover, agency relationships with most fathers and mothers of the children in care are such that, if parental conditions are to be modified, the process will have to be one of self-healing. [5:5–9]

Ten years later, following up on children in placement 10 or more years, Maas found:

> . . . half of all the children and 46% of long-term care children were placed voluntarily. . . . We found no evidence of uniqueness in the level of agency treatment given the children in long-term care. . . . There were, however, significant associations between long-term care and the agencies' treatment of the parents. More of the parents of long-term care children (73%) had little or no agency treatment; 55% of these parents had, as of 1957, no contact at all with the agencies. Only about 15% of these parents had adequate or better contact with the agencies, and relationships of significance. Most of the children in long-term care, thus, seem to have remained in care while their parents and the child welfare agencies were not in contact with one another. [6:329–331]

That same year, 1969, Jenkins reported:

> The importance of giving serious attention to the needs of mothers and fathers when children enter care goes beyond the perception of them as individuals in need of help. Unless expressed needs and feelings have been worked out so that the parent can understand the placement experience, it is likely that the trauma suffered by the child upon separation from the mother or father will only be reinforced upon return home by the unresolved problems suffered by the parent upon separation from the child. [3:339–340]

Certain facts stood out. There is a direct relationship between immediate, intensive work with parents and early discharge of children from foster care [7:3–9]. "In community after community it is clear . . . that unless children move out of care within the first year to year and a half of their stay in care, the likelihood of their ever moving out sharply decreases. Early diagnoses and clear planning are essential" [4:390].

The Intake Department of Children's Services therefore stated in its 1970 report: " . . . the very real shortcomings for parents, foster parents and children in full-time foster home placements . . . would . . . cause an agency to experiment, innovate, modify, and generally come up with an innovative use of foster home placement" [1:4]. Five-day foster care, a program of supportive, supplemental help to parents and children, was one result. Two additional services, a family day care program and services to children in their own homes, were also started.

## WHAT IS 5-DAY FOSTER CARE?

Five-day foster care assists parents unable to carry the total child rearing responsibility through placement of their children in professionally supervised foster homes. For 24 hours a day, 5 days a week, children live with and receive care from foster parents. On weekends, holidays and vacations they live with their own parents. This service seeks to reduce the trauma of separation for parents and children, and to maintain children's identities and relationships with their relatives.

Traditional child welfare services—counseling for unmarried mothers, preadoptive foster care, adoption, long-term guardianship foster care, and treatment in residential institutions—rest on the concept of substitute care for children. With this conceptual base, practice tends to replace natural parents, to provide "better" parent figures, and to enforce separation of children from their families. Five-day care, based on the concept of child care supportive of and supplemental to that provided by natural parents, capitalizes on the natural parents' potential for part-time parenting. The program design assures that natural parents continue to share physically and psychologically in the lives of their children, even though the children are away from their families part of the time.

Viewed as a short-term plan not to exceed a year, the program measures its success by the steps taken to reunite the child with his or her own family, at a better level of functioning. From the beginning, parents, foster parents and social workers are aware that the child must eventually return home. The goal is to enable parents to fulfill their parental role on an independent, continuous basis—and that objective is advanced in day-to-day practice.

Since Children's Services is a voluntary, nonsectarian agency, the decision to start to terminate placement is mutually agreed upon by parents and the agency's representative, the social worker. Parents provide financial support according to ability for the 5-day foster care.

## WHICH CHILDREN CAN 5-DAY CARE HELP?

Five-day foster care can best serve children whose families face situational or emotional crises. The following broad groupings illustrate the clientele: children of parents who temporarily lack physical or emotional resources to handle full-time parenting or day care arrangements; children of parents who work on rotating or night shifts, making it impossible for them to use community child care facilities; children of one-parent families where the parent has not yet adjusted to the roles involved in the altered status created by illegitimacy, divorce, death or desertion; children of two-parent families where one spouse is hospitalized or imprisoned. Aside from the situational crises, these families share other characteristics: the parents are capable of carrying out child care on a part-time basis; they desire to participate in their children's lives; and they can form the kinds of relationships needed to make use of short-term help through counseling and child care arrangements.

Five-day foster care can also serve other children with special problems: children of fragile emotional balance who cannot tolerate the daily separations from parents occurring in day care programs, children who need relief from home situations as part of their treatment; children discharged from institutions and 7-day foster care programs who temporarily require a protective setting as a step toward returning home; and some ambulatory handicapped children who cannot function in regular child care programs.

## PROGRAMMING ASPECTS

To achieve the goal of the child's return home, safeguards are built into the program from the start of the client-agency relationship. Paramount among these are the altered roles of social workers, the altered roles of foster parents, the careful selection of participating parents and children, and a cooperative method of working.

### Role of Social Workers

Essential are social workers who can counsel parents, struggling with emotional deprivation, loss of significant relationships, and dysfunctioning social behavior. While fully understanding personality dynamics,they must zero in on aspects of the individuals involved and the environment that influence child rearing. Their role is to make parents aware of these aspects, to help them recognize their current means of coping, suggest sounder alternatives, and support parents as they try new ways on the weekend visit. Workers also must understand the effect of separation on both children and parents, and help them establish relationships with foster parents and reestablish relationships with each other. It is essential that social workers choose foster parents who can accept the challenges and limitations of a 5-day program, operate within its framework, and make use of workers' support. Workers (as the agency's representatives), foster parents and natural parents should be working together as a team toward a total parent-child reunion as soon as practical.

Some of these broad tasks have always been part of the child welfare worker's role; others derive from an altered philosophy. Traditional foster care—substitute care—envisioned child care as provided by a conjugal pair, functioning in cooperative, if sex-restricted, roles. This was viewed as the desirable standard. Where such care was not present in the child's own family, the parents were viewed as deviant. This frequently led to worker overidentification with children and foster parents, and hostility to parents. Workers excluded parents from the child-rearing process, and eventually lost them.

Five-day foster care—supportive, supplemental care—demands an end to the myth of a united family. For social workers, this means a recognition that family life styles have changed, and that societal supports for child nurture and rearing are long overdue. This can be expressed in practice as ways are found to assist the solo parent.

## Role of Foster Parents

Basic to the program are foster parents who "deal with reality in a reasonable way" [1:9 ff.]. They are assistant parents, not substitute parents. Awareness of this role enhances performance of the implied tasks: to refrain from criticizing the natural parents or joining children in their rejection of them; to help children see their parents as persons with heavy burdens in some areas; to assist children in recognizing that they can be different from and still love and respect their parents.

The program's structure reinforces this foster parent role. Foster parents participate in arranging for the weekend visit home, communicate with parents about routines, allow children either to share or to withhold information about weekend activities, respect children's rights to privacy, and help children to accept that homes are different because people are different.

Foster parents must complement the parental role, not compete for it. As Hutchinson pointed out in the 1940s, "The foster parent who must dominate the situation to the exclusion of the agency and of the worker has little use in a practical situation, where mutual responsibility in the job and sharing of the child are essential" [2:92]. This is particularly true in 5-day foster care.

## Selection of Clients

Five-day foster care requires a careful assessment of client strengths and potential at the outset. It calls for a prediction of behavior based on an analysis of past performance. Parents showing severe pathology or the inability to carry out weekend child rearing cannot utilize this service.

Although the goal is to return the child home, there of course are family situations in which the child should not return home. Silverblatt describes such situations: "There are some situations in which the best help to child and parent comes when a parent can acknowledge his real feelings of rejection or inability to cope with the child, and frees the child to make new ties in a foster home or in adoption. There are some parents, fortunately in the minority, who can neither accept help for themselves nor allow their children to live satisfactorily in foster care" [8:24]. The screening of clients focuses on eliminating such parents from the 5-day program.

The families selected are those experiencing situational crises. They nevertheless exhibit certain strengths: a history of achievement, the capacity for personal relationships, periods of at least minimal functioning, current ego strengths. Their current functioning is adequate to provide satisfactory child care on weekends.

## Method of Work

Parents and children are seen initially in the intake department for evaluation. When 5-day foster care is selected as appropriate after consultation with the foster care department, the intake worker prepares the parents and the children for the program and for the relationship to the ongoing foster care worker. In intake, a contract is established with parents as to the reason for placement, expectations of the client and the agency, and length of placement—not to exceed a year. A beginning is made in intake in outlining goals to be worked toward so that the child can return home. An agreement for financial support, on a sliding scale based on parents' income, is signed. The full cost is made up through the federated fund campaign.

The ongoing social worker discusses with the foster parents information about the children to be placed, and clarifies further with parents the reasons for placement; the goals; and the roles of parents, foster parents and the agency. The social worker, natural parents and foster parents then meet to review the children's needs and details of placement. Preplacement visits for the children and natural parents are arranged. The children are seen by their own pediatrician or that of Children's Services to obtain medical approval for placement.

The ongoing worker subsequently provides supervision of the children in foster care and casework service to children, parents and foster parents. Work is directed toward helping parents and children view placement as a means of solving a family problem—not as rejection or punishment—and toward freeing parents of guilt and feelings of inadequacy. Supportive help is provided to enable parents to take responsibility for their children. To aid the children's adjustment and insure a team approach, workers keep communications open between natural parents and foster parents. Where 5-day foster care is selected for children currently in the agency's 7-day foster care or day care programs, planning is handled by the social worker already assigned to the family.

## CASE ILLUSTRATIONS

A *divorced mother.* Twenty-year-old Linda Adams requested foster care for her 2-year-old daughter Jeannie. Recently separated from her husband, whom she had married after Jeannie's birth, she felt despondent and defeated over the breakup of her marriage. The $15 weekly child support payment was inadequate to feed and clothe the child. In desperation, she had moved back into the central city apartment of her mother, a widow employed days at a factory. This move provided shelter, but reactivated hostile-dependent feelings.

Not a high school graduate—pregnancy ended her schooling in her senior year—untrained in any vocation, never employed, burdened with child care and support, Mrs. Adams' energies were scattered as she struck out in many directions. Finish high school; get office skills or college training; take care of Jeannie; find a job; get along with her own mother: all these themes ran through her conversation with the intake social worker. Intelligent but immature, Mrs. Adams was clearly overwhelmed by many tasks and goals.

Five-day foster care was selected as appropriate. It would provide care for Jeannie, enable Mrs. Adams to work on her problems one at a time. It would also retain for Jeannie on the weekends home the warm relationship she had with her mother prior to her parents' separation. The verbal agreement between the agency and Mrs. Adams stipulated that Jeannie would be in placement for up to a year, returning home from Saturday mornings to Sunday evenings, and that Mrs. Adams would use the rest of the week to complete high school, acquire vocational skills, and then obtain employment.

In September 1971 at the age of 2 years, 10 months, Jeannie was examined in the agency's clinic prior to placement and found to be a well-developed, well-nourished child, with behavior appropriate for her age. On the visit to the foster home, with her mother and her ongoing social worker, Jeannie first appeared shy, but gradually revealed a sense of humor. Three days after the visit Jeannie returned to the foster home to stay.

The transition was hard for everyone. Jeannie cried when her mother telephoned during the week and left her in the foster home Sunday evenings. Although toilet-trained, Jeannie had some embarrassing accidents. Gradually she became more comfortable with the foster family. She progressed as she accepted reassurance that her mother loved her but needed time to go to school and to find work.

Mrs. Adams reacted with mild depression and a sense of loss. With the help of the social worker, she enrolled in a high school class for adults, was graduated, then moved into an office skills course at a community college.

Mrs. Bart, the foster mother, was upset when she found that Jeannie was undisciplined: poor table manners, inadequate personal hygiene, and the use of street language. With help from the social worker, she gained understanding of Jeannie's previous environment and began sharing her knowledge of child care with Jeannie's mother. Jeannie's language and manners gradually took on the characteristics of her new neighborhood.

Mrs. Adams' mother initially refused to involve herself in Jeannie's care. When placement occurred, she berated her daughter. However, as Mrs. Adams' schooling progressed and her mother saw tangible achievements, the women began to be more positive toward each other. Gradually the grandmother began to show interest in Jeannie. In June 1972, with Mrs. Adams enrolled in the last quarter of her course and with job applications on file for fall, the two women decided they could manage Jeannie's care evenings and weekends. Jeannie was then placed in an agency family day care home, while her grandmother worked and her mother attended college full time. In October 1972, when Mrs. Adams completed her first month on her new job, Jeannie's grandmother quit work to remain home days to care for her.

After 9 months of 5-day foster care, 4 months of day care, and simultaneous counseling and supportive help to her mother, Jeannie returned to a full-time home with her own relatives. The last contact with Mrs. Adams was in November 1972. At that time no services were needed from the agency.

A *father, abandoned with three children.* George Polsky was 31 when his wife deserted him and their three children, 6-year-old Sandra, 3-year-old Steve, and 18-month-old Don. His efforts to find a live-in housekeeper failed. No one wanted the job for $30 weekly, plus room and board—all he could afford. His wife's parents in Indiana sided with him against their daughter, but they were old and had chronic health problems. Temporary sitters helped out; neighbors pitched in on an emergency basis; but days missed from work would mean the loss of his job and the home he had purchased with a big mortgage because it had room for the children. He asked Children's Services to help him find a foster home in his neighborhood so Sandra could continue in the same school, and he could be near his children. No such home was immediately available and placement in another school district was considered. The Polskys were still legally married and shared custody, but Mrs. Polsky consented to placement, and confirmed that she did not want reconciliation. (An uncontested divorce action later granted Mr. Polsky custody.)

Mr. Polsky wanted eventually to make a home for his children. Once he had hoped to take college classes to improve his position. His technical skills as a company repairman brought him commendation, but his spoken and written English was a handicap, and he was bypassed for promotion. He and the intake worker arrived at this agreement; the agency would provide care for the children in a foster home 5 days weekly; Mr. Polsky would provide care for them in his own home from Friday evening to Sunday evening; he would study English in evening college classes, under the GI Bill. If he upgraded his position, his increased salary would enable him to hire a full-time housekeeper. If not, other means of utilizing his technical skills would be explored. A $30 weekly payment toward the cost of foster care was set, with the fee to be reevaluated if his income changed.

Ten months have passed since the Polsky children were examined in the agency's clinic and visited the Howard home prior to placement. Sandra, the 6-year-old, quickly became friends with the foster mother's 6-year-old daughter. She now mothers and protects her younger brothers less, plays more with her friends. Rarely does she mention her mother, except to recall that her parents fought constantly. Described as an inattentive, tired child by her kindergarten teacher, Sandra performs better than average in the first grade despite the change in schools. On weekends she tries to help her father.

Three-year-old Stevie came to the foster home with a respiratory infection and a history of asthma, but has been symptom-free in the foster home. Toilet-trained before placement, he had to wear diapers for a time after placement. His father had viewed Stevie's headbanging temper tantrums and fights with his brother as typical boy behavior. With help from the social worker, he and the foster mother perceived this behavior as related to Stevie's being upset. They tried new approaches. Stevie now talks more, smiles more, is less fearful of strangers, hurts himself less. He looks forward to visits with his father but shows no difficulty in returning to the foster home.

Eighteen-month-old Don related affectionately to the older Howard daughters from the start. An active child, he eats and sleeps well, and speaks rapidly in complete sentences. He identifies with the foster father, but also is anxious to return to his father on weekends.

Mr. Polsky has been responsible in dealing with the foster parents and the agency worker. He follows through quickly on suggestions made by the foster mother, expressing gratitude for her help. The foster parents identify sympathetically with him, and take pride in the children's progress and their role in it. Since the placement, Mr. Polsky has completed two college English courses, earning Bs. He appears more confident. An increased salary now enables him to pay $50 weekly toward the cost of foster care. He is also looking into the possibility of earning more by working part time for a friend who repairs radios and television sets. And he is again looking for a housekeeper.

## PROGRAM TO DATE

Of 28 children served from April 1971 through June 30, 1974, 17 have been discharged from placement. Of these, 16 have returned home to their natural parents, and one child was surrendered for adoption. Table I shows the time in 5-day care needed to assist these families.

**TABLE 1**

**Time in 5-Day Foster Care, and Outcome**

| No. of Children | Time in 5-Day Care | Outcome |
|---|---|---|
| 1 | 1 mo. | Home to mother |
| 1 | 5 mos. | Surrendered for adoption |
| 3 | 6 mos. | Home to mother or father |
| 6 | 7 mos. | Home to mother or both parents |
| 2 | 8 mos. | Home to mother |
| 2 | 10 mos. | Home to mother |
| 1 | 19 mos. | Home to mother |
| 1 | 23 mos. | Home to mother |

It should be noted that 12 of the 17 children required additional services before or after 5-day foster care. For example, the child who returned home in 1 month received 2 months of agency day care subsequent to 5-day foster care. The child who was surrendered for adoption in 5 months had received 6 weeks of 7-day foster care prior to 5-day foster care. One of the children who left 5-day care after 6 months had received 3 months of 7-day foster care before the 5-day care and 8 months of agency day care after the 5-day care.

Eleven children were in 5-day foster care as of June 30, 1974. Table 2 shows their length of time in 5-day foster care and the other services utilized.

## SOME REFLECTIONS

Five-day foster care is a relatively new service program. It has been tried with a comparatively small number of families. Considering the criteria that led to inclusion of these particular families in the program, they undoubtedly

**TABLE 2**

**Time in 5-Day Foster Care; Other Services Utilized**

| No. of Children | 5-Day Care | Services Other Than Counseling |
|---|---|---|
| 1 | 3 mos. | 8 mos. prior day care |
| 2 | 5 mos. | None |
| 2 | 6 mos. | None |
| 1 | 10 mos. | 10 mos. prior 7-day care |
| 2 | 7 mos. + 4 mos. | Returned to 5-day care after 2 mos. at home |
| 3 | 13 mos. | None |

represent a select group. Therefore no major conclusions can be drawn at this time. However, several significant elements stand out. In the situations of 27 of the 28 children served, the child's relationship with his own relatives was maintained on an ongoing basis. We believe that the program's structure and methods of work contributed to this and, consequently, to the child's having a home to which he could return. In the case of the child surrendered for adoption, the experience of 5-day foster care contributed to the mother's recognition of the need to make a permanent plan for her child.

The time limit of 1 year may need further evaluation in practice. Although a structured use of time may be helpful in mobilizing parents, foster parents and social workers toward specific tasks and goals, time should not be used as an arbitrary measure. Some families may need more than a year; many parents—particularly solo parents—may need varying forms of societal supports for child rearing over varied periods as family life styles and economic conditions change.

Our findings indicate that a flexible use of child welfare resources in new combinations—parental counseling combined with 7-day foster care, 5-day foster care and/or day care—can benefit many parents in crises. By revising our thinking and our methods—sharing parental burdens rather than assuming them—we can assist parents eventually to fulfill their parental roles on a full-time basis.

## REFERENCES

1. Children's Services, Unpublished report of Intake Department, January 1970.
2. Hutchinson, Dorothy. In Quest of Foster Parents. New York: Columbia University Press, 1943.
3. Jenkins, Shirley, "Separation Experiences of Parents Whose Children Are in Foster Care," Child Welfare, XLVIII, 6 (June 1969).
4. Maas, Henry S., and Engler, Richard E., Jr. Children in Need of Parents. New York: Columbia University Press, 1959.
5. Maas, Henry S. "Highlights of the Foster Care Project: Introduction." Child Welfare, XXXVIII, 7 (July 1959).
6. ———. "Children in Long-Term Foster Care," Child Welfare, XLVIII, 6 (June 1969).
7. Shapiro, Deborah, "Agency Investment in Foster Care: A Followup," Social Work, XVIII, 6 (November 1973).
8. Silverblatt, Florence. "The Child Welfare Agency's Services to Own Parents," in Polk et al., Today's Child and Foster Care. New York: Child Welfare League of America, 1963.

# 25

# Involuntary Clients' Responses to a Treatment Experience

GENEVIEVE B. OXLEY

Today, therapists are paying more attention to their clients' perceptions of the treatment experience [1]. This trend coincides with the growing emphasis on accountability and with the demystification of the treatment process. One source of client feedback is the followup study. This article reviews the findings of one such study, based on the reactions of parents and boys to treatment in a boys' residential center. It also includes those aspects of the study relevant to clinical intervention and the clients' specific suggestions for increasing treatment effectiveness [2]. Although the setting of the study is residential, the implications for effective clinical intervention apply as well to outpatient facilities. The findings are of particular interest in considering ways of reaching the nonvoluntary client.

## THE STUDY SETTING

The Edgewood Children's Home in San Francisco is a residential treatment center that houses a maximum of thirty-two boys, who are admitted between the ages of six and eleven. Of the group studied, the average

Reprinted by permission of the Family Service Association of America, publisher, from *Social Casework*, Vol. 58, No. 10 (December 1977), pp. 607–614.

admission age was eight and one-half years, and the average length of stay was thirty-four months. The boys came to the program because of behavioral difficulties at home and in school. Many were in special classes or on limited day programs at school, although all were of average or better-than-average intelligence. Forty-three percent of the boys were from single-parent families and 26 percent were adopted children.

A unique feature of the treatment given in the home is the requirement of active participation by the parents; as a part of the treatment contract, the parents agree to weekly counseling sessions for themselves. The boys go home for weekends and for a one-month summer vacation. The program is well staffed with experienced social workers, a medical director who is also the consulting psychiatrist, and trained child-care counselors. A school staffed by the San Francisco school system is located on the premises.

In an effort to assess the degree of effectiveness of the program, Edgewood's board of directors proposed a followup study which was carried out by an independent consultant. The study was undertaken ten years after the inception of the present program format. Of the ninety boys who had entered and left this program during the first ten years, followup interviews were held with at least one member of the family in seventy (77 percent) of the cases. At followup, the boys ranged in age from eleven to twenty-one, with a mean age of fifteen and one-half. The average time since the boys had left the treatment center was just under four years.

## SUMMARY OF FOLLOWUP FINDINGS

The clients' perceptions of their treatment experience need to be considered in the context of the outcome findings of the study. As is generally true in followup studies, the subjective impression of service recipients was positive. Ninety-one percent of the parents perceived their boys as better now than when they had entered the program, and 82 percent of the boys rated the Edgewood experience as helpful to them. These positive, subjective client reactions were substantiated by more objective data. For example, at followup, 92 percent of the boys were appropriately productive (that is, in school or at work) according to their age. Eighty percent of the boys were living with their parents. A rating on a twenty-four point numerical scale at admission, discharge, and followup yielded a positive pattern of growth in 83 percent of the boys studied [3].

These results were considerably more positive than those of other studies using involuntary clients as subjects [4]. Although there was no control group with which to compare the behavioral adjustment of the Edgewood boys, there was some verification of the general accuracy of the results of the study. Unlike many followup studies of residential treatment [5], the findings indicated a significant relationship between a boy's adjustment at discharge from the institution and his adjustment at followup. That is, those boys who made good use of the treatment experience were making significantly better adjustment when seen at followup than those boys who had not been doing well at discharge [6]. There was a minimal relationship between behavior at admission and discharge, or admission and followup. The only items at admission which were found to be predictive of successful outcome were: the problem had existed for less than four years, and the boy had experienced fewer than two significant separations or losses prior to admission. These findings suggest that treatment influenced outcome.

Both the parents and the child came to the agency as involuntary clients in that neither requested treatment for themselves. The parents had made application to the agency for treatment of their sons, often because of pressure from outside sources, and the boys came to the agency because their parents had brought them.

What accounts for the positive outcomes reported by clients? A study of the clients' responses in the followup interviews suggests dynamics of treatment which were important in facilitating positive change.

## ENGAGING THE INVOLUNTARY CLIENT

The parents came to Edgewood in a state of crisis. They felt overwhelmed—often they were pressured by school authorities to do something about their son. Eighty-three percent of the parents had been to other social agencies for help without finding desired solutions. They were emotionally ready to agree to almost any terms if someone would help their child. Edgewood had much to offer: an excellent physical plant, a sound and well-staffed program, and a strong conviction and commitment to the importance of parents to children. The psychiatrist and the social work staff respected the role of the parents. They involved the parents and the child in a long and carefully planned preplacement study and preparation period. Parents had to agree to come to the center at least once each week for counseling throughout the period that the child was in placement. Children were not accepted for admission if the parents did not agree to these terms, or if the staff concluded that the parents would not be able to carry through on their responsibilities. These conditions limited the population of the institution to those children who were fortunate enough to have parents who were willing to be involved and who lived in sufficient proximity to the agency to make the involvement feasible. Many parents commuted substantial distances each week to meet with the social worker.

The basis of the treatment contract was the requirement of parent participation in return for child care service. A basic question is whether this kind of mandatory involvement can be effective. This contract assured the bodily presence of parents. It assured no more, and, with a few parents, it got no more. The transformation of a required presence into an involved and goal-directed commitment to growth and change rested with the skill and creativity of the social worker or psychiatrist. The followup study revealed some factors which appeared to facilitate this process.

## CLIENTS' RESPONSES TO THE EXPECTATIONS OF THE THERAPIST

There are two major points of view regarding parents in the child care field. Bruno Bettelheim is a well-known proponent of the point of view that, if parents create problems in their children, the children should be removed and treated away from parents [7]. Salvatore and Patricia Minuchin state the opposite view; they see pathology as:

> . . . located in the child in his context. Therefore the intervention and the responsibility for change would be located in the child, in his family, in the school and in the way they affect each other. The social system is considered dysfunctional and the intervention is conceptualized in these terms. [8]

There is also a third position, which might be described as a nebulous area, in which mental health professionals emphatically speak of the importance of family to children but do little to include parents in their treatment efforts [9].

Edgewood focused on the "child in his context." Such a focus, of course, is not without complications. Helping the child learn to cope with the intertwining subsystems of cottage life, school, administration, and treatment teams places a heavy demand on the social worker. The burden may seem overwhelming if the social worker is also asked to include the parent system when working with the child. In order to treat "the child in context," it is necessary for an agency to support its philosophical commitment with sufficient funds and allocation of staff time for work with the parents. It is also necessary for the social workers to have a very firm belief in, and commitment to, the importance of parents in the treatment system of children. These last two factors were present at Edgewood, and they are the basic ingredients of a successful involvement of parents in the treatment program.

Role theory lends understanding to the importance of the worker's expectations of the client [10]. If a worker thinks of the parents as dispensable, they will feel unimportant and uninvolved and expect the institution to "cure" their child. If, on the other hand, the worker assigns the parents an important role, they will feel more important to the child and be more interested in becoming partners in the treatment endeavor. The social worker who requires weekly interviews says, in effect, to the parents, "I consider you so important that I want to spend an hour a week of my time with you." Even reluctant parents cannot escape this message. Comments of parents to the followup interviewers underscored the effect upon them of the worker's implicit statement, "You, parent, are important to your child." One parent recalled:

> They were trying to give some semblance of order to his [the boy's] life at a time when there was chaos. As well as order to the parents' lives. This is important. It wasn't just that they helped the children; they also tried to help the parents. So Edgewood served a dual purpose, I think—for the family, his brothers and sisters in the family too. . . . After he had been there for awhile my social worker and I had some discussions and I came to realize that I was too angry at him. I was too harsh on a little boy, because of all my problems. . . . There's no perfect solution, of course, but when we left, I felt a lot more in control than I did in the beginning. I felt more confident, and my son was different. He was much improved.

Another worker's consistent expectation that a parent come for interviews was rewarded by this retrospective view of the experience:

> I dreaded every time I had to go for my interview, but I enjoyed them. It was after I got out of them that I enjoyed them. I just went there because it was my duty. But some of them were really good—finally seeing why I was doing things.

## EGO ENHANCEMENT FACILITATES GROWTH

The social worker's first message to the parent is, "You are important to your child." The second message is, "You are important as a person, a separate individual with your own needs, hopes, and abilities." This belief in, commitment to, and respect for the parents as important individuals in their own right was a curative force for many parents. A mother described her perception of this attitude: "Of course their goal is more strengthening of yourself so you'll be happier too. You're not just a mother, you're a person.

You're a woman. Work on that level. If you're happier, of course then you'll make your kids happier."

Another mother told the followup interviewer of her experience with Edgewood:

> When I first went there I was so guilt-ridden about so many things, primarily the kids. They helped me. When I first went there they put me on antidepressants. They thought I was suicidal although I wasn't aware. But things were really at an all time low and they made me see that I wasn't as bad as I thought I was. I wasn't doing that bad a job as a mother. There were things I could grow on. I could improve on. I think they reinforce you a great deal. They give you hope and strength. It's still very hard. But when you get constant good reinforcement, it helps. I know what comes from bad reinforcement. That's what happened when I was growing up. Edgewood made me put pieces together. Made me see that although I had always gotten along with people and had friends, I couldn't really see why they liked me, that kind of thing. Edgewood points this kind of thing out. In the group they all liked me and they looked up to me. They respected what I said, and when you get constant reinforcement, good feedback, no matter if you want to reject it or not, it gets in there.

The sensitivity of clients to any negative reinforcement was illustrated by a parent who recalled what her social worker had said to her about mothering: "I know you want to be a good mother." The client interpreted this comment as an indication that she was not seen as a good mother; she heard the comment as a put-down.

Listening and understanding enhances the self-esteem of parents. For example,

> They acknowledged that we had a problem when no one else would listen. They understood. They took the time to evaluate us and our boy. And they gave constructive help, not just verbiage. Real help. Understanding and acceptance is a tremendous thing. They listened, then took the time to help. They listened to what we felt and thought.

Another parent spoke of the importance of the social worker's concern even after his boy left the institution:

> I think that I would go to the social worker with any major problem that I would have. Maybe there wouldn't be an answer, but just somebody to talk to that really cares. It's just nice to know

> that somebody who isn't connected to you financially, or doesn't have your child in school, cares that much. It just makes it all worthwhile.

There were some negative comments from parents about workers who were overly passive in their approach. A more active, give-and-take interchange between client and social worker was viewed by the parents as more helpful. For example, parents expressed appreciation for the social worker's interest and help with family and economic problems. A father told the followup interviewer that his social worker was responsible for his ownership of a very comfortable home, of which he was obviously proud. "She helped us set goals—how to spend money and not go into debt. It was one of our big problems and she helped us out. She taught us how to work out problems for ourselves. . . ."

## TREATMENT FOCUS FACILITATES CHANGE

The findings of the study suggest that a conscious self-focus enhances treatment outcome. It appeared to be true for both parents and for boys. For example, the sons of those parents who had developed a focus of treatment on self-change were doing significantly better at followup. This comparison was made between those parents who, at followup, recalled that they had problems of their own to work on and those parents who saw their son as the only problem. These findings support the view of family therapists who emphasize the importance of helping the family move away from a concern with the identified patient [11]. Case records did not distinguish between those parents who came to Edgewood with a recognition of their involvement in their son's problems and those parents who were helped to this recognition by their social worker. It is the author's impression that, initially, the majority of parents perceived their son as the identified patient. If true, then the skill of the social workers in assisting the parents to become involved directly in the treatment endeavor was highly significant to their son's outcome adjustment. In other words, as the social worker was able to shift the treatment focus to strengthening the parent and reinforcing the family system to which the child would return, she was increasing the boy's chances of a brighter future.

One parent described her work on her own problems:

> I needed to talk to someone who was impartial and unbiased about the things that were really deep inside, and bring them out and see them for what they were. I couldn't do this by myself, because I didn't know if I was thinking the right way. I know how I was thinking, but I was thinking with malice and with anger. I just

> about needed to be told as a child would be told, "Don't you consider this factor? Have you thought about this side of the issue? What about your own reactions?" This sort of thing I couldn't do myself. I couldn't be objective. I needed somebody outside.

A conscious focus was also important in successful work with the boys. The boys were brought to Edgewood by their parents; they were in trouble; they were unhappy but did not seek to live away from home or to talk with a social worker or psychiatrist about their problems. The social work staff was faced with the task of gaining the confidence of these boys and actively involving them in the treatment process. Anna Freud [12] describes the steps so aptly in her material on the introductory phase in the analysis of children. She discusses her preparatory work with six young people between the ages of six and eleven, the same age group as that of this study. The boys at Edgewood were not in analysis, but the importance of their active involvement in the counseling process is similar. Freud writes, "I succeeded in making the small patient 'analysable' in the sense of the adult, that is to say inducing insight into the trouble, imparting confidence in the analyst, and turning the decision for analysis taken by others into his own" [13].

The Edgewood study highlighted the importance of this initial phase of treatment. Case readers were asked to rate the record material for indications of the worker's efforts to help the boy understand the purpose of his being at Edgewood. These ratings were then compared with the boy's gross adjustment at followup: that is, occupation, living plan, experience with law enforcement authorities, and medication. A boy whose worker recorded a focus on establishing the reason why the boy was in treatment was doing better at followup than those for whom the records did not show this emphasis.

Some of the boys gave the followup interviewers clear reasons for being at Edgewood and the help they received.

> I used to get real violent in fights, but I didn't like it when I got that way . . . Edgewood helped me stop getting into arguments and fighting with people.
>
> I made instant enemies.
>
> Edgewood helped me to face up, not run away anymore, but face up to what I did.
>
> I knew I couldn't get along with other people in school, so I had to find out why I couldn't get along.
>
> I learned to listen to and talk to people, and try to see their point of view.

## RECOMMENDATIONS AND SUGGESTIONS OF CLIENTS

Parents and boys generally received the followup interviewers with interest and warmth. They appeared to be pleased to have the opportunity to reminisce about Edgewood and to share their ideas and reactions to their experience. Their suggestions for changes tended to cluster in three areas. These suggestions would seem to have relevance for therapeutic situations in many settings.

### Choice

Parents accepted the requirement of treatment but would have liked a choice within that requirement. They asked for participation in the choice of their therapist and the freedom to request a change of therapist if they could not work well with the one to whom they were assigned.

Parents also requested more choice in the selection of modalities of treatment. Family treatment and group treatment were made available during the later years of the program, and many parents who had not been given a choice of participating in these modalities suggested them as options for future clients. There were many positive comments about experiences with group and family treatment. Study findings showed that participation in family treatment increased the chances of successful outcome as measured by the boy's adjustment at followup.

Both parents and boys requested greater flexibility and choice in determining the schedule of appointments. For example, some parents felt that regular appointments were essential early in the treatment process. They suggested a middle period when appointments should be scheduled on an "as needed" basis. As the time approached for the boy to be returned to his own home, they thought that parents would want to see their social worker with increased frequency.

The boys, initially involuntary clients, requested greater availability of their social workers so they could see them more often, and as needed, rather than on a weekly appointment schedule only.

### Increased Participation in the Total Program

This request was made most often by the parents. Essentially, the parents liked their involvement and requested more. The Edgewood program was structured so that the majority of parent contacts with the institution were made through the social worker. The parents accepted the importance of the social work role but, in addition, requested that they be invited to visit the cottages, talk with the boys' counselors and teachers, and give and receive more direct feedback on their son's progress. A parent who generally felt positively about her experience with Edgewood described feeling excluded from her son's life in the cottage:

> They showed me where he was going to be—the house he was going to live in. I put his duffel bag on the floor and then left. That was it. I never met the people he was going to live with. Never saw the lady who washed his clothes or helped take care of things. Indirectly she was taking my place, but I never saw her. This was a painful experience for me.

Parent-teacher conferences were held twice yearly. In recent years, the Edgewood program has included family nights, and these were discussed in enthusiastic terms by the parents who had participated.

## Planned Followup Appointments

It is interesting that these clients, initially forced into a treatment situation, asked for a structured expectation of return appointments after their boy was discharged from the institution. Most parents described a honeymoon period of six months following the boy's return home. After that, old problems were apt to begin reappearing. The policy of the agency was to invite parents to return on an "as needed" basis, but very few parents acted on that invitation. Some parents heard but expressed their ambivalence about calling for an appointment:

> I might think of calling Edgewood but I don't. I never have since we left. I thought of it though. But I know he's out of the age level for Edgewood now. He hasn't really been that much of a problem. It's not that dramatic. But there might be family problems where they might be able to help me and I might have thought of them. I haven't done it though. I would like to talk with my social worker. We became like friends. I would like to talk to her just as a friend and let her know how things are going for me. I didn't want to lose touch, in other words, once I left. I have a feeling toward the people. It isn't just like a school where at the end of the term you say goodbye and never think about them again. It's different at Edgewood. They're much more important to you. I feel that way. I don't know why. I just never have called

> them. I'm not saying I never would. Because I guess I figure we're out of their care. Not that I think they wouldn't offer to help. I'm sure they would. I've never called them, though.

This poignant example of ambivalence illustrates how the client who is enthusiastic about a service is reluctant to accept an open-ended invitation to call for further help.

The treatment philosophy of the agency may influence the message from worker to client about returning. Often intensive treatment efforts following the medical model place greater emphasis on beginnings and leave clients with unrealistic expectations of "cure" at the point of discharge from treatment. If the client accepts this implicit message, then he will be embarrassed to call to report that his child or he, as parent, has failed to meet the expectations of the agency and again, or still, has a problem. One way of handling this possible confusion in expectations is to plan check-up appointments at three- or six-month intervals following formal discharge from treatment. This followup plan was the nature of the recommendation from many parents and has now been adopted by the Edgewood staff.

## POLICY IMPLICATIONS

Many of the parents' suggestions are in line with the current emphasis on consumerism and the right of the purchaser of any service or commodity to have more effect on that product. Most Edgewood parents paid a fee for service on a sliding scale. Although the social worker may agree philosophically with this stance and wish to offer the client increased participation, some of the parents' suggestions raise policy issues. Is it possible to run an orderly and efficient institution if the parents are permitted to request changes in their assigned workers, if the boys can see their social workers at any time, and if the parents are invited on the grounds to further complicate the lives of the counselors? Such policies would present more challenge and difficulty than explicit structured rules on these points. The comments made by the parents and boys, however, suggest that flexibility within some structured expectations could increase the very commitment and involvement of parents, which is the core of the agency's philosophy.

A request for a change of social worker would need to be evaluated within the context of transference and resistance to treatment. The worker should know within his own counter-transference reactions whether the client might move more rapidly in a relationship with another person on staff. If parents were invited to visit the cottages and to talk with counselors more often, there would be an added educational opportunity as parents observed the counselors interacting with the boys and dealing with crises. There would also be a further demonstration of sharing and partnership between parent and institution.

Planning time schedules for the workers becomes much more difficult if boys are free to see their workers at irregular times. It is possible, however, that such a plan might reduce the overall number of necessary contacts by utilizing the crisis situation for understanding and growth.

Another question relates to costs. Is it possible to meet any of the parents' suggestions for flexibility, for more structured followup, without increasing the already high cost of treatment? Additional appointments for boys and parents cannot be added to the current plan of regular weekly appointments. If the parents' suggestion of flexibility in reducing appointments during the middle period in treatment were adopted, however, then more hours would be available for life-space interviews with the boys and for scheduled checkup appointments after discharge. The findings of the study suggest that some shifting in priorities in the use of clinical time might yield increased benefits without increasing costs. One specific finding of the study was that there was no advantage for those boys who remained the longest in the program. The agency has, in recent years, been reducing the average length of stay and this trend might be further accelerated with the adoption of the suggestions made by the clients. Finally, there is the question of how an institution can change policy and practices which have been inherent in its program for years. The very pressure of day-to-day client needs leaves little staff time for longer-range planning or experimentation. Openness to hearing the feedback from clients is a first essential. Creativity, flexibility, and a goal of excellence can transform that feedback into meaningful policy actions.

## REFERENCES

1. For example, see Hans H. Strupp, Ronald Fox, and Ken Lessler, *Patients View Their Psychotherapy* (Baltimore: Johns Hopkins University Press, 1969); and Irving Yalom and Ginny Elkin, *Every Day Gets a Little Closer* (New York: Basic Books, 1974).

2. For the overall findings of the ten-year followup study of Edgewood Children's Home, see Genevieve B. Oxley, A Modified Form of Residential Treatment, *Social Work* 22: 493–98 (November 1977).

3. Ibid.

4. See Anthony Davids and Peter Salvatore, Residential Treatment of Disturbed Children and Adequacy of Their Subsequent Adjustment: A Followup Study, *American Journal of Orthopsychiatry*, 46: 62–73 (January 1976); Joel Fischer, Is Casework Effective? A Review, *Social Work*, 18: 5–20 (January 1973); and Ellen Handler, Residential Treatment Programs for Juvenile Delinquents, *Social Work* 20: 217–22 (May 1975).

5. Melvin Allerhand, R.E. Weber and M. Haug, *Adaptation and Adaptability: The Bellefaire Followup Study* (New York: Child Welfare League of America, 1966); and Delores Taylor and Stuart Alpert, *Continuity and Support Following Residential Treatment* (New York: Child Welfare League of America, 1973).

6. Oxley, A Modified Form of Residential Treatment, pp. 493–98.

7. Bruno Bettelheim, *The Empty Fortress, Infantile Autism and the Birth of Self* (New York: The Free Press, 1967); and *Truants from Life, the Rehabilitation of Emotionally Disturbed Children* (Glencoe, Ill.: The Free Press, 1955).

8. Salvatore and Patricia Minuchin, The Child in Context, A Systems Approach to Growth and Treatment, in *Raising Children in Modern America*, ed. Nathan B. Talbot (Boston: Little, Brown, and Co., 1976).

9. Kermit Wiltse and Eileen Gambrill, Foster Care, 1973, A Reappraisal, *Public Welfare*, 23: 7–15 (Winter 1974).

10. Genevieve B. Oxley, Caseworkers' Expectations and Client Motivations, Social Casework, 47: 432–37 (July 1966).

11. Virginia Satir, *Conjoint Family Therapy* (Palo Alto: Science and Behavior Books, 1964 and 1967).

12. Anna Freud, *The Psycho-Analytic Treatment of Children* (New York: International Universities Press, 1946), pp. 1–14.

13. Ibid., p. 6.

# 26

# The Use of Foster Parents as Role Models for Parents

LINDA J. DAVIES AND DAVID C. BLAND

Child and Family Services, Hartford, Connecticut, is a private, multifunction agency serving children, families and individuals. The agency's clinical services division includes an outpatient child guidance clinic, a residential treatment unit for emotionally disturbed children, a group home for adolescents, and a specialized foster care program for emotionally disturbed children.

The foster care program provides both long-term and time-limited care. The time-limited program is intended to lead to a permanent home within a year for children between the ages of 3 and 10, permanency being defined as belonging to a biological or adoptive family. The long-term program serves children for whom the adoption option does not exist because of age, legal difficulties or emotional disturbance.

The short-term program's commitment to permanency grows out of concern over the current drift of children into long-term foster care [2;4:1]. In addition to individual and family therapy provided by the clinical social worker, specially trained foster parents work with agency staff on individual treatment plans to prepare the children to return to their own homes or to go to adoptive homes.

---

Reprinted from *Child Welfare*, Vol. LVII, No. 6 (June 1978): 380–386.

## USE OF CONTRACTS

Contracts are used as a way of committing foster parents, parents and social workers to plan for placement, treatment and return home of the child [3:28–36].

After the social worker evaluates the child and family diagnostically, a written contract is developed, outlining the treatment process. The purposes are to: 1) underscore agreement on establishing a permanent plan for the child within a specified time, usually a year; 2) clearly define the responsibilities of the parents, foster parents and social worker; 3) explicate the work to be done in developing child management techniques; 4) set time limits for both placement and frequency of visits home (usually every weekend); 5) require that parents keep weekly therapy appointments (children are also seen weekly). The contract also provides that parents and foster parents meet regularly with the social worker.

## ROLE MODELING

Some foster care programs have discouraged contact between parents and foster parents. In this time-limited program, both agency resources and foster couples are used to help the parents regain control of their child's life. Role modeling of parenting behavior by foster parents for natural parents is the major technique when the goal is to return the child to his/her own home. There is an attempt to match foster parents and parents whenever possible, to promote a positive working relationship.

The basic assumption in role modeling is that many parents have deficits in parenting, and are unclear as to what is expected of them as parents. Many parents in the program would be diagnostically classified as character disordered, borderline or schizophrenic, and come from multiproblem families. The children in placement are emotionally disturbed, and have many special needs.

Difficulty in child management is common to many of the parents with children in placement. Typical is the case of Mary T.

> The behavior of Mary, 5½, included defiance of authority, stealing, fire setting, sexual acting out, and aggression toward peers and siblings. Mary's mother is a single parent. Her anger at Mary's behavior led to severe beatings, followed by periods of remorse, guilt and overindulgence. Mary's reactions to this absence of clear limits was to test with new vigor until mother

> responded with violent outbursts. In her own family, Ms. T. had experienced a lack of clear limits with her own mother. Her actions can be viewed in part as a neurotic need to repeat a trauma, and in part as learned behavior. Ms. T. sought the help of the agency voluntarily and Mary was placed with a foster family. The contract called for weekly therapy appointments for the mother and Mary, and biweekly meetings of the mother, foster mother, and social worker (role modeling sessions). A limit of a year was set to effect a permanent plan for Mary. Mary was to spend every weekend home with her mother.
>
> During the role modeling sessions, a rapport developed between the mother and the foster mother to the point that the mother would ask for suggestions about what to do when Mary stayed out late or what to do when Mary was sent home from school for poor behavior. Foster mother gave specific suggestions, which the mother followed. Ms. T. began to feel more in control. For the first time she was able to use positive attention as a reinforcer. She was also able to send Mary to her room for "time out," during which they both regained control of themselves. The foster mother modeled this calm approach to provocative behavior by the child.

Another major component, in addition to role modeling, brings about behavioral change: a corrective emotional experience usually occurs through the parents' identification with foster parents [1:329]. The case of Johnny S. illustrates this.

> Johnny was a 7-year-old whose father deserted the family when the boy was 4. Johnny's mother, a depressed woman whose own father had recently died, remarried in an attempt to provide a father for Johnny. This marriage was extremely destructive, but Ms. S. was unable to separate from her second husband. Johnny exhibited disturbed behaviors, such as setting fires, being cruel to animals, not relating to peers, and demanding excessive attention. He was placed in the foster home of a middle-aged couple. Ms. S. and the foster father rapidly developed a father-daughter kind of relationship. Ms. S's depression gradually lifted and she began to forgo the destructive relationship with her husband, establishing more positive supports with other family members and friends. She worked out a permanent plan for Johnny and was able to take total responsibility for his care after 6 months of placement. Both Johnny and Ms. S. continued to have frequent contacts with the foster parents after the placement ended.

## STAGES OF ROLE MODELING

There are usually four stages in the relationship between parents and foster parents. In the first, the natural parents teach the foster parents what their child is like. In the second, the social worker facilitates a shift in the roles whereby the foster parents take over the role of teachers. In the third stage, the social worker becomes less active, allowing the rapport that has developed between the parents and foster parents to grow. In the fourth, the social worker helps the foster parents and the parents to separate. The meetings often take place in the foster home.

### Stage I

Competitiveness, hostility, mistrust, and fear frequently arise in the relationship between the parents and foster parents. Parents, feeling threatened by the foster parents' ability to parent effectively, often attack both their methods of childrearing and their values. Foster parents react with anger and hurt. Much of the social worker's energy is directed toward helping the parents and foster parents share their feelings with each other. The foster parents need support to avoid counterattacking the parents; the parents need to feel that their anger is heard, but they are basically accepted as caring parents. The major part of the social worker's role is to interpret the parents' behavior in such a way that foster parents can feel compassion for the parents. During early contacts of the social worker, foster parents and parents, the social worker asks the parents to put themselves in the role of teacher and describe the child to the foster parents. The foster parents are encouraged by the social worker to ask about the child's bedtime, playing patterns, food preferences, and so forth. In doing so, the foster parents model listening and acceptance. At the same time, the message is given to the parents: "What you have to say is important; I can learn from you." The foster parents model the role of learner, saying, "It's okay not to know." This beginning process cuts through much of the hostility inherent in the relationship.

### Stage II

In the second stage, which begins soon after placement, the social worker facilitates a shift in roles. The foster parents begin to teach the parents child management techniques, with emphasis on the parents' strengths. The social worker sets limits for the parents in the early stages. Many parents initially test the limits set in the contract, for instance, by being late in picking up the child for a weekend visit. When parents act in this way, the social worker helps them express their anger, interprets their acting out, and sustains the limits. The message is, "I am not intimidated by your anger." This is, in fact, the message the parent will eventually have to give the child. Individual therapy is used with the parents to help them understand their feelings, including anger.

## Stage III

The third stage begins 2 to 3 months into placement, and reduces the social worker's importance in the relationship between parent and foster parent. The social worker encourages the foster parents to become the primary role models. The social worker continues an ongoing relationship with the parents through weekly therapy sessions, separate from the role modeling sessions. The purpose of the individual therapy is to help the parents understand their feelings and gain support to change their behavior. The social worker's role between the parents and foster parents continues to be that of facilitator. In most cases, the social worker relinquishes some control once a positive relationship between parents and foster parents is established. Meetings often occur at the foster home without the social worker present. However, the social worker retains the responsibility for control should difficulties arise. The case of Sara illustrates both the positive relationship between the parents and foster parents and the social worker's relinquishment of control.

> Sara, a 7-year-old with a failure-to-thrive syndrome, was referred by a children's hospital. She had not grown significantly since age 2. Symptoms prior to hospitalization included refusal to talk or cooperate with adults, stealing food, stubborn and uncooperative behavior with parents, and an inability to play with her peers. Sara was placed in a highly structured foster home. The relationship between the parents and foster parents developed positively and rapidly to the point where the families were spending much of their leisure time together. Although the social worker was involved weekly, her activity was important mostly during times of crisis. Parents and foster parents often discussed major planning decisions together before discussing them with the social worker.

## Stage IV

The fourth stage involves separation and termination. During the last few months of the year of placement, it is necessary for the social worker to meet more frequently with the parents and the foster parents.

Relationship is again tested, with the parents trying to determine if the placement can be prolonged or terminated prematurely. The social worker's role is to support the plan and to prepare the parents for the child's testing and the foster parents for the parents' testing. Because of trust and closeness that have developed between foster parents and parents, it is not uncommon for the foster parents to feel hurt and rejected if the parents become angry with them. When the foster parents are helped to anticipate the testing and anger, they can generally deal with it. Their task is to model separation without rejection.

Because of the number of persons involved, the separation process is complex. The social worker's task is to help all involved deal as directly as possible with their feelings about separation, and to confront their natural tendency to avoid the issues.

Because of the many difficult decisions in each case over a relatively short time, the social worker needs much support. The foster care support group, consisting of three social workers involved in the program and an administrator, meet weekly, with the psychiatrist and psychologist available as consultants.

## QUALITIES OF FOSTER PARENTS AND PARENTS

Training for foster parents takes the form of group meetings between the social worker and the foster parents. In addition to a genuine liking for children, foster parents in a time-limited program doing role modeling must have a capacity for understanding and accepting persons. They must be nonjudgmental as to values different from their own. Foster parents must be secure in their own childrearing ability, particularly since parents frequently choose this as the focus for criticism and hostility. Finally, they must have a strong commitment to the use of a time-limited foster care program. The agency facilitates this by considering them members of the treatment team, where their role is similar to those of other professionals in working for the child's return to the parents. The foster parents' commitment is severely tested when the child is returned to a home where the parenting is not so effective as that the foster parents had provided.

Qualities common to parents who have been able to use the program effectively are difficult to identify. There are no fixed diagnostic criteria for screening out parents; the intake process is flexible. However, parents sometimes screen themselves out due to 1) unwillingness to remain in therapy; 2) inability to allow another family to be involved with their child; 3) inability to accept the agency's goal of a permanent plan for their child.

## CONCLUSION

The major goal of a time-limited foster care program is to give each child a permanent home. Parents must be helped as quickly and effectively as possible to make decisions concerning their own capacities to provide long-term care for their child. In the effort to minimize the length of the child's "limbo state" in foster care, all potential helping resources must be utilized fully. The use of foster parents as teachers of parenting behavior is a powerful resource that can help develop and strengthen the child-management skills of parents.

## REFERENCES

1. Alexander, Franz. The Scope of Psychoanalysis. New York: Basic Books, 1961.
2. Fellner, Irving, and Solomon, Charles. "Achieving Permanent Solutions for Children in Foster Home Care," Child Welfare, LII, 3 (March 1973).
3. Maluccio, Anthony, and Marlow, Wilma. "The Case for the Contract," Social Work (January 1974)
4. Shapiro, Deborah. Agencies and Foster Care. New York: Columbia University Press, 1976.

# 27

# Home Management Services for Families with Emotionally Disturbed Children

LAUREN A. SPINELLI AND KAREN S. BARTON

After providing care and shelter for the neglected and dependent children of Philadelphia for over 100 years, Southern Home for Children in 1954 became a psychiatric residential treatment center for emotionally disturbed boys and girls and their families. Since 1970 when a multifunction approach was established through the addition of its Day Care Center, Southern Home has gradually expanded its treatment population from 56 children and their families to, at present, over 500 child clients and their family members. Children and their families receive the direct services of more than 400 social work, psychiatric, psychological, child care, home management, creative arts, educational/vocational and Community Home staff, coordinated by M.S.W. social workers through 10 agency programs.

## POPULATION CHANGES

Although the overall orientation of these treatment programs is eclectic, an emphasis on psychoanalytic theory has led to a conviction that work with

Reprinted from *Child Welfare*, Vol. LIX, No. 1 (January 1980): 43–52.

families is an essential component in the treatment of emotionally disturbed children and adolescents.

In recent years the kinds of child and family referred for treatment at Southern Home has changed dramatically; the staff have therefore had to adapt to the special needs of its present client population. Although agency programs are equally available to children and their families from all races, economic strata, and living environments, the current clientele is predominantly adolescent, black, poor and socially disorganized.

The children and adolescents manifest acting-out behavior, mild to moderate mental retardation, and poor academic performance. They are often abused, neglected, undisciplined and inadequately disciplined. Their largely single-parent families are seriously deprived of income, housing, clothing and food. Emotional and physical disorders often render caretakers further unable to meet the needs of their children. An understandable mistrust of authority, bureaucracy, institutions and so-called helping professionals compounds their problems and impedes the treatment process.

## RESPONSE TO CHANGING NEEDS

A survey of family participation of Southern Home, conducted in the winter of 1975–76, revealed waning parent interest in family therapy, declining attendance at Parent Association meetings and activities, and no participation at all in group therapy. Attempts to increase attendance through encouragement and explanation failed; only five mothers attended a luncheon to which 50 families had been invited to learn about the programs. A simply written brochure and a monthly newsletter listing regular and special activities (and offering to pay babysitting fees for parents who took part) met with little response. Advertisement of a program to financially reward parents of current clients for visiting families new to Southern Home elicited no inquiries.

A newly hired black male M.S.W. Parent Activities Coordinator visited parents at home to stimulate interest through describing Southern Home's services, cochaired Parent Association meetings, and led the weekly activities groups. Attendance increased moderately for a short time but it was obvious these efforts did not meet the needs of the most disturbed families.

More home visiting by social workers increased family contacts but proved an imperfect solution. The existing assignment of social work duties left little time for either the increased demands of home visiting or fulfillment of the basic needs identified through such contacts. Perhaps more important, parents obviously had difficulty trusting and confiding in the predominantly middle-class, childless, young social workers (black and white) who choose to work in such an intense and demanding setting.

## HOME MANAGEMENT SERVICE BEGUN

The Home Management Service for Families with Emotionally Disturbed Children was conceived in 1975 as a continuation of the agency's family focus in treatment and as an addition to and enrichment of its resources. In the past, family intervention had concentrated on individual and interpersonal psychological problems. This proved insufficient, however, to deal with all the problems clients face daily. Through development of Home Management Service, the agency could attack such social and environmental factors as poverty, poor housing, and unemployment, which are frequently of primary importance in family disorganization and disintegration and are all too often ignored by treatment agencies.

Through utilizing the Home Management Service to deal with these concrete issues and to develop and maintain parents' child and household management skills, these results may occur: 1) some children initially referred for residential treatment might remain in their own homes while receiving services; 2) children currently in residential treatment programs might return home sooner; and 3) re-placement of children who returned home following residential treatment might be prevented.

The service was begun in May 1976, following receipt of a grant from the United Way of Greater Philadelphia. A gift from the William Penn Foundation allowed expansion, and continuation has been possible through United Way grants and the inclusion of the service in the cost of all agency programs.

The interface between Home Management Service and family therapy can best be understood in the context of Abraham Maslow's hierarchy of needs [1:461–462]. Maslow contends that the most basic needs of food, shelter and safety must be met before the individual can turn attention to psychological needs for belongingness and love, esteem and self-actualization. A "lower" need must be sufficiently gratified before the next "higher" need can fully emerge in an individual's development. The majority of Southern Home families are unable to participate in meetings and activities or in family therapy, not because of "resistance" to change in a psychological sense, but because of preoccupation with overwhelming subsistence issues.

Every effort is made to eliminate the need for the Home Management Service through the family's attainment of a reasonable minimum level of social functioning, determined during the initial evaluation process and reassessed periodically thereafter. For the most seriously disorganized families, however, ongoing Home Management Service may be necessary to help the family approach a level of existence satisfactory for the return of their children to and/or maintenance of their children in their home.

## THE HOME MANAGEMENT SPECIALIST

Home Management Specialists teach, support and motivate the caretakers with whom they work. For very severely deprived parents, they often provide a parental type of concern, acceptance and nurturance that may have been lacking in their lives. Home Management Specialists are, in a most important sense, enablers who whenever possible do *with* rather than *for*. No matter how inadequate the caretaker, the focus is always on assisting the client to develop and sustain knowledge and skills that may lead to independent, mentally healthy functioning.

Each Home Management Specialist is assigned to an average of 10 active cases. The specialist spends approximately 3 hours a week with each family in its own home and community. The remaining time is spent traveling, attending training sessions and conferences, collaborating with other treatment staff, writing progress notes, receiving supervision, and attending the regular department staff meeting.

Time spent with a family may be used in such activities as helping to define a caretaker's goals, demonstrating and participating in such child and household management skills as disciplining children, budgeting money, writing shopping lists, purchasing and preparing food, searching for more suitable housing, and applying for employment, or meeting with staff from other agencies regarding benefits to which the client may be entitled.

At the program's inception, cases needing the services of a Home Management Specialist were identified by the social work staff, but it soon became clear that virtually every client family could in some way benefit from Home Management Service. Currently, the "family treatment team" of social worker and Home Management Specialist is introduced to every family at the time of the initial evaluation. Cases in which a serious need is identified during screening can be assigned a Home Management Specialist even before the formal social work interview takes place. In addition, Home Management staff have served as cotherapists with social workers in a weekly evening group of new families to acquaint newcomers with agency services and further identify areas of need.

In addition to direct work with parents and other adult caretakers, Home Management staff have proved invaluable in preparing older adolescents (including teen-age mothers) for independent living. Home Management Specialists accompany youngsters on job interviews and shopping excursions and hold regular group discussions and activity sessions on household management skills, use of leisure time and care of newborn infants.

## STAFFING

There are at the time of this writing 18 Home Management staff, including the director, two supervisors, two Youth Counselors, and 13 Home

Management Specialists. The success of the Home Management Service is directly related to the quality of the personnel selected. The choice of an M.S.W. social worker as director provides a professional identity and self-image for the department, reinforces its link to Southern Home's treatment services, and adds the necessary balance of advocacy and objectivity discussed at greater length later.

Home Management supervisory and line staff combine skills in child and household management and knowledge of and expertise in using community resources. Home Management staff members are all over 30 years old, and have reared children of their own; most have experienced the emotional tragedy of separation and divorce. All but two are black, as are 90% of the client families. Two are Spanish-speaking and work primarily with Spanish-speaking clients. Several Home Management staffers are parents of children who have had successful treatment for emotional disturbance.

Many of the staff have received supplemental income benefits, several have lived in public housing, and all have encountered discrimination and the hardships of urban life. They have joined the Home Management staff after experience with the Model Cities Program and the Welfare Rights Organization, and following work in mental health counseling, child care, and homemaking positions. Most important, they have overcome barriers and learned to manipulate the "system" in their own behalf and in behalf of others.

Youth Counselors were added to the Home Management Service to fill the need for a "male figure," role model, and motivator for siblings of identified child clients who are themselves truanting school and displaying generally disorganized behavior. The Youth Counselor, along with social workers and Home Management Specialists, works with adolescent and preadolescent boys in their own homes to prevent the need for their placement, and with older adolescents who are on their way to independent living.

Integration of a variety of programs within one multifunction treatment agency causes the least hardship to the child and family in terms of time, travel and repetition in the development of service plans.

## OTHER SERVICE ASPECTS

Home Management Specialists have experimented widely through emphasizing their availability to the parents and children with whom they work as a "friend" or "sister" or "brother." Home Management staff members usually, and by their own choice, give parents their home phone numbers. As a result, they are frequently called upon early in the morning, late at night, and on weekends for support and assistance. They often work voluntarily many more than the 40 hours for which they are paid. Home Management

Specialists have accepted the role of godparent to children in the families with whom they work, have entertained families in their own homes on such special occasions as Christmas and Thanksgiving, and have been dinner guests in the homes of their clients. They have taken parents to movies and museums, to lunch and to dinner, and for walks in the park in an effort to stimulate their interest in themselves and to escape their daily drudgery.

The possible negative effects of a loss of objectivity through such "unprofessional" intervention are well documented in social work literature and the availability and supervision of the "more objective" social work practitioner become crucial to lend balance in each case. Home Management staff members tend, by their nature, selection and assignment, to "overidentify" with parents. There is a need for recurrent reminders that the program involves a very special type of advocacy without adversaries. Home Management Specialists work in behalf of the child and the family, with other members of the Southern Home treatment team, and with community service personnel who control benefits that parents may use. Through continuing collaboration, training and supervision, Home Management staff come to understand the tendency for guilt-ridden parents to unconsciously undermine their child's progress in treatment.

## SUPERVISION AND COLLABORATION

The Home Management Specialist is now an integral part of the Southern Home treatment team. Supervision on each case is provided by the social worker who coordinates all services provided the child and family and by Home Management supervisors who meet weekly with each specialist. Self-carbonized progress notes written after each Home Management contact inform social workers of case developments between periodic collaborative sessions. Home Management Specialists present reports in regular intake and progress evaluation conferences attended by all clinical staff working with a particular child and family. Their minimum high school education and previous experience are supplemented and strengthened through attendance at an individualized combination of such agency training courses as Child Management, Abnormal Child Psychology, Normal Child Growth and Development, and Management and Understanding of Childhood and Adolescent Sexuality. Home Management staff members themselves serve as trainers for the agency's own social work staff and staff of other agencies serving similar client families, explaining the techniques and approaches they have found useful.

## CASE EXAMPLES

### The B Family

The Home Management Service became involved with the B family at the request of the agency's day care center intake worker, who had not been able to complete the social history required prior to admission of 13-year-old Robert to the center. Mrs. B had missed several appointments at the agency and the home situation was so chaotic that the social worker was unable to obtain the needed information during specially scheduled home visits. Prior to the existence of the Home Management Service, the case would have been closed because of the family's inability to complete the necessary formal procedures.

After assignment to a Home Management Specialist, Mrs. B was not home on several early occasions when attempts were made to visit her, but gradually a relationship of trust developed and the Home Management Specialist was able to bring in both Mrs. B and Robert to complete their evaluation appointments. On one home visit, the Home Management Specialist was unexpectedly called upon to accompany Mrs. B to a juvenile court hearing at which Joseph, Robert's 9-year-old brother, was committed to a juvenile detention center following his fifth arrest for burglary. Notified that afternoon by the Home Management Specialist, the agency social worker contacted the court and developed an alternative plan for Joseph that enabled the agency to work with the entire family. Robert now attends the agency's day care center. Joseph is temporarily placed in a Southern Home-affiliated community group care facility while receiving psychiatric services from agency staff. The social worker/Home Management Specialist team continues to assist Mrs. B with health problems, alcoholism, and inadequate parenting. Upon recommendation of the agency and with the court's permission, Joseph will return home when his home situation is sufficiently strengthened.

### Kevin

Kevin, a 16-year-old ward of DPW, had refused to accept previous public and voluntary agency placements and had also failed to adjust to the Southern Home campus residential program. After weekend and holiday visits to his 54-year-old grandmother and stepgrandfather, he did not return to the agency but remained in the community for days and sometimes weeks, not attending school, avoiding police notified of his AWOL status, and never revealing his whereabouts during occasional calls to his social worker at the agency. When Kevin said that he could not remain at the agency due to his concern about his alcoholic grandparents, who had been robbed several times in their inadequately protected apartment, a Home Management Specialist was assigned to work with his grandparents on problems of housing, finances and drinking.

Following the location and furnishing of a rented house for them in a safer neighborhood near his grandmother's niece, Kevin reappeared. The increased stability of his grandparents led to his placement with them through an agreement with DPW. Kevin began attending school regularly and accepted the responsibility of caring for a dog, for whom he and the Home Management Specialist built a house in the yard.

Today, 2 years later, Kevin continues attendance at a special community private school and receives services in his own home. The Home Management Specialist continues to work with his grandparents, and Youth Counselor services provide Kevin with a male role model after which to pattern his behavior.

## SUMMARY

To date, the Home Management staff have worked with over 300 families. Achievements can be measured both in hundreds of thousands of dollars in benefits obtained for parents and children and in warmth, acceptance and increased self-esteem felt by formerly alienated parents. Day care centers have been found for toddlers while mothers attended high school diploma classes and training sessions or worked at new jobs. Several mothers enrolled in college following receipt of their diplomas. SSI, VA, DPA, and Food Stamp payments have been granted or increased with the assistance of Home Management personnel, better housing has been located, and rent supplement payments have been obtained. Parents have begun to assume the competent authority role that provides their children with the direction and support necessary for mentally healthy growth and development.

Through their personal characteristics and their valuable approaches, Home Management staff members have overcome many of the barriers of mistrust that prevented the most disturbed families from using the help available through the agency. There is little question that the carefully chosen Home Management staff member does understand these parents, is understood by them, and has deep meaning in their lives.

In the 3 years since the inception of the Home Management Service, the average length of stay in residential treatment at Southern Home has been reduced by 6 months, from 18 months to 12. We have every expectation that further refinement and expansion of this service, along with refinement and expansion of other agency services, will result in still further reduction.

## REFERENCE

1. Krech, David, and Crutchfield, Richard S. Elements of Psychology. New York: Alfred A. Knopf, 1961.

# 28

# A Program for Parents of Children in Foster Family Care

DOROTHY A. MURPHY

Our classes for parents whose children have been placed in foster care through court order began in January 1976. They are an outgrowth of the classes for foster parents which have been sponsored since January 1974 by the San Francisco Department of Social Services, Foster Parents United and the San Francisco Community College District.

During these latter classes, which consisted of three series of eight sessions each, foster parents had expressed their concerns and feelings about the natural parents of the children in their care. Their first, predominant attitude had been one of resentment, if not outright hostility, toward the natural parents. At the end of the first eight sessions, however, there was a marked change in the foster parents' attitudes. Role-playing was one technique used and it was fascinating to watch the persons who had played the natural parents become truly angry with a foster parent and even show some resentment after being "de-roled."

In the latter part of 1975, the Advisory Committee for Foster Parent Training, comprised of foster parents who have completed the classes and representatives from our agency, the college district and other community agencies and groups concerned with foster care, voted to explore the

Reprinted from *Children Today*, Vol. 5, No. 6 (November–December 1976), pp. 37–42. By permission of the author and the journal.

possibility of conducting classes for natural parents. Staff members of the foster care division of the Department of Social Services were asked to select a group of parents from their caseloads, discuss the classes with them and submit their names to me. Since it was our first attempt to involve natural parents in training classes, we felt that the selection of the parents was most important. We decided to focus on parents whose children had recently returned home and those who had progressed to a point where a return home would probably occur in the near future. However, workers were cautioned against giving the impression that parents' participation in the classes would insure the return of their children.

I received the names of 20 parents and sent them information about the classes and an invitation to participate, together with a return slip and postage-paid envelope. Thirteen of the 20 indicated an interest in attending and did attend some of the classes. Although the college usually requires a minimum of 15 students before it will provide a teacher, an exception was made for this program.

The first course consisted of eight 2½-hour sessions. Classes were held in the agency's building because it is easily accessible by public transportation and an appropriate room was available. We provided coffee and donuts at each session.

Like the classes for foster parents, these were also led by Mary K. Jones, the late director of parent classes for the college district [1]. Ground rules for class listening and participation were outlined [2], then parents were asked to bring up areas which they wanted to discuss in the classes. Twelve pages of newsprint paper were covered with questions and complaints by the end of the first class!

It was apparent that these concerns had to be addressed in order to drain off some of the parents' hostility before Mary K. could work effectively with them. I attended the next two sessions and attempted to answer the questions and comment on the complaints they had listed. There were lengthy and heated discussions of the problems, and arrangements were made to meet after the classes to work out specific plans to solve some immediate problems. For example, within a week four families who had been trying for several weeks to find suitable housing within the limits imposed by AFDC had been helped to locate new homes and they had made arrangements to move.

During the discussion of the questions and complaints, the extreme deprivation and emotional needs of the parents were evident. It was not difficult to overlook their focus on their own needs and the obvious distortions in their discussion, for their hurt was so obvious. They were presenting the problems as they saw them. They were not role playing; their pain was real.

Among the concerns expressed most often and with the greatest amount of feeling were:

- Foster parents' intrusions during parents' visits to their children and their setting up of a competitive situation between themselves and the natural parents. One example cited frequently was that of a foster mother coming into the room and asking the foster youngster such a question as "Did you show Mary (the natural mother) what Mommie bought you when we shopped yesterday?"
- The failure of foster parents and/or social workers to invite a parent to attend or even to notify him or her of a special event in the child's life, such as a school graduation ceremony.
- Situations when foster parents permitted their own children to tease and sometimes hit a foster child.
- The natural parents' pervasive feeling of being treated like "dirt" by foster parents and social workers.
- Situations when decisions which significantly affect their child's life are made without consulting the natural parents.
- Complaints that foster parents were sometimes guilty of the same actions which had resulted in their child's being removed from home; yet the foster parents were permitted to care for the child and were paid for doing so. Examples cited were failure to take the child to a dentist and/or a doctor or the use of corporal punishment.
- Instances when natural parents had given their child clothes or a toy and learned that the item had been immediately given to a "poor" child.

This is a small sample but it represents concerns voiced by all of the parents.

At the end of these two sessions the parents were asked if we could present their questions and complaints to the foster parents and social workers who attended monthly alumni classes. (These classes had been established at the request of the foster parents and social workers who were in the first two classes to complete the 24 sessions in "Basic Techniques In Foster Parenting." Each graduating class is invited to join the group.)

The natural parents were pleased to have their concerns brought to the attention of this group and their questions and comments had a tremendous impact on the foster parents and social workers. Since these meetings combine a social occasion—a pot luck supper—with discussion, spouses are included regardless of whether or not they had also attended the classes. The differences in the reactions to the natural parents' comments between those who had attended the classes and those who had not was remarkable. In general, those who had attended the classes were understanding and compassionate; those who had not were angry and defensive.

Mary K. reported on the discussion with the alumni group when she met with the natural parents the following week. Although the reactions of some of the foster parents and social workers were negative and tended to be critical of the natural parents, the class was able to accept and deal with their comments. They had reached the point where they had some understanding of foster parents' feelings. I believe that this indicated tremendous growth in a period of five weeks.

After the first three sessions it was possible to proceed with more structured discussion and training in the "ages and stages" of children's development and with techniques to enhance parenting skills. Parents whose children had returned home talked about their problems and this, in turn, prompted much discussion and sharing of experiences.

Parents were very explicit in describing the problems their children presented at home. Although they were supportive of other parents' efforts to re-establish their families, they were honest in saying that they would not listen to the advice of social workers and foster parents before the children were returned to them. Parents working toward the return of their children were much better able to accept from other parents the warning that all would not be peaches and cream when the family was reunited.

We were able to offer very little help with one problem which emerged during many discussions, i.e. , the difference in living standards between the foster and parental homes. Children's comments on even such small items as the "wrong" brand of hair shampoo were constant reminders of the change in a child's situation. The parents admitted that it was difficult not to become angry and resentful when their children talked about the material advantages they had enjoyed in the foster home, particularly since the parents had worked so hard to bring the children home and were willingly giving up small extras themselves so that the children could have more. They were not hopeless and despondent; they did tell those parents whose children would be returning home about the positive aspects of having them back, but they hoped to reduce the feelings of disappointment which they knew those parents would experience on occasion by giving them a realistic description of life with children.

All of the natural parents who had participated in classes were invited to attend a closing graduation ceremony. The 10 who had attended at least five sessions received certificates from the Community College District, presented by Mrs. John Douglas, Vice President of the Social Services Commission.

Other guests included agency administrative staff members, the social workers who had selected the parents for the classes and foster parent teacher trainees. The ceremony was followed by a luncheon prepared by agency staff members.

The parents were eager to continue with the classes. A new series was started but, unfortunately, two days after the first session a city strike was called. No public transportation was available in most areas of San Francisco; some parents walked as far as six miles to come to the second class.

The strike was a prolonged one and since only four parents either had access to a car or lived within easy walking distance it was decided to suspend classes until September. In the meantime, four parents who were able to come to the office decided to form a Committee for Natural Parents. The committee met weekly with Mary K. and I was included whenever the parents felt that I was needed.

As its first project, a flyer was prepared by the Committee, announcing its formation through the Department of Social Services.

"We are a group of parents whose children have been placed in foster homes and are going through the process of getting them back . . ." the flyer read.

"Our purpose is to help other parents whose children have been placed in foster homes to get them back as soon as possible and to give assistance and support to parents immediately after their children are returned.

"We also wish to give attention to any problems concerning foster homes and parents, suspected child abuse, the rights of the natural parents, etc."

The flyer concluded by suggesting that those who needed help or were interested in attending classes should contact one of the four parents whose names and telephone numbers were listed, along with the words:

WE ARE HERE TO HELP!!! NEW MEMBERS WELCOME!!!

The agency reproduced the flyer, which was distributed to agency staff with a memo from me noting that the committee would appreciate it "if you would distribute the attached flyers to any of the natural parents in your caseload who would benefit from attending the classes or who might need and be able to use the support of the Committee." Parents also distributed the flyers.

Almost immediately the committee was presented with two opportunities to assist parents who had participated in the classes. The first occurred when one of the women, unable to cope with both the new changes in her life and the problems presented by her 4-year-old daughter who had been in foster care since she was six months old, decided to relinquish her instead of continuing with plans for her return. While none of the committee members had considered this decision themselves, they understood why Katy had made the choice and their support, affection and concern were a source of comfort and strength to her. Later, when another woman was seriously injured when she was struck by a car, two of the committee members immediately contacted the agency to see what needed to be done to prevent Joan's child from returning to foster care even temporarily. They kept in touch with Joan's boyfriend, helped her child to visit her regularly in the hospital, and kept the agency informed about what they were doing for Joan and her family.

At the request of the committee and Mary K., a meeting with agency staff was arranged. Most of the staff members who attended were those who did not have parents in their caseloads who were attending the classes. All were delighted with the committee's presentation. They were impressed by the manner in which committee members answered questions, including those which were fairly provocative. As a result of this meeting, several parents were referred for enrollment in the next series of classes.

Last June the Advisory Committee sponsored a one-day conference and the Committee for Natural Parents was asked to put on a workshop. Although they were apprehensive, the members agreed to do so. The workshop was well-attended by social workers and foster parents from 10 counties in northern California. Mary K. and I were proud and delighted. It was hard to believe that in not quite five months these four people had come so far. In January, one mother had been overwhelmed by the problems she was having with her 7-year-old daughter who had been at home with her only a short time. By the time of the workshop, she was able to present a synopsis of laws related to the rights of natural parents. She had gone to the law library, selected the pertinent code sections and prepared a summary. Initially she appeared to be a bit nervous but she quickly relaxed and made a presentation worthy of a veteran workshop panelist.

A few participants from the other counties were defensive and challenged the panelists. All but one of the parents handled this beautifully. Louise, the one who responded angrily, was going through the legal process for return of her children, and she was extremely anxious. She seemed to realize that she was not responding well, however, and, after one hostile and argumentative reply, she confined her responses to those comments and questions which were presented objectively.

Our new series of classes, which began with about 15 parents in mid-October, were planned with the help of Rosemary Darden, Director of Parent Programs of the Community College District. After the first eight sessions, we hope to continue with another series.

Our experience certainly proved that problems affect learning ability. Because we were dealing with adults, not children, we were shocked at first when we were faced with a group whose needs were so great that they were unable to absorb anything new or to refresh their memories about facts they had learned earlier. We had selected those we had felt to be our strongest parents, but we had forgotten that they were the strongest among a group who had been severely battered physically and emotionally throughout most of their lives. Since it was apparent from the initial session that no progress would be made until we dealt with some of their problems, we lost no time in proceeding in this direction. If we had not done so our classes would not have been successful. I believe that the results justified our providing such small touches as the coffee and donuts at each session and the graduation ceremony and luncheon.

I realize that I have stressed the needs and problems of our parent group. I believe that most groups of parents whose children have been placed by court order would present similar difficulties for anyone who is attempting to set up and conduct classes with them. We hope that others can learn from our experience. Perhaps the parent-formed committee is the most significant result, because it reflects the gains made by parents in all areas, not only in learning and in parenting skills.

## NOTES

1. A missing ingredient of this article is the input of Mary K. Jones, the master teacher and planner of our foster parent and natural parent training classes. She and I were making plans to collaborate on the article when the cancer which Mary K. had fought so valiantly for almost two years gained momentum. Mary K. was hospitalized last July and died within three weeks.
2. Five basic rules were posted on the classroom walls, including "One person speaks at a time and is really heard"; "Every person listens with care . . . ," ". . . no side conversations . . . Side conversation can mean 'I don't care what you're saying'"; "Differences of opinion are welcome . . ."; and "A person has the right to remain silent."

# Part IX
# Special Aspects

# Part IX

## Special Aspects

Two aspects of child welfare that have become especially prominent in recent years are worker burnout and parent-child visitation. The authors in this section contributed original articles on these topics.

Although much has been written about the phenomenon of burnout, authors have only lately addressed the many stresses confronting the child welfare practitioner or the impact of worker burnout on clients. In Chapter 29, Bertsche examines this phenomenon within a public child welfare context, especially as its relates to parents of children in foster care.

Viewing burnout as a multidimensional problem, the author defines it as a dynamic condition caused by the interaction of a variety of factors, including excessive physical and emotional stress in the work setting, organizational variables such as bureaucratic constraints, and qualities of the client-worker relationship such as the extreme dependence of some parents. Noting the frequently adverse effect of worker burnout on parents, Bertsche delineates a variety of strategies to prevent or ameliorate burnout at the individual and organizational levels.

This volume ends on a positive note with Chapter 30, in which White concentrates on the advantages of parent-child visiting in foster care. Citing evidence from her own research, as well as other studies,[1] the author underlines the powerful role of visiting in achieving permanent plans for children in foster care.

Especially useful is her discussion of the problems and benefits of visiting as perceived by parents, children, foster parents, and social workers. On the basis of these findings, White offers thoughtful implications for agency policy, practice, and training of child welfare personnel. She emphasizes in

[1]See Fanshel's chapter on visiting elsewhere in this volume.

particular that the visiting experience can be effectively used as a natural opportunity to provide social services that meet the developmental needs of children and promote the competence of parents.

## SUGGESTIONS FOR FURTHER READING

Daley, Michael R., "'Burnout': Smoldering Problem in Protective Services," *Social Work*, 24:5 (September 1979): 375–79.

Fanshel, David, "Parental Visiting of Children in Foster Care: Key to Discharge?" *Social Service Review*, 49:4 (December 1975): 493–515. (Reprinted elsewhere in this volume.)

Fanshel, David and Shinn, Eugene, *Children in Foster Care: A Longitudinal Investigation*, New York: Columbia University Press, 1978. (Especially pp. 85–110.)

Maluccio, Anthony N., "Promoting Client and Worker Competence in Child Welfare," in *Social Welfare Forum—1980*, New York: Columbia University Press, 1981.

Maslach, Christine, "Job Burnout: How People Cope," *Public Welfare*, 36:2 (Spring 1978): 56–58.

White, Mary S., "The Role of Parental Visiting in Permanency Planning for Children," in *Social Welfare Forum—1980*, New York: Columbia University Press, 1981.

# 29

# Worker Burnout in Child Welfare and Its Effects on Biological Parents

ANNE VANDEBERG BERTSCHE

At 5:45 P.M. a young child welfare worker sits at her cluttered desk staring at the ringing phone. The office is empty—no one would know whether or not she answers. Guilt rises in her, and she abruptly picks up the receiver. It is a young mentally retarded mother asking if she can visit tonight with her four-year-old son who lives across town in a foster home. The worker answers coldly, "You are not one of my cases. Your caseworker will be out of the office the rest of the week. Call her next week."

In the past, this worker had energy, enthusiasm, and great concern for clients. Burned out, the same worker appears to have changed her entire philosophical approach, rationalizing that "hand holding" or "chasing clients" is detrimental and that sitting back and waiting for clients to demonstrate initiative is, in fact, in the client's best interest.

It has long been acknowledged that child welfare workers function in a uniquely stressful environment. A classic in child welfare literature, Ner

---

An original article prepared for this volume. An extended version appears in *Social Work Practice with Parents of Children in Foster Care: A Handbook*, by Charles R. Horejsi, Anne V. Bertsche, and Frank W. Clark, Springfield, Ill.: Charles C Thomas, 1981.

Littner's "The Strains and Stresses on the Child Welfare Worker" [1956], chronicles the emotional stresses confronting the worker.

The difficulty in working hour after hour with abused and neglected children is compounded by the necessity to intervene with often-hostile parents. In addition, workers must operate within a bureaucratic structure that offers little support and is beset with rules and regulations that may hinder their effectiveness. A former child protective services worker writes:

> From champion and protector of children's rights to tranquilized victim, the child protective service worker's ability to make sound decisions dies under the cancer-like frustrations of ever increasing caseloads (the better you do, the more difficult cases you get), insensitive administration (you're doing a good job, but document it with these forms so we can justify keeping your position), the demands of clients (you promised me that I could have my child back!), and failing physical and mental health.
> Justifiable anger properly aimed at the impossibility of the job, lack of community and agency support, and negative feedback from involuntary and hostile clients turns inward and jeopardizes the worker's competency as a social worker and human being. [Lee, 1979]

Although much has appeared in the literature concerning the phenomenon of burnout, few authors have addressed the multiple stresses faced by the child welfare worker and fewer still have discussed the impact of worker burnout on clients. This article is an exploration of the burnout syndrome in child welfare workers, especially as it relates to parents of children in foster care.

## DEFINITIONS

Burnout is not a new phenomenon, nor is it limited to workers in the social work profession. Job-related stress is a part of nearly all occupations [Selye, 1956]. Maslach [1976], a leader in the study of burnout in human services, conducted extensive research on the dynamics of burnout and found that all professional groups studied (poverty lawyers, physicians, prison personnel, psychiatrists in mental hospitals, and psychiatric nurses) experienced some degree of burnout. However, burnout has become a pedestrian term in the human services, used to describe anything from simple worker fatigue to total system dysfunction.

Freudenberger [1975] described burnout as the exhaustion that results from excessive demands on energy, strength, and resources. Maslach [1978a] further refined this definition and described burnout as the emotional exhaustion that results from the stress of interpersonal contact in the helping professions when the worker is unable to meet expectations for job performance. Pines and Maslach [1978] asserted: "Burnout can be defined as a syndrome of physical and emotional exhaustion, involving the developing of negative self-concept, negative job attitudes and loss of concern and feeling for clients."

## THE STAGES OF BURNOUT

Daley [1979] conceptualizes burnout as a dynamic force with various developmental stages: "Burnout might be defined as a reaction to job-related stress that varies in intensity and duration of the stress itself. It may be manifested in workers becoming emotionally detached from their jobs and may ultimately lead them to leave their jobs altogether." Daley also offers a useful adaption of Costella and Zalkind's [1963] stress model as it relates to burnout. Accordingly, environmental stressors interact with aspects of the individual's personality to produce tensions that may vary in intensity and duration. In this context, burnout can be seen as having three stages:

*Alarm stage:* The initial stage of reaction to increased stress is characterized by an emergency mobilization of the body's defenses. This often results in an increased striving to maintain the earlier level of performance.

*Resistance stage:* If unchecked, the alarm stage may progress into the resistance stage in which the individual's energies are constantly exerted to manage stress.

*Exhaustion:* Unrelieved exhaustion from continual energy demands leads to breakdown in the individual's adaptive capability. Daley's use of this three-stage stress model allows one to view burnout not as a static state (e.g., "I am burned out—I must leave the organization") but as a dynamic, changing state open to assessment, prevention, and amelioration.

## THE SIGNS OF BURNOUT

The signs of burnout have been well documented and researched; indeed, Maslach [1976, 1977] and Freudenberger [1975] have identified the various components. The author's experience in working with burned-out practitioners suggests that these signs can be viewed in context with the three stages mentioned above. Table 1 presents the author's conceptualization of the relationships between the stages and signs of burnout. Although these relationships tend to be consistent, variance can occur. For example, termination of the job may occur in the alarm stage, but it is almost inevitable in the exhaustion stage. Early signs of worker burnout may include physical complaints such as headaches, colds, and fatigue. Low worker morale, another early sign, is particularly important to recognize as burnout; even in its early manifestations it can spread throughout the agency: "Burnout has a contaminating, depressing effect on the atmosphere of the agency, and one worker's burnout behavior intensified tendencies toward burnout in others" [Kadushin, 1980:693].

Some early signs of burnout may seem paradoxical. Increased time spent on the job or overconfidence may appear to be dedication and increased productivity, but can also be an early signal of worker burnout. Watch for the deceptiveness in these signals.

Signs of burnout likely to surface during the resistance stage involve the loss of concern for the people with whom one works. Workers develop a cynical and dehumanized perception of clients. Stereotypes—"the alcoholic," "the schizo," or "my case"—are used to label clients. Workers lose

**TABLE 1**
**Stages and Signs of Burnout**

| **Signs** | **Stages** | | |
|---|---|---|---|
| | **Alarm Stage** | **Resistance Stage** | **Exhaustion** |
| Physical ailments (headache, fatigue, insomnia, etc.) | X | X | X |
| Low morale | X | X | X |
| Overconfidence | X | | |
| Increased time on job | X | | |
| Loss of concern and feeling for client | | X | X |
| Negative self-concept | | X | |
| Dehumanizing clients | | X | X |
| Feeling of being "locked in" | | X | |
| Lowered job performance and productivity | | X | X |
| Increased use and abuse of drugs | | X | X |
| Absenteeism | | X | X |
| Physical and emotional exhaustion | | | X |
| Termination of job | | | X |
| Depression | | | X |

respect, sympathy, and concern for their clients and clients are seen as somehow deserving of their problems and responsible ultimately for their own victimization [Ryan, 1971]. One worker describes this loss of caring for clients as the "if you have a dime, call someone who cares" phase of burnout.

In the exhaustion stage of burnout, the worker is emotionally and physically fatigued and faces a choice of either leaving the job or breaking down.

## DETACHMENT TECHNIQUES

Ironically, many of these signs of burnout may have originated in necessary and helpful coping techniques. Maslach [1977] discussed several detachment techniques used by helping professionals to reduce the amount of personal stress in their relationship with clients. The techniques include:

*Semantics of Detachment*—using terms that objectify people. For example, "the poor," "my caseload."

*Intellectualization*—recasting situations in less personal terms. For example, an abusive mother blames the child for everything: "He's a rotten kid." The worker might pull back and examine the situation more analytically: "She doesn't mean it, she's just in the denial phase of separation."

*Situational Compartmentalization*—workers attempt to make sharp distinctions between their job and personal life. Workers do not talk shop at home or talk to co-workers about personal matters.

*Psychological Withdrawal*—workers try to minimize psychological involvement in stress situations, for example, avoiding eye contact, sitting behind a desk, cutting down length of interviews.

*Social Techniques*—workers turn to colleagues for advice and comfort, joking (e.g., sick humor).

These techniques can be functional for workers but they become dysfunctional when they begin to serve the worker's self-interest at the expense of the client. Workers then become petty bureaucrats hiding behind rules and regulations.

Conceptualizations of burnout are varied and complex. However, the author's experience in working with public social service employees requires a more comprehensive definition of burnout: Burnout is a dynamic condition caused by excessive physical and emotional stress on the individual that results in worker exhaustion, negative job attitudes, and ultimately, reduced service effectiveness. Further, stressors to the individual are not limited to client interactions but include organizational variables, worker style, and individual responses to stressors.

## SOURCES OF STRESS

Stressors on individual workers come from a variety of sources. Although it is acknowledged that the emotional strain of working with people who have problems is great, organizational life is also a source of stress for workers. Coping with rules and regulations, paperwork, crowded working conditions, and intra-office conflict intensify symptoms of burnout. [Bertsche, et al., 1979].

No two individual workers will react identically to a specific stressor. For example, a particularly difficult confrontation with a hostile parent may involve a stress reaction in one worker, whereas another worker may not perceive this situation as unusually stressful and will react accordingly. Worker style and coping ability must then be addressed in discussing sources of stress. Personal expectations and individual assertiveness are only two of the variables that determine how an individual may react to a given stressor.

## STRESSORS IN WORKER—BIOLOGICAL PARENT RELATIONSHIPS

*Role Conflicts*. Dealing with foster parents and other professionals may at times be a source of stress for workers. Certainly, the worker-client relationship with the abused or neglected child can be tremendously stressful at times. But one of the most trying stresses encountered by the worker in the relationship with the parent is the basic contradiction in the prescribed roles of investigator and helper. In many agencies the same worker who investigates a report of child abuse or neglect must also provide followup services to this same family [Drews and Hare].

In addition to the roles of investigator and therapist, the worker is also called upon to perform the roles of advocate, broker, mediator, and case manager. The worker who cannot reconcile the demands of these often conflicting roles will undoubtedly experience overwhelming stress.

*Diverse Clientele*. Although all parents who need social services have serious problems that preclude their children from remaining in their home, the problems may range from acute mental illness to alcoholism, mental retardation, or chronic illness. This heterogeneity may be frustrating to workers who see their knowledge and skills as limited and feel unable to meet the needs of such a diverse clientele.

*Lack of Progress*. The likelihood of change in a client's situation is also related to burnout. The perceived unwillingness or inability to change on the part of parents may be particularly stressful to the worker. The lack of change may be related to the nature of a client's problem (e.g., chronic illness) or to unrealistic expectations by the worker. Sometimes, however, this lack of change by the worker is seen as failure in performing his/her job or he/she may attribute cause of failure to the client's weaknesses [Maslach, 1978a].

*Client Dependency.* Another stressful element of the worker-client relationship is the extreme dependency of some parents. Clients of bureaucracies are often conditioned to be passive and dependent. As the recipient of help, they cast the worker into the role of authority figure, expecting him/her to respond to every query. Although passive clients are more manageable and less likely than others to resist actions of the agency, Maslach [1978b] warns that this passive-dependent client stance can be a "double-edged sword."

*Negative Feedback.* Positive feedback from clients to workers is rare. The hostile and sometimes threatening parent can be a genuine source of stress for the protective services worker. Whether the anger and hostility are a result of their own sense of guilt and failure, or are aimed at the bureaucracy for poor services, the worker usually bears the brunt of the client's anger.

## ORGANIZATIONAL SOURCES OF STRESS

Child welfare workers are required daily to negotiate the stresses and constraints of organizational life. Although few social workers have been trained in the skills necessary to cope with bureaucratic life, all must eventually develop some competence in this area in order to survive and achieve service delivery goals.

The stresses of organizational life can be a primary source of burnout for workers. Poor supervision, large caseloads, intra-office conflict, and role ambiguity are only a few of the sources of stress. Just as organizations contribute to worker burnout, worker burnout also affects organizations. High turnover, low productivity, and absenteeism result in lowered organizational effectiveness with clients and constitute a major drain on scarce agency resources for recruiting and training new workers or revitalizing older workers.

*Poor Supervision.* Supervision in many social service agencies is grossly inadequate. Seniority, a time-honored principle in organizations, often results in promotion of the "oldest" worker rather than the "best" to supervisory rank. It is not uncommon for a worker experienced only in adult services or developmental disabilities to be promoted to foster care supervisor simply on the basis of seniority. In addition, few supervisors have had formal training in theories and techniques of supervision. Consequently, it is not uncommon for a new worker to be supervised by a "survivor" who has had little or no experience in child welfare and who has little knowledge of the dynamics of supervision. Also, a supervisor who is uncomfortable with or inadequate to his/her responsibilities creates stress for other workers, regardless of their personal strengths [Thompson in Glicken and Katz, 1979].

*Size of Caseloads*. Large caseloads are a constant source of stress for most workers. Few agencies adhere to standards recommended by national groups such as the Child Welfare League of America and the American Public Welfare Association to limit the caseload to the number of cases that can be handled realistically by workers. Although caseloads continue to increase, budget constraints do not allow for additional staff. Research findings reveal that the ratio of clients to staff is a factor in burnout. As the number of clients increases, the worker experiences more cognitive, sensory, and emotional overload [Maslach, 1977].

*Nature of Caseloads*. The crisis-oriented nature of their caseloads compounds the problems of large caseloads for child welfare workers. The immediacy of a new case, or an old case with a new crisis, often takes priority. Dealing continually with clients in acute crises, the worker seldom has time to do more than "check up" on those clients who, although their problems may be serious, place few demands on the worker. This, unfortunately, is the situation for many biological parents.

*Lack of Support*. Lack of feedback and recognition are major sources of organizational stress. As mentioned earlier, clients seldom give workers positive feedback. The organization itself is not designed to provide feedback to workers. "Complex organizations are notoriously inefficient distributors of appreciation and recognition" [Pruger, 1973:29]. Not finding support from clients or the system, workers often turn to their colleagues for support and feedback. If support is not found there, the worker may experience feelings of isolation and added stress.

*Red Tape*. Red tape, characterized by voluminous paper work, is often decried by workers in public social service agencies. Not understanding why paper work is necessary for agency functioning, the worker often sees it as an unavoidable burden that diminishes precious time that might be spent with a client.

*Lack of Resources*. Lack of resources, particularly in rural areas, is often a source of stress for workers. In child welfare, the need for appropriate supportive services is especially acute. The parents whose children are repeatedly removed from the home because the parents did not receive supportive services is a constant source of discouragement for the worker.

## INDIVIDUAL WORKER CHARACTERISTICS AS SOURCES OF STRESS

Many factors unique to each worker may exacerbate feelings of burnout. Personal and professional values, personal needs, job expectations, and even early childhood experiences may be sources of stress.

If the worker meets the needs and demands of the organization and the organization meets the needs of the individual, then there is "fit" between individual and organization. When the individual's skill does not meet the organization's demands or the organization cannot meet the individual's needs, stress is likely to occur.

*Lack of Knowledge and Skills*. The knowledge and skills needed by the worker in working with parents are varied and many. Knowledge of child development, family functioning, theories of separation, legal rights and responsibilities, cultural and ethnic differences in families, as well as knowledge of specific conditions such as alcoholism, schizophrenia, mental retardation, and other handicapping conditions, is essential if the worker is to meet the demands of the job. Skills needed by the worker include communication and assessment, community resource utilization, counseling, court referral, and values clarification. Without these, making complex decisions daily will undoubtedly generate stress. This is unfortunately the case for many workers who have, at best, a generalist education in social work but who are expected to meet the job demands of the specialized field of child welfare.

*Personal Attributes*. Personal attributes that draw people to social work, such as sensitivity and capacity for empathy may contribute to burnout because these same attributes cause individuals to be more vulnerable to job-related emotional stress [Reid, 1979].

*Work Expectations*. Another dimension of individual characteristics that may induce burnout is the kind of fulfillment an individual expects from work. Some expect that their work will provide them with autonomy, intellectual stimulation, personal fulfillment, and appreciation from clients and the organization. Further, they expect that their training has equipped them to handle any situation that may arise. These expectations are influenced by what is called the "professional mystique," in which the individual imputes to the job positive qualities that may or may not be based in reality [Cherniss et al., in Reid, 1979]. When the worker recognizes that the reality of the job differs from his/her expectations, the disillusionment may be stressful.

People often choose a particular job or profession on the basis of how well it meets their own needs. A desire to work with children and help society often motivates young people to become child welfare workers. However, once on the job, they find that their personal needs and values in working with children are not met by the organization. Only a part of their job involves direct work with clients. Organizational and bureaucratic roles require much of their time and energy. Daley [1979] states that protective service workers spend probably only 25% of their time in direct contact with clients.

## EFFECTS OF BURNOUT ON BIOLOGICAL PARENTS

Today, reliance on family and friends during times of crisis is often not feasible and people must turn to strangers for help with their personal problems. The bureaucracies designed to meet these needs have grown unwieldy. Although staffed in large part by caring professionals, bureaucracies are inadequate surrogates for loved ones. Faced with long lines and red tape, clients have criticized services as demeaning and dehumanizing. Most workers try hard to counteract the negative effects of bureaucracy, but the burned-out worker augments them and may destroy the already tenuous relationship between the source and recipient of help.

## THE SEPARATION PROCESS

Interviews conducted by the author with both workers and parents reveal that consistency is essential to the successful worker-parent relationship. The separation process, in particular, from the decision to place the child until the child returns home, requires consistent follow-through by the worker. This is typically a time of crisis for the parents. This crisis period is usually very short, lasting from one week to one month and it is an opportunity for effective workers to support the parents and assist them in defining and evaluating the situation. It is essential at this time to mobilize the parent's crisis-generated energies for positive action but workers who are experiencing burnout may not take advantage of this opportunity. Further, burned-out workers who have distanced themselves from clients may compound the guilt and anguish felt by the parents by being judgmental and responding to them as stereotypes. Denial of responsibility by parents, which is natural during this early phase of separation, may be viewed by cynical burned-out workers as proof that the parents are unwilling or unable to change and that further intervention would be futile. Thus, the process of remediation of the problems that precipitated the separation is aborted, and the chance of the children returning home is diminished.

During the phases following the initial separation, effective workers continue active outreach with the parents. Referral to other resources may be necessary. Visiting between parents and child must be arranged, progress monitored, and emotional support of the parents maintained. Burned-out workers, hiding behind rules and regulations, may be inflexible about visiting. Visits arranged according to the convenience of the workers, rather than the welfare of the parents and children, may result in frustration and possible further weakening of familial bonds. If burned-out workers terminate their job during this time, parents are left in mid-air until a new worker is assigned. Establishing a relationship with the new worker, adjusting to his or her style, and often backtracking to bring the worker up to date may reopen old wounds for the parents as well as lose valuable time.

## STRATEGIES FOR PREVENTING AND REDUCING BURNOUT

Both individuals and organizations can take specific steps to prevent or ameliorate burnout: it is neither inevitable nor irreversible. Just as the source of stress may vary from worker to worker, so too the remedies selected from those offered below should address the specific needs of the individual or agency. For example, attempting to improve the client-worker relationship will only result in frustration if office conditions are chaotic and deny privacy for the worker and client. It is, therefore, imperative that the true source of stress be recognized so that an appropriate strategy is employed.

## INDIVIDUAL SOLUTIONS

The first and perhaps the most important step in dealing with burnout is recognizing the early signs of stress in an individual, which have been described earlier, assessing its sources, and taking appropriate measures to prevent burnout from developing into a more serious stage.

*Time-Out*. One way the individual worker may deal with pressures at work is to withdraw physically from the stressful situation in order to recoup emotional strength. Withdrawal in its positive form is known as time-out.

Time-outs may take several forms. The most common [Maslach, 1977; Pines and Maslach, 1978] occurs when the worker chooses to do some less stressful, nonpersonal work (e.g., paperwork) while other workers temporarily cover the caseload. Other forms of time-out may include taking a planned "mental health" day away from the job to recharge one's energy or going to a foster home and playing with the children. Using time-outs is a positive coping technique in that good client care can be maintained while the worker gets an emotional breather. The critical element here is that the worker's withdrawal does not come at the expense of the client.

*Peer Support*. Seeking peer support is another way that workers can successfully cope with job stress. Burnout may be exacerbated for the worker who feels isolated and believes he/she is the only one who is experiencing the symptoms of burnout. Support groups may be as informal as what one agency calls a "hug club" where a worker feels free to go to a fellow worker for reassurance and emotional solace, or as formal as regularly scheduled support groups established by the agency. Maslach [1978a] reports that burnout seems to be lower under such formal or informal arrangements.

*Assertiveness Training*. Assertiveness training can help workers who have difficulty saying "no" to excessive demands from clients, supervisors, and the community. It is a simple technique that may prevent much unnecessary stress. The assertive worker may also encourage clients to be more independent, reducing the stress of client dependence.

*Time Management*. For many child welfare workers a major source of stress is not enough time to do too many tasks. The Pareto Principle [Schular, 1979] asserts that most people spend 80% of their time performing duties that relate to only 20% of the total job results. In other words, many workers spend most of their time on the wrong (or less important) duties. These workers are also faced with doing the important 80% of their job in only 20% of the total time. Understanding one's own skills, needs, abilities, and job duties assists the worker in conserving and controlling valuable time.

The strategies mentioned thus far deal with coping with stress rather than actively changing the source of stress. Most line workers believe changing organizational sources of stress are beyond their ability. Inadequate supervision policies and procedures that hinder service delivery and poor working conditions are facts of life for many workers who feel powerless to effect change. A growing body of literature suggests that line level workers can indeed accomplish organizational change (see, for example, Horejsi et al., 1977; Patti, 1978; Patti and Resnick, 1972; Weissman, 1973). Workers skilled in organizational change techniques can effectively eliminate many sources of organizational stress not only for themselves but for future workers.

## ORGANIZATIONAL SOLUTIONS

Many recommendations for reducing worker burnout emphasize organizational remedies [Daley, 1979; Glicken and Katz, 1979; Kahn, 1978; Maslach, 1977, 1978a, b]. They range from reducing the client/staff ratio to inservice training and career ladders. Organizations must be sensitive to worker burnout and begin to recognize their role in preventing and reducing burnout. It is not only the human thing to do but the only rational alternative to organizational deterioration.

*Reduced Client Hours*. Reducing time spent on the job or in direct contact with clients can help prevent stress from becoming unmanageable. This can be accomplished by shortening the work hours through allowance for a larger variety of worker activities, and by employment of more part-time professionals. Reducing the number of caseload days a year by special leaves, sanctioned mental health days, attendance at conferences, and so on, should be viewed not as a reward but as an available way to replenish the energies of the depleted worker. Reducing the number of years of concentrated client contact may be accomplished through implementing career ladders or tapered retirement plans [Kahn, 1978].

*Role of the Supervisor*. Adequately trained and supportive supervisors are essential in preventing worker burnout. Supervisors should avoid assignment of difficult cases to new workers or workers who are showing signs of burnout and encourage the use of time-outs, mental health retreats, and peer support groups for workers. Fostering open lines of communication between supervisors and staff members can prevent the isolation felt by many workers in the process of burnout [Daley, 1979]. The teaching supervisor can provide the individualized training in knowledge and skills that are often lacking in the new worker. Especially important in child welfare, supervisors can share decision making with workers in cases that are particularly stressful. A plan for case sharing or case rotation of difficult clients can be implemented and allowances made for specialization among the staff. For example, a worker may not feel so overextended or overwhelmed when handling only investigation or a certain type of caseload. Finally, supervisors can support their workers through respect, encouragement, and appreciation of the tremendous pressures they face.

*Job Advancement*. Most jobs in child welfare are entry level positions that require little previous experience. Although there may be a few salary and rank advancements within the caseworker level, most workers will not advance unless they choose supervisory or administrative positions. Many skilled workers choose to remain at the caseworker level rather than advance to supervision, in which they have no interest or training. The development of career ladders would provide incentives for workers who would prefer to remain in direct service. Advanced caseworker positions should carry increased salary and status rewards that would allow workers to remain in the agency. The single remedy of establishing career ladders may do much to retain agency personnel.

*Inservice Training.* Many child welfare workers come to the job without appropriate education or experience. Inservice training and opportunities for continuing education should be supported by agencies through carefully planned sequential training for new workers and advanced specialty courses for older workers.

## REFERENCES


1. Bertsche, Anne; Bernau, Elly; Deaton, Robert; and Vestre, John. "A Training Model for Preventing and Reducing Staff Burnout in Public Social Service Personnel." Paper presented at the Annual Program Meeting of the Council on Social Work Education, Boston, MA, March 1979.
2. Cherniss, C.; Egnatios, E.; Wacker, S.; and O'Dowd, B. "The Professional Mystique and Burnout in Public Sector Professionals." In Kenneth E. Reid, "The Management of Job Related Stress in Social Work." Paper presented at the Sixth Professional Symposium, National Association of Social Workers, San Antonio, November 1979.
3. Costello, W., and Zalkind, S., eds. Psychology in Administration: A Research Orientation. Englewood Cliffs, NJ: Prentice-Hall, 1963.
4. Daley, Michael. "Burnout: Smoldering Problem in Protective Services." Social Work 24 (September 1979): 375–379.
5. Drews, Kay, and Hare, Isadora. "Worker Burnout in Child Protective Services." National Professional Resource Center on Child Abuse and Neglect, NASW, APWA (undated).
6. Freudenberger, H.J. "The Staff Burn-Out Syndrome in Alternative Institutions." Psychotherapy: Theory, Research and Practice 12 (Spring 1975): 73–82.
7. Glicken, Morley D., and Katz, Susan. "Undoing Bureaucratic Pathology: Responding to Worker Burnout in Public Settings." Paper presented at the National Association of Social Workers Professional Symposium, San Antonio, November 1979.
8. Horejsi, John E.; Walz, Thomas; and Connolly, Patrick. Working in Welfare: Survival Through Positive Action. Iowa City: University of Iowa, 1977.
9. Kadushin, Alfred. Child Welfare Services (3rd ed.). New York: Macmillan Publishing Co., Inc., 1980.

10. Kahn, Robert. "Prevention and Remedies." Public Welfare 36 (Spring 1978): 61–63.
11. Lee, Dalton, "Staying Alive in Child Protective Services: Survival Skills for Worker and Supervisor," Part I. Arete 5 (Spring 1979): 196.
12. Littner, Ner. The Strains and Stresses on the Child Welfare Worker. New York: Child Welfare League of America, 1956.
13. Maslach, Christina. "Burned-Out." Human Behavior 5 (September 1976): 16–22.
14. ———. "Burn-out: A Social Psychological Analysis." Paper presented at the annual convention of the American Psychological Association. San Francisco, August 1977.
15. ———. "Job Burnout: How People Cope," Public Welfare 36 (Spring 1978(a)): 56–58.
16. ———. "The Client Role in Staff Burn-Out." Journal of Social Issues 34 (Fall 1978(b)): 111–123.
17. Patti, Rino J. "Organizational Resistance and Change: A View from Below." Social Service Review 48 (September 1978): 367–383.
18. Patti, Rino J., and Resnick, Herman. "Changing the Agency from Within." Social Work 17 (July 1972): 48–57.
19. Pines, Ayala, and Maslach, Christina. "Characteristics of Staff Burnout in Mental Health Settings." Hospital and Community Psychiatry 29 (April 1978): 233–237.
20. Pruger, Robert. "The Good Bureaucrat." Social Work 18 (July 1973): 26–32.
21. Reid, Kenneth E. "The Management of Job-Related Stress in Social Work." Paper presented at the Sixth Professional Symposium, National Association of Social Workers, San Antonio, November 1979.
22. Ryan, W. Blaming the Victim. New York: Pantheon Books, 1971.
23. Schular, Randall, S. "Managing Stress Means Managing Time." Personnel Journal 58 (December 1979): 851–854.
24. Seyle, Hans. The Stress of Life. New York: McGraw-Hill Book Co., 1956.
25. Weissman, Harry. Overcoming Mismanagement in the Human Service Professions. New York: Jossey-Bass Publishers, 1973.

# 30

# Promoting Parent-Child Visiting in Foster Care: Continuing Involvement within a Permanency Planning Framework

MARY S. WHITE

The full potential of parental visiting in foster care to meet the developmental needs of the child and the service needs of his or her family has not yet been realized. Although parental visiting is receiving increased attention and its significance is recognized, we need to know more about the many factors that help shape the actual visiting experience.

The immediate impetus for addressing this subject is three-fold: 1) research demonstrates that visiting is the best predictor of discharge from foster care, and that maintaining contact is critically important for the well-being of the child; 2) even though permanency planning for children is a national goal, it is far from being realized for every child in care; 3) in

---

Original article prepared for this volume. Adapted in part from Mary S. White, "The Role of Parental Visiting in Permanency Planning for Children," *Social Welfare Forum*, 1980. New York: Columbia University Press, 1981.
This work was supported by Child Welfare Services Training Grant TEMN 9038 T21, U.S. Department of Health and Human Services, Office of Human Development Services, Administration for Children, Youth & Families.

response to the problems of prolonged foster care and inappropriate placements, there is a new awareness of the necessity of working more effectively with each child's family.

Because research strongly suggests the need to examine further the dynamics in parental visiting, this chapter is an examination of the role of visiting in working with families within a permanency context and contains suggested guidelines for practice. The premise for promoting parent-child visiting is based upon observations from a recent study conducted at Hennepin County Community Services, Minneapolis, Minnesota [White, 1981], as well as related research.

## RESEARCH FINDINGS

Parental visiting is the best indicator of the long-term fate of children in foster care. In their five-year longitudinal investigation of 624 foster care children in New York City, Fanshel and Shinn [1978] found that children who were visited frequently were almost twice as likely to be discharged as those children who were not visited or whose parents visited only minimally. Sixty-six percent of children who received no visiting during their first year in placement were still in care five years later. Although the association between visiting and discharge decreased over time, there was still a relationship even after five years.

Only a modest amount (23%) of the variance in the frequency of visiting was accounted for by the variables utilized in the investigation, including age of child, number of children in placement, ethnicity, reasons for placement, evaluation of mother, and caseworker contact rate. Further work needs to be done to illuminate what Fanshel has called the unknown factors that affect the frequency and quality of visiting. In interpreting the results of his investigation, Fanshel concludes:

> Like the frequent monitoring of body-temperature information for assessing the health of patients in hospitals, the visitation of children should be carefully scrutinized as the best indicator we have concerning the long-term fate of children in care. [Fanshel, 1975:513].

### Effect of Visiting on Children

Research also shows a relationship between visiting and the child's sense of well-being and adjustment. In the Fanshel-Shinn investigation, visiting proved to be a relevant variable in the analysis of changes shown by I.Q.

scores of the children and in their personal and social adjustments. Although visiting did not emerge uniformly as a significant predictor of changes in the children, Fanshel and Shinn were impressed nevertheless with the frequency with which significant changes were accounted for by parental visiting. In comparisons between frequently and infrequently visited children, those who were visited more frequently showed greater gains in I.Q. scores, in emotional adjustment tests, and in Child Behavioral Characteristics (CBC) [Fanshel and Shinn, 1978:486–487].

In Weinstein's study of 61 children in foster care [Weinstein, 1960], the average well-being of those who were visited was higher than those who were not visited. Weinstein speculates that unvisited children may develop feelings of being unwanted and, therefore, may feel inferior and unworthy. Eisenberg reported on 499 foster children for whom psychiatric consultation was requested in Baltimore [Eisenberg, 1962]. These children received few visits from their parents and had experienced multiple placements.

## Effect of Visiting on Parents

Visiting appears to have positive effects on parents as well as children. The Jenkins-Norman study [1975:65–69], a major component of the longitudinal investigation in New York City, reported that frequent visits were associated with positive changes in parental feelings toward the placement. Parents who visited frequently believed that they felt closer to their children since placement. Moreover, a large number of those who visited infrequently stated that they did not know how to arrange the visit and the agency did not provide help or that agency policy did not allow visiting. In conjunction with the same New York City investigation, evidence was found that the mother's visiting pattern accounted for a significant degree of variance in the improvement of her status [Shaprio, 1976:104].

## Obstacles to Parent-Child Visiting

Although the implications from research for the encouragement of visiting are clear, studies have persistently documented the overwhelming failure of parents to visit their children.

Maas and Engler found that in approximately one-half of the foster care cases they studied, parents visited infrequently or not at all [Maas and Engler, 1959]. In his study of over 5,000 foster care children in Massachusetts, Gruber [1973] found that less than 30% of the children had seen one of their parents within a 3-month period. Approximately 38% of the children had seen their parent(s) sometime during the previous six months. The remaining children had no substantial parental contact. Although the reasons for the low rate of visiting were not known, 60% of the parents interviewed reported that they did not see their children as often as they would like. In a study of foster children in Arizona [Mech, 1970], less than 30% of the children had received visits from their parents and only 14% reported visiting their parents in their own homes.

A number of reasons have been suggested for the failure of parents to visit: discouragement by the agency and/or social worker, difficulties with foster parents, worsening of the child's behavior, negative reaction of the biological parents, and transportation and scheduling problems. It is generally assumed that, at least in the short run, visiting can be problematic for all those involved.

## THE CONCEPT OF PERMANENCY FOR CHILDREN WITHIN FAMILIES

The importance of visiting cannot be understood as an isolated phenomenon but can be best examined within the framework of permanency for children within families. The goal of permanency is to reduce foster care drift by developing a plan to reunite children with their families or free them for adoption or long-term foster care within a specified time period. The concept of permanency is significant because it integrates knowledge of child development with legal, social, and cultural norms. The essence of the concept goes beyond the placement decision regarding the long-term fate of the child. Within the permanency framework, the objective is to meet the developmental needs of the child and to act in the child's best interests.

Permanency has been defined by the Oregon Project [Pike, et al., 1977:1–2] as the following:

> Permanency describes intent. A permanent home is not one that is guaranteed to last forever, but one that is intended to exist indefinitely. When the expectation of permanence is lacking, a child experiences doubt, uncertainty and hesitancy. Permanency planning means clarifying the intent of the placement, and during temporary care, keeping alive a plan for permanency. . . Permanent homes give commitment and continuity to the child's relationships. . . Permanent homes are rooted in and sanctioned by cultural norms and the law. . . Children in permanent homes are recognized . . . as having a respected social status.

The concept of permanency is derived from an understanding of a child's developmental needs in relation to attachment, belonging, and continuity [Bowlby, 1969, 1973; Ainsworth, 1973; and Sroufe & Waters, 1977]. It is further embedded in legal and cultural norms regarding the rights of children to a "permanent home" and to a respected social status [Goldstein, et al., 1979]. A number of states are moving toward permanency through legislation to reduce the drift in foster care by mandating case planning and periodic court review [Jones, 1978]. The passage of the Adoption Assistance and Child Welfare Amendments [P.L. 96–272] should further the objectives of permanency. States would be encouraged to require practices that favor prevention and permanency and discouraged from the practice of custodial foster care.

Permanency provides an evolving framework for a continuum of services in the child welfare field: prevention, protection, placement, and outcomes (return home, adoption, or long-term foster care). However, in implementing the law there is a new danger of becoming concerned primarily with legal and agency procedures and overlooking the substance of permanency as defined by the Oregon Project. Working within this context, the fundamental importance of parent-child visiting should not be underestimated. Visiting could become a cornerstone in the development of a permanent plan and in fostering a sense of permanency for the child whether or not the child returns home.

## Permanency and Family Services

The need to improve services for families is at the heart of the permanency concept. The visiting issue is one example of problems encountered in the foster care system in which studies show a striking gap between service objectives and outcomes. A number of reports document the fact that families are often ignored by child welfare workers. Illustratively, Stein and Gambrill [1977] found that county social workers spent more time with foster parents than with biological parents. Gruber [1978] found that over 30% of the parents had not even seen a social worker.

*The National Study of Social Services to Children and Their Families* [Shyne and Schroeder, 1978:61–65] reported that specific services for families were recommended for only 42% of the children receiving child welfare services. Counseling was the service most frequently recommended and utilized. Although this included all children receiving services and not just those in foster care, it nevertheless documents the dismal failure of the system to provide services for biological families. Capitalizing on the opportunities provided by visiting is a natural way to upgrade services for this neglected population. Frequent visiting, used creatively, offers an opportunity to improve services to parents and to shape the development of permanency for the child. To this end, an exploratory study (results of this study were presented at the National Conference on Social Welfare Annual Forum,

Cleveland: May 1980) was conducted to identify elements that affect visiting from the perspective of social workers, foster parents, biological parents, and adolescents in placement.

## METHODS OF STUDY

Through the cooperation of Hennepin County Community Services, Minneapolis, group interviews were conducted with social workers, foster parents, and adolescents in placement. Individual interviews were arranged with biological parents. Participants in the study were asked to identify factors from their own experience that deter and those that facilitate visiting. It should be noted that difficulties were encountered in arranging interviews with biological parents and further work remains to be undertaken with this group.

A questionnaire was used to solicit information on the following topics:

- understanding the purpose and importance of visiting
- agency policies and procedures
- agency and worker encouragement and facilitation of visiting
- type of visiting plan and scheduling procedures
- visiting arrangements including place, time, frequency, transportation, geographic distance
- persons who have had contact, including parents, siblings, other family members, and friends
- expenses related to travel, child care for siblings, support for a child who visits at home and activities associated with the visit
- types of activity pursued during the visit, including play, recreation, television, sharing meals, entertainment, shopping, household tasks, and participation in church, school, or other organizational activities
- communication, including discussion of everyday events, problems, and feelings
- feelings about visiting and separation
- quality of relationships among the parents, child, foster parents, and social worker

## RESULTS AND DISCUSSION

Analysis of information gathered from the four groups shows substantial areas of agreement about the problems and the benefits of visiting. Results confirm earlier findings about the importance of maintaining contact to promote long-term gains, while recognizing the impact of the short-term problems. In practice, the potential of visiting is often overlooked by agencies and workers. Inadequate policies and procedures are reinforced by parents who have assumed a passive role in their acceptance of visiting restrictions. That foster parents and parents do not understand why visiting is important is understandable because the actual visit creates immediate problems, particularly for the foster parents and the child. It causes a temporary worsening of the child's behavior and ability to function. Relationships between the parents and the child or the foster parents create conflict and bring to the surface negative feelings about separation and placement. Visiting is disruptive to family schedules and functioning. Social services are usually not available to help deal with these problems as they occur.

## Problems of Visiting

Foster parents cited the following problems most frequently:

- Visits are disruptive to the child and result in changed behavior. The child may experience continuing fears of rejection and separation that result in anger, aggression, withdrawal, psychosomatic symptoms, and acting out in the family or in school.
- Behavior of the biological parents can be problematic. They are uncooperative and unpredictable; use alcohol and drugs irresponsibly; make unrealistic promises to the child; are disorganized and have standards and schedules for the child who visits at home that are different from those of the foster family; miss appointments without calling, arrive late and return the child late; do not know what to do during the visit, particularly when visiting an infant or very young child. For example, instead of interacting with their child, they spend the time talking to the foster parents.
- Agencies and social workers do not do enough to encourage visiting and to help the foster parents cope with the problems, particularly those immediately resulting from the child's worsened behavior and the parents' behavior.
- Foster parents feel ambivalent about visiting. They may recognize its importance but are frustrated, confused, and often angered by the problems created by the visit.

Adolescents in placement called attention to these problems:

- Visits bring to the surface painful feelings about the realities of their situation. Because they are often unable to cope with these realities and their relationship with their parents, adolescents and children may refuse or balk at visiting. Maintaining contact precipitates overwhelming feelings about separation and loss. Children and adolescents are not given the help they need to deal with these feelings. Those who are physically afraid of their parents fear the dangers involved in a visit home; one adolescent reported that she always brought a friend along on home visits as a protective measure.

- Visiting schedules and activities are arranged to meet the needs of the foster parents or biological parents and do not take into consideration the child's or adolescent's needs.
- The frequency and scheduling of visits are used by foster or biological parents to reward or punish the child's behavior. For example, foster parents restrict visits if the child is acting out or disobeying in-house rules.

Biological parents identified these problems:

- Parents have not been helped to understand the importance of frequent visiting nor the purpose of visiting. Generally speaking, they assume a passive attitude.
- To allow for the child to "settle in," visiting is often not encouraged early enough in placement.
- Because the child refuses to visit or reacts negatively to the visit, frequent visiting is often not permitted. Telephoning and other means of communication are not encouraged.
- Visiting brings out feelings of guilt, inadequacy, and anxiety. Parents suffer from the separation. They have ambivalent feelings about their ability to be parents and to give the child "as good a home as the foster family's." For instance, a father stated that he worried about his child's adjustment upon returning home because he could not compete in material ways with the foster family.

Social workers reported the following problems:

- A gap exists between the visiting plan and the reality of the visit. The purpose of maintaining contact needs to be better clarified for all those involved.
- Worsening of the child's behavior as a result of visiting is disruptive in the treatment process. If visiting becomes too disruptive, it is difficult to retain foster homes.
- Because of the problems involved, foster parents do not cooperate, and sometimes sabotage the visiting plan.

- The low level of functioning and behavior of many parents makes the visit problematic.
- Problems created by geographic distances often occur, especially when the child is placed in an institution. Lack of money for travel and support of the child who visits at home can also be a problem.

### Benefits of Visiting

Results show strong agreement among the four groups that, despite the problems, maintaining contact is critically important because it allows the child, parents, and other siblings an opportunity to see each other realistically and to work out feelings about separation and loss. Illustratively, an adolescent reported that she initially rebelled at being required to visit her home. However, with the support and help of her social worker, she was able to work through her feelings of grief and anger, and eventually accept the reality of her family situation. Dealing with the realities lessens the tendency to suppress separation feelings and the necessity of developing irrational explanations. The need for fantasy (both idealizing the good and exaggerating the bad) decreases.

Frequent visiting was also seen as beneficial because it provides opportunities for the parent and child to maintain or develop a relationship that meets the developmental needs of both. An understanding of these needs can help determine the visiting purpose, frequency, persons who visit, the place, and activity. Foster parents said that successful visiting helped them to be more effective. In discussing the benefits, the importance of providing appropriate social services was stressed by the four groups.

All agreed that the immediate problems are outweighed by the long-term benefits. However, the benefits can be realized only by working through the negative factors. To do this successfully, workers, parents, foster parents, and children need a better understanding of the benefits and must work together on the development and implementation of a visiting plan.

## PRACTICE IMPLICATIONS AND GUIDELINES

That research findings concerning visiting have not yet had a substantial impact on practice has implications for the development of agency policies and practices. What stands out most significantly is the lack of commitment to the importance of maintaining contact. The potential of visiting has been overlooked in promoting permanency for the child and in the provision of casework services to the family. It is encouraging to note, however, that Fanshel and Shinn's investigation showed that frequency of casework contact, independent of the evaluation of the mother, is associated with greater frequency of visiting [Fanshel and Shinn, 1978:111].

The following guidelines are offered to stimulate the use of visiting as a natural medium for working with parents and children. Recognizing that each child's situation is unique and complex, professional judgment is needed to apply the guidelines to individual cases.

## Agency Policies

Agencies should promote ways to increase the frequency and improve the quality of visiting. Policies to support visiting should be developed at all levels of the agency: administration, staff development, supervision, and line worker. Agency policies that encourage and facilitate visiting are in keeping with a growing emphasis on client rights and agency accountability. Limiting or restricting visits should be prohibited unless there are specific reasons that are communicated to all involved. In such cases, visiting should be viewed as a goal to be worked toward. Visiting should be allowed during the early phase of placement. In general, the younger the child, the more frequent the visits should be. Visiting should not be used as a reward or punishment for behavior.

A visiting plan that is incorporated into the overall case plan should be required in all out-of-home placements. Foster parents, parents, and the child, if of appropriate age, should participate in developing the plan and be educated about its importance. The plan should specify arrangements such as transportation, specific activities, and, if needed, the source of financial support for the child who visits at home; and should clarify how the visit will be used in the therapeutic intervention. A visiting record should be maintained, including an evaluation of visits that can be used in case and court review. This is particularly important in states such as Minnesota that have legislated that "neglected and in foster care" are grounds for termination of parental rights [MN. Session Laws: 1978].

## Training

Agencies should offer training to supervisors, workers, foster parents, parents, and children in placement on the benefits, problems, consequences, and significance of visiting. A training model that focuses on visiting has been developed recently at Hennepin County Community Services for foster parents and workers (Rebecca Richardson, Foster Parent Training Coordinator).

This type of training should be offered also to parents and their children in placement. Meeting parental needs through educational and self-help groups has been seriously neglected. The visiting experience provides a natural forum for the discussion of broader issues, and feelings related to the parent-child relationship.

## Planning and Arrangements

Planning for the visit can provide an avenue of entry to the development of a comprehensive case plan. Before the child is actually placed, the worker can begin to prepare the parents, child, and foster parents for visiting. Potential negative and positive consequences should be discussed. It is important to promote their participation in the actual development of a plan. Two visiting models should be considered. To meet changing needs, the models are offered as a continuum that recognizes the rights and needs of all those involved.

In the Open Model, foster and biological parents and the child work out visiting arrangements informally and on demand. The worker is kept informed and is involved in structuring activities for the visit; offering appropriate social services; helping with problems; and assessing the quality of the visit.

In the Mediated Model, the social worker takes pressure off the clients by facilitating or mediating the visiting arrangements. Time, place, persons to visit, transportation, and activities for the visit are carefully spelled out. The worker is available to provide social services, help with problems, and assess the visit.

## Use of Visiting in Intervention

Visiting can be used effectively as a therapeutic tool in the intervention process. As a real life experience, visiting offers an opportunity to work with families in the context of their natural life situations. Using visiting in intervention is an example of how competence-oriented social work can be applied to child welfare services. In the competence model, clients are viewed as partners in the helping process [Maluccio, 1981]. Workers are defined as change agents who use varying approaches to enable clients to achieve goals, engage in developmental processes, and carry out their tasks [Studt, 1968; quoted in Maluccio, 1981]. The visit can serve as a central focus in efforts to work more effectively with parents. Client competence can be enhanced through utilizing the visit to meet developmental needs of parents and child and to work through the separation and loss related to the placement.

*Child Development.* Visiting provides natural opportunities for helping the parent understand the child's needs within the framework of Eriksonian developmental stages and tasks [Erikson, 1950]. Working through the stages in a predictable sequence is essential for the child's healthy development. In planning the visit, the purpose, persons who visit, activity, and interaction should be carefully structured and monitored to conform with the particular developmental stage of the child. In promoting permanency for the child, developmental tasks should be integrated with the child's need for attachment, continuity, and consistency.

Ways can be found to promote tasks that are developmentally appropriate. For instance, parents with infants should be encouraged to visit frequently and to understand the critical importance of physical interaction with the child in establishing basic trust. Ideally, the mother or father might spend a substantial period of time every week in the actual care (i.e., feeding, bathing, clothing, playing) of the infant or young child. If a sense of trust has developed, shared activities away from the foster home such as recreation or church/school functions can contribute to continuing growth in the child's development and the relationship. When visits take place in the foster home, some privacy with the child is recommended. Worker observation of the visit, with feedback, might be helpful in certain cases.

In working with the older child and adolescent, an understanding of the need for the development of ego-identity and intimacy can be used to plan age-appropriate visits. The importance of including siblings, other family members, and peers in the visiting plans should be stressed. The tasks of normal adolescence, which include physical, social and psychological changes, are complicated by out-of-home placement. The worker should help the parents and adolescent understand the significance of normal acting out and striving for independence and how these issues relate to the placement situation.

*Parent Development.* In Fanshel and Shinn's investigation, children of mothers who received more positive evaluations by the caseworkers showed significantly higher frequencies of visiting [Fanshel and Shinn, 1978:107]. This has implications for services for parents who can be helped to become more competent in their parental roles and functions. The visit can be used to involve them in problem solving and decision making about practical matters related to parenting. For example, foster parents might include them in making decisions with the child about purchase of clothing, school/social activities, peer relationships and other concerns. When possible, parents, siblings and other family members may be included in special occasions, holidays, birthday celebrations, school conferences, church and other organizational activities. These efforts will help children and parents preserve their family identity and continuity and help them increase their sense of control over their situation.

Because approaches to working with families have been severely limited, parents have not had sufficient help in developing or strengthening their parenting skills. Visiting provides opportunities to use foster parents in a natural setting as role models [Maluccio and Sinanoglu, 1981]. If the environment is supportive, parents will have a chance to try out new skills and to gain competence in their parental roles. Individual efforts should be supplemented by parent education groups for parents, modeled after self-help groups such as Parents Anonymous. This type of resource has been sadly overlooked, due perhaps to restrictions from privacy laws and regulations. However, such groups could provide a learning-awareness experience in such areas as child development and behavior; child management and discipline; family roles and dynamics; self-esteem in children and parents; and expectations about separation and loss related to the placement. Subsequently, the actual visit generates a natural opportunity to apply the learning to life experience.

*Separation and Loss.* The centrality of the separation experience has been widely recognized. Painful feelings of rejection, loss of identity, anger, and guilt, which are associated with the separation, place the parent and child in a highly vulnerable situation. Littner has detailed the traumatic effects [Littner, 1956]. After effects include increased sensitivity of the child to later separations; the child's increased fear of emotional closeness; development of irrational explanations and fantasies; and the development of behavior based upon the painful feelings and fantasy. There is evidence that the child exposed to sustained separation in long-term care is vulnerable to the development of cognitive and emotional problems.

More precise information is needed about the effects of separation within the context of permanency. How can workers help the parent and child deal with the pain of the separation in relation to the goal for the placement? Assessment of the degree of attachment is pertinent to case planning and the visiting plan. Efforts should be made to work through the trauma of the separation, whether the placement goal is return home, adoption, or long-term foster care.

Current thinking about the importance of the grieving process in relation to loss has implications for practice. To work through the stages of grieving that accompany the separation, it is crucial that the parents and child have opportunities to see each other and to interact in real life experiences. The study at Hennepin County Community Services [White:1980] revealed that children, indeed, do seriously grieve. Immediately following the visit, children may show signs of disturbance, anger, or withdrawal, which result in disruptive behavior.

Because it is so painful to see a child grieve and because this creates severe strains on the foster family, a common reaction has been to curtail the visiting. The natural grieving process, then, is cut off and the child and parent are not permitted to work through the stages of denial, anger, and depression to a level of acceptance. Workers have an essential role in helping the parents, child, and foster parents to understand their feelings and to cope with this very difficult, life-shaping process.

## CONCLUSION

Visiting has been underutilized in the delivery of services related to placement. In the face of increased concern for the rights and needs of biological families, the use of visiting as an important intervention tool deserves greater attention since it offers a natural opportunity to provide social services that meet developmental needs. As a first step, it is recommended that the term "parental visiting" be changed to a designation that better connotes the idea of continuing parent-child involvement within a framework of permanency. Continuing involvement will make reentry easier if the child returns home. If the child does not return home, but remains in long-term foster care or is adopted, visiting will have helped the parents and child accept a relationship that is changed but can never end in its truest psychological sense.

## REFERENCES

Ainsworth, Mary D. Salter. "The Development of Infant-Mother Attachment," in Betty M. Caldwell and Henry N. Ricciuti (eds.) *Review of Child Development Research*, *Vol.* 3. Chicago: University of Chicago Press, 1973.

Bowlby, John. *Attachment and Loss: Vol. 1, Attachment*. New York: Basic Books, 1969.

Bowlby, John. *Attachment and Loss: Vol. 2, Separation*. New York: Basic Books, 1973.

Eisenberg, Leon. "The Sins of the Fathers: Urban Decay and Social Pathology." *American Journal of Orthopsychiatry* 32 (January 1962): 5–17.

Erikson, Erik H. *Childhood and Society*. New York: W. W. Norton and Company, 1950.

Fanshel, David. "Parental Visiting of Children in Foster Care: Key to Discharge?" *Social Service Review* 49 (December 1975): 493–515.

Fanshel, David and Shinn, Eugene. *Children in Foster Care: A Longitudinal Investigation*. New York: Columbia University Press, 1978.

Goldstein, Joseph; Freud, Anna; and Solnit, Albert J. *Beyond the Best Interests of the Child*. New York: Free Press, 1973.

Goldstein, Joseph; Freud, Anna; and Solnit, Albert J. *Before the Best Interests of the Child*. New York: Free Press, 1979.

Gruber, Alan. Foster Home Care in Massachusetts. Boston: Governor's Commission on Adoption and Foster Care, 1973.

Gruber, Alan. *Children in Foster Care: Destitute, Neglected . . . Betrayed*. New York: Human Sciences Press, 1978.

Jenkins, Shirley and Norman, Elaine. *Beyond Placement—Mothers View Foster Care*. New York and London: Columbia University Press, 1975.

Jones, Martha L. "Stopping Foster Care Drift: A Review of Legislation and Special Programs," *Child Welfare* LVII, No. 9, (November 1978): 571–579.

Littner, Ner. *Some Traumatic Effects of Separation and Placement*. New York: Child Welfare League of America, 1956.

Maas, Henry S. and Engler, Richard E. *Children in Need of Parents*. New York: Columbia University Press, 1959.

Maluccio, Anthony N. "Promoting Client and Worker Competence in Child Welfare," in *Social Welfare Forum, 1980*. New York: Columbia University Press, 1981.

Maluccio, Anthony N. and Sinanoglu, Paula A., Editors. *The Challenge of Partnership: Working with Parents of Children in Foster Care*. New York: Child Welfare League of America, 1981.

Mech, Edmund V. *Public Welfare Services for Children and Youth in Arizona*. Tucson, Arizona: Joint Interim Committee on Health and Welfare, 1970.

Minnesota Session Laws, Chapter 602, 1978.

Pike, Victor, et al. *Permanent Planning for Children in Foster Care: A Handbook for Social Workers*. Portland, Oregon: Research Institute for Human Services, Portland State University, 1977: 1–2.

Shyne, Ann W. and Schroeder, Anita G. *National Study of Social Services to Children and Their Families*. Washington, D.C.: DHEW Publication No. OHDS 78-30150: 61–65.

Shapiro, Deborah. *Agencies and Foster Care*. New York: Columbia University Press, 1976.

Sroufe, L. Alan and Waters, Everett. "Attachment as an Organizational Construct," *Child Development* 48 (December 1977): 1184–1199.

Stein, Theodore J. and Gambrill, Eileen D. "The Alameda Project: Two-Year Report," *Social Service Review* 51 (September 1977): 502–513.

Studt, Eliot. "Social Work Theory and Implications for the Practice of Methods." *Social Work Education Reporter* 16 (June 1968): 22–24 and 42–46.

Weinstein, E. A. *The Self-Image of the Foster Child*. New York: Russell Sage Foundation, 1960.

White, Mary S. "The Role of Parental Visiting in Permanency Planning for Children," in *Social Welfare Forum, 1980*. New York: Columbia University Press, 1981.